THE WORLD
IS A TEXT

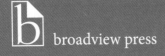

broadview press

THE WORLD IS A TEXT

WRITING ABOUT VISUAL AND POPULAR CULTURE

UPDATED COMPACT EDITION

JONATHAN SILVERMAN
DEAN RADER

broadview press

BROADVIEW PRESS – www.broadviewpress.com
Peterborough, Ontario, Canada

Founded in 1985, Broadview Press remains a wholly independent publishing house. Broadview's focus is on academic publishing; our titles are accessible to university and college students as well as scholars and general readers. With over 600 titles in print, Broadview has become a leading international publisher in the humanities, with world-wide distribution. Broadview is committed to environmentally responsible publishing and fair business practices.

© 2018 Jonathan Silverman and Dean Rader
Reprinted with corrections 2019.

This text was previously published by Pearson Education, Inc.

Library and Archives Canada Cataloguing in Publication

Silverman, Jonathan, 1965-, author
      The world is a text : writing about visual and popular culture / Jonathan Silverman and Dean Rader. — Updated compact edition.

Includes bibliographical references and index.
ISBN 978-1-55481-379-7 (softcover)

      1. English language—Rhetoric. 2. Culture—Problems, exercises, etc. 3. Readers—Culture. 4. Critical thinking. 5. College readers. 6. Report writing. 7. Semiotics. I. Rader, Dean, author II. Title.

PE1408.S517 2018   808'.0427   C2018-901389-3

Broadview Press handles its own distribution in North America:
PO Box 1243, Peterborough, Ontario K9J 7H5, Canada
555 Riverwalk Parkway, Tonawanda, NY 14150, USA
Tel: (705) 743-8990; Fax: (705) 743-8353
email: customerservice@broadviewpress.com

Distribution is handled by Eurospan Group in the UK, Europe, Central Asia, Middle East, Africa, India, Southeast Asia, Central America, South America, and the Caribbean. Distribution is handled by Footprint Books in Australia and New Zealand.

 Broadview Press acknowledges the financial support of the Government of Canada for our publishing activities.

Edited by Juliet Sutcliffe
Book Design by Em Dash Design

PRINTED IN CANADA

CONTENTS

PART 1

Writing about the World

INTRODUCTION

The following conversation took place via text messaging between the two authors of this book, Jonathan Silverman and Dean Rader, as they began writing the introduction to the new edition of *The World Is a Text*:

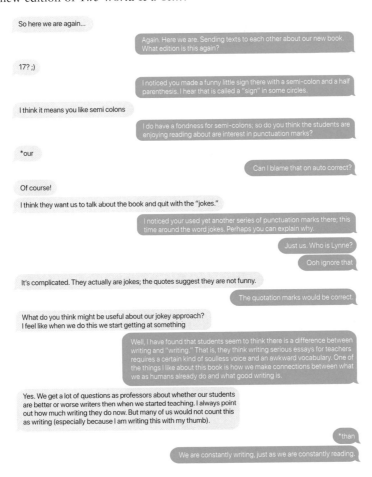

So here we are again...

Again. Here we are. Sending texts to each other about our new book. What edition is this again?

17? ;)

I noticed you made a funny little sign there with a semi-colon and a half parenthesis. I hear that is called a "sign" in some circles.

I think it means you like semi colons

I do have a fondness for semi-colons; so do you think the students are enjoying reading about are interest in punctuation marks?

*our

Can I blame that on auto correct?

Of course!

I think they want us to talk about the book and quit with the "jokes."

I noticed your used yet another series of punctuation marks there; this time around the word jokes. Perhaps you can explain why.

Just us. Who is Lynne?

Ooh ignore that

It's complicated. They actually are jokes; the quotes suggest they are not funny.

The quotation marks would be correct.

What do you think might be useful about our jokey approach? I feel like when we do this we start getting at something

Well, I have found that students seem to think there is a difference between writing and "writing." That is, they think writing serious essays for teachers requires a certain kind of soulless voice and an awkward vocabulary. One of the things I like about this book is how we make connections between what we as humans already do and what good writing is.

Yes. We get a lot of questions as professors about whether our students are better or worse writers then when we started teaching. I always point out how much writing they do now. But many of us would not count this as writing (especially because I am writing this with my thumb).

*than

We are constantly writing, just as we are constantly reading.

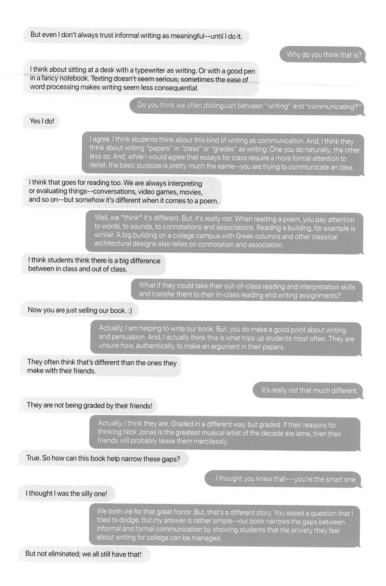

But even I don't always trust informal writing as meaningful--until I do it.

Why do you think that is?

I think about sitting at a desk with a typewriter as writing. Or with a good pen in a fancy notebook. Texting doesn't seem serious; sometimes the ease of word processing makes writing seem less consequential.

Do you think we often distinguish between "writing" and "communicating?"

Yes I do!

I agree. I think students think about this kind of writing as communication. And, I think they think about writing "papers" in "class" or "grades" as writing. One you do naturally; the other less so. And, while I would agree that essays for class require a more formal attention to detail, the basic purpose is pretty much the same--you are trying to communicate an idea.

I think that goes for reading too. We are always interpreting or evaluating things--conversations, video games, movies, and so on--but somehow it's different when it comes to a poem.

Well, we *think* it's different. But, it's really not. When reading a poem, you pay attention to words, to sounds, to connotations and associations. Reading a building, for example is similar. A big building on a college campus with Greek columns and other classical architectural designs also relies on connotation and association.

I think students think there is a big difference between in class and out of class.

What if they could take their out-of-class reading and interpretation skills and transfer them to their in-class reading and writing assignments?

Now you are just selling our book. :)

Actually, I am helping to write our book. But, you do make a good point about writing and persuasion. And, I actually think this is what trips up students most often. They are unsure how, authentically, to make an argument in their papers.

They often think that's different than the ones they make with their friends.

It's really not that much different.

They are not being graded by their friends!

Actually, I think they are. Graded in a different way, but graded. If their reasons for thinking Nick Jonas is the greatest musical artist of the decade are lame, then their friends will probably tease them mercilessly.

True. So how can this book help narrow these gaps?

I thought you knew that---you're the smart one.

I thought I was the silly one!

We both vie for that great honor. But, that's a different story. You asked a question that I tried to dodge, but my answer is rather simple--our book narrows the gaps between informal and formal communication by showing students that the anxiety they feel about writing for college can be managed.

But not eliminated; we all still have that!

    While we do not recommend you begin your essays for your college classes as we just did; this is, after all, an introduction to a book about writing and the writing process. And there is something to our chat that might be worth thinking about as you begin to write your own papers. We wrote informally as part of a dialogue, even though our topic may have seemed rehearsed. It was. We wanted to mimic the process of discovery and informality that often guides our own writing and thinking. When the two of us write books, essays, and scholarly articles, we have to adopt a slightly more academic tone for our audiences to take us seriously. But almost no writing we do begins in this manner—the process we undergo in order to get our thoughts in order often begins haphazardly, nonlinearly (not in a straight line), and in fragments. Sometimes we scribble portions of ideas, half-brained concepts, ridiculous ideas, just to get them down on paper so that we can come back to them and turn them into something meaningful. And sometimes, two writers send silly texts to each other to help get things going.

By now, most of you have been introduced to the idea of brainstorming and free-writing by high school or college teachers, and soon enough, all of you will be. While we have always endorsed this process when writing about anything, such an approach seems particularly appropriate for writing about non-traditional texts such as movies, television, race, and fashion because this kind of free association mimics the way we actually begin our discussions of these texts. Many of you have engaged in heated arguments about the bands and television shows you like. You no doubt have read posts on Facebook about movies and even texted snarky comments about One Direction or Miranda Lambert to other people. These informal ways of arguing can themselves be the beginning of more formal arguing. Put more simply, your crabby tweets can be the very seeds that will eventually turn in to your essay. For *college*.

How?

Keep reading. This book helps you build on skills you already have as well as helps you acquire new skills in writing and interpretation. We think it is important to learn how to write a good essay, whether it is about *The Simpsons* or Shakespeare. But we think writing about popular culture has a few advantages that writing about other subjects may not. For one, writing papers develops skills you may often use in everyday life—both in terms of your informal critiques AND your more formal writing process. By now, you may be tired of writing informational research papers and endless essays of literary analysis. Looking at a fresh subject can also help you rethink your thinking process, which, by extension, forces you to reimagine your writing process.

Because we want you to both write and read better, this book is both a guide to writing and a guide to reading. In the first part, we begin by talking about semiotics as a way of interpreting popular culture. Then we move to a detailed explanation of how the writing process works. In the second part, the book switches modes. In a series of short how-to chapters, we walk you through the process of writing papers on specific topics like sports, fashion, race, movies, and music.

In a way, this chapter you are currently reading is not only the result of a dialogue between us but also between our readers (both teachers and students) and us. We want the book to serve your interests as students and ours as teachers. That is why we think dialogue and discussion, as well as more formal writing, are key to this process.

As you can tell from the chat above, we're eager to make sure you understand the main objective of our book and this introduction. If that objective is not clear, we'll restate it here: our goal is to help you read and write about texts (movies, pieces of art, experiences, people, places, ideas, traditions, advertisements, etc.), in much the same way you would read and write about traditional texts. Many of these texts are visual or have visual elements, and your past tendencies probably have been to "see" them rather than "read" them—that is, you likely simply regarded them rather than interpreted them. In this book, however, instead of looking at texts, we ask you to *see* them—to slow down and decode texts in ways you may not have done previously. In addition, we want you to try formalizing this reading process. What we mean by "formal" here is the process we undertake when analyzing literature (or, depending on your training, math formulas, a painting, or research data).

We have several goals in this book. First, we want you to become a better writer. Second, we want to help you become a better reader of the world generally and a better reader of texts like television and movies specifically. We also want to make you a better reader of essays about those topics. We remain confident that your increased abilities as a reader will, of course, translate into better writing.

One of the primary elements of formal reading is the breaking down of a text into smaller elements and interpreting them. Analyzing a short story for themes, character development, and figurative language (symbols, metaphors, etc.) is formal reading, as is the process of poring over a Supreme Court decision. Explicating a poem is a classic example of formal "decoding." Looking at a poem's rhyme, meter, symbolism, tone, structure, and design is a decoding process that involves posing questions about what the poem is trying to do and how it does it. Although it may feel natural to think of reading or interpreting poems in this way, approaching an advertisement or a television show or a gender may feel a bit foreign at first. Over the course of reading this book, we hope that this process ceases to feel alien and begins to seem natural, especially as you become more familiar with analyzing the elements associated with these cultural and visual texts.

To sum up, the traditional analytical work you have done in English classes is something we want to imitate here. We believe that texts, including those that are non-traditional, such as public spaces, songs, and advertisements, have meanings that can be uncovered through the exploration of their elements. You may sense that a certain mall is ugly or that a sports mascot might be racist, but we want you to understand why. You may already sense that advertisements use sex to sell products, but we want you to understand how. The idea is not only to slow the interpretive process down but also to make more conscious your meaning making, a process you undertake all the time—whether you intend to or not. Understanding how texts make meaning is the most important step toward writing your own texts about this world.

CHAPTER 1

SEMIOTICS:
THE STUDY OF SIGNS (AND TEXTS)

All reading we do, perhaps anything we do, is backed up by various ideas or theories—from the simple belief that the acts we undertake have consequences both good and bad to the more complex theories about relativity and gravity. In this book, we rely on a theory that the world itself is open to interpretation—that we can make meaning out of just about anything. The notion that the world is a text open to interpretation is itself a theory, which has a strong connection to semiotics, the study of signs. In this part of the book, we elaborate on the idea of semiotics as a way of helping you understand some of the assumptions we made when writing this book. You can use the rest of the book without focusing on semionics, but you may find that this section will prove helpful when thinking deeply about your paper subject.

In semiotics, the main idea is that everything is a "sign." You already know what signs are, because you encounter them everywhere. There are traffic signs, signs telling whether something is open or closed, signs in your classroom urging you not to smoke or cheat, or informing you where the exit is. You do very little work in trying to understand these signs, which seemingly need no interpretation. Once you understand what "stop" means, or that the color red means "stop," or that green means "go," or that yellow means "slow down" or "caution," there is no need to stop, think, and interpret these signs each time you see them. Of course, you did not always know what these signs meant; at some point in your childhood, you picked up the ideas behind these signs and now take them for granted. The important thing to realize, however, is that our culture has come to a common understanding that a number of random signs and symbols—a cross, a red octagon, a round green light, a stick figure with the outline of a skirt—stand in for or symbolize specific concepts.

We have a broader idea of signs (or texts) in this book, although how we talk about signs here is based on the most rudimentary cultural symbols. A sign is an object or idea or combination of the two that refers to something besides itself, and it depends on others to recognize that it is a sign. The red octagon and the letters S–T–O–P mean "Stop" to most of us through the combination of the shape, color, and letters. A blue diamond with "HALT" on it would catch our attention, but we would not treat it in the same way, despite the fact that "halt" and "stop" are synonyms, or that a blue diamond is a perfectly fine combination of color and shape. The stop sign as we now know it carries a meaning beyond a simple combination of word, color, and shape. It carries the weight and force of history, law, and ubiquity.

Another example: we know an "Open" sign at a store means the store is transacting business. But "Open" itself is an arbitrary sign, unique to English-speaking cultures. The symbols O–P–E–N are characters English speakers have identified as "letters," and those letters, when put together in a certain way, create "words." If we were to put these symbols together, "Δ• ≠ »," and hang them on the door of a coffee shop, we would just confuse people because our culture has not assigned specific meanings for these symbols. But what if we came across this sign: "ABIERTO"? In Spanish, "abierto" means "open." So, if we read Spanish, then we can decode the sign. Or, if we live, say, in San Diego, and we have grown up knowing that these seven letters mean "open" in Spanish, then we can also decode it. And in some places, a sign contains both abierto and open to indicate that it is signifying to two different sets of clientele. "Open" and "Abierto" can both be signs, but so can their presence together be a sign. If we saw an abierto and an open sign in one place, we might draw conclusions about where we were (a neighborhood where English and Spanish are spoken), who owned the restaurant or store (bilingual owners?), and who their audience was (primarily speakers of Spanish and English). In other words, the presence of both signs is itself a sign—taken together they create meaning.

Semioticians ("sign-studiers") have a more formal way of referring to signs. Ferdinand de Saussure, a Swiss linguist working in the nineteenth and twentieth centuries, believed that signs contained two elements: the signifier and the signified, which, when taken together, create meaning. The **signifier** is the object that exists, and the **signified** is what it means. In other words, the letters O–P–E–N are the signifier, and the message that a place is open for business is the signified, and the external reality is that the store is ready to receive customers. Similarly, using our stop sign example, the actual red sign with the STOP written in white letters is the signifier. The signified is the message that you must bring your car to a complete halt when you approach this sign.[1]

SYSTEMS OF READING: MAKING SENSE OF CULTURAL TEXTS

Sometimes the same signifiers (physical signs) can have different signifieds (meanings). For instance, what do you think of when you see the word "pan"? Most of you probably imagine an item for cooking. Or you might think of a critic "panning" or criticizing

---

[1] The terms signified and signifier are well known; a good introduction to the work of the complicated idea of semiotics is Daniel Chandler's *Semiotics: The Basics* (Routledge, 2002), particularly page 19.

a bad movie. However, a Spanish speaker who saw the word "pan" in our bilingual store would most likely imagine bread. The signifier "pan" in Spanish cultures refers not to an item for cooking but to what English speakers think of when they see the signifier "bread." Thus, people from both cultures would experience the same signifier, but what is signified would be entirely different.

However, we do not even need other languages for there to be various signified meanings for the same signifier. Photographers may think of a pan or wide-angle shot. Scholars of Greek mythology may think of the Greek god who is half goat and half man. The letters p–a–n remain the same, but the meanings change; the sign—the word "pan"—has different meanings. We also can have the same signified but with different signifiers. For example, "soda," "pop," or "Coke" are all different signifiers that different people from different parts of the country use to refer to a flavored carbonated drink.

So when we talk about signs, we are not talking only about physical signs but also about a system of reading. In this system, we can interpret images, words whose letters are arbitrarily assigned meaning, and experiences—really just about anything. Sometimes we make these interpretations with little or no effort and sometimes with a lot of work. Many semioticians believe that everything is a sign, including the way we are writing this introduction. The words are signs, and so is the way you are reading them (it is simply a more complex way of saying that everything is a text).

And more complex signs of course do not reveal themselves so easily. For example, let us consider a very famous sign (or text)—the *Mona Lisa* (see Fig. 1a), Leonardo da Vinci's painting that hangs in the Louvre in Paris. Its power in some part comes from its simplicity and its unreadability. We do not know why the woman in the painting is smiling, we only have a vague idea of who

FIGURE 1a
Leonardo da Vinci, *Mona Lisa*, c.1503–06

she is, and we will likely never know. That smile, or half-smile, has become so famous that its life as a sign has transcended even its power as an image. The painting is a signifier, but its signified is ambiguous and difficult to determine. If we look at the various images of the *Mona Lisa* on shirts, mouse pads, posters, even variations of the original (we like the version where *Mona Lisa* has a big black moustache), we can agree that the *Mona Lisa* has become a symbol of something 1) traditional, 2) artistic, 3) commercial, and 4) universal, and perhaps 5) modern. We can agree that something about its power has not diminished despite or because of its age. But our signified—our mental concept of what "*Mona Lisa*–ness" is—depends on what perspective we bring to the reality of this artwork. Does it signify our definition of a masterpiece? A commodity? A self-portrait by the artist?

We do not know exactly (but people guess all the time). And that's why sometimes sign reading is so frustrating. Some signs are so easy to read and understand that we do not even know we are reading. Others, like paintings—and more importantly, human relationships—are more difficult. One of the most complex components of reading texts is suspending judgments about a text's values. In your initial semiotic analysis—your initial reading of a text—try to consider all aspects of a text before applying a label like "good" or "bad" (or "interesting" or "boring"). Such labels are earned only after a thorough reading of the text under question. Later, if you want to argue that a text has problems, then you would use the details, the information you gleaned from your reading, to support these assertions in your papers. In attacking the *Mona Lisa*, for example, it would be acceptable to most professors for you to speculate about what you thought da Vinci was trying to accomplish in his painting if you can defend your ideas—your *guess*. Reading visually, in fact, often means such guessing is a natural part of writing any sort of paper.

Overall, the basic idea behind semiotics should not be foreign to you—on a fundamental level, it simply means reading and interpreting nontraditional objects like you would a short story or a poem.

THE "SEMIOTIC SITUATION" (OR THE "MOVING TEXT")

As you may have realized, you do this type of work all the time. You read people and relationships every day, having developed this skill over years of reading the world. For instance, say you are walking down Wall Street in New York City. You see a man dressed in a suit, talking on a cell phone, carrying a copy of the *Wall Street Journal*, and yelling "Sell Microsoft at 42! Sell! Sell! Sell!" What would you assume his profession is? He could be a lawyer. He could be a banker. But given the context (where you are, Wall Street), what he's talking about (stocks), and how he's dressed (a suit), the best interpretation of this text might be that he is a stockbroker. You could be wrong, but based on the clues of the text, that is a pretty good reading.

We perform this work constantly. For example, on first dates we try to read the other person for cues of attraction and enjoyment; quarterbacks read a defense before every play and pass; we read a classroom when we enter it; we read a friend's house, and especially his or her room, by scanning posters, its cleanliness, its odor, and the collection of books and music. These moments are what we call "semiotic situations"—when we try to make sense of our surroundings or interpret one aspect of our surroundings based on the signs or texts we see. The copy of the *Wall Street Journal*, the cell phone, the man's comments—all are signs that represent a text that can be read. And when we put these signs together, they help us make sense of the larger text (the man) and the larger text (Wall Street) and an even larger text than that (America). As you may have guessed by now, this act of reading can even help you make sense of the largest text of all—the world—in both literal and mythical ways.

Because we are always trying to make sense of the world, because we are always reading, we are almost always in semiotic situations. This book builds on your own methods of reading and tries to sharpen them so that you become more critical and thoughtful readers of the complex text that is our world. We keep returning to the reading metaphor because it aptly describes the process of making sense of our surroundings, and because it is the first step toward crafting an excellent essay. When we read a poem or a short story, we pay attention to detail: we look for symbols, metaphors, and hidden themes. We "read between the lines." To read between the lines, both in literature and in conversation, means that we read not only what is there but also what's not there. We do this frequently as well; we "read into things." Beer commercials never come right out and suggest that attractive, straight, single women will immediately be drawn to straight men if the men drink a certain kind of beer, but that is implied in almost every ad. People we are interested in dating may not tell us what kind of people they are, where they come from, what kind of music they like, or what their political leanings are, but by paying attention to the clothes they wear or the comments they make, or the bumper stickers on their cars, we may be able to begin to piece together a better interpretation of the text that is this person. In other words, we already know how to read books and poems, and we also know how to read the world itself. This book will help you merge your experiences from formal and informal, as well as conscious and unconscious reading.

CHAPTER 2

TEXTS, THE WORLD, YOU, AND YOUR ESSAYS

We hope by now that you understand what we mean by reading the world as a text, and that this notion seems both comfortable and interesting to you. However, you are probably wondering how any of this figures into your writing course. As you have no doubt realized by this time in your academic career, writing is fundamentally connected to reading and thinking. To our knowledge, there has never been a great writer who was not also a great thinker. What's more, to be a great thinker and a great writer, we must also be great readers. Writing is so intimately tied to thinking and thinking so intimately tied to the act of reading the world and one's surroundings, that the three form a kind of trinity of articulation and expression:

Of course, by "reading" we mean not only reading books and newspapers and magazines but also the semiotic situation or the nontraditional text, the practice of reading the world. Writing, thinking, and reading are a symbiotic process, a cycle in which they feed off and influence each other. Thus, if we are reading and thinking, then the chances are we will be better prepared to do good writing.

RHETORIC: WRITING'S SOUNDTRACK

Good writing is also grounded on solid rhetorical principles, as is good reading (especially as we have broadly defined reading so far). Rhetoric comes from the Greek word *rhetorik*. Its literal definition means "speech" or "speaking." In English, "rhetoric" has come to refer to the art of speaking or writing effectively—usually with an emphasis on persuasion. This book considers rhetoric broadly, exploring how it works not only in cultural and visual texts but also how you can apply rhetorical principles and strategies to your writing to make your papers more effective.

The history of rhetoric is a long and complicated one, and it is worth knowing a little about its background. Generally, scholars link the birth of rhetoric with the Sophists (Greek thinkers from the fifth century BCE), who first began studying and theorizing the concept of public speech. Later, rhetoric became one of the three pillars of the liberal arts and a foundation for classical education. The great Greek philosopher Plato (427–347 BCE) had issues with rhetoric being considered an art; for him it was more of a cheap skill—essentially, fancy flattery. He considered medicine a true art and compared rhetoric to cooking. Given the current popularity of The Food Network, that is not so bad, but at the time, it was a bit of an insult. Ultimately, Plato argued that rhetoric could never be an art, because it had no subject; it had nothing to ground it. Thus, when you hear a pundit describe a political speech as "all rhetoric," the pundit is using rhetoric in much the same way Plato saw it—as empty, content-free verbiage.[1]

However, Aristotle (384–322 BCE), also a famous Greek philosopher and Plato's student, argued that rhetoric was one of the great arts and that its subject was all things. In fact, Aristotle found the subjects of medicine and warfare rather narrow, whereas, in his mind, rhetoric had no bounds. For him, rhetoric cast the widest net and, because it could encompass so much, it was worthy of study. In fact, in his famous study *On Rhetoric*, Aristotle advances a concept of rhetoric ("the art of finding the possible means of persuasion in reference to any given situation") that informs current rhetorical theory and much of this book.

Indeed, with the advent of the modern media, advertising, and visual culture, rhetoric has grown to encompass all persuasive techniques, strategies, and approaches beyond mere speaking and writing. Any ad, commercial, or political slogan that tries to get you to do, buy, think, or feel anything is using rhetoric. One of the main goals of our book is to help you to detect various strategies of persuasion in any situation, whether it is an advertisement, a movie, a building, or fashion. To that end, *The World Is a Text* is interested in both cultural and visual rhetoric—how cultural and visual texts make arguments. As you will see, we discuss the "rhetorical moment" or the "rhetorical situation" a great deal. By this, we mean the many different situations Aristotle refers to that will require you to use new interpretive skills. You cannot read all texts the same way—you must adjust your reading to meet the signs of the text. For example, commercials for heart medication may make different arguments than those for Match. com. Beer ads in *Maxim* rely on an entirely different set of images, codes, and associa-

---

1   Much of the work on rhetoric can be found in a variety of sources, including James L. Golden et al., *The Rhetoric of Western Thought: From the Mediterranean World to the Global Setting* (Kendall Hunt Pub. Co., 2007).

tions than those for Diet Coke in *Cosmopolitan*. Thus, the rhetorical tools advertisers use and that readers (like you) employ can change dramatically in any given situation.

In addition, the study of rhetoric carries with it a sense of the *polis* (Greek for "city" or "public") that the authors of this book find appealing. Originally linked to public oratory, rhetoric now subsumes under its umbrella political speeches, public art, television shows, commercials, billboards, and now, the internet. Plato and Aristotle could never have imagined the degree to which rhetoric has been stretched. Nevertheless, rhetorical approaches help make sense of everything from graffiti to buildings to video games to movies to clothing. In short, any text designed to make meaning or have an effect incorporates some aspect of rhetoric. An awareness of the history, reach, and goals of rhetoric make you better readers of the world. Ultimately, rhetoric is about civic engagement.

The World Is a Text is a visual and cultural rhetoric, meaning that this book is a kind of a playbook or how-to manual of rhetorical principles, with emphases on texts and approaches that make meaning in both cultural and visual realms. This book is primarily about writing, but it argues that no good writing can happen without good reading skills. In the remaining pages, we address both. We offer strategies for decoding cultural texts; we provide various strategies for reading and writing; and we offer step-by-step instructions on both reading and writing. Later in this section, we discuss various ways of making arguments and provide strategies for identifying how other texts make arguments with the ultimate goal of rounding out your vocabulary and your facility in regard to persuasion in discourse. One of the most famous scholars of rhetoric, Kenneth Burke, describes rhetoric as the "use of language as a symbolic means of inducing cooperation in beings that by nature respond to symbols."[2] By cooperation here, Burke means that we use language to *understand each other.* That's the basis of all communication—we want to understand each other. Burke's emphasis on symbols points to the importance of signs, signifiers, and the visual language on which so much of the communication in our world relies. His interest in cooperation reveals the degree to which rhetoric is woven into the fabric of a culture, part of the garment that humans wear in the world. The visual and cultural implications of rhetoric and their importance for undergraduate education and writing undergird the larger scope of this book—understanding each other and the world.

FROM RHETORIC TO WRITING

As you have no doubt gleaned by now, our goal is to help you learn to see the rhetorical strategies of various texts and also to get you started writing your own. We are firm

---

2   Burke's quote appears in Golden, *The Rhetoric of Western Thought*, and many other sources.

believers that textual analysis (reading) and textual formation (writing) jointly contribute to the larger process of knowledge making. Thus, we are interested in helping
you to ask not simply what something means but how something means. This is why
reading will help your writing: it teaches you how to be savvy consumers and producers of texts. You will get to know texts from the inside out, so that when it comes to
writing your essay, you will know, intimately, how arguments work.

Here is also where our instructions about reading and your assignments for writing
intersect, because learning to identify rhetoric in cultural and visual texts better enables
you to use rhetoric in your papers. In fact, writing is itself an important component
of interpretation. Writers and thinkers have long seen writing as a means of helping
us arrive at ideas. When we think abstractly, we tend to gloss over ideas so fast that
we do not slow down and articulate them. They are more sensations than thoughts.
To put them down on paper, to compose them into sentences, ideas, and reasons, is
harder than thinking. Indeed, if you have done freewriting exercises, you may have had
no idea what you thought about something until you wrote it down. It is no surprise
that journaling or keeping a diary is vitally important to writers. The act of writing
can often be an act of unlocking: the door opens and ideas, reactions, fears, and hopes
walk right out of your head and on to the page and say, "Here I am!" Sometimes we
wish they had stayed inside, but this is where the interesting work happens, and here
is where learning to read the world as a text can help you learn to write on a college
level. Learning to write well allows us to move into the world of ideas, interaction, and
exchange. And learning to read outside our traditional ideas of what it means to read
will expand your mind even further.

Writing about the world as a text may not only facilitate writing and thinking but
also writing and feeling. Although we certainly do not want to diminish the logical
aspect of writing, we want to pay attention to a component of writing that is often
overlooked, and that is the emotional component. Stephen King, Franz Kafka, Emily
Dickinson, Pablo Neruda, Toni Morrison, and dozens of other writers turned and
continue to turn to writing because it helps them get a handle on the world. Writing
is or can be rewarding, rejuvenating. In part, writing means sharing, participating in
a community of language and ideas. We learn about others and ourselves through
writing because writing is simultaneously self-exploration and self-examination. We
see ourselves in a larger context. Of course, we may not always like what we discover
(perhaps traces of sexism or racism or classism), but uncovering those elements of our
personality and understanding them is a rewarding experience. Writing that is honest,
candid, and reflective attracts us, because those are traits we value.

At the same time, we do not want to neglect the idea that writing is a difficult process to master. Between us, we have authored thousands of papers, articles, handouts,
tests, reports, and now, this book. In almost every case, we went through multiple
drafts, stared at the computer screen, cursed whatever picture was on the wall for its

interference, and struggled at various points along the way. In fact, this very chapter has been through between fifteen and twenty drafts, and we revised it again for this new edition. In some ways, writing is very much like exercising: It does not always feel great when you are doing it, but when you are finished, it is both rewarding and good for you. The authors are drafters by nature—we believe that whereas writing is a form of thinking, several drafts are often needed to convert that thinking into something worth showing the public.

By now, you should be beginning to see some direct connections between writing and reading. Only by reading well can you write well. A good essay makes sense of a topic using detail, insight, and purpose—the same traits one uses to read. We believe that the readings and questions in this book are a good springboard for that writing process. Some of the essays may anger you, but that is okay. Some will make you laugh, some will confuse you, and some will make you see a movie or a place or a gender in ways you never have before. We hope that these readings and images not only show you what writing can do, but also that the texts in this book spark your imagination and push you toward the writing process so that your own work will be as vigorous and as provocative as the texts presented here.

In the next section, we provide some hands-on examples of visual and cultural rhetorical readings so that you can see first hand how you might make the transition from the act of reading to the act of writing.

CHAPTER 3

READING THE WORLD AS A TEXT:
THREE CASE STUDIES ON INTERPRETATION

In this section, we walk you through the act of interpretation, of reading semiotically; that is, we help you read certain texts in ways that you may find unfamiliar. However, as stated earlier, we believe that living critically in the world means living as an informed, questioning, and engaged person. Learning to read the world as a text is a good way to begin, and it is critical for writing a solid essay.

CASE STUDY 1: READING PUBLIC SPACE: STARBUCKS

One of the most familiar places in our modern world is the coffee shop, and in particular, Starbucks. As a ubiquitous presence, it could make for an interesting "read"—many ideas about the world might come from reading a Starbucks. With this in mind, we sat down one morning in a Starbucks and read it as a text. All things have authors of sorts, even a coffee shop. In fact, scholars often talk about a painting or a room or a design or a sign having a "visual grammar"—a series of rules that help us figure out its messages.

We decided the best place to begin figuring out Starbucks's messages was to take notes. So we just started writing down what we saw and thought. We wrote down our impressions, which is really the first level of communication. Below is a transcribed version of our notes:

> Note taking: brown, green, red, brown patterned carpet. Green
> Lighting non-fluorescent Curves
> Wood—metal
> Tables different types Products art—decoration
> Logo "coffee-related art" photos Baby chairs, modern garbage cans
> Advertisements, baskets, games, "Cranium" wood
> Handicapped bathrooms—the New York Times, windows, mahogany, metal
> door handles, pull to get in, push
> Music: "cool," varied

With this information, we can begin to construct a series of observations that could develop into ideas for interpretation and, therefore, for writing:

> Starbucks relies on moderate earth tones for decoration. Their seating places are made of durable materials.

> Their artwork is a mix of coffee photographs and advertisements—primarily for Starbucks items.

> There is lots of light. The lighting they use is bright but not harsh, avoiding fluorescent light.

> Their advertisements are prominent within the store. Their products are geared to the middle and upper classes both by design and content. (Hey—an argument slipped in!)

As you can see by the last statement, in the process of writing down observations, *ideas* about the text itself sneaked into our document, which is what we were hoping for. In this case, the idea that Starbucks is geared toward a particular target audience is an argument, and potentially one that you might pursue in a paper. How could you make this a paper? You could expand the idea of a target audience into multiple paragraphs: one about products, another about décor, maybe one about music, and perhaps another about the location of the particular Starbucks you are in.

If we were going to construct a thesis statement, it might look something like this: "Starbucks appeals to the middle and upper classes through a combination of its décor, music, products, and location."

While this thesis statement is okay and would work to organize a paper, it is still pretty vague. We could ask why Starbucks wants to sell its wares to a particular demographic through its design. We know the answer to this already—they are a commercial venture. But the question of "how" still raises itself—we can see the target audience and the tools, but how Starbucks is using them is a different story. Maybe another question is this: What is Starbucks trying to sell besides coffee? What experience can someone hope to get by entering Starbucks? We would argue that Starbucks is trying to sell an idea of "cool" or "hip" to its customers. And for its target audience of middle- and upper-class people, cool is something these people may feel they need to buy. So a new thesis could be: "Starbucks tries to sell its idea of cool to the middle and upper classes through its hip music; sturdy, smooth décor; and its sleek and streamlined products."

This could still improve, but notice that this thesis gives you an automatic organization of paragraphs about décor, music, merchandise, and location. From here, you could work on incorporating the details of your observations as evidence for the points you are making. For example, you could describe in some detail the nature of the furnishings, the various songs that play over the loudspeaker, and the general location of this particular Starbucks. If you wanted to, you might research how companies use these elements to make their businesses more profitable.

We hope, through this example, that you can see how this sort of thing might work. We began with a trip to Starbucks and ended up talking about demographics and public space. Not all such experiences could end up as papers, but you would be surprised how many can.

CASE STUDY 2: READING FONTS: HOW TYPE CAN SAY A LOT ABOUT TYPE

Although you are only a few words into this section, the shift in font has already altered your reading experience. We associate many things with certain fonts; more than we might expect. Even though you know this is a book for a class, the simple change of font may have made you think of Game of Thrones or some older European manuscript, although no reference to either appeared until just now. **If we were to ask you what fliers written in this font were advertising, what would you say? Even if you have never been to a jazz concert or a Broadway play, you would likely guess one of those two options.** *Similarly, if an invitation appeared in your mailbox engraved in this script, what would you think? Does this font suggest a luau? A Bachelorette watching party? Probably not. In fact, we are willing to bet that your attitude, your general happiness, even your basic anxiety level has altered a bit simply through an alteration of font.* For example, those of you who have relied on Courier to make your essays appear longer may be visited with a sense of joy, nostalgia, or anxiety at seeing it here, in a textbook, where it is just not supposed to be.

In putting this book together, we had several conversations about the most appropriate font. We wanted to express seriousness and scholarly competence, but at the same time, we hoped for a font that would convey a sort of contemporary edginess that we thought the book embodied. THAT FONT PROBABLY WOULD HAVE LOOKED MORE LIKE THIS THAN WHAT WE SETTLED ON, BUT ULTIMATELY, WE DECIDED THAT THIS IS A FONT FOR ADVERTISING OR MENUS—NOT A BOOK. PLUS, THE ALL-CAPS SITUATION MAKES IT LOOK LIKE WE ARE YELLING AT THE READER. That something as small as font can carry so many associations, hang-ups, and biases speaks to the unspoken power of semiotics and the importance of visual rhetoric.

Fonts tell us how the designers of a text want their text to be seen, what associations they want us to have with that text (and perhaps their product). Retailers, advertisers, designers, T-shirt manufacturers, sports franchises, and alcohol producers take full advantage of fonts to influence the public. For example, what if the Oakland Raiders began the 2018 football season with the same famous black and silver pirate logo, but with all the lettering on the uniforms, helmets, and memorabilia in this font:

The Oakland Raiders

Or, if the Raider Nation, considered by sports aficionados to be the craziest, rowdiest fans of any professional American franchise, suddenly changed their promotional and web font to

The Raider Nation
Win, Lose or Tie: Raiders til We Die!!!

In both cases, the groups would lose all credibility—even if the play of the team or the insanity of the fans remained the same—because neither of these fonts suggest dominance, fear, or aggression. The first evokes formality, such as you might find on an invitation to a tea party; the second is somewhat juvenile, wholly playful.

These two examples reveal yet another truism about semiotics—signs are almost never value free. This is certainly the case for fonts. Every font carries associations and assumptions. Take the examples used previously. One reason they seem so ludicrous is that both are somewhat stereotypically feminine. The humor comes in the gap between the values we associate with professional football and the values we associate with curly font. **THE OAKLAND RAIDERS AND THE RAIDER NATION** might work, because we tend to associate this Stencil font with the military, and we tend to associate the military with masculinity, force, power, strength, and victory. THE OAKLAND RAIDERS AND THE RAIDER NATION probably would not work because this Desdemona font calls up art deco, France, and all kinds of associations that are antithetical to the image of American football. Thus, how seriously we take a font is often related to its perceived femininity or masculinity. Consider what traits in font we might link with femininity and which we might consider masculine. Pay attention to flourishes, curls, and fat and wide lines.

Just as fonts often carry gender values, they also frequently carry cultural values as well. For example, why would this sign seem incorrect?

**Jean Luc's
French Bistro**

For better or worse, when we see this font, we tend to think of one kind of cuisine, but when we think of French food, we never consider this font as even a remote possibility for an effective medium of communication. Similarly, we may also carry prejudices toward cultures without even knowing it. To some, an odd juxtaposition of appearance and content can come off not simply as discordant, but offensive as well.

Even though the sentiment may be genuine and completely in line with traditional American Christian values, the Arabic font—a source of fear and anxiety to some

God Bless the United States of America

Americans—somehow sends a different message than if the same phrase appeared in a less loaded font:

God Bless the United States of America

or

GOD BLESS THE UNITED STATES OF AMERICA

If both of these last two examples feel more appropriate than the Arabic-influenced font, it might be useful to examine how and why this might be.

In Chapter 1, we distinguish between the signified and the signifier, and the font/message equation is a perfect example of this complex linguistic and visual coding. If fonts carry positive or negative associations, it is because, over time, a culture has imbued them with meaning—a kind of stereotyping. Our culture would like to think of words and language in nonvisual terms, but the font issue points to ways in which even the written word sends messages.

One final example. Imagine a restaurant called "Beverly's." Based on the font used in the sign in front of the restaurant, think about what kind of food and ambiance is suggested by each sign:

Beverly's

BEVERLY'S

Beverly's

BEVERLY'S

B e v e r l y ' s

BEVERLY'S

Beverly's

Guessing what kind of place the various fonts evoke is relatively easy and fun, but the harder part is figuring out why a certain font sends the message it does. The Beverly's signs are another instance of cultural and visual rhetorics merging. For your papers, if you decide to read an advertisement or a commercial or a movie poster or a building, remember that a font is not merely a means of delivering the written message, it is also a visual cue along with photographs, logos, brands, and illustrations that underscores the larger argument the text is making.

CASE STUDY 3: CAN WE LAUGH? READING ART AND HUMOR IN GEICO COMMERCIALS

Geico is funny. From the talking gecko with the undetermined British accent (Cockney?) to the celebrity "interpreters," to the "It's What You Do" series, Geico has made viewers laugh perhaps harder than any other advertiser in recent memory.

But …

Geico is a commercial enterprise that makes us laugh only to sell us something. Is there anything wrong with this? And more importantly, how might we write about such a phenomenon? Thinking about the Geico ads raises all sorts of questions about art, entertainment, and commerce, not to mention the nature of humor.

In sitting down to write this, we thought about how we might take our reaction to Geico's commercials and convert it into an argument for an essay. We already know that the commercials engage topics that are popular targets of semiotic analysis—art and advertising. A number of influential writers have read billboards, ads in magazines, and television commercials—especially those broadcast during the Super Bowl—in an attempt to make sense of corporate strategies, cultural mores, and common assumptions about race and gender. But the Geico ads complicate these lenses. In fact, the caveman ads produced by Geico not so long ago have very little to say about Geico at all, so selecting the right lens for reading these commercials is important. To help you make sense of the Geico ads, we have provided a sample semiotic reading, taking as our point of departure their most obvious trait—humor.

One way of beginning a reading of the Geico commercials might be to inquire into why these commercials are funny, and to do that, we should determine what types of humor they use. In this situation, as in any such reading, we begin with the obvious. In this case, it is the gecko. The gecko himself has made it clear that he's a pitchman for the company solely because of the similar name. "Because Geico sounds like gecko— that's the only reason I'm here," he says in one commercial. From the start, then, the commercial is asking to be read through a lens of comedy. Despite their charm, geckos do not know anything about car insurance. They cannot even drive. The gecko does not provide price quotes or consumer satisfaction statistics. Geico's use of the gecko is merely for humor's sake. What makes this interesting is that the Geico commercials derive their humor from the fact that they are commercials about commercials. In other words, the commercials in many ways are advertising themselves with only a secondary hook to the product of insurance.

So part of the humor is meta-commentary. Meta-ness simply means acknowledging the subject of what you are talking about as you are talking about it. When the gecko refers to his role in the commercial during the commercial, it is a form of a meta-commentary. Part of the humor here has to do with the way we perceive advertising, as something that is supposed to be forced on us to pay for the television we are watching or the periodical we're reading. Instead, Geico lets us know that we are indeed watching a commercial, and that the commercial may not tell us anything useful about the product.

In turn, this suggests that Geico is not trying to deceive the customer. You might ask yourself whether this is actually true, or whether it matters, or whether Geico is being "honest"—or even whether this question matters in trying to evaluate the commercials. To do this, you should consider what kind of appeal the commercial makes. In the language of rhetoric, one might argue that Geico appeals to both our ethos—our common sense, our sense of ethics, or the credibility of the company itself—as well as our pathos, our emotions: it is making us laugh. The logos, or logic, of the appeal is less apparent; indeed, what we are doing here is trying to decode the logos, so one could argue that its appeal is minimal if we cannot readily perceive it. (We talk more about ethos, pathos, and logos later in this book—"How Do I Formulate Arguments about Popular Culture Texts? A Rhetorical Guide.")

The commercials' ethos appeal builds through a cumulative trust of a company that so willingly makes light of itself. Such an appeal thirty years ago might not have been as effective, because these commercials might have seemed inappropriate in a culture that believed that a company that jokes about itself cannot be taken seriously, but to increasingly savvy consumers, such an approach punctures our usual resistance to companies that do nothing but brag about their products (almost all car companies' commercials do this). Geico trusts its viewers to understand the commercials on multiple levels.

You also might ask why it is important to laugh at insurance commercials. To do that, inquire into the cultural associations surrounding insurance. We often perceive insurance salesmen and insurance companies negatively. Insurance generally is often associated with misfortune; no one calls an insurance company unless something terrible happens. So, when anything insurance-related makes us laugh, the company has already broken down some viewer resistance because so little about insurance is positive, funny, or engaging.

A closer reading of these commercials shows other humorous appeals. Not too long ago, Geico ran "celebrity interpreter" commercials that paired a celebrity with a "Geico customer," who is labeled on-screen as a "real person," whereas the celebrity is labeled as an "actor," or in the case of Burt Bacharach, a "celebrity." The commercial humorously implies that Burt Bacharach is not a real person and suggests that celebrities are somehow more equipped to endorse products rather than real users. That Geico plays with this idea has little to do with insurance but rather entertainment. Of course, in these commercials, celebrities are silly—Bacharach's second line is the hilarious, but nonsensical, "Lizard licks his eyeball," which is, again, a meta-commentary, as it refers to previous Geico commercials when the gecko does, in fact, appear to lick his eyeball.[1] And other celebri-

---

1   This commercial and many other Geico commercials are widely available online.

ties are similarly of no help in validating Geico's competency as an insurance company, like Charo, Little Richard, and Don LaFontaine, the famous announcer for action movie trailers. We likely laugh at these commercials because of the juxtaposition (re-ordering) of traditional ideas of insurance and an absurdist humor, but we could only come to that conclusion through a process of thinking and writing. If we were making this into an actual paper, we might start with a summary of the commercials (it is better to be specific in the introduction rather than general), have a thesis about this juxtaposition, and perhaps write paragraphs about humor, insurance, the specific humor involved in the commercial, and the way the two aspects combine. Taking notes on all of these things, writing down your reactions (no matter how silly they may seem) is a way of applying language to association. It is a form of articulating what you are thinking and feeling.

You might also think about Geico ads as a larger project that involves research. Watch past commercials on YouTube. Track down Geico sales numbers. Read articles about their ad campaigns. From this perspective, it is clear that Geico has established a reputation through humor—the parody of the reality show *Tiny House*, the gecko himself, and the "It's What You Do" series, all of which emphasize branding over information. Geico likely hopes humor, a form of absurdity, will emphasize the importance of consumers for the company, but it is also mainly designed to help emphasize the Geico name, building brand awareness. The messages can be somewhat contradictory—does Geico want its customers to laugh or purchase? Is humor consonant with good insurance service? In a business sense, the Geico ads have paid off, adding two million customers from 2002 to 2006, for a total of seven million.[2]

We know why Geico made these commercials, but why do we laugh—and buy? And should we be laughing at something that is so explicitly commercial? In writing a paper, you could argue either side of the question that underlies this—whether commercials are art—pretty convincingly. On the negative side, you could argue that you should be skeptical of the motives of a producer of art that means to sell you something—it means that the art is not "pure." This is a variation of an argument that has been made many times over the years. Some even argue that the Geico ads are not art but commerce. This raises even more complicated questions about the interplay between commerce and entertainment. What if the Geico commercials are substantially more fun than reruns of *Big Bang Theory*?

However, you could point to the fact that people who do not drive have no financial stake in the ads, and so the ads are really just entertainment for those viewers. Others could argue that most, if not all, art does not have a pure basis, and that to be entertained is a primary consideration in terms of whether to evaluate a piece of art.

---

2   Theresa Howard, "Gecko Wasn't First Choice for Geico," *USA Today*, 16 July 2006.

CHAPTER 4

HOW DO I WRITE A TEXT FOR COLLEGE?
MAKING THE TRANSITION FROM HIGH SCHOOL WRITING

Patty Strong

Writing is thinking. This is what we teachers of college writing believe. Hidden inside that tiny suitcase of a phrase is my whole response to the topic assigned me by my colleague, Jonathan Silverman, one of the authors of the textbook you are currently reading. Knowing my background as a former teacher of high school English, Dr. Silverman asked me to write a piece for students on the differences between writing in high school and writing in college. I have had some time to ponder my answer, and it is this: Writing is thinking. Now that's not very satisfactory, is it? I must unpack that suitcase of a phrase. I will open it up for you, pull out a few well-traveled and wearable ideas, ideas that you may want to try on yourself as you journey through your college writing assignments.

Writing is thinking. I suggest that this idea encompasses the differences between high school writing and the writing expected from students on a college level, not because high school teachers do not expect their students to think, but rather that most students themselves do not approach the writing as an opportunity to think. Students might construct many other kinds of sentences with writing as subject: Writing is hard. Writing is a duty. Writing is something I do to prove that I know something.

When I taught high school English, I certainly assigned writing in order to find out what my students knew. Did they, for example, know what I had taught them about the light and dark symbolism in Chapter 18 of *The Scarlet Letter*? Did they know precisely what Huck Finn said after he reconsidered his letter to Miss Watson ("All right, then, I'll go to hell!") and did they know what I, their teacher, had told them those words meant in terms of Huck's moral development? Could my students spit this information back at me in neat, tidy sentences? That's not to say I did not encourage originality and creativity in my students' writing, but those were a sort of bonus to the bottom-line knowledge I was expecting them to be able to reproduce.

College writing is different precisely because it moves beyond the limited conception that writing is writing what we already know. In college, students write to discover what they do not know, to uncover what they did not know they knew. Students in college should not worry about not having anything to write, because it is the physical and intellectual act of writing, of moving that pen across the page (or tapping the keyboard) that produces the thoughts that become what you have to write. The act of writing will produce the thinking. This thinking need not produce ideas you already know to be true, but should explore meanings and attitude and questions, which are the things that we all wonder and care about.

My discussion of these matters has so far been fairly abstract, caught up in the wind of ideas. Practical matters are of importance here, too, so I will address some points that as a college student you should know. First, your professors are not responsible for your education—you are. While your teachers may in fact care very much that you learn and do well in your coursework, it is not their responsibility to see that you are successful. Your college teacher may not do things you took for granted like reminding you of assignments and tests and paper deadlines. They probably won't accept your illness or the illness of a loved one or a fight with a girlfriend as legitimate excuses for late work. Sloppy work, late work, thoughtless work, tardiness, absences from class—these things are the student's problems. Successful college students accept responsibility for their problems. They expect that consequences will be meted out. Successful students do not offer excuses, lame or otherwise, although they may offer appropriate resolutions. Successful students understand that their education is something they are privileged to own, and as with a dear possession, they must be responsible for managing it. If you wrecked your beloved car, would you find fault with the person who taught you how to drive?

On to the writing task at hand. You will want to write well in college. You probably want to write better and more maturely than you have in the past. To do this, you must be willing to take thinking risks, which are writing risks. I read an interesting quote the other day that I shared with my writing students because I believed it to be true and pretty profound. The American writer Alvin Toffler wrote that "The illiterate of the twenty-first century will not be those who cannot read and write, but those who cannot learn, unlearn, and relearn." And so it is true that when you come to the university for your "higher education," you must be willing to unlearn some old things and relearn them in new ways. That is probably true for just about every academic subject you will explore during your university career, and it is certainly true about the writing courses you will take.

Writing is thinking. Writing will lead you toward thought. Your college writing teachers will expect more of your thinking, thinking you have come to through the process of writing and rewriting. In order to get where you need to be, you must relearn what writing is. You must see that writing is not duty, obligation, and regurgitation, but opportunity, exploration, and discovery. The realization that writing is thinking and that thinking leads to writing is the main idea behind this book—the simple notion that the world is a text to be thought and written about. The successful college writer understands that he or she writes not just for the teacher, not just to prove something to the teacher in order to get a grade, but to uncover unarticulated pathways to knowledge and understanding.

CHAPTER 5

FROM SEMIOTICS TO LENSES:
FINDING AN APPROACH FOR YOUR ESSAYS

Earlier in this book, we talk a great deal about semiotics as a pathway to knowledge and understanding. Formal and informal decoding of cultural and visual cues can be pretty interesting stuff, but you may be wondering what bearing this has on college, grades, and your class. You are going to have to write for this course, and these concepts will help you land on a topic for your essay. Your next step, however, is to select an approach for that paper. Only rarely can essays be simply observational; most of the time you have to turn those observations into arguments. Thus, in order to make an argument, you have to have an approach, or what the talk show host Jim Rome might call a "take." There are any number of approaches or lenses when writing about nontraditional/popular culture/ visual texts. We began with semiotics as it explains how texts make meaning through signification and connotation. But there are other ways of thinking about texts beyond their theoretical components. In this and the following chapters, we devote some time to helping you with the micro aspects of your arguments, and here we give you a broad introduction to the macro aspects of your papers by providing some of the language you need in order to approach these texts.

The main approaches we consider here are those of lenses, microscopes, and windows; language and elements of literary interpretation; context, historical and otherwise; social and political approaches, such as race, class, gender, sexual orientation, region, age—and more; and finally, academic disciplines.

LENSES, MICROSCOPES, AND WINDOWS

The idea of a lens is a metaphor for "putting on" a particular point of view in order to think, read, and write, in much the same way you might put on sunglasses or reading glasses to see the world in a different way. Aside from the major lenses of race and gender, which we address later, there are other lenses you might put on when reading texts, such as college student or consumer; Democrat or Republican (or independent); rural, urban, or suburban; Western or Eastern European or Asian; gay/lesbian/ trans/bi; immigrant; athlete; and so on. By thinking either with or through your own perspective or someone else's, you can put into words the point of view you may have already been using.

A microscope takes something small and makes it bigger. In much the same way, you might take a portion of a text or short contained text, examine it closely, and reveal some larger truths. For example, one might examine a particular image, such as Lady Gaga's clothes or Lisa Simpson's pearls, or the images in your university logo and write about how they represent a particular value. Such an approach can be part of a larger paper or an examination of its own. For instance, one could write an entire essay on the fashion choices in *Empire* or *Portlandia*. Or you could write about feminism in Beyoncé videos. Either way, these essays require close attention to detail.

A window allows one to look outward from a particular perspective, also as a way of exploring a larger truth. One could look at a television show as a way of writing about race or ethnicity or politics. You might, for example, use cable news as a window for the way Americans view politics, a popular song as a window for a way young people view gender attitudes, or a new shopping mall as a window for how Americans currently view consumption. Later in this chapter, we talk about the movie *Office Space* as a window onto the mind-numbing corporate job.

Your professor may point out that these approaches overlap with some of the ones we discuss later—that's true. But we find that sometimes we as scholars and students get untracked when trying to apply the language of traditional interpretation to non-traditional texts.

LANGUAGE AND ELEMENTS OF LITERARY INTERPRETATION

In a sense, each text has an argument and narrative that invites interpretation, whether it is a movie, an advertisement, or a building. One way of thinking about this is to figure out the grammar of whatever the text is. If stories are made up of words and sentences, buildings are made up of beams, concrete, and other materials that are almost always chosen deliberately for effect. Movies are made up of scenes, advertisements of discrete images, specific editing choices, camera angles, and soundtracks that, when taken together, create a kind of cinematic grammar. Now, think about what a particular element of a building could mean. For example, what effect does a new building constructed entirely of brick have on the viewer? What connotations or meanings do bricks have? Why might a designer put in columns? Why build a new building to look like an old warehouse? When a movie character wears a cowboy hat, what does it mean? A critic in *Rolling Stone* makes the argument that the trumpets in Sufjan Stevens's "Casimir Pulaski Day"—an ode to a dead childhood friend—signal Stevens's displeasure with God. For the critic, that particular sound—the blast of trumpets, which are mentioned in the Bible—is similar to a way a writer might use a description of landscape to make a larger point in a novel or short story.[1]

Metaphor remains one of the most popular approaches to any text. A metaphor is a part of a narrative or text that can be taken for the whole of the text itself or as a small indicator of a larger trend. For example, commentators often describe reality shows as metaphors for the decline in quality television (some suggest such shows reflect a culture's lack of interest in story in favor of spectacle) or as metaphors for the postmodern world we live in (everything is edited, everything is performance). Some argue that the hit show *Lost* was a metaphor for the sense of directionlessness and entrapment felt by young people in the new millennium. In the 1990s, grunge music became a metaphor for Generation X's need for controlled catharsis. The Washington Monument, you might argue, is a metaphor for America's soaring ambitions, its towering strength, and, as some have argued, its masculine value system. One could even argue that the movie *The Hangover* is a wacky metaphor for waking up in a post 9-11 world in which nothing makes sense. Metaphors can be tricky, because sometimes they lead a writer to read too much into a text or to over-interpret, but metaphor can be an excellent lens for making sense of a popular text.

CONTEXT, HISTORICAL AND OTHERWISE

Reading a work through the lens of context is another way of making sense of a text and of establishing an argument about that text. For instance, understanding the historical situation of the Old South, slavery, and black/white relations helps make sense of *The Adventures of Huckleberry Finn*. Knowing a bit about William Randolph Hearst and the newspaper business in the 1920s, 1930s, and 1940s makes viewing *Citizen Kane* more meaningful. To place something in context means in essence to put something in perspective, often through comparison. If you were writing about *The Big Bang Theory*, you could put the show into any number of contexts: sitcoms, comedies that featured science, the 2010s generally, workplace comedies shows, California sitcoms, and so on. The reason you put nontraditional texts, or all texts for that matter, into context is to gain perspective by looking at similar items. Typically, we think of context in historical or temporal terms—comparing a building to others built in the same era, for example—but context could also mean comparing all baseball stadiums in terms of their playability, seating, and vistas. Finally, context can also refer to genre—the kind of text it is. For instance, if you want to write about Metallica, you probably would not compare them to Kronos Quartet, Iron and Wine, or Céline Dion, because those acts are all operating in different genres. For the purposes of your paper, it would be most

---

1   Rob Sheffield, review of *Illinois* by Sufjan Stevens, *Rolling Stone*, 28 July 2005.

fruitful to place Metallica in context—perhaps reading them alongside Iron Maiden, Nirvana, or Black Sabbath.

RACE, CLASS, GENDER, SEXUAL ORIENTATION, REGION, AGE—AND MORE

One's experiences affect one's perspective. As we see in Chapter 12, about race and ethnicity, and Chapter 15, concerning gender, people often write from the larger perspective of these groups, which have been historically discriminated against. But discrimination does not need to drive one's group perspective. As a college student, you probably see things differently from your professor; if you come from a working-class background, you may see things from a different perspective than someone from a more wealthy background. In a famous essay on economic class, the critic Michael Parenti reads *Pretty Woman* through the lens of class, arguing that the movie upholds traditional upper-class patriarchal values. On the opposite end, the wonderful British comedy *The Full Monty* can be read as a celebration of working-class men and women, while the popular series *Downton Abbey* looks at how these two strata of society interact (or don't).

ACADEMIC DISCIPLINES

This book might be part of a course called "Writing Across the Disciplines." Although there are different definitions of what that means, generally it signals that your professor or department wants you to learn to write in your chosen discipline or major. Social scientists read texts differently than artists. Scientists approach information in a distinct way, as do semioticians, literary scholars, and cultural critics. The components of disciplinary readings are vocabulary, prose style, and citation. Sometimes this simply means that you need to be attuned to the citation style of your discipline; English departments, for example, use the Modern Language Association style, known as MLA, whereas psychology departments use the American Psychology Association style, or APA. History departments often use Chicago (or Turabian), whereas other disciplines may have their own styles.

Disciplinary approaches can also affect issues of subjectivity and objectivity. For example, in literary studies, film studies, and media studies, writers often ground their writing in argument, interpretation, and insight. But in many social sciences, soft sciences, and the hard sciences, scholars rely on data and objective proof. Thus, a scientist, a film scholar, and a political scientist would each read Al Gore's movie *An Inconvenient Truth* through three very different lenses, because they work in three distinct disciplines.

LANDING ON AN APPROACH

Your professor may have a specific approach in mind for you, but then again, he or she may not. In general, the approach you take will probably mirror your own lenses. If you were raised on a farm in Ohio, you will likely always, in some way or another, look at people, places, and things through the Ohio-rural-farm lens. Thus, you may read a movie like *Field of Dreams* (even though it is set in Iowa) quite differently than a baseball player who grew up in Puerto Rico. As you try to land on an approach for your essay, think about what sort of lenses you tend to look through on a daily basis.

But we would also be lax if we did not suggest that such essential perspectives can be changed. For example, most people who live or work in Manhattan will tell you that New York has transformed them, has made them look at the world differently—even if they came from small towns in the Midwest. Perhaps more important is your willingness to try on approaches or lenses. One of the foremost experiences one of your authors had was learning about others' developed, theoretical perspectives on the world around them; fellow graduate students were feminists, or had race-oriented perspectives, or were highly political, or had completely absorbed even more obscure perspectives. By trying to understand others' perspectives, both through reading and discussion, one can become a better reader of texts.

CHAPTER 6

HOW DO I WRITE ABOUT POPULAR AND VISUAL CULTURE TEXTS?
A TOUR THROUGH THE WRITING PROCESS

We begin by underscoring how important being a good reader is for the writing process. Both processes are about discovery, insight, ordering, and argument. The process of writing, however, differs from the product of writing. When we say product, we mean the produced or finished version—the completed paper that you submit to your instructor. The writing process is the always complex, sometimes arduous, often frustrating, and frequently rushed series of events that eventually lead you to the finished product. There are a lot of theories about writing, so we will not bore you with an overview of all of them. Chances are your instructor or your institution's writing center has a series of handouts or guidelines that will help you along the way, but we thought we would take you on a quick tour of what we see as the highlights of the writing process, with an added emphasis on building a good first paragraph and building sound arguments.

That begins with understanding the assignment.

UNDERSTANDING THE ASSIGNMENT

This is usually the easiest part of the writing process, but it, too, is important. And because you are learning how to be savvy readers of various texts, this task should be easy for you. First, you should read the assignment for the paper as you would read a poem or an advertisement. Look for textual clues that seem particularly important. In fact, we recommend making a list of questions about the assignment itself, such as:

What questions do I have to answer in order to complete or answer the assignment? Do I have a research or writing question that my paper must answer?

Does my assignment contain any code words, such as "compare," "analyze," "research," "unpack," or "explore"? If so, what do these terms mean?

What text or texts am I supposed to write about? Do I understand these texts?

What is my audience? For whom am I writing?

What are the parameters of the assignment? What can I do? What can I not do? Is there anything I do not understand before beginning?

One of the biggest mistakes students make is paying too little attention to the assignment. Like any text, it contains textual cues to help you understand it.

FREEWRITING AND BRAINSTORMING

Freewriting and brainstorming are crucial to the writing process because they generally produce your topic. Freewriting involves the random and uncensored act of writing down anything that comes into your mind on a particular topic. There are any number of ways to freewrite; some teachers and students like visually oriented methods, whereas others prefer a straightforward "Write all you can down in five minutes" approach. Some of our students set a stopwatch at two minutes and write down anything and everything that pops into their heads during that time. When the two minutes are up, they review the list to see if any patterns or ideas emerge. From this list of random stuff, you can generally narrow down a topic. Let us say your assignment is to analyze the popular series *Game of Thrones*, and you see that you jotted down several things that have to do with the way the show looks. From that, you could decide that you want to write on the innovative "look" of *GoT*.

At this point, you can move on to brainstorming. Here, you take a blank piece of paper, or sit down in front of a blank computer screen, and write the topic of your paper across the top: The "look" of *Game of Thrones*. Now, write down everything that pops into your head about the look of the show. See if you can come up with 10 to 20 ideas, observations, or questions. When you are done, look closely at your list. Does a pattern emerge? Are there certain questions or ideas that seem to fit together? Let us say you have written "cool effects," "lots of action," "scary creatures," "mythical overtones," "religious symbols," "good vs. evil," "darkness vs. light," "beautiful scenery," "the camera angles were very unique," "very serious," "it felt like fantasy," and "good wins, evil loses," "dragons!," "zombies!" Based on these observations, you could write a paper about good versus evil, or perhaps certain symbols in the film, like light and dark or white and black. Or you could take things in a different direction and talk about how the "look" of the movie (camera angles, setting, colors, and effects) makes a certain argument or contributes to the theme in some way. Yet another possibility is to combine these observations into a paper that looks at the theme and the form.

The goal here is to try to home in on your topic—the overall subject of your paper. At this point, your topic does not have to be perfectly formulated, but you should be getting an idea of how you might narrow your topic down to something that you can feasibly write a paper about. It is possible—even likely—that as you start plotting an outline, a more defined topic will emerge.

OUTLINING

Once you have your topic, you need to organize your paper. Outlines are helpful because they provide a visual map of your paper so that you can see where you're going and where you have been. An outline is also useful in helping you see if your ideas fit together, if the paper is coherent, and if the paper is equally distributed among your various points. If you find yourself getting stuck or suffering from writer's block, an outline might help push you along. In addition, an outline presents your ideas in a logical format, and it shows the relationship among the various components of your paper.

The truth is that deciding on these various components is a process of trial and error. We change our minds all the time. So, as authors of this text, we are reluctant to say that one approach is better than another. Writing is always an organic process—that is, it grows at its own pace in its own way, and as a writer, you will likely need to adjust to accommodate where your ideas want to go.

No doubt, your instructor will talk a great deal about developing a thesis (which is the main argument or focus of your essay—what you argue about your topic), and he or she may encourage you to make this thesis part of your outline. This is a common strategy. The only problem is that you may make an outline with an idea of a thesis, finish the outline, and decide you need to change your thesis. At that point, you should make yet another outline. During the writing process, you may hone your thesis yet again, at which point, you will probably want to draft another outline so that you stay on course given your new thesis. Our point here is that there is no definitive process when you are talking about the very fuzzy beginning stages of writing a paper. You should do whatever works for you—whatever leads to the most organized product.

Unlike the authors of most other books, we decided to combine a section on outlining and thesis making because, for us, the two go hand in hand. Most suggest that writers figure out a thesis before doing an outline. Our experience, however, tells us that arriving at a thesis is often hard, and we do not always know exactly what we want to say about our topic until we get a visual map of the paper. In fact, most of the time, you arrive at your thesis after the first draft of the essay. Just remember that the first outline you make does not have to be the last outline—you can and should change it as you see fit.

Now to that visual map. Traditionally, an outline states your topic (maybe states your thesis), enumerates your main points and supporting arguments in Roman numerals and, beneath the Roman numerals, lists your evidence in letters. For an essay with two main points, an outline might look something like this:

THE TITLE OF MY ESSAY
Introduction (1–2 paragraphs)
Thesis: This is my thesis statement, if I have one at this point

My first point (2–4 paragraphs)
My supporting evidence
My supporting evidence
My second point (2–6 paragraphs)
My supporting evidence
Further evidence, graphs, statistics perhaps
My supporting evidence
Further evidence
My smart conclusion (1–2 paragraphs)

Notice how the outline helps flesh out an organizing idea, even if it is in the most general way. The final outline almost never matches up with the first version, but an outline can help you see the strengths and weaknesses of your organization, and it can help you think in an organized way.

Still, outlining in this manner may not suit everyone. Some students (and professors) do not like outlining because they do not refer to the outline when writing, and they feel like the whole process is a waste of time. Others like to outline at various stages of writing; some outline after they have written a draft to make sure they have covered everything they wanted to cover. Those approaches are okay as well; so is writing an outline that is less formal in nature. At various times, we have written outlines that are barely outlines—just a mere list of points. Other times, we have written outlines with topic sentences of every one of our paragraphs. The approach you take will depend not only on class requirements, but also on the topic of your paper, your knowledge of the topic, and the amount of research required.

The reason we are committed to outlining is that it separates to some degree the thinking and composing stages of writing; if you know more or less what you want to say before you start putting words on paper, the more likely you are to write a clear and thoughtful draft, one that needs less extensive revision. The thinking aspect of outlining is why it is at once difficult and rewarding.

CONSTRUCTING A GOOD THESIS

Now that you have an idea of the work an outline can do, we can move on to helping you construct a thesis. As stated earlier, a thesis is the argument that you make about your topic. It is the main point, the assertion, you set forth in your essay.

We should say at the outset that the term "thesis" is only one possible word for the paper's argument. Some instructors like the term "claim," some like "focus," still others like "controlling idea." Regardless of what term you use, the concept is the same. The thesis is the idea you propose in your paper—it is not a statement of fact but rather a claim, an idea.

The most important first step is to distinguish among a topic, a thesis, and a thesis statement. One of the great mistakes students make is that they assume a topic is a thesis. A topic is merely the avenue to the freeway that is the thesis, the appetizer to the main course. Let us say you are writing a paper about affirmative action. The topic is what your paper concerns, which is affirmative action. Your thesis is the argument you make *about* affirmative action. Your thesis statement is the actual articulation, the statement or statements in which you unpack or explain your thesis. Now, a thesis statement does not have to be (nor should it be) one simplified sentence; in fact, it could and probably should be two or three sentences, or even a full paragraph. (A book can have a thesis statement that goes on for pages.)

We might break down these three components as follows:

Topic: What you are writing about (Affirmative action)

Thesis: What you argue about your topic (Affirmative action is a necessary law)

Thesis statement: The reason for or explanation of your overall thesis—this usually appears in the first or second paragraph of your essay (Affirmative action is a necessary law because it prevents discriminatory hiring practices. Minorities, women, people with disabilities, and gay and lesbian workers have suffered discrimination for decades. Affirmative action not only redresses past wrongs, but also sets a level playing field for all job applicants. In short, it ensures democracy.)

Generally, the topic causes you the least anxiety. Your instructor will help you with your topic and may even provide one for you. In any case, you cannot start a paper without a topic.

The real task is figuring out your thesis. Many students feel anxious if they do not have a thesis when they begin the writing process, but that is normal and in a way preferable in the quest to find a solid argument. Sometimes it is enough to have what we might refer to as a thesis question—a question that when answered through writing and research, actually reveals your thesis to you. Or you might have what we call a "working thesis," one that is too broad for a final paper but is specific enough to guide you through the writing process. Often you must write a first draft of your essay before a thesis finally emerges. Remember that writing is exploration and discovery, so it may take some freewriting, brainstorming, outlining, and drafting before you land on a thesis. But stay with the process—you will eventually find what you want to say.

Perhaps the most confusing aspect of the thesis for students is the realization that a good thesis means you might be wrong. For example, an ineffective thesis might be something like, "The sitcom *Black-ish* is about an African American family." This sentence is not a thesis statement because it is a statement of fact—it is not a statement you actually need to support. What would be a thesis is something like "The real audience for *Black-ish* is not African Americans but middle-class white Americans." This is a good thesis because there is something at stake. You need to provide evidence to make your point. And scariest of all, you might be wrong!

In fact, you know you are on the road to a good thesis if you think someone might be able to argue against your point. That may sound counterintuitive, but it's true. Writing is grounded in rhetoric, which, as we discussed earlier, is the art of persuasion. Your goal in your papers is not necessarily to change your audience's mind but to get them to consider your ideas. Thus, your thesis needs to be something manageable, something reasonable that you can argue about with confidence and clarity.

The most effective strategy we found with helping our students understand a thesis is to use the example of the hypothesis. As most of you know, a hypothesis is an educated guess. A thesis is the same thing. In Greek, *thesis* means "a proposition" or "an idea"; *hypo* is Greek for "under" or "beneath." So, literally, a hypothesis is a "proposition laid down." Your thesis is the same thing. It is not a fact; it is not a statement. It is an idea, a proposition that you lay down on paper and then set out to support. You are not absolutely sure that affirmative action is a necessary law, but you believe it is. You are pretty confident in your stance, but you also know that someone could write an essay arguing why affirmative action should be abolished. This possibility of disagreement is how you know you have a good thesis, because you must provide sound reasons and convincing examples to support your assertion about the necessity for affirmative action.

Why must a thesis be an educated guess? Because if a thesis is a statement of fact, there is literally nothing to argue. If your thesis is "affirmative action is a law that was designed to prevent discrimination," you have simply stated a fact. There is nothing at stake, nothing to debate. Even a thesis like "affirmative action is an important law" is rather weak. Virtually no one would suggest that affirmative action is not important. It has been extraordinarily important in American culture. So, again, that is not the best thesis you could come up with, although it remains better than our first example. However, arguing that it is a necessary law makes your thesis more provocative, more risky. Therefore, it is likely to draw interest and get people excited. Readers will want to see your reasons and think about the examples you provide.

To help, we will break it down even further, using an example from current American popular culture—*Star Wars: The Force Awakens*. You've probably seen the movie, and you probably had some sort of opinion about it.

Weak thesis: *The Force Awakens* is the first *Star Wars* movie to feature a black actor and a Latino actor in starring roles.

This is a weak thesis statement because it is a statement of fact. No one would debate this point.

Better thesis: *The Force Awakens* makes race and ethnicity part of its plot structure.

This is a better thesis statement because it proposes something a bit controversial. It is possible to argue against this point, since the characters in the film don't really talk too much—if at all—about race and ethnicity. However, there is evidence in the movie to suggest your thesis could be supported by casting choices and themes within the film.

Even better thesis: Director J.J. Abrams took the *Star Wars* franchise in a new direction by making race and ethnicity an important part of the film both through themes and casting. By making the First Order reminiscent of the Nazis and by casting a black actor as Finn and a Latino actor as Poe, Abrams makes the values of *The Force Awakens* match current American values on race and racial equality.

This thesis statement is even better because it provides a bit more precision, and it gives a reason for the author's stance. It is easier, then, for this writer to prove the thesis because the reason is already articulated. Homing in on a good thesis is the foundation for building a good paragraph—which, in turn, is the foundation for building a good essay.

BUILDING AN OPENING PARAGRAPH: A CASE STUDY

The opening paragraph for your essay does a great deal of work, both for your thesis and for your audience. For your audience, it sets up your argument and informs them what is going to happen in the remaining pages. In the paper, it functions as the road map, pointing readers down certain avenues, and telling them to avoid others. If your reader is confused after the first paragraph, she may remain confused for a good bit of your essay, and that is never what you want.

An opening paragraph should do a number of things—it should engage the reader's interest with an entertaining or provocative opening sentence, and it should provide the road map for the rest of the paper. In addition, your opening paragraph is typically the home for your thesis statement (although some professors might have different preferences on whether your thesis must go in the first paragraph). It is also the face for your paper, so it should be well organized, moving from a general observation to the more specific thesis statement (think of an upside-down pyramid—broad going down to narrow). For the writer, the opening paragraph is critical because it provides the formula for working through the issues of the essay itself. A vague opener provides too little direction; a paragraph that tries to argue three or four different topics never gets on the right track; and a paragraph that does not make an argument has a tendency to go nowhere, because it keeps restating facts instead of staking out a position and making an argument.

The purpose of this section is to avoid these pitfalls. Here, we provide some models of opening paragraphs before and after revision to show you how a thorough revising process can improve your opening paragraph, strengthen your thesis, and provide a good entrée into your essay.

As an example, we chose to write about the movie *Office Space*. You like the movie. You think it is funny, and all of your friends think it is funny. During parties and over lunch, you trade lines with each other. You agree that the movie speaks to your generation in some odd way, but you are having trouble figuring out what you want to say about it. You decide to make a list of all possible observations and some questions about those observations:

Office Space speaks to people of my generation. (Why is this important?)

Office Space is funny. (But that's not an argument.)

Office Space is the funniest movie of the last 15 years. (But how would I prove that?)

Office Space makes a connection with college students like no other movie. (Is this true? What about *Lord of the Rings* or *Caddyshack*? Or *Old School* or *Step Brothers?*)

Office Space was not a huge box office hit, but it is wildly popular among college students. (Maybe its biggest audience is college students?)

We like *Office Space* because it is funny.

We like *Office Space* because it is about rebellion. It is anti-establishment, anti-corporate.

Maybe we identify with it because it is also anti-institution, like school or college.

Office Space appeals to college students because they can identify with the anti-institution theme. (But we are all part of institutions—school, jobs.)

We like *Office Space* because it is anti-institution and yet not. (It is kind of subversive, but not really. The people in it are kind of lazy.)

This is a pretty good list. We can likely get the beginnings of an argument from it. The trick is finding something that is truly an argument. Saying that *Office Space* is funny is not much of an argument. Most would agree with this, and really, who cares if it is funny or not? That does not help us understand the movie any better. Arguing that college students like it is also overstating the obvious. The key is to explain why this particular movie appeals to college students at this particular time. Of course, one could talk about the fantasy of stealing a million dollars or getting a date with Jennifer Aniston, or the bigger fantasy of enjoying working construction over being in a cubicle, but those kinds of ideas occur in other movies. What sets this movie apart is the idea of being subversive (sort of) in an institutional setting. You want your paper to be unique, and you want it to tell your readers something they might find compelling. Readers can usually tell after an opening paragraph if there is anything in there for them, so as you craft your essay, ask yourself—Am I giving pertinent information? Is my argument interesting?

So the first try at an opening paragraph might look like this:

Office Space, directed by Mike Judge, has become a classic movie for college students. It's funny plot, it's witty dialogue and stance on corporate life appeals to students across disciplines and states. One might wonder why a movie that was not a box-office sensation has become a cult sensation among college students, but it's clear that *Office Space* appeals to students in a number of ways. Perhaps the biggest way is the movie's theme of rebellion. Students can identify with the movie's anti-corporate message.

Okay, so what do we see here? On a micro level, there are some problems with the prose: the rogue apostrophe in "it's" (two instances in the second sentence) has to go; the phrase "across disciplines and states" is vague and not really helpful; "box-office sensation" is a cliché and also vague; "number of ways" also does not do much work. Still, there is also a great deal of information here to work with. The beginnings of our thesis probably rest in the last two sentences—it is there that we make our argument. On closer examination, however, it would appear that the last sentence is not really an argument. Almost no one would disagree with that statement, so proving it would be easy but ultimately pointless. Essays that merely sum up what everyone agrees with do little to further our understanding of the issue or topic at hand. From an entertainment perspective, a good opening paragraph needs to give us reasons to keep reading, so the next version should incorporate some reasons why the movie appeals to students. It should also be a bit more sophisticated and precise. So, in the next version, list some reasons the movie appeals to college students, and give the date of the film, for starters. And do a bit of research and see what you can come up with.

Draft two might come out like this:

Office Space (1999), directed by Mike Judge of *Beavis and Butthead* fame, has become an underground classic among American college students. It is not uncommon to overhear students quoting entire passages from the movie, and there is even an *Office Space* drinking game. Though the movie features a couple of funny subplots involving dating and stealing a million dollars, the real draw of the movie lies in the fact that it is rather anti-establishment. The main character of the film does not simply quit his job—he actually stops working. What's more, he gets rewarded for it through a promotion. Thus, *Office Space* sends a message to college students that when they enter the same corporate environment, they too can be rewarded for rebelling against the corporate mindset.

Wow, what happened here? On one hand, the paragraph is much stronger. Notice the increased specificity: American college students, examples of how students enjoy the movie, more active verbs instead of being verbs (is, are); even some details from the movie itself. But, beyond all that, the thesis has gone off in a different direction! Our argument was that students relate to the movie's theme of rebellion; now, it would appear that we are arguing that students like the movie because they will get rewarded for rebelling. Is that what we want to argue? Is that the reason students like the movie? Does the appeal of the movie lie in the fact that students relate to it, or that it gives them hope? What if it is both? Is there a way to work both into the thesis? Generally, the more precise you are, and the more thorough your thesis is, the better; however, yours has gone off in a different direction! In truth, probably both things appeal to students, so why not strengthen the thesis and the essay by making arguments about both?

The resulting third draft:

Mike Judge took slacking to new heights with his hilarious cartoon *Beavis and Butthead*, which chronicled the lives of two under-achieving teenage boys who had a great deal of fun doing a great deal of nothing. Judge's first movie involving real humans is also about doing nothing, but this time it is recent college graduates who find themselves working in cubicles for a mind-numbing corporation. Despite the fact that *Office Space* (1999) was not a huge hit at the box office, it has become an underground classic across university campuses. Students quote entire scenes to each other from memory, *Office Space* T-shirts abound, and there is even an *Office Space* drinking game. One might wonder why a movie with no real stars except for Jennifer Aniston has made such an impact on this generation of students. Though there are some funny subplots involving dating and stealing a million dollars from a corporation, the main action of the movie comes when the main character, Peter, decides to stop working but winds up getting a promotion. Thus, the movie appeals to students not simply because it champions rebelling against the man, but it suggests one might get rewarded for doing so. On one hand, students identify with the desire to completely stop working, and they like the idea that things might turn out better for them if they do. Ultimately, students are drawn to *Office Space* because it tells them they can be anti-establishment and successful at the same time.

This version is better not because it is longer, but because it provides detail, it is precise, and it features a thorough three-sentence thesis statement. Readers know from this opening paragraph that we are going to read an essay that makes an argument and makes an argument about the two ways/reasons the movie appeals to college students.

Because we have a focused thesis, we can now go into a lot of detail in the rest of our paper about how and why students relate to specific scenes and concepts, and we can also make some interesting observations about "safe rebellion" and rewards. From here on, the writing process involves "proving" and elaborating on the thesis we just wrote.

A note here on opening paragraphs: One of the authors believes that writing the opening paragraph should come closer to the end of the composing process rather than the beginning. Although getting a thesis early is important, writing an opening paragraph before you know what you want to say might mean you must extensively revise the paragraph or scrap it altogether. Some writers, however, need to "begin with beginning"—they cannot go on until they know exactly what their argument is going to be. Ultimately, your preference regarding the writing process is less important than the finished product.

Finally, avoid writing a clichéd introduction. Do not use phrases like "since the beginning of time," which is much too general and tells us little. Also resist using a dictionary definition of an important word. These two strategies should almost never be used in college writing. If you want to use a time construction, confine it to specific knowable time, such as "the recent past" or "in the 1990s." If you find yourself drifting toward a dictionary definition, try defining the word yourself, looking in a more specialized source such as a book about the subject (but be careful to cite), or engaging the definition you find by arguing with it or refining it. Never write: "The dictionary defines [your subject here] as ..."—there are many different dictionaries, all of which define words slightly differently.

If you take your opening paragraph seriously, use it as a method of organization, and make it interesting, you will be off to a good start with your paper.

BUILDING GOOD PARAGRAPHS

Building a good paper is relatively simple, once you understand the formula. By formula, we do not necessarily mean a standard five-paragraph essay. Instead of thinking of your paper in terms of numbers of paragraphs, think in terms of points or reasons. By "points," we mean ideas, concepts, observations, or reasons that support the argument you make in your thesis. The units that help you organize these points are the paragraphs themselves. This section helps you get a handle on how to structure your paragraphs so that you make the most of your supporting points.

For a typical undergraduate essay, you do not want too many or too few points. If you are arguing about affirmative action, how many reasons do you want to include in your paper to support your thesis? Do you want seven? No, that's too many. One? That's too few. Generally, we suggest two to four points or reasons for a standard three-to-six page essay. For a longer assignment, like a research paper, you may want four or five points to drive home your argument. But the danger of including too many points in your paper is that, unless you can supply ample evidence for each point, an overabundance of points winds up having the opposite of the intended effect. Rather than bolstering your argument by the sheer number of reasons, you tend to weaken your argument because you dilute your points through an overabundance of reasons and a lack of evidence. In other words, it is better to write three or four paragraphs for one or two points than to write five paragraphs for five points.

One very good bit of advice: write more about less as opposed to less about more. By this we mean, go into great detail about two or three claims rather than five or six.

The key to making and supporting your assertions is the paragraph. Paragraphs are the infrastructure of your essay; they frame and support the arguments you make. Every paragraph is like a mini-essay. Just as your essay has a thesis statement, so does your paragraph have a topic sentence—a sentence in which you lay out the main idea for that paragraph. Once you write your topic sentence, then you have to provide evidence to support the claim you have made in your topic sentence. Each paragraph has its own topic and its own mini-assertion, and when taken together, all of these paragraphs work together to support the overall thesis of the entire essay.

Topic sentences should establish the mini-argument of your paragraph. Try to make them assertive and focused, because they serve as a small map to the theme of your paragraph. Some examples:

Weak topic sentence: This is a plan one finds in the library.

Weak topic sentence: *Family Guy* first aired in 2002.

These are weak topic sentences because they simply state facts rather than advance an argument. Note the topic sentences of the previous two paragraphs. Neither are over-the-top in terms of making an argument, but they both make assertions. Following are topic sentences from a freshman essay on the overuse of medication in the United States:

- The increasing overuse of medication has been made possible by the "quick-fix" mentality that has become prevalent in our society.
- A big factor leading to the increasing amount of over-medication is the rampant advertising of new drugs by the pharmaceutical companies.
- In addition to our desire for quick and easy solutions, America's preoccupation with youth and physical perfection is also to blame for the overconsumption of drugs in our society.

This last example is particularly good because it includes a transition ("in addition to our desire for quick and easy solutions") in the topic sentence. The topic of the preceding paragraph focuses on America's desire for quick and easy solutions, and the author used the topic sentence not only to advance her idea about youth and physical perfection, but she also reminded the reader of her previous topic, making her overall argument feel connected, part of a piece. Remember—make assertions in your topic sentences.

Once you have a clear, focused topic sentence, it is time to move on to the rest of your paragraph. For instance, say your topic sentence is: "*Scandal* is a revolutionary show because it challenges traditional notions of race in Washington, DC." What might be your next move? You could talk about how Washington is portrayed in older shows like *The West Wing*. You could describe the ethnicity of Olivia Pope. You could even talk about the relationship between race and gender. Perhaps there are key scenes you can describe and explain.

This is also a good time to bring in quotes from other writers that support your assertions. What are TV critics saying about *Scandal* and race? What about websites like *The Root?* Remember, if you quote from another source, or if you quote from a primary text, be sure you explain how the passage you quote supports your thesis. (And, of course, cite the quote's origin.) The quote cannot explain itself—you must tell your audience why that quote is important, why and how the statistics you include are evidence the reader should pay attention to.

Finally, end your paragraphs well. The most common mistake students make when writing paragraphs is that they tend to trail off. Make that last sentence a kind of connector—make it tie everything in the paragraph back to the topic sentence. When possible, also reinforce the fact that your paragraphs are working together by writing transition sentences from one paragraph to the next. For example, a good transition in the essay on *Scandal* would acknowledge the topic of the preceding paragraph and lead into the topic for the paragraph at hand. Such a sentence might look like this: "Not only does *Scandal* break new ground in regard to race, it also makes headway in terms of gender. Note how this sentence refers to the subject of the previous paragraph (race) and also how it informs us of the topic we are about to engage (gender).

Start on your next paragraph with the same model. Keep doing this until you have built yourself a paper. Then go back and revise and edit, revise and edit, revise and edit. The key to building good paragraphs is using them to make arguments. The next section walks you through that process.

DRAFTING THE WHOLE ESSAY

Although we spend a great deal of energy explaining various strategies for composing a paper, it still comes down to the actual work of thinking about a topic, doing your own method of prewriting (outlining, brainstorming, etc.), and putting the words on paper. In other words, you still have to write that first draft.

Sentence by sentence, and paragraph by paragraph, you start building your paper. Remember to give as much detail as possible. Include examples from the text you are writing about, and try to avoid plot summary or unnecessary description. Remember: Analyze, do not summarize. In other words, do not simply provide information—make sense of information for us.

Once you finish your first draft, you may discover that buried somewhere in your closing paragraph is the very good articulation of the thesis you have been trying to prove for several pages. This happens because, as we have said, writing is a discovery process. So by working through your ideas, your arguments, your textual examples, you start to focus on what you have been trying to say all along.

Now that you have a better idea of what you want to say, it is time for the real work—editing and revising.

EDITING AND REVISING, EDITING AND REVISING, EDITING AND REVISING

The single biggest mistake student writers make is turning in their first draft. The first draft is often little more than a blueprint—it is merely an experiment. In the editing and revising stage, you convert the process of writing into the written product. Here, you turn a bad paper into a decent one, or a good paper into a great one. You can clear up confusing sentences, focus your argument, correct bad grammar, and, most important, make your paper clearer and more thorough. Students think that they are good writers if papers come easily. This is the biggest myth in writing. A good paper happens through several stabs at editing and revising.

There are a number of strategies for editing and revising, so we'll give you a couple of our favorites. First, when you are ready to edit and revise, read your paper through backward. Start at the very end, and read it backward, one sentence at a time. This forces you to slow down and see the sentence as its own entity. It is probably the most useful strategy for correcting your own writing. Even more helpful is getting a peer to read your paper. Another person can point out errors, inconsistencies, or vague statements that you may miss because you are too close to the process. An often painful but very effective way of editing is reading your paper out loud. The authors often do this, especially when presenting our work to other people.

Finally, we also recommend that although you may write hot, you should edit cold. What we mean by this is that you need to step back from your paper when you edit. Look at it objectively. Try not to get caught up in your prose or your argument. Work on being succinct and clear. Practically, this means not working on your essay for a period of time, even if that period is hours, not days. As professors, we are well aware that you may wait until the last minute to write a paper. Although we are not endorsing this way of composing, you still need to find a way to step away from the essay and come back to it to get some perspective on what you have written.

This is also the time to go to back over the arguments you made. (Here we introduce some terms that you see again in Chapter 7.) Look at your logos and pathos—are they appropriate? Have you made argumentative errors? Are you guilty of using fallacies? Do you supply enough good evidence to support your assertions? Do you end your paragraphs well?

It may take several drafts (in fact, it should) before you feel comfortable with your paper. So we recommend at least three different passes at editing and revising before turning in your paper. We advocate going back over and looking at your language one last time. Do not use words that are not part of your vocabulary; try to avoid stating the obvious. Be original, be honest, and be engaged. We urge you, above all else, to think complexly, but write simply. In writing a recent book, one of us has, conservatively, rewritten the introduction to a chapter more than thirty times. Revising is often a great deal of work, and sometimes rewriting takes multiple drafts.

Finally, we want to reiterate here that writing is not easy or simple for anyone. Although you may think that you are not a strong writer, and that others write more easily and naturally, the truth is that all "good" writers spend a significant amount of time revising their work. In fact, most good writers enjoy this part of the composing process, because it is the time when they see their writing actually turn into something worth sharing with someone else.

TURNING IN THE FINISHED PRODUCT

The most enjoyable part of the process! Double-check spelling and grammar issues. If you did a research paper, check your citations and go over your Bibliography or Works Cited pages. Make sure you have cited all the material from outside sources you used in your paper—not to do so is to plagiarize!

Turn in the paper and go celebrate!

SOME FINAL TIPS: A RECAP

- Distinguish between a topic and a thesis.
- Your thesis does not have to be one concise sentence; it can be several sentences, perhaps even an entire paragraph. It might even be helpful to think of your thesis as your focus, your idea that you are trying to support.
- "Thesis" comes from "hypothesis." A hypothesis is an educated guess. So is your thesis. It is an educated guess, an idea that you are trying to support. You do not have to develop an over-the-top airtight argument; you simply want your reader to consider your point of view.
- Writing is conversation; it is dialogue. Keep asking questions of yourself, your writing, and your topic. Ask yourself, "Why is this so?" Make sure you answer. Be specific; be thorough.
- Consider your audience. You should never assume they have read the text you are writing about, so do not toss around names or scenes without explaining them a little. It is called "giving context." There is a big difference between giving context (valuable information) and summarizing the plot (regurgitation).
- Make good arguments. Use logos, pathos, and ethos appropriately. Try to avoid fallacies.

CHAPTER 7

HOW DO I FORMULATE ARGUMENTS ABOUT POPULAR CULTURE TEXTS? A RHETORICAL GUIDE

KNOWING YOUR ARGUMENTS

As we suggest in the previous section, building a good essay is dependent on making good arguments and supporting them with solid evidence. In contemporary American culture, "argument" tends to carry negative connotations. Few like getting into arguments, and no one wants to be seen as an argumentative person. However, in writing, argument has a slightly different meaning. When we talk about arguments or argumentation, what we mean is staking out a position or taking a stance. In writing and rhetoric, to argue means to put forth an assertion or a proposition and to support that position with evidence. If you are using this book, then most of the writing you do in your class involves making an argument and backing it up. So, in your regular, non-writing life, feel free to go on avoiding arguments, but in your writing life, we urge you to think positively about the prospect of making a compelling argument.

Before we go into specific kinds of arguments, it might be useful to think about why we make arguments. In academic settings, it is important to be able to argue a specific point because almost all information is debatable, particularly in the arts, humanities, and social sciences. Should welfare be abolished? Is capital punishment moral? Is Picasso's *Guernica* transgressive? Is the Transamerica pyramid in San Francisco an ugly building? Is Johnny Depp a jerk? Why are the Kardashians famous? Is Beyoncé a feminist? Is there a relationship between Christianity and Buddhism? Should we discount the poetry of Ezra Pound, T.S. Eliot, and e.e. cummings because they wrote anti-Semitic material? These are important questions with no clear answers. Accordingly, you need to be able to justify or explain your opinions on these issues. Holding an opinion and backing up that opinion is argument, and we engage in this kind of argumentation all the time. What is the best song of the 2000s? What is the best horror movie? What five books would you take to a desert island, and why? These are fun arguments, and perhaps mostly intellectual exercises, but down the road, being able to argue persuasively might be important in a job ("Here is why we should choose Bob's marketing strategy"), a relationship ("Honey, I know you think I should get an MBA, but let me tell you why an MFA in creative writing is better for me and the kids"), to making purchases ("Let me give you seven reasons why you do not need that Hermes bag"). In fact, as we put this book together, we had daily (but friendly and funny) arguments over what readings to publish, the tone of this very chapter, and what should go on the cover. Finally, knowing how arguments work also helps you discover more fully your own stance on a particular issue. Often, understanding how you feel about a topic is difficult if you do not write or talk about it.

The question is, how does one make an effective argument? There are two ways to look at this question. The first is to approach it from the perspective of the argument; the other is to approach it from the perspective of the audience. When we think of arguments, we tend to break them down into two types—logical and emotional. Arguments that appeal to our sense of logic are arguments of *logos* (Greek for "word" or "reason"); those that cater to our emotions are arguments of *pathos* (Greek for "suffering" and "feeling"). Both are effective forms of persuasion, but they function in different ways and sometimes serve different purposes. Although you should use both in your essays, your main focus should be on building an argument based on logos.

Arguments of logos appeal to our sense of reason and logic. They tend to rely on facts, statistics, specific examples, and authoritative statements. Your supporting evidence for these kinds of arguments is critical. It must be accurate, valid, and specific. For instance, while looking over essays we thought might be useful, we came across a study arguing that long-distance romantic relationships among college students generally did not last very long. Based on this description, what kinds of evidence do you think the authors of the study relied on? Rumor and innuendo? A survey of people who graduated from college in 1979? A close examination of TV shows about college students? A review of the film *Everybody Wants Some*? Of course not. The authors were sociologists who surveyed hundreds of college students who were or had been involved in long-distance relationships. They provided almost six pages of statistics; they allowed for differences in age, race, gender, and location; and they did their survey over a respectable amount of time. In short, they relied on objective data, scientific reasoning, and sound survey practices to help make their argument that long-distance relationships in college tend not to work out.[1]

Think about what kinds of information would persuade you in certain situations. What would make you buy an iPod over some other MP3 player? Or, more importantly, what would convince you to buy a Volvo over a Hyundai for driving around your newborn twins? If you were going to write a paper on fire safety, would you rely on the expertise of a fire marshal or a medical doctor? If you were writing an essay on water pollution, would you consult scientific journals and EPA studies, or would you

---

1   David Knox et al., "Absence Makes the Heart Grow Fonder?: Long Distance Dating Relationships among College Students," *College Student Journal*, vol. 36, no. 3, 2002, p. 364ff.

rely on the websites of chemical corporations? Readers are more likely to be moved by the soundness of your argument if your supporting evidence seems logical, objective, verifiable, and reasonable.

Having said that, it would be a mistake to dismiss arguments of pathos outright. In fact, we believe that many teachers and writers have too easily separated intellect and emotion when talking about arguments. Arguments of pathos can be unusually powerful and convincing because they appeal to our needs, desires, fears, values, and emotions. The statement, "You should get an iPhone because they are just plain cooler than anything else out there" is an appeal to pathos. Notice how this claim ignores any information about warranties, durability, price, or functionality. Rather, the statement plays on our desire to be cool—a most powerful appeal. If you are truthful with yourself, you might be surprised just how often such arguments actually work.

Most television commercials and advertisements in popular magazines play on our sense of pathos. If you have found yourself moved by those Michelin tire commercials in which nothing much happens except a cute little baby plays around in an empty Michelin tire, then the good folks in the marketing department at Michelin have been successful. If you have fought back a tear at an image of an elderly couple holding hands, or believed (if even for an instant) that drinking a certain light beer might get you more dates, then you have been moved by an appeal to your sense of pathos. Now, appeals to pathos are not necessarily bad or manipulative; on the contrary, they can be effective when statistics or logic feels cold and inhuman.

We believe that the most effective arguments are those that combine logos and pathos, and, as we discuss next, ethos. Emotional appeals without facts feel incomplete, and scientific data without human appeal feel cold. We still maintain that your essays should make appeals to logos over pathos, but we encourage you to build arguments in which emotion supports or enhances logic. Arguments that feature good combinations of logos and pathos make you and your essay appear both smart and human—a good mix.

Not only do you need to create an appropriate mix of logos and pathos for your intended audience, but you must also create an appropriate *ethos*. Greek for "character" or "disposition," a writer's ethos is his or her sense of credibility. For most conservative Republicans, Rachel Maddow has little credibility, so for them she would have a low ethos. However, someone like Colin Powell, a four-star general who was the former secretary of state for President George W. Bush, enjoys the respect of many Republicans and Democrats. Most Americans trust him; they find him credible. Therefore, Powell's ethos is high. The ethos of public figures like Powell and Maddow are easier to talk about than relatively unknown personalities, so as a beginning writer, you should be mindful of how you want to establish credibility and authority. If you are going to argue that the Vietnam Veterans Memorial is the ideal example of public art, it might undermine your argument if your best friend is the architect (or if you conceal that your best friend is the architect). Alternatively, if you argue that the Washington Redskins should not change their mascot from the potentially offensive epithet "redskin" but fail to mention that you own stock in the Redskins, then your credibility might be in jeopardy, and people might not take your argument seriously. Ethos, pathos, and logos make up what we call the "rhetorical triangle," and most arguments are made up of some combination of the three. Based on your audience, you need to adjust your own rhetorical triangle so that your argument contains the right mixture of reason, emotion, and credibility.

It is also helpful when reading to understand whether or how a writer is effective by analyzing their argument on whether they are writing from logos, pathos, or ethos. For example, if Powell writes about the need for international diplomacy in the Middle East, it would automatically carry more weight than one made by your local city councilwoman, even if she had her master's degree in international relations.

MAKING CLAIMS

A claim is a kind of assertion that you make based on evidence, logical and emotional appeal, and solid reasoning. Other words for claims are "thesis" or "assertion." It is important to distinguish between a claim and a fact, and a claim and an opinion. The sentence "Pearl Jam is a band from Seattle" is a fact. It is a true statement, and as such would not make a good thesis or a good topic sentence. The sentence "I think I prefer Pearl Jam to Soundgarden" is an opinion and, again, would not make a particularly good thesis or topic sentence, in part because this is not a disprovable statement. Maybe someone who knows you well could argue that in your heart of hearts you prefer Soundgarden to Pearl Jam, but the topic is so personal and so narrow, it holds little interest for other readers. However, the sentence "Although most critics prefer Nirvana, Pearl Jam has emerged as the most socially conscious Seattle grunge band" is a claim because it is something you could spend an essay supporting. It emerges from the small world of personal opinion ("I prefer") to the world of more universal interest.

Generally, there are three different types of claims—policy, value, and fact—and these claims are frequently linked to the kinds of appeals you make (ethos, pathos, logos). Policy claims are those claims that the writer thinks should happen. Often, one sees policy claims made in terms of "ought," and they usually advocate action. These claims must be supported by a justification, and it is usually a good idea to address potential opposing ideas. Essays that argue for more funding for public art or that demand harsher penalties for graffiti are examples of policy claims.

The value claim is among the most popular of all claims; in fact, the Pearl Jam thesis is a value claim. These claims assert worth and value. If you were to argue that *The Simpsons* carries positive messages or that a certain building embodies anti-human architecture, you would be advancing a value claim. Although emotion can go a long way in these kinds of claims, it is never advisable to hinge value claims on pathos or emotion.

For many beginning writers, the most common claim is a fact claim (sometimes called a claim of truth). These types of assertions focus on classification or definition, and they assert that X is or is not Y. In fact claims, the thesis is incredibly important, because you do not want to argue something that is not provable, nor do you want to argue for the obvious. For example, making the claim that the movie *Talladega Nights* is a parody of NASCAR is pointless, because it is so clearly a parody of NASCAR. One of the most common mistakes writers make is confusing truth with argument (see our section on thesis statements for more help here). Fact claims attempt to clarify. They assert that a thing or idea should be seen in a certain way or considered from a particular perspective.

The key to making supportable claims lies in framing your assertions with balance and reason. Students often feel as though their arguments must be extreme in their coverage. Those kinds of claims tend to be less convincing because so little in life is absolute. Instead of arguing that Pearl Jam is the "best" Seattle band (because concepts like "best" and "worst" are impossible to prove), make a claim that Pearl Jam is the most socially conscious band (citing their lyrics and political activism), or argue that they are the most influential Seattle band (citing other songs that mimic them, interviews with other bands that mention Pearl Jam, and the opinion of music critics). In addition, make sure your claims are reasonable in scope. Do not be afraid to use qualifiers. Limiting the Pearl Jam argument to Seattle bands or grunge bands circumscribes your claim and makes it doable in a five- or six-page essay.

Finally, now that you have made a claim, you must support that claim. The most common types of support include:

- Expert opinion: Citing the opinion of top scholars in a field or established experts is one of the most persuasive forms of support.
- Statistics: Readers like numbers, facts, and percentages. Use credible statistics to lend objectivity and data to your claims.
- Analysis: Close readings of a text by an insightful person can be quite convincing. This is where being a savvy semiotician is useful.
- Analogies and comparisons: One way of illustrating what something is, is to show what it is not. Comparing and contrasting can highlight the values you want to explore.

In the next section, we expand our discussion of support, claims, and evidence to discuss how one implements these strategies to build a comprehensive argument and actually write that essay.

USING CLAIMS AND SUPPORT TO MAKE ARGUMENTS: SOME HELPFUL TIPS

Honesty and trust come into play when you make your arguments. You do not want to mislead your potential audiences, you do not want to alienate them, and you do not want to manipulate them in an unethical way. Making up facts, inventing sources, and leaving out important details are not merely bad argumentation—they are often unethical acts. More positively, writing is all about engagement. We write to make connections with others; we read to learn more about the world and our place in it. Next we provide some basic tips for making solid, convincing, ethical arguments.

DO NOT BE AFRAID TO ACKNOWLEDGE DIFFERING OPINIONS

Some students think that if they acknowledge any aspect of the other side of their argument that they poke a hole in their own. Actually, just the opposite is the case. Letting your readers know that you are well informed goes a long way toward establishing your credibility. What's more, if you are able not only to identify a differing opinion and then refute it or discount it, your argument could carry even more weight. For instance, if you want to argue that Kanye West is an important artist, you should probably acknowledge early on that some of his lyrics can be considered sexist and violent. In fact, you may decide to write about their problematic nature to help you make your own assertions.

USE CREDIBLE, DETAILED INFORMATION AND SOURCES TO HELP SUPPORT YOUR ARGUMENTS

This is perhaps the most important tip we can provide. Think about what kind of information convinces you to do anything. Are you persuaded by vagueness, or by specificity? If we wanted to convince you to meet us for dinner at a specific restaurant, which of the following would be the most persuasive?

- We heard from someone that the food is really good.
- A restaurant critic we respect said this is some of the best food in town.
- A restaurant critic, two chefs, and a group of our friends all recommend this place.
- We have been there a number of times, and the food is great, the service is fantastic, the scene is relaxed but cool, and the prices are reasonable.
- The restaurant's website claims it is the city's favorite restaurant.
- Your grandparents raved about it.

In general, we are persuaded by thorough, objective data. Although we trust people whose tastes are similar to our own, we tend not to trust people we do not know or who might have a stake in a certain argument. The best kinds of evidence are expert opinions, statistics from a reliable source (such as a scientific study), facts from an objective source (such as a newspaper or peer-reviewed journal), personal experience, and the testimony of others. However, if your grandparents previously recommended good restaurants, their ethos could match the so-called experts who recommended the place. Then again, their tastes may be much different than yours. Understanding the criteria that one uses in judging restaurants, movies, and television shows is crucial. For example, Roger Ebert, the well-known critic, admitted before some Adam Sandler movie reviews he wrote that he is no fan of Adam Sandler, giving his readers a warning that his criteria may not match their own.[2]

ESTABLISH YOUR OWN CREDIBILITY AND AUTHORITY, BUT TRY NOT TO OVERDO IT

There are two different ways to establish authority—explicitly and implicitly. In the explicit method, you say up front that you are a specialist in a certain area. For instance, if you are going to write about the influence of Tejano music in South Texas, you might say in the opening paragraph that you are a Latina from Texas who grew up listening to your dad play in Tejano bands around San Antonio. The audience then knows your background and is likely to give your arguments more weight than if a white guy from Boston was making the same argument—unless, of course, the white guy in question was a scholar of Tejano music (which lends a different kind of credibility). Establishing authority implicitly may have less to do with you and more to do with the research you have done. Implicit authority is revealed to the reader slowly, in pieces, so that you carefully fill in gaps over the course of your essay.

There are, of course, many ways to establish authority—by being an expert, by quoting experts, and by building a knowledge base as a result of research—but however you establish authority, do so within reason. If the essay becomes more about how much you know and less about your topic, you will alienate your reader. You want to keep your reader engaged.

TRY TO AVOID FALLACIES

Fallacies are, literally, falsities, gaps, and errors in judgment. Sometimes called logical fallacies, these missteps are mistakes of logic, and they have been around for centuries.

---

2   Jim Emerson, "Ebert on Sandler: All Thumbs," *Roger Ebert's Journal*, 22 June 2006.

We are all guilty of falling into the fallacy trap now and then, but avoid that trap if possible. Here are a few of the most common:

The straw man fallacy: When the writer sets up a fake argument or a "straw man" (an argument that does not really exist), only to refute it later.

The *ad hominem* fallacy: Latin for "to the man," this occurs when a writer attacks a person and not an argument. When a politician accuses his detractors of personal attacks in an attempt to avoid the real issues, he is claiming that his opponents are making *ad hominem* assertions.

The hasty generalization: When a writer jumps to a quick and easy conclusion without thinking through the leap logically. A hasty generalization would occur if one made an argument that Parker Posey appeared in every independent movie in the 1990s.

The *post hoc ergo propter hoc* fallacy: Latin for "after the fact therefore because of the fact," this fallacy is a favorite among beginning writers. Literally, it means that because X comes after Y, Y must have caused X. In other words, it is a faulty cause-and-effect relationship. For example, someone observes that teen violence seems to be on the rise. This person also is beginning to notice more video games at the local video store. The *post hoc* fallacy would occur when this person concluded that the rise in teen violence was because of the increased video games.

The vague generality: Also a favorite among college students, the fallacy or generalization takes place when a writer makes sweeping claims about a group but provides no specific detail or evidence to back up his claim. This can happen on a micro level with an overuse of the passive voice ("It is agreed that ..." or "It is assumed that ...") that does not attribute responsibility. It happens on a macro level when a writer makes a broad generalization about a group of people, like immigrants, lesbians, Republicans, Jews, professors, or students. In some ways, this fallacy is the cause of racism, as it assumes that behavior (or imagined behavior) of one person is shared or mimicked by an entire group. This is a dangerous strategy.

The *non sequitur* fallacy: This is not a particularly common fallacy, but it is still useful to know. Latin for "it does not follow," a non sequitur is a fallacy of conclusion, like a faulty assumption. An example would be, "The Polar ice cap is melting quicker than expected, so let's play *Mortal Combat*."

USE INDUCTIVE AND/OR DEDUCTIVE REASONING WHEN APPROPRIATE

As you write your essay, as you make your arguments and present your evidence, your reader must think through your arguments. However, before that happens, you must also think through your arguments so that you can develop them in the most cogent way. The two types of argument organization are inductive and deductive. Deductive reasoning begins big and moves to small; or, in other terms, deductive reasoning starts with the macro and moves to the micro. In classic rhetoric, this is called a syllogism. A classic syllogism might go something like this:

- Most Hollywood movies have a happy ending.
- *Forrest Gump* is a Hollywood movie.
- Therefore, it is likely that *Forrest Gump* has a happy ending.

A typical syllogism begins with two broad statements and arrives at a narrower proposition based on those statements.

Inductive reasoning resembles detective work. You start with many small observations or bits of evidence, and then, based on that conglomeration, you make a generalization. For instance, you notice that actress Parker Posey starred in *Party Girl, Best in Show, The House of Yes, Short Cuts, Broken English*, and *A Mighty Wind*. You also then realize that all of these movies are independent films. Therefore, based on all of this information, you make an argument about Parker Posey's contribution to independent film. Both approaches are valid, but each has its own pitfalls. Be sure you do not make big leaps in logic (see hasty generalization) that you cannot support.

Papers that use deductive reasoning almost always begin with a thesis or main argument. Most professors prefer this type of reasoning because it indicates that the author has thought about his or her argument in advance. However, the inductive approach can also be effective in certain situations, particularly those where the writer has established credibility. Typically, essays that follow the inductive model build an argument over the course of the essay and position the thesis near the end. Although this strategy is valid, it can be more difficult for beginning writers to execute. Writing instructors tend to favor essays written in the deductive model because the formula is simpler—the writer places the thesis near the beginning of the essay and spends the rest of the paper unpacking, proving, and supporting that thesis.

CONSIDER THINKING LIKE A LAWYER WHEN BUILDING AN ARGUMENT—MAKE A CASE AND PROVE IT

One of the best ways of making and proving an assertion with insight, clarity, and thoroughness is through what rhetoricians have come to call the Toulmin system. This term was derived from Stephen Toulmin, a British philosopher, who argued that the best way to win an argument is by making a strong case.[3] This may sound like stating the obvious, but it really is not. Rather than relying on airtight data to make an argument, Toulmin argued that in real-life situations, you can never be 100 percent certain of something. Someone always has a comeback or an opposing view to counter yours. So, for Toulmin (and many writing teachers), you make an argument by building a case, like a lawyer would in a trial. And, in essence, Toulmin's system resembles legal reasoning in that it makes a case and lays down evidence rather than pretending you have achieved complete certainty. Toulmin's system is useful because it does not insist on absolutes, which is important when writing about texts as subjective as those in popular culture. It is next to impossible to be "right" about what a movie like *Get Out* means, but it is possible to be convincing about your particular interpretation. You cannot say with complete certainty why someone liked *Get Out*, but it is possible to make a strong case about why students like *Get Out*.

According to Toulmin, one makes a convincing case by first making a claim (see "Making Claims," page 60) then by citing a "datum," or evidence, that would prompt someone to make a claim in the first place; then, one offers support for that datum via what he calls a "warrant." A warrant is a statement that underscores the logical connection between the claim and evidence. For instance, if you park your car outside a store, go inside, and return and it is gone, and say, "My car has been stolen," you are relying on the warrant that a car that is missing from a place one has left it must be stolen.

- Your claim: "My car has been stolen."
- Your datum: The car is missing.
- The warrant: Cars that are missing must have been stolen.

But of course, another warrant could be argued—"A car that is missing might have been towed." The warrant is legitimized by what Toulmin calls "backing," or additional evidence.

How would this system work when arguing about popular culture? Let us use another film example. Say that you notice something about recent gangster movies. You observe that since *Reservoir Dogs* and *Pulp Fiction* were released, the gangster genre has become increasingly popular. Based on this observation, one could make an argu-

---

3   See Stephen Toulmin, *The Uses of Argument* (Cambridge UP, 1964).

ment that Quentin Tarantino, the director for both movies, has had a rather significant impact on gangster films. In doing some research, we discovered that a number of recent directors cited either *Reservoir Dogs* or *Pulp Fiction* when asked about their films.[4] In the car example, the backing might be that you have parked in a high-crime area or in a tow-away zone, depending on the warrant you use. According to Toulmin, we have here all the necessary information to make a convincing case:

- **Claim:** Quentin Tarantino has had a significant impact on the gangster movie genre.
- **Datum:** Two popular gangster movies, *Reservoir Dogs* and *Pulp Fiction*, were directed by Tarantino.
- **Warrant:** Several directors cite either *Reservoir Dogs* or *Pulp Fiction* when talking about their own movies.
- **Backing:** These comments appeared in respectable, reviewed publications.

Of course, if you were to build a paper out of this system, you would need one to two more pieces of data (what we called points or reasons earlier) and additional warrants; in this case, perhaps discussing how recent movies or television shows resemble specific scenes from the Tarantino movies.

The Toulmin system cannot be used for every type of essay, but it does provide a model for argumentation, and it is particularly useful for making claims about popular-culture texts, or any text for which there is no clear "right" or "wrong" answer.

SYNTHESIS: PULLING IT ALL TOGETHER

Writing is about synthesis—combining differing elements—so learning to synthesize makes you a much better writer (and a better thinker). In the world of composition, synthesis refers to a couple of different things. First, a writer must synthesize her ideas; that is, she must pull together the various half-baked premises, vague notions, and uncompleted thoughts into one cohesive, central concept. Usually, this concept becomes your thesis, but sometimes it may take a draft or two of writing and condensing and collapsing before you arrive at what you want to say.

Another form of synthesis involves combining all of the secondary sources you amass into the body of your essay. This is one of the hardest things to master—weaving other voices into the tapestry of your own. How much of another quote do you include? Should you paraphrase or quote precisely? How does one lead into a quote succinctly and elegantly? We would love to provide some sure-fire tricks here, but, alas,

---

4 A simple Google search of "influenced by Quentin Tarantino" and "interview" brings up a few dozen references.

that is impossible, as integrating secondary quotes, paraphrases, and ideas into your own work remains a kind of art that gets easier only with practice.

However, do not fear, because you engage in synthesis every day. Whenever you relate to your roommate what each person in your group thought about a concert or a movie, you synthesize. Take the process of deciding what movie to see. The entire process is one big act of synthesis—from seeing what's playing, to locating the best theater, to juggling the various reviews, to deciding whether you trust the opinion of your friends and family who have either seen the movie or talked to someone who has. You synthesize when you take all of the disparate material in your head, combine it, and from that whorl of data, arrive at a kind of personal claim: *I am going to see the new Harry Potter movie at the Balboa Theater at 9:15.*

Because synthesis is so important to becoming an inclusive, informed writer, increasingly more instructors require a synthesis essay. A synthesis essay is an essay that asks the writer to synthesize various kinds of information into one unified document. Typically, this means researching, paraphrasing, and presenting differing forms of data. That data could be opinions about a piece of art, quotations from experts on a new movie, or data from surveys on television use. How a writer delivers that information, however, is critical. A writer must either paraphrase (restate an idea in his or her own words) or quote (reprint the phrase or sentence exactly, using quotation marks) the material; in both cases, the writer must cite the passage by indicating where the material comes from. The writer cannot pass this information off as his or her own work. Most instances of plagiarism occur in the synthesizing process—because students do not know how to cite, do not know how to paraphrase, or think they do not need to do either one.

To illustrate synthesis in action, we use synthesis itself as an example. To do this, we consulted the Drew University On-Line Resources for Writers and the Bellevue College Online Writing Lab. The Drew site offers a full definition of synthesis writing:

> Although at its most basic level a synthesis involves combining two or more summaries, synthesis writing is more difficult than it might at first appear because this combining must be done in a meaningful way and the final essay must generally be thesis-driven. In composition courses, "synthesis" commonly refers to writing about printed texts, drawing together particular themes or traits that you observe in those texts and organizing the material from each text according to those themes or traits. Sometimes you may be asked to synthesize your own ideas, theory, or research with those of the texts you have been assigned. In your other college classes you'll probably find yourself synthesizing information from graphs and tables, pieces of music, and art works as well. The key to any kind of synthesis is the same.

It also enumerates these three features of synthesis:

- It accurately reports information from the sources using different phrases and sentences;
- It is organized in such a way that readers can immediately see where the information from the sources overlap;
- It makes sense of the sources and helps the reader understand them in greater depth.

Our decision to cut and paste the definition and the three features exactly as they appear on the Drew site is a form of quotation or citation. Acknowledging Drew lets the reader know that the features come from a reliable source and that they are not the products of Silverman and Rader.[5]

However, the Bellevue site includes this explanation of synthesis:

WHAT IS A SYNTHESIS?

A synthesis paper is a certain kind of essay.

According to the *Little, Brown Handbook* (Aaron & Fowler, 2001, p. 133), a synthesis is a way to "make connections among parts or among wholes. You can create a new whole by drawing conclusions about relationships and implications." What this means is, in order to write a successful synthesis paper, you must conduct research on your chosen topic, contemplate what this unique collection of knowledge may mean to you and the world, and develop an argument about it. Specifically, this means discussing the implications of the knowledge you have gathered. You have amassed a collection of information on a certain topic, and now you must say something unique and interesting about it.

A synthesis is not: A summary

A synthesis is: An opportunity for you to create new knowledge out of already existing knowledge, i.e., other sources. You develop an argument, or perhaps a unique perspective on something in the world (a political issue, how something works, etc.), and use your sources as evidence, in order to make your claim (thesis statement) more believable.[6]

5　Sandra Jamieson, "Synthesis Writing," *Drew University On-Line Resources for Writers*, 1999 (users. drew.edu/sjamieso/webresources.html).

6　"What Is a Synthesis?" Bellevue College Writing Lab, 3 Apr. 2010.

Thus, at the risk of confusion, here is how one might synthesize two different takes on synthesis in college writing:

> Though the Drew On-Line Resources for Writers Lab and the Bellevue Online Writing Lab approach the concept of synthesis differently, they ultimately have more similarities than differences. What connects the two sites is an emphasis on combining information from various sources in order to make connections. Drew tends to focus on synthesis as it applies to written texts and as a means of presenting and collating sources so that readers can better understand varying information. In addition to a generous definition of synthesis, the Drew site lists three key features of synthesis, all of which focus on accurate presentation of source material. Despite the fact that Bellevue distinguishes between summary and synthesis (something Drew does not), their site underscores Drew's argument that synthesis can perform important work by taking existing information and combining it in a way that makes it rounder, more comprehensive, and more fresh.

At its core, synthesis is a type of interpretation. In order to write this paragraph, we had to interpret what both sites had to say about synthesis. Notice how we did not just regurgitate the two sites. We made connections between the two (synthesized), and we unpacked the data from each so that we could 1) make it our own, and 2) distill it so that we could better explain it to you.

Synthesis takes work; one must be conscientious and careful while doing it. Do not take shortcuts and simply cut and paste—that's plagiarism. Consider each source separately, unpack each source, then present the theme of each source in your synthesis. This helps you avoid the traps of plagiarism and summary, and it enables you to connect with your audience.

KNOW YOUR AUDIENCE

An outspoken advocate of the internet's capacity to share vast amounts of information has been invited to speak at a gathering of music company executives who are nervous about the thousands of people downloading free music. What kind of tone should she take when addressing this potentially hostile audience? Next, that person is going to speak to a gathering of college students, who are among the most avid downloaders of music. How would her presentation differ? Would she give the same presentation to both audiences? What strategies would she use with the hostile audience that she would not need for the sympathetic one? Keeping the assumptions, education, political leanings, and culture of your audience in mind helps you write a more appropriate essay than if you ignored these issues altogether.

When we were writing the introduction for the third edition, Michael Moore's controversial movie *Sicko* had just been released nationwide. A scathing indictment of America's healthcare industry, Moore's film polarized viewers and critics. There is no doubt that the film makes a powerful argument, but one might ask who the audience of the movie is. Is Moore making the movie for Republicans, Democrats, or those in the middle? Many believe that because the movie is so one-sided it will change few people's minds, whereas others contend that it could move people to actually do something about America's healthcare shortcomings. We would argue that Moore's audience is mainstream America: people who are most affected by nonexistent or poor insurance. Moore knows that his movie will probably be seen by those on the right as propaganda, but his persistent arguments in the movie seem aimed at those who defend the status quo. If Moore was interested in a broader audience, there are any number of ways he might have kept his message but changed his method of delivering it—including interviewing sympathetic and thoughtful defenders of HMOs, insurance companies, and the healthcare lobby, toning down some of his own antics, and most importantly, editing the film differently.

These examples reflect the three types of audiences you should consider when writing your papers—a sympathetic audience, an undecided audience, and an antagonistic audience. You would likely not write the same paper for the three kinds of audiences but tailor your arguments based on who would be reading your essay. We do this kind of tailoring all the time. For instance, when you tell the story of a fabulous date you had the previous night to your mother, your best friend, and your ex, you probably tell three radically different stories. The potentially hostile audience (the ex) gets one version, the undecided audience (mother) gets another, and the sympathetic audience (best friend) gets yet another. All your stories might be accurate but shaded and delivered differently based on what you know about each listener.

When writing for a sympathetic audience, you already have them on your side, so you do not need to try to win them over. In this case, an argument grounded in pathos may be the most effective. Chances are, they already know the information that might make them think a certain way, so giving them facts, statistics, and details they are familiar with is ineffective because it could come across as overstating the obvious or simply appearing repetitive. However, an emotionally powerful appeal supported by a strong ethos could be incredibly successful. If you are going to write an essay on Taylor Swift's contribution to American music, would you write the same essay for *Rolling Stone* and *Taste of Country*? What about for *Seventeen*? The *New York Times*?

What if you get invited to write an article on the importance of Kurt Cobain (the lead singer of the band Nirvana) for *Country Music Today*? How would you approach your audience and your article? The audience is likely going to be less sympathetic to your topic. In this instance, you need to adjust your ethos and your approach. First, you could establish credibility by informing your readers that you are a fan of country music, perhaps even mention the important contributions of various artists you know these readers appreciate. When addressing a potentially antagonistic or skeptical audience, it is best to avoid an overly pathos-driven argument. You may come across as ill-informed and even irrational. Instead, you might want to point to specific Nirvana songs or chords that resemble country songs. A good strategy might be to make connections thematically, arguing that even though the music is different, Cobain, Willie Nelson, Lyle Lovett, Garth Brooks, and Blake Shelton all write smart, catchy songs about disaffected, blue-collar Americans. Look for instances of overlap. If you have time to research, you might find out that Cobain listened to country music or that the people in the area he grew up in have a strong affinity for country music. With these kinds of audiences, the best way to establish credibility is to let your audience know that you have done your homework, and that you know their world as well as you know your own.

In some ways, writing for an antagonistic audience is easier than writing for an uncertain one, because you know what you are getting into. Writing for the vast middle can be truly challenging. When writing for an undecided audience, the best strategy is to establish strong ethos and logos. How much you rely on ethos or logos depends on you and your topic. If you are arguing that advertisements featuring skinny, near-naked female models are empowering to women, you might need to adjust your argument based on your gender or age. If you want to argue that the Names quilt, a quilt made by the loved ones of AIDS victims as a memorial, should be taken seriously as art, focus not simply on the formal or artistic qualities of the quilt, but mention how the quilt affected you, that it fostered an interest in folk art and a love for art that inspires social change. Your audience responds more favorably to your claims if they trust you and your evidence. Be honest. Do not try to manipulate. Write in your own voice.

USE COMMON SENSE

You know what arguments are likely to persuade you. You have examples of documents in this book and elsewhere of compelling, sound, reasonable arguments. Use them as your models. The best argument is one that comes from a position of reasonableness.

Overall, making an argument is a key element of writing successful papers, perhaps more important than any other. For one, knowing what you are arguing often leads to clearer writing; it allows you to separate to some degree the processes of thinking and actually putting those thoughts onto paper. In an attempt to impress professors, students use big words and write in what they imagine a scholarly voice to be. Do not worry so much about tone. Write in your own voice. Remember: The best writing is complex ideas rendered in simple language—not the other way around.

CHAPTER 8

RESEARCHING POPULAR CULTURE TEXTS

Thus far we have focused on the process of making arguments largely from processing and elaborating on one's observations. However, nontraditional texts can also be fruitful entry points for researching questions, both large and small, about culture.

For one, nontraditional texts often raise questions about the medium from which they come. When you watch a sitcom, it might make you think about other sitcoms. When you see a painting, it might make you think of other paintings. When you walk through another university's student union, you might think about how the two student unions are related—maybe a similar type of student goes to each university, or perhaps the student unions were built in different times. You might also notice that your student union has university-owned food and drink places, but your friend's union has chain restaurants. Researching the history of student unions would produce one type of essay, probably one more historical in nature, whereas researching the presence of corporations on campus would produce a paper that explored more explicitly political issues (the presence of corporations on campus is a highly sensitive issue for many associated with higher education). In either case, your walk through a public space might suggest to you some avenues for research.

Nontraditional texts can also raise issues about gender, race, and class, among other things. When observing stereotyped behavior on sitcoms, it can make you think about how other television shows present the same behavior and perhaps how other creative genres do as well. Nontraditional texts can also be places where one might explore how abstract concepts play out in practice, through portrayals of popular culture.

There are other ways of using nontraditional texts to engage research, but these methods are worth talking about further, because they offer relatively straightforward ways of using research to enhance understanding of both the texts at hand and the culture at large. In the first method of researching popular culture, the one about student unions, the text is a window to further exploration of such issues as the corporatization of universities or the function of the environment in student lives.

In the second approach, examining the text and stereotypes in it, the text itself is the focus. In the third approach, the lens used to look at the nontraditional text is the focus; the nontraditional text is more a means to further discussion and elaboration of the concepts. All three approaches share the idea that these texts matter—that they reflect larger concerns in society.

There are other reasons why researching nontraditional texts might seem daunting. You may ask yourself what scholarly writing could possibly exist about Barbie dolls or *The Big Bang Theory*. Or you may not have written a paper that engages popular culture as a research topic. After all, is not research about "serious" topics? Traditionally, you have probably written research papers about historical events or movements, or about the author of a literary work, or perhaps literary movements. Although research of nontraditional texts may seem more difficult, students writing research papers about popular culture have a lot of resources at their disposal. There is a large and ever-increasing amount of work written on popular culture, such as music, the movies, technology, art, found objects, and television. There is even more work done on the more political elements of this textbook, such as gender and the media.

Because researching popular culture topics seems daunting, you might be tempted to amass as much information as possible before beginning your writing. However, we believe that one of the best ways of researching a paper about popular culture is to make sure you have already preliminarily interpreted whatever text you are analyzing before researching. That way, you have your ideas to use as a sounding board for others that might come your way. Finding out what you think about the text also allows you to research more effectively and probably more efficiently.

Generally, the trick to researching papers about popular culture is not only to find work that engages your specific topic but something general or contextual about your topic. In the case of *The Matrix* (2000), a film popular with both viewers and critics, science fiction movies might be a good general subject to research but so might computers and culture. Broadly defined, *The Matrix* is a science fiction movie, but it is also a movie about the roles of computers in society. One of the movie's primary arguments is that our culture is quickly moving toward one that is run by computers with decreasing human control. That is the subject of more than a few movies, including *2001: A Space Odyssey* and *I, Robot*, but its message is even more crucial given the remarkable growth of the internet since the mid 1990s. One could research the philosophical argument the movie is making, that humans and computers are somewhat at odds. One could research how other movies or books treat this subject, both within the science fiction genre and outside it. The movie also has a political bent, about the nature of not only computers but also of corporations, who seem to run Neo's life before he realizes what the Matrix is. It is also about the culture of computers, which Neo is immersed in before his transformation. In addition, it engages the idea of the future as well as the present, a temporal argument (about time). All these contexts—philosophical, genre-based, cultural, political, temporal—have strong research possibilities. You could write compelling papers on each of these topics, and each would be very different from the others. You can also see why understanding what you are arguing affects how you research a topic.

Another possibility for research comes fom music. Instead of thinking of particular contexts right away, you might begin by asking some questions of the text. For example, take as a text Johnny Cash's album *American III: Solitary Man*, which he released in 1999. Johnny Cash was a musician who recorded music for almost 50 years; he received his start about the same time and in the same place as Elvis Presley but later had the same record producer as the Beastie Boys, a popular rap group. Such biographical constructions may shape your paper's direction, or they may not. In either case, in writing this paper, you might listen to the album and note some of the themes, symbols, and ideas. You might ask yourself: Was Johnny Cash writing about issues he had written about before? You could find this out by listening to other albums or seeking research materials about his recording career. You could also ask: What is it about Cash's life that made him write songs like this? Material contained either in biographies of Cash himself or in general histories of country music could help this paper. Another question: Is Johnny Cash part of the recognizable genre of country music or a different genre altogether? Again, a general work about country music enables you to answer this question. Any of these questions can be the beginning of a good research paper. If you decided to focus only on the album, you could also read other reviews, and after you have staked out your own position, argue against other readings of this album.

Movies and music are good choices for research because they are texts that in some ways mirror traditional texts—movies have narratives like novels, and songs have lyrics that resemble poetry. But even found objects have strong possibilities for research. Objects like cars or dolls are not only easily described but have long traditions of scholarship, especially within cultural contexts. In the case of dolls, histories of dolls in American culture or the role of toys would provide historical contexts for your arguments; the same would be true for cars. As you get closer to the present, your methods of research may change. In the case of cars, current writers may not be writing about the context of a new model, but they certainly review them, and examining the criteria of car reviews may give you insight into the cultural context of a car. So might advertisements. Researching popular culture can include placing different primary sources (the source itself, like *Solitary Man* or *The Matrix* or advertisements for either of these texts) in context with one another, or using secondary sources—sources about the primary text, such as reviews, or scholarly articles, ones that are peer reviewed, reviewed by experts, and often have footnotes. Of course there are movies and music to write about: one could write about Kendrick Lamar's 2017 album *Damn* or Beyoncé's 2016 *Lemonade*, the renewed Marvel superhero franchise(s), or *Game of Thrones*; almost *all* popular culture texts can benefit from cultural examination through research.

The most difficult thing about doing this research, somewhat ironically, is its flexibility; once you decide on researching popular culture, many different avenues, sometimes an overwhelming number, open to you. We have encountered students who enjoy this type of work but are overwhelmed by the possibilities in approaching popular culture texts as researchable topics. However, most students eventually come away with not only a better understanding of their particular text but of researching generally.

RESEARCHING NONTRADITIONAL TEXTS: ONE METHOD

There are any number of ways to undertake the research process with nontraditional texts, given the complexities of the intersections among texts, issues, and culture. At Virginia Commonwealth University, where Dr. Silverman once taught, the department used the same approach in the university's required sophomore researched-writing class. Each student focused on what instructors called a "cultural text," which, for their purposes, meant nonliterary texts.

For the class, students were required in a four-step process to 1) identify and explore a particular cultural text and write about it; 2) choose research angles or avenues and write about the arguments between sources they encountered; 3) reread and write about the text through the research; and 4) merge the first three assignments (a kind of synthesis). The approach mimics to some extent the way many academics work, with a focus on text and context. This may involve doing a close reading of a text. A close reading examines the text details by paying attention to all of its inner workings, its colors, shapes, sounds, and symbols. When combined with research and larger cultural insight, a close reading can become a comprehensive paper.

The advantages of this approach are many. For one, you get a sense of how to do in-depth research that's not done for its own end but to provide better understanding of a particular topic. It also makes you as a writer learn how to incorporate others' ideas into your essay—which is what you have to do in school and long after you leave, when you have to complete market research and prepare reports.

From a purely academic perspective, this approach also demonstrates the diversity and depth of research being done on nontraditional texts and the even deeper well of information for issues of cultural significance (such as race, gender, and class). When faced with the prospect of doing in-depth college research, not to mention research on popular culture topics, students often believe there is not enough information for their topic. Sometimes this is true, but most times the process requires some cleverness and ingenuity.

NUTS AND BOLTS RESEARCH

Clearly, your university library is the place to start. Books have a much more comprehensive perspective on any possible text than most websites. Think broadly when approaching what books you might look at; think about what category the books you are looking for might fall into. One of the best ways of doing this is through a keyword search involving "the perfect book." For a book about Coco Chanel, a simple keyword search on "Coco Chanel" might yield some useful sources. If not, a keyword search with "history," "fashion," and "international" might provide some results. If it does, write down a call number (the physical address of the book in the library) and head for the stacks; most libraries have separate floors or sections for their collection of books. When you get there, find the book number you have written down, but also be careful to look around on the shelves for other possibilities. Some of the best sources often come from browsing on the shelves of libraries.

Then it is on to periodicals.

Use an electronic database your university subscribes to; search engines like Google, Google Scholar, or Yahoo! are limited in what they come up with and may lead users to sources that are not reliable. When we talk about reliability, we are not actually saying that people are trying to deceive deliberately (though they might be). Academic publication requires a type of scrutiny—work is often reviewed by two or more experts in the field—that sets it apart from work posted on the internet without such vetting. This peer review is what your professors are talking about when they refer to scholarly sources. We like electronic databases such as Infotrac (or Academic Search Premier), JSTOR, Proquest, Omnifile, and LexisNexis, which many universities subscribe to (usually you can access these indexes through your library's website). The overall difference between Infotrac and LexisNexis and standard internet searching is that Infotrac and LexisNexis, for the most part, have articles that appear in print form—generally, although not always—making them more reliable sources. Infotrac is an index to periodicals that tend to be scholarly, with footnotes, although some more popular magazines are there as well. Some of the articles on Infotrac are full-text articles, which means the full version appears on the screen; some you have to head to the library to find. LexisNexis contains full-text articles from most large American and European newspapers as well as many magazines. It has a database geared toward general news and opinion and other databases geared toward sports, arts, science, and law.[1] If you are working with popular culture sources, the arts index, which contains reviews, may be helpful. Speaking of computers, you may also find the Library of Congress website, http://www.loc.gov, or WorldCat, a database of the holdings in major libraries, helpful to find if there are any books on the subject; you can then use your library's interlibrary loan to request a needed book. Be aware, however, that some books may take some time to arrive from another library to yours. The Library of Congress site also has an excellent collection of images. Overall, in doing research, be creative and thorough.

---

1   *The Reader's Guide to Periodicals* is a complete non-electronic guide to periodicals such as newspapers and major magazines. You may be tempted to skip anything not online, but electronic sources generally go back only a decade, so for any type of historical research, you should probably hit the *Reader's Guide*.

GUERILLA RESEARCH

Okay, if you have exhausted your library options and you still cannot find what you need, try bookstores—they still exist! Or look at Amazon.com, where you can research books, movies, and albums; sometimes you can see what you need, especially bibliographic information, in Amazon's "look inside the book" feature.

CHAPTER 9

KNOWING WHAT A GOOD
PAPER LOOKS LIKE :
AN ANNOTATED STUDENT ESSAY

Oftentimes, students have the ability to write good essays; they just cannot visualize them. They simply do not know what a good paper looks like, what its components are.

An annotated student paper appears on the following pages. You see that we have highlighted the positive aspects of the essay and also some elements that need work. (Careful readers might notice additional stylistic and formatting inconsistencies.) One thing we like about this piece is a good move from general information to specific. The best papers are those with a clear, narrow focus. This student's thesis is also clear and well developed.

SAMPLE ESSAY

Compton 1

Matt Compton
Professor Silverman
English 101
9 December 2001

"Smells Like Teen Spirit"

In 1991 a song burst forth onto the music scene that articulated so perfectly the emotions of America's youth that the song's writer was later labeled the voice of a generation (Moon). That song was Nirvana's "Smells Like Teen Spirit," and the writer was Kurt Cobain; one of the most common complaints of the song's critics was that the lyrics were unintelligible (Rawlins). But while some considered the song to be unintelligible, to many youth in the early 90s, it was exactly what they needed to hear. Had the song been presented differently, then the raw emotions that it presented would have been tamed. If the lyrics had been perfectly articulated, then the feelings that the lyrics express would have been less articulate, because the feelings

The title appears in quotes because it represents a song title.

Good beginning—the "burst forth" is passive, but here it seems to work.

Good clarification, although he almost moves too quickly into unintelligibility.

This is a strong explanation, although it probably could have been condensed a bit.

Compton 2

that he was getting across were not clear in themselves. One would know exactly what Kurt Cobain was saying, but not exactly what he was feeling. The perfect articulation of those raw emotions, shared by so many of America's youth, was conveyed with perfect inarticulation.

1991 was a year when the music scene had become a dilute, lukewarm concoction being spoon-fed to the masses by corporations (Cohen). The charts and the radio were being dominated by "hair bands" and pop ballads; popular music at the time was making a lot of noise without saying anything (Cohen). Behind the scenes "underground" music had been thriving since the early eighties. Much of this underground music was making a meaningful statement, but these musicians shied away from the public eye. The general public knew little about them, because they had adopted the ideology that going public was selling out (Dettmar). Nirvana was a part of this "underground" music scene.

In 1991 Nirvana broke the credo, signing with a major label, DGC, under which they released the chart-smashing *Nevermind.* "Smells Like Teen Spirit" was the first single from the record, and it became a huge hit quickly (Cohen). Nirvana stepped up and spoke for the twenty something generation, which wasn't exactly sure what it wanted to say (Azerrad 223–233). A huge part of America's youth felt exactly what Cobain was able to convey through not just "Smells Like Teen Spirit" but all of his music. Nirvana shot into superstar status and paved the way for an entire "grunge" movement (Moon). No one complained that they could not hear Cobain, but many did complain that they could not understand what he was saying.

Kurt Cobain did not want his music to just be heard and appreciated; he wanted it to be "felt" (Moon). His music often showed a contrast of emotions; it would change from a soft lull, to a screaming rage suddenly. And few could scream with rage as could Cobain (Cohen). There is a Gaelic word, "yarrrrragh," which "... refers to that rare quality that some voices have, an edge, an ability to say something about the human condition that goes far beyond merely singing the right lyrics and hitting the right notes." This word was once used to describe Cobain's voice by Ralph J. Gleason, *Rolling Stone* critic (Azerrad 231). It was that voice, that uncanny ability to show emotions that Cobain demonstrated in "Smells Like Teen Spirit."

Cobain's raging performance spoke to young Americans in a way that no one had in a long while (Moon). Michael Azerrad wrote in his 1993 book, *Come as You Are: The Story of Nirvana,* "Ultimately it wasn't so much that Nirvana was saying anything new about growing up in America; it was the way they said it" (Azerrad 226). Cobain's music was conveying a feeling through the way that he performed. It was a feeling shared

Compton 3

by many of America's youth, but it was also a feeling that could not have been articulated any other way than the way that Cobain did it (Cohen).

"Smells Like Teen Spirit" starts out with one of the most well-known guitar riffs of the 90s. The four chord progression was certainly nothing new, nothing uncommon. The chords are played with a single guitar with no distortion, and then suddenly the bass and drums come in. When the drums and bass come in the guitar is suddenly distorted, and the pace and sound of the song changes. The song's introduction, with its sudden change, forms a rhythmic "poppy" chord progression to a raging, thrashing of the band's instruments (Moon), sets the pace for the rest of the song.

The chaos from the introduction fades, and it leads in to the first verse, which gives the listener a confused feeling (Azerrad 213). In the first verse the tune of the song is carried by the drums and bass alone, and a seemingly lonely two-note guitar part that fades in and out of the song. The bass, drums and eerie guitar give the listener a "hazy" feeling. Here Cobain's lack of articulation aids in the confused feeling, because as he sings, one can catch articulate phrases here and there. The words that the listeners can discern allow them to draw their own connections. Cobain's lyrics do in fact carry a confused message, "It is fun to lose, and to pretend" (Azerrad 213).

The pre-chorus offers up clear articulation of a single word, but this articulation is the perfect precursor to the coming chorus. As the first verse ends, the pre-chorus comes in; Cobain repeats the word "Hello" fifteen times. The repetition of the word Hello draws the confusion that he implicates in the first verse to a close, and in a way reflects on it. As the tone and inflection of his voice changes each time he quotes "Hello," one is not sure whether he is asking a question or making a statement, or both. It is like he is saying, "Hello? Is anybody at home?" while at the same time he exclaims, "Wake up and answer the door!"

The reflection that he implicates in the pre-chorus builds to the raw raging emotions that he expresses in the chorus, as the guitar suddenly becomes distorted, and he begins to scream (Azerrad 214, 226). In the chorus he screams, but somehow the words in the chorus are actually more articulate than those in the verse. As Cobain sings, "I feel stupid, and contagious," anyone who has ever felt like a social outcast understands exactly what Cobain is saying (Cohen), and they understand exactly why he must scream it.

I remember the first time that I heard that line and thinking about it; I was about thirteen, and I thought that there was no better word than "*contagious*" to describe the way it feels being in a social situation and not being accepted. Because no one wants to be around that person, they

---

The strong final sentence supports not only the topic sentence of the paragraph, but also the thesis of the paper.

This topic sentence is a bit on the narrative side and does not connect well with the previous paragraph.

The passage does an excellent job of describing how the song sounds. It is a very difficult task to do this well.

This is a very good topic sentence—it not only leads us from the last paragraph, but also sums up the current one.

Good quote from the song. (He might have cited the song itself, but wanted to include Azerrad's ideas.)

Another good topic sentence, and here the transition is much better implied than in those mentioned earlier.

An insightful analysis of what seems to be a pretty simple lyric. This is excellent work—complicating the simple is a staple of good work in reading culture. The writer also makes a good analogy here.

Omit unnecessary "actually." Again, good reading of the song. So far the writer has done a lot of strong work in (1) contextualizing the song, (2) studying its music, and (3) analyzing its lyrics. It is almost a formula for doing this type of work.

This personal aside adds to the paper, in our opinion—but you should check with your teacher before including it.

Compton 4

will look at the person with disgust, as if they have some highly *contagious* disease. There is certainly a lot of anger and confusion surrounding those feelings. People needed to hear Cobain scream; they knew how he felt, because they knew how they felt.

People who were experiencing what Cobain was expressing understood what he was saying, because they understood how he felt. In much the same way when someone hits their hand with a hammer that person does not lay down the hammer and calmly say, "Ouch, man that really hurt." They throw the hammer down, and simultaneously yell an obscenity, or make an inarticulate roar, and one knows that they are going to lose a fingernail. Anyone who has smashed their finger with a hammer understands why that person is yelling; in the same way anyone who has felt "contagious" or confused about society knows why Cobain is screaming about feeling "stupid and contagious." Cobain is not examining society. He is experiencing the same things as his audience (Moon); he is "going to lose a fingernail." As the chorus draws to a close, the music still rages, but it changes tempo and rhythm slightly.

The chorus is the most moving part of the song; it is a display of pure emotion. In the chorus Cobain demonstrates what it was that connected with so many; his lyrics said what he meant (Moon). But what he said had been said before, and whether he was articulate or not, people felt what he meant. It was the articulation of that feeling that gained the song such high praise (Moon).

The chorus ends with the phrase, "A mulatto, an albino, a mosquito, my libido"; this line is a reference to social conformity. Cobain is referring to things, or the ideas associated with them that are "outside" of social conformity, and then relating those things back to himself with the phrase "my libido" (Azerrad 210–215). This end to the chorus again goes back to reflect on the feelings expressed in the chorus, and ties them together with a return to the confusion expressed in the verses.

The articulation of the lyrics in the second verse gives the confusion more focus than in the first verse. He begins the second verse with the lyric, "I'm worse at what I do best, and for this gift I feel blessed." Although the lyrics are more articulate in the second verse, the feelings of confusion are still there, due to the tempo and rhythm of the music. After Cobain has sung the second verse he returns to the pre-chorus, the repetition of the word Hello. The cycle begins anew.

"Smells Like Teen Spirit" in its entirety gives the listener a complete feeling after listening to it, especially if that listener is feeling confused and frustrated. The song carries one through an entire cycle of emotions,

Another analogy—comparison, done in reasonable doses, is an effective technique in doing analysis, particularly if one does it thoughtfully.

The move back to narrative is jarring.

Good topic sentence, although it could be condensed into one sentence.

See previous comment—the topic sentence is doing excellent work but not doing it as "writerly" as it could be done.

We like the way the writer connects ideas, music, and lyrics together again.

Compton 5

from confusion, to reflection, to frustration. Tom Moon, a Knight-Ridder Newspaper writer, described Nirvana's music as having moments of "tension and release." Being carried through those emotions allows the listener to "vent" their own feelings of confusion and frustration, and at the same time know that someone else feels the same way (Azerrad 226–227). Despite the connection that Cobain made with many there were still many who did not "get" the song; these people often complained about the inarticulation of the lyrics (Azerrad 210).

Good summary of the song's meaning/content. The writer does a good job of making sure the reader is following his argument.

Weird Al Yankovic utilized the common criticism of the song in his parody "Smells Like Nirvana"; Yankovic parodied "Smells Like Teen Spirit," based entirely on Cobain's obscure articulation. Yankovic is known for parodying popular music, and with lines such as, "And I'm yellin' and I'm screamin', but I do not know what I'm saying," Yankovic stated exactly what so many of the song's critiques had, though he did it with a genuine respect for the song, and its impact (Rawlins).

Now, he switches to other voices. Because the choice is both surprising and apt, the use of Weird Al is a good choice for a source/comparison.

Weird Al Yankovic's version struck a note with many who liked Cobain's music but could not understand his lyrics (Rawlins). There were many people who did not understand the feelings of confusion, frustration, and apathy that Cobain was getting across. In 1991 when "Smells Like Teen Spirit" first came out I was only 9, and I did not like that kind of music at all. I remember my brother, who is nine years older than me, and who listened to a lot of "heavy metal," bought Yankovic's *Off the Deep End*, with his parody "Smells Like Nirvana" on it. He thought it was funny because he did not like Nirvana. He never really connected with Cobain's message; even though he did not get what Cobain was saying, he could still enjoy the music. When I became older I did connect with Cobain's music, and Nirvana was one of my favorite bands. My brother never did understand, like many people who never did understand what it was that Cobain was saying (Azerrad 210).

Again, we like the personal reference. It is not as relevant as the other one, but it somehow gives the argument more weight if we know where the writer is "coming from."

Nirvana made the generation gap clear. It was Nirvana that spoke for a large part of that generation (Moon), where no one else had ever really addressed the confusion and frustration about growing up in America at that time, or at least no one had expressed it in the same way that Nirvana did. They were not the first to vocalize a problem with corporate America, but they were the first *popular* band to convey the feelings that many were feeling *because* of growing up in corporate America, in the way that they did. Cobain did not just show that he has experienced those feelings, but that he was still *experiencing* them, and many young people connected with that (Moon).

The transition is not strong here, but the topic sentence is good. It again summarizes—this time the band, not the song.

The "corporate America" reference is not clear here. As readers, we know vaguely what he is talking about, but he does not use sources in the same way he has previously when making similar points.

Compton 6

In 1992 singer-songwriter Tori Amos illustrated why Cobain's "Smells Like Teen Spirit" had connected with so many by making a cover of the song that was a clear contrast to the original. She rendered the song with a piano, and a clear articulate voice. Her cover of the song became fairly popular, because it was different, and because many people could now understand the lyrics that Cobain had already popularized (Rawlins). The cover was interesting, to say the least; however, it would have been impossible for her version ever to have had the same impact as Cobain's (Rawlins). The lyrics to the song have meaning, and depth, but the emotions that the song conveyed were in and of themselves abstract.

Amos's version of the song articulated each word clearly, her clear voice hit each note on key; her song was comparable to a ballad. Cobain's "Smells Like Teen Spirit" could be described as "sloppy," his guitar distorted through much of the song; he either screamed or mumbled most of the song (Azerrad 214). The two versions of the song illustrate a clear contrast: it is as if Cobain is "angry about being confused" (Azerrad 213), while Amos sings the song to lament Cobain's feelings.

Amos's version of the song became popular for the same reason that it could never have paved the way as Cobain's version did. It was like a ballad, and after everyone heard what Cobain was saying, about society, about America, about growing up, there is one clear emotion that follows the confusion and frustration: sadness. Her "ballad-like" cover of "Smells Like Teen Spirit" exemplified that sadness. But at the same time, people had written ballads about being confused or frustrated, and performed them as Amos performed "Smells Like Teen Spirit"; that was nothing new. However, no one had yet demonstrated such clear and yet abstract confused, frustrated emotions as Cobain did, and at that moment in time that was exactly what America needed to hear (Azerrad 224–225).

Cobain had written and performed a song about his own confusion, and in the process he had connected with young people all over the United States (Moon). He had helped those people to understand their own confusion better. The problem with "Smells Like Teen Spirit" was not that Cobain was not articulate; he could not have articulated his point more clearly than he did. The problem was that not everyone knew what he was talking about, just like not everyone knows what it is like to strike their finger with a hammer. And in the same way, if someone does not know what it is like they might say something foolish like, "That couldn't *hurt* that bad;" or "What's *his* problem?" when someone else hits their finger with a hammer, and they make an inarticulate roar. That roar expresses exactly what that person is feeling, but only those who know that feeling, can really understand it. As Michael Azerrad, author of *Come as You Are: The Story of Nirvana*, put it, "you either get it, or you do not" (Azerrad 227). Thus was the case with Cobain's music. "Smells Like Teen Spirit" was his inarticulate roar; it was articulate in that it expressed exactly what he was trying to point out; however, not everyone could grasp what that was.

Overall, the work this paper does is outstanding—it approaches a "cultural text," a famous song, and brings the reader multiple perspectives on it, using comparison, literary and sound analysis, and analogy. It is a good model for doing this type of work.

Works Cited

Azerrad, Michael. *Come as You Are*. New York: Doubleday, 1993.

Cohen, Howard, and Leonard Pitts. "Kurt Cobain Made Rock for Everyone but Kurt Cobain." *Knight Ridder/Tribune* 8 Apr. 1994. Infotrac.

Dettmar, Kevin. "Uneasy Listening, Uneasy Commerce." *The Chronicle of Higher Education*. 14 Sept. 2001: 18. LexisNexis.

Moon, Tom. "Reluctant Spokesman for Generation Became the Rock Star He Abhorred." *Knight Ridder/Tribune* 9 Apr. 1994. Infotrac.

Nirvana. *Nevermind*. David Geffen Company, 1991.

Rawlins, Melissa. "From Bad to Verse." *Entertainment Weekly* 5 June 1992: 57. Infotrac.

CHAPTER 10

HOW DO I CITE THIS CAR?
GUIDELINES FOR CITING POPULAR CULTURE TEXTS

As you probably know, you must cite or acknowledge any kind of text (written or otherwise) that you use in an academic or professional essay. Most students think that citing work has mostly to do with avoiding plagiarism—and that is certainly an important part of it—but there are other reasons why citing work is important.

As a researcher, your job is often to make sense of a particular phenomenon and, in doing so, make sense of the work done before you on the same subject. When you do that, you perform a valuable service for your reader, who now not only has your perspective on this phenomenon but also has an entry into the subject through the sources you cite. For this very reason, professional researchers and academics often find the works cited pages and footnotes as interesting as the text itself.

As writers in the humanities, you typically use MLA (Modern Language Association) formatting in your papers. There are two other major forms of citing—APA (American Psychological Association), often used in the social sciences and science, and Chicago (named for its association with the University of Chicago Press, which publishes *The Chicago Manual of Style*) or Turabian, often used in history and political science.

All three ways of citing are part of a system of citation. How you cite (say where information comes from) is directly related to the bibliography or, in the case of MLA, the works cited page. You indicate in the text who wrote the article or book, and at the end of the paper, the sources are listed in alphabetical order, so the reader can see the whole work, but without the intrusion of listing that whole work within the text; seeing (Alvarez 99) is much easier than seeing (Alvarez, Julia. *How the Garcia Girls Lost Their Accents*, New York: Plume, 1992, 99.) in an essay.

USING PARENTHETICAL REFERENCES

In MLA, you cite using parenthetical references within the body of your essay. The format for the parenthetical reference is easy. If you know the author's name, you include the author's last name and the page number(s) in parentheses before the punctuation

87

mark. For instance, if you are quoting from LeAnne Howe's novel *Shell Shaker*, your parenthetical reference would look like this:

> The novel *Shell Shaker* does a great job of conveying Choctaw pride: "I decide that as a final gesture I will show the people my true self. After all, I am a descendent of two powerful ancestors, Grandmother of Birds and Tuscalusa" (Howe 15).

If the author's name has already been used in the text in that particular reference (not just earlier in the essay), then you simply provide the page number (15). If there are two or three authors, then list the authors' last names and the page number (Silverman and Rader 23). For more than three authors, use et al. (Baym et al. 234).

The same holds true for citing an article. Simply list the last name of the author of the article or story or poem, followed by the page number (Wright 7). You do not need to list the title of the book or magazine.

If you use works from the internet, the system of citing is the same, except you sometimes do not have page numbers, and you often cannot find authors (although you should look hard—sometimes the authorship appears at the end of the text, rather than the beginning). In citing an article from the internet, use if you can the page's title, rather than the home page. For example, if you are looking at admissions policies at Virginia Commonwealth University, you come to the page and it says "Admissions" at the top. You would then in the text, after your information, type: ("Admissions")—not "Virginia Commonwealth University" and definitely not the webpage URL: http://www.vcu.edu/admissions. This form of citing also applies to non-internet articles without authors. Some of your professors may ask you to tell them from which paragraph the information comes. If that is the case, your in-text citation might look like this: ("Admissions" par. 2).

BUILDING THE WORKS CITED PAGE

A works cited page consists of an alphabetized list of the texts that you cite in your paper. This list goes at the end of an essay in MLA format. This list tells your readers all of the pertinent publication information for each source. It is alphabetized by the last name of the author or, if there is no author, by the title or name of the text. Generally, works cited pages start on a new page and bear the heading "Works Cited." For books, you use the following format, not indenting the first line but indenting the remaining lines.

Clements, Brian. *Essays Against Ruin*. Texas Review Press, 1997.

Goldstone, Dwonna. *Integrating the 40 Acres: The Fifty-Year Struggle for Racial Equality at the University of Texas*. University of Georgia Press, 2006.

Notice the crucial aspects in this citation—the author's name, the title of the work, who was responsible for publishing it, and the date it was published. The general rule of citing work is to find all four of these elements in order to help a fellow researcher (or your teacher) find the source and to give appropriate credit to both those who wrote the book and those who brought the book to the attention of the general public. Of course, citing a magazine requires a different format, but with the same idea, as does citing a webpage or a song or a movie. We provide examples of many different sources later.

PLAGIARISM

Citing your work is critical. If you quote from a text in your paper, or if you use information in any way but do not cite this source, the use of this material is plagiarism. At most institutions, plagiarism is grounds for failing the assignment and even the class. At many universities and colleges, students can be dismissed from the institution entirely if plagiarism can be proved.

A student can commit plagiarism in several different ways. One is the deliberate misrepresentation of someone else's work as your own—if you buy a paper off the internet, get a friend's paper and turn it in as your own, or pay someone to write the paper, you are committing the most serious form of plagiarism.

Then there is the previous example of using someone's work in your text but without citing it, which is also a serious offense. Some students do this inadvertently—they forget where their ideas came from or mean to find out where the information came from later but do not. Still others want their teacher to think they are intelligent and think that using someone else's work may help. The irony of the last way of thinking is that teachers often are more impressed by the student who has taken the time to do research and incorporate those ideas thoughtfully into a paper—that is what real researchers do.

It is also possible to commit plagiarism without such intent. If you do not paraphrase a source's work completely—even if you cite the source—that is also plagiarism.

Besides the general ethical problem of using someone else's work as your own, the more practical issue with plagiarizing is that you are likely to get caught. As teachers, we become so familiar with the student voice in writing, and a particular student's voice, that it is often not very difficult to catch a cheating student.

WORKS CITED EXAMPLES

The examples shown here cover most citation contingencies; however, if you have trouble deciding how to cite a source, there are a number of options, the best of which is to consult the *MLA Handbook for Writers of Research Papers*, which your library owns, if you do not. Otherwise, you can find any number of webpages that provide examples of MLA documentation. We recommend the Purdue Writing Center site (http://owl. english.purdue.edu) and the award-winning "Guide for Writing Research Papers" site at Capitol Community College (http://webster.commnet.edu/mla.htm).

Citing Books

Book entries include the following information:

Author's last name, Author's first name. Title. Publisher, year of publication.

A BOOK BY A SINGLE AUTHOR
Clements, Brian. *Essays Against Ruin*. Texas Review Press, 1997.

A BOOK BY TWO OR THREE AUTHORS
After the first author, list subsequent authors' names in published (not alphabetical) order.

Levitt, Steven D., and Stephen J. Dubner. *Freakonomics: A Rogue Economist Explores the Hidden Side of Everything*. William Morrow, 2005.

TWO OR MORE BOOKS BY THE SAME AUTHOR
Arrange entries alphabetically by title. After the first entry, use three hyphens instead of the author's name.

Garber, Frederick. *Thoreau's Fable of Inscribing*. Princeton UP, 1991.

---. *Thoreau's Redemptive Imagination*. New York UP, 1977.

AN ANTHOLOGY OR COMPILATION
Driver, Martha W., and Sid Ray, editors. *The Medieval Hero on Screen: Representations from Beowulf to Buffy*. McFarland, 2004.

A BOOK BY A CORPORATE AUTHOR
Bay Area AIDS Foundation. *Report on Diversity: 2001*. City Lights Books, 2001.

A BOOK WITH NO AUTHOR
A History of Weatherford, Oklahoma. Southwest Publishers, 1998.

A GOVERNMENT PUBLICATION
If no author is known, begin with the government's name, and then add the department or agency and any subdivision. For the US government, the Government Printing Office (GPO) is usually the publisher.

United States, Forest Service, Alaska Region. *Skipping Cow Timber Sale, Tongass National Forest: Final EIS Environmental Impact Statement and Record of Decision.* USDA Forest Service, 2000.

THE PUBLISHED PROCEEDINGS OF A CONFERENCE
Ward, Scott, Tom Robertson, and Ray Brown, editors. "Commercial Television and European Children: An International Research Digest." *International Perspectives on Television Advertising and Children: The Role of Research for Policy Issues in Europe*, July 1–3, 1984, Provence, France, Gower, 1986.

AN EDITION OTHER THAN THE FIRST
Gibaldi, Joseph. *MLA Handbook for Writers of Research Papers*. 5th ed. Modern Language Association, 1999.

Citing Articles
Articles use a similar format as books; however, you must include information for the article and the source of its publication. They follow the following format:

Author(s). "Title of Article." Title of source, day month year, pages.

For newspapers and magazines, the month or the day and the month appear before the year, and no parentheses are used. When quoting from a scholarly journal, the year of publication is in parentheses. When citing articles from periodicals, the month (except May, June, and July) is abbreviated.

AN ARTICLE FROM A REFERENCE BOOK
Deignan, Hebert G. "Dodo." *Collier's Encyclopedia*. 1997 ed.

Voigt, David G. "America's Game: A Brief History of Baseball." *Encyclopedia of Baseball*. 9th ed., Macmillan, 1993, pp. 3–13.

AN ARTICLE IN A SCHOLARLY JOURNAL

Crawford, Rachel. "English Georgic and British Nationhood." *ELH*, vol. 65, no. 1, 1998, pp. 23–59.

Ingrassia, Catherine. "Writing the West: Iconic and Literal Truth in *Unforgiven*." *Literature/Film Quarterly*, vol. 26, no. 1, 1998, pp. 53–60.

A WORK IN AN ANTHOLOGY

Begin with the author of the poem, article, or story. That title goes in quotation marks. Then, cite the anthology, as before. Include the page numbers of the text you use at the end of the citation.

Haven, Chris. "Glimmers of Hope in the Economy." *99 Poems for the 99 Percent*, edited by Dean Rader, 99: The Press, 2014, pp. 27–28.

AN ARTICLE IN A MONTHLY MAGAZINE

Sweany, Brian D. "Mark Cuban Is Not Just a Rich Jerk." *Texas Monthly*, Mar. 2002, pp. 74–77.

AN ARTICLE IN A WEEKLY MAGAZINE

If the article does not continue on consecutive pages, denote this with a plus sign (+).

Gladwell, Malcolm. "The Coolhunt." *The New Yorker*, 17 Mar. 1997, p. 78+.

AN ARTICLE IN A NEWSPAPER

Hax, Carolyn. "Tell Me about It." *The Washington Post*, 29 Mar. 2002, p. C8.

AN ARTICLE WITH NO AUTHOR

"Yankees Net Bosox." *The Richmond Times–Dispatch*, 1 Sept. 2001, p. D5.

A LETTER TO THE EDITOR

McCrimmon, Miles. "Let Community Colleges Do Their Jobs." Letter. *The Richmond Times–Dispatch*, 9 Mar. 1999, p. F7.

Silverman, Melvin J. "We Must Restore Higher Tax on Top Incomes." Letter. *The New York Times*, 8 Mar. 1992, p. E14.

A REVIEW

Smith, Mark C. Review of *America First! Its History, Culture, and Politics*, by Bill Kauffman. *Journal of Church and State*, vol. 39, 1997, pp. 374–75.

A CARTOON

Jim. Cartoon. *I Went to College and It Was Okay.* Andrews and McNeel, 1991.

Electronic Sources

A BOOK PUBLISHED ONLINE

If known, the author's name goes first, followed by the title of the document or page in quotation marks. If the document/page is part of a larger work, like a book or a journal, then that title is italicized. Include the date of publication, the date of access if known, and the address or URL (uniform resource locator) in angle brackets.

Savage, Elizabeth. "Art Comes on Laundry Day." *Housekeeping—A Chapbook. The Pittsburgh Quarterly Online,* edited by Michael Simms, Dec. 1997, http://trfn. clpgh. org/tpq/hkeep.html. Accessed 20 Mar. 2002.

AN ARTICLE FROM A WEBSITE

Silverman, Jason. "2001: A Re-Release Odyssey." *Wired News,* 13 Oct. 2001, http:// www.wired.com/news/digiwood/0,1412,47432,00.html. Accessed 20 Mar. 2002.

A REVIEW

Svalina, Mathias. Review of *I Won't Tell a Soul Except the World,* by Ran Away to Sea. *Lost at Sea,* July 2001, http://lostatsea.net/LAS/arctosea.htm. Accessed 2 Mar. 2002.

A MAILING LIST, NEWSGROUP, OR EMAIL CITATION

If known, the author's name goes first, followed by the subject line in quotations, the date of the posting, the name of the forum, the date of access and, in angle brackets, the online address of the list's website. If no website is known, provide the email address of the list's moderator or supervisor.

AN EMAIL TO YOU

Brennan, Brian. "GLTCs." Received by Dean Rader, 21 Mar. 2002.

AN ELECTRONIC ENCYCLOPEDIA

"Play." *Encyclopædia Britannica,* 2007. *Encyclopædia Britannica Online,* http://www. britannica.com/eb/article-9060375. Accessed 27 July 2007.

AN ARTICLE FROM A PERIODICALLY PUBLISHED DATABASE ON INFOTRAC

Gordon, Meryl. "Truly Deeply Maggie." *Marie Claire,* 1 Sept. 2006, *LexisNexis Academic.* Accessed 31 July 2007.

(Some of your professors will ask for a more complete version of this, which includes the place you found it and the original page number.)

Gordon, Meryl. "Truly Deeply Maggie." *Marie Claire*, Sept. 2006, p. 208+. *LexisNexis Academic*. Henry Birnbaum Library, Pace University, http://www.lexisnexis.com.rlib. pace.edu/universe. Accessed 31 July 2007.

Other Sources

A TELEVISION OR RADIO PROGRAM
List the title of the episode or segment, followed by the title of the program italicized. Then identify the network, followed by the local station, city, and the broadcast date.

"Stirred." *The West Wing*. NBC, WWBT, Richmond, VA, 3 Apr. 2002.

A PUBLISHED INTERVIEW
Morrison, Toni. Interview with Elissa Schappell. *Women Writers at Work: The Paris Review Interviews*, edited by George Plimpton. Modern Library, 1998, pp. 338–75.

A PERSONAL INTERVIEW
Heinemann, Alan. Personal interview. 14 Feb. 2001.

A FILM
Olympia. Directed by Bob Byington. King Pictures, 1998.

Or (depending on emphasis in your paper)

Byington, Bob, director *Olympia*. Performances by Jason Andrews, Carmen Nogales, and Damien Young, King Pictures, 1998.

A SOUND RECORDING FROM A COMPACT DISC, TAPE, OR RECORD
The Asylum Street Spankers. *Spanks for the Memories*, Spanks-a-Lot Records, 1996.

A PERFORMANCE
R.E.M. Walnut Creek Auditorium, Raleigh, NC, 27 Aug. 1999.

A WORK OF ART IN A MUSEUM
Klee, Paul. *A Page from the Golden Book*. Kunstmuseum, Bern.

A PHOTOGRAPH BY YOU
United States Post Office. Bedford, NY. Personal photograph by author, 15 Aug. 2001.

AN ADVERTISEMENT
Absolut. Advertisement. *Time*, 17 Dec. 2002, p. 12.

CARS, BUILDINGS, OUTDOOR SCULPTURES, AND OTHER ODD TEXTS
Although many of your teachers would not require you to cite a primary text like a car or a building, if you have to do so (or want to), we suggest you follow the guidelines for a text like a movie, which has a flexible citing format, but always includes the title and the date, and hopefully an author of some kind. For example, if you were going to cite something like a Frank Lloyd Wright building, you might do something like this:

Wright, Frank Lloyd, architect Robert P. Parker House, Oak Park, IL, 1892.

If, for some reason, you were to cite a car, you might do something like this:

Toyota Motor Company. Camry. 1992.

Or, if you knew where the car was built:

Toyota Motor Company. Camry. Georgetown, KY, 1992.

But if you knew the designer of the car, you could use that person as an author, similar to the way you can use a screenwriter or a director or an actor for the "author" of a movie.

CHAPTER 11

HOW AM I A TEXT?
ON WRITING PERSONAL ESSAYS

We think the best papers come from one's own viewpoint—after all, writing is thinking, and for the most part, the thinking you do is your own. The texts you have been writing about, however, were texts you read from a more general perspective.

But say your professor wants a personal essay, as many freshman composition instructors do. Is it possible to write one using the ideas and techniques of reading texts? Indeed—you are a text, and so are your experiences, feelings, ideas, friends, and relatives. What's more, your experiences and emotions are not culture neutral—they have in some ways been influenced by the expectations living in our culture has generated. Take, for example, one of four ideas often used as personal essay topics in freshmen classes: the prom, the class trip to the beach, the loss of a loved one, or coming to college.

Just so you know, these are the topics we instructors often brace ourselves for, because students often have so little new to say about them. The essays are often laden with description of familiar landscapes, emotions, and events at the expense of any real reflection—they do not tell us anything new about the prom or grief.

Yet, in some way, even going to the beach should be a rich textual experience. Here is why: Not only are you going to the beach, but also you are going to the beach with ideas of the beach in mind, with cultural expectations of what beaches are like, what people do at beaches, and so on. For example, how do we know to wear bathing suits, put on sunscreen, and play volleyball at the beach? Not only have we done these before, but because we have seen others do these things, we have incorporated their ideas about beachgoing into our beachgoing.

So if you write about the prom or a loved one getting ill or dying, try to focus not only on the emotions attached to such an event, but your emotional expectations as well. Did you "not know how to feel"? Why? Was it because you had expected to feel a certain way? How did you know how to act? Were there cultural clues? Did you see a movie about a prom or about death? Proms are a particularly American phenomenon, and have been featured in any number of movies, usually teen romances. Use that knowledge about the prom (or any other subject) in your own writing.

Take another common example. Dying in America has any number of traditions attached to it, depending on what American subculture you belong to. Foreign cultures have very different ways of looking at death. How you view death or illness may also have to do with religious beliefs, the closeness of your family, and so on. But even these ideas about illness and death come from somewhere, and you owe your reader your best guess at how you came to them. You should approach ideas about brothers, mothers, fathers, and grandmothers with the same approach if you write about them.

What we are talking about here is what personal essayists often call reflection—the idea that we are not only describing our lives but also contemplating them at the same time. Entering college is a particularly ripe time for contemplation; at a minimum, you have a new learning environment, but for most of you, there is a change in friendships and social environments as well. For some of you, it is time for even more upheaval—you may change your career path or your worldview. You probably will not know all this if you decide to write about entering college, but you have some ideas about what your expectations for college are and where you received them. The university setting is a rich cultural text; reading it may provide you additional insight into your own experiences there.

There are more subjects that are worthy of personal reflection than we can count here (the ones we already named are some of the hardest). The idea is to take an experience or event, put it in your own perspective, and reflect on how your perspective may fit in with others. Anything from a trip to the grocery store to a road trip to a phone call to a visit can be the subject of a reflective essay; so can relationships with other people. But what you have to do in these essays is to make sure they matter not only to you but to others as well—that is why focusing on putting your experiences in a cultural perspective can make your writing worth reading (not just worth writing).

Some of you might object to this sort of self-analysis and wonder why you cannot just simply describe your experiences in a paper. For some papers and some teachers, that might be acceptable. But if writing is thinking and writing about oneself is thinking and self-discovery, you owe your reader—and yourself—your best shot at unearthing cultural expectations.

One last note about personal essays: Students often misunderstand their purpose. Although the topic of the personal essay might be your experience, the personal essay is not written for you but for your audience. The story that you tell about the beach or the prom or the death of a loved one is not as important as what you learned from the event. Simply recounting your trip to the beach is not nearly as interesting as what you saw, observed, and learned from your trip to the beach. Even more important is to consider what your audience can learn from what you learned. How can your experiences help the reader? The two great advantages you have as a personal essayist are recognition and discovery. In the best personal essay about a prom, the reader recognizes something familiar (an awkward moment, a romantic dance, the smell of hairspray), but also discovers something new about the text that is a prom because of your essay. So, as you sit down to draft a personal essay, think about how you might use this opportunity to help your readers learn something new about a topic they think they already know.

PART 2

Writing about Specific Types of Texts

READING AND WRITING ABOUT THE WORLD AROUND YOU

"There was a time when meanings were focused and reality could be fixed; when that sort of belief disappeared, things became uncertain and open to interpretation." This observation, from the British painter Bridget Riley,[1] serves as a way into the second part of *The World Is a Text* and, in particular, to this chapter. Here and elsewhere we emphasize the possibility and importance of "reading" and interpreting the world around you by paying attention to the arguments texts make.

In the introduction, we gave you a theoretical basis for reading the world as a text; here we want to say a bit more about how you, as a writer, might perform such a task. As you will recall, we suggest that the world itself is a structured, "authored" place that is full of buildings, signs, people, laws, advertisements, and spaces that are always making some kind of argument. Again, this is not to say that office buildings are *arguing* with you, but rather each in their own way is suggesting something or trying to guide you in some way, either as a consumer or a citizen. If a house has a fence in front of it, that might be a different argument than if it has a bench. A classroom with desks in a circle might make a different argument—or establish a different tone—than one where desks are arranged in rows. A cafe that features pour-over coffee, kale salad, contemporary art on the walls, and music by Wilco, The National, and Death Cab for Cutie is making an argument about its edginess, its hipness.

The idea behind this chapter is to introduce you to the act of thinking about common texts as thought-out constructions designed to enable some kind of effect or reaction. Or, put in the language of rhetoric—we want you to learn to recognize how texts—even seemingly small texts—make arguments, and we want to help you begin to write your own smart, insightful essays about these texts.

The world around you is often structured or even authored. Most of us go about our daily lives paying very little attention to how structures and patterns in our homes, campuses, work places, dorm rooms, and restaurants get us to behave a certain way, walk a certain direction, or look at a certain vista. One reason we tend not to think of land-

---

1   "Op Art," *The Art Story*, www.theartstory.org/movement-op-art.htm, accessed 13 Dec. 2017.

scapes or suburbs as being authored texts is that we never really know who the "author" is. A developer? A financer? A city council? And who is the author of your apartment building? Your dormitory hall? A person (or persons) went to great trouble (and great expense) to create these structures. Similarly, popular stores like Target or Wal-Mart are meticulously authored, as are museums and theme parks. Each one is designed to get you to stay and, hopefully, spend. Is it a coincidence which items are near the checkout lane? Where the souvenir shops are located? Where the food is? Because so much of our lives in America takes place in communities, very little of our built environment is left to chance.

While this may make for less than exciting day-to-day experiences, it makes for great writing topics. One of our favorite exercises in our classes is to have students take a step back from or out of their daily routines and look at their surroundings as though they were a visitor from another country or an alien planet. Begin by taking a lot of notes. If you are reading, say, the most prominent building on your campus, begin with its external characteristics. How big is it? What color is it? What is its shape? Is it old? Is it only sort of old but trying hard to look old? Does it evoke classical architecture of Greece or Rome? Does it resemble a church? Does it look friendly or intimidating? Does it look like a place where learning happens?

If you are writing about your neighborhood, you might begin by looking at small details like street names. Many neighborhoods around America have streets with names like "Harvard Street," "Yale Court," or "Oxford Place." Why might they do this? Is your street a "terrace," or an "avenue," or a "court?" Does that distinction matter? Are there sidewalks? Fences? Well-manicured lawns? Cul-de-sacs? You might also pay attention to the cars people drive. Are they American? Japanese? German? How close is a highway or busy road? Is there a Starbucks near? Is the closest store Whole Foods or Safeway? Are there parks? Speed bumps? Fountains? The answers to these questions may not tell you much about the author of your subdivision or suburb or neighborhood, but they may give you an idea of the feeling that space is supposed to create. You can bet that very little—perhaps nothing—about your neighborhood is pure chance.

Students who live in an urban area may have a harder time defining a neighborhood or narrowing a focus to an authored building or space. But they can still become educated readers of city landscapes. For example, what visual markers designate your neighborhood? What sounds tell you you are home? What smells? What about your neighbors? Often, there are also historical and political traces as well, like what distinguishes "good" blocks from "bad" ones? Does your city have a history of segregation? Is that history visible in its civic design; its access to green spaces, grocery stores, schools, and hospitals? Are there gardens and trees? Our point is that what is familiar to you is usually what you examine the least. We want you to think about the thinking that created the space and spaces you take for granted.

Once you get a list of details (colors, shapes, sizes, design, ornamentation, access), you can begin to start making sense of them. That is the first step in learning to read the world around you not simply as the world around you but as a text.

The world around you is full of symbols and symbolism. Consider the following list:

- columns
- steeple
- streetlamp
- flower bed
- fountain
- tenement house
- strip mall
- town square
- fence
- statue
- gate
- police
- ivy

What associations, feelings, or emotions are created by each of these items? When reading the world around you, it is often a good idea to pay attention to the symbolism of objects. You may think this sounds odd, but it is a great deal like the way you would think through literary symbolism in a poem or novel. City planners might design a fountain in a town square to connote European civilization; they might erect statues to call attention to a place's history (and importance); they might build a fence to create a sense of exclusivity. Not everything will necessarily be deeply symbolic, but many things ranging from flags to gazebos to cobblestones to public art to skyscrapers to simple signage can tell you a great deal about the intent or theme of a place.

One way to begin is to think about what the place you are going to write about thinks of itself. What we mean by this is, what kind of argument is your place trying to make? For example, let's say you want to write about your campus. When you look at your campus, when you walk through it or drive around it, what words or images come to mind? Is your campus more urban or more rural? Are there tall buildings with lots of parking lots? If so, your campus might be trying to send the message that studying there is about ease or that it recognizes it serves a large population. If you are at a small, expensive, liberal arts college, your campus might be trying hard to look "quaint" or "stately" or "safe" to justify the high tuition. Perhaps you attend a large state school where an enormous football stadium is either at the center of campus or is the largest thing on campus or both. Does that make an argument about the centrality of football at your campus? What if a church or chapel is at the center of your campus? What symbolism does that carry? How big is your library? What kinds of signs are around campus? What colors are they? What fonts are used? All of these details may seem insignificant, but you can be sure that a great deal of planning, discussion, and forethought went into each.

Now, think about where your campus is situated. Often, campuses are on a hill or along the most prominent landmass of an area. Why might that be? Many of the community colleges in California are located near major highways. Is this coincidence? Have you ever wondered why so many major state universities like Ohio State, University of Kansas, University of Illinois, University of Georgia, Oregon State, SUNY-Binghamton, and Cal-Berkeley are located in smallish or even out of the way towns? Of course, over time, some of these have grown to be more than college towns but all began as places away from thickly settled areas. Do you have any idea why this may be? Now think about urban institutions—university or community colleges in the hearts of Chicago, Philadelphia, Miami, and Detroit. What are they like? What about community colleges in the suburbs? Small liberal arts colleges in tiny towns? Do institutions reflect the values and environment of a place? Why? How?

This kind of approach can be applied to any mode of nontraditional reading because so much our world relies on symbolic communication. With some practice, attention to detail, and a willingness to read the world around you as a text, you will become a savvy reader of the community of symbols.

Everything has a specific grammar. We think of grammar as a series of rules for writing and language, but that concept extends to most of our world. Paying attention to the "grammar"—the internal and external structure—of an object, place, city, or sign is key to understand how it makes meaning.

Let's take the inside of a car, for example. This is a place we are all familiar with. Cars may differ slightly inside and in the makeup of their dashboards, but all passenger vehicles share a grammar—the steering wheel is always in the same place, there are four windows and a windshield, the radio and climate systems are generally in the middle of the dashboards, our seatbelts are over our outside shoulder, the gas and brake pedals appear in the same places. On those rare occasions we can't find the headlights or the windshield wipers, we become aware of the fact the car is using a different grammar than what we are used to. Shopping malls are similar. Malls tend to employ the same grammar from mall to mall, whether it's in Hawaii or New Jersey or Florida. Big department stores are located at the ends, food courts are in the middle, and the cellphone and sunglass kiosks pepper the wide aisles between the stores. The maps generally look the same and all malls smell more or less the same. There are few surprises.

When it comes to malls, the predictability and uniformity may be tedious or comforting, depending on your personality, but when it comes to something like traffic signs, consistent grammar is critically important. Octagons, triangles, and Xs all signify specific things. Yellow means one thing, red another, green yet another. But none are accidental. Red never means go. A triangle never means stop. A seemingly uninteresting topic but one that can be strangely intriguing is that of safety. For a day, just one day, pay attention to as many details as you can that have to do with your safety and the safety of others. Fire exits, crosswalks, safety belts, security guards, passwords, fire extinguishers, warning bells, sprinklers, helmets, lights, etc. To be sure, our society relies on a grammar of safety, and some neighborhoods or buildings feature more of these than others.

Lastly, each of us participates in our own brand of personal grammar through our clothes, glasses, shoes, hairstyle, bags, jewelry, tattoos, nose rings, fingernails, hats, and all of our other accessories. As we suggest in the previous section and later in our chapter on fashion, we author the texts of ourselves every day. In doing so, we create and adhere to our own individual grammar. However, we might also argue that we have inherited a fashion grammar that we did not ourselves create. A classic example is the kind of clothes that are acceptable and unacceptable for men to wear. Strangely, fashion options for women have evolved faster and more dramatically than for men. Women can now wear pants, boots, and ties, but it is still a bit of a faux pas for men to wear dresses or high heels, especially in a professional setting. In other words, many of us adhere to fashion grammar without, perhaps, understanding why. Paying attention to the rules of authorship and organization can prove tremendously helpful when trying to read the world around you.

The world around you incorporates technology. Cellphones, iPads, and other devices have altered how people behave around us. On the bus, the subway, in the line for coffee, even walking across campus, more and more people seem engaged in their devices and disengaged from the larger world around them.

But there are other technologies as well: cars, video monitors, cellphone towers, surveillance systems, bicycles, headphones, step counters, pencils and pens—the list goes on and on. The micro technologies we wear on our bodies and the macro technologies that make towns, cities, and universities function have increased power over us and our surrounding environment (see our Chapter 13 for more on this).

As you consider the world around you, think about how that world is mediated by our various forms of media and technology.

Here are some things to think about as you write *about* the world around you. All genres have conventions, vocabularies, structures, and patterns. As you begin taking notes, making outlines, and figuring out your perspectives, you might consider the following:

- Semiotics: Semiotics is the study of signs and their meanings. For a refresher, refer back to pages 13–17.

- Signifier: A signifier is the sign or symbol itself. For example, a stop sign is a signifier. The Mercedes logo is a signifier. The American flag is a signifier. A cross is a signifier.

- Signified: The message, value, or idea communicated by the signifier. The signified of the stop sign is "stop." The signified of the Mercedes logo is "affluence," perhaps, or "sophistication." The signified of the American flag will differ depending on who you are. If you are a proud Vietnam veteran, the signified of the flag might be "pride," "freedom," and "honor." If you are a refugee from another country, the signified of the flag might be "hope," "promise," "safety." If you are a member of ISIS or al-Qaeda, the signified of the American flag might be "evil," "violence," or "infidel." Similarly, the signified for the cross, could range from "holy" to "oppressive" depending on your religious and political beliefs.

- Intentional vs. unintentional: When reading the world around you, it is necessary to pay attention to the intentional and unintentional arguments a place, building, neighborhood, or campus makes. For example, a smartly designed public square in the middle of a city is a good example of an intentional project, but graffiti or a homeless person on the benches might be an unintentional component of the square yet one which may affect your reading of it nonetheless. Similarly, you may *intend* for your Sanskrit tattoo to convey a respect for ancient languages or a deep reverence for the sacred, but to someone who associates tattoos with criminals, the unreadable tattoo may, unintentionally, send the *opposite* message.

- Natural vs. unnatural: We are not talking about cyborgs here but rather, the so-called "natural world" and the so-called "built world," or as they are sometimes referred to, "the natural environment" and "human-made environment." It is easy to distinguish between a national forest and a baseball field, but a farm or a maintained tall grass prairie can be more complicated in these terms.

WRITING ABOUT THE WORLD AROUND YOU: THE GENRES

Writing about the world around you is not really an official topic like film or television or public space. Writing about what surrounds you is just *writing*. So the genres we write about below are applicable to any of the rest of the chapters and topics. Similarly, any of the genres you see in other chapters are also applicable to this one.

The Review

In a review, an author evaluates a text or a series of texts and makes recommendations about the success or failure of the item or items under review. We are most familiar with book and movie reviews, but there are also concert reviews, television reviews, dance and recital reviews, reviews of sporting events, political speeches, and fashion shows. While one doesn't really review "the world," there are instances of critics, scholars, and writers reviewing the external world. For example, the *San Francisco Chronicle* runs regular reviews of buildings by its architecture critic, John King. Popular magazines often run snarky and short reviews of celebrity fashion choices. Many newspapers and magazines publish long and incredibly detailed reviews of cars. Electronics is one area where reviews have exploded. You can now find all kinds of reviews

A QUICK GUIDE TO WRITING ABOUT THE WORLD AROUND YOU

1. Define your space or object: We talk about this throughout the book, but the most important first step is to narrow down to a specific area. "My hometown" may be too broad, but "my block" or "my subdivision" or "my house" may not be. "My hat" might be too vague, but "My New York Yankees hat" is better.

2. Think about argument and intention: As we suggest above, built environments make arguments. A park may try to argue for its serenity or its playfulness. A person may argue for her edginess by wearing vintage cowboy boots, aviator sunglasses, a heavy metal T-shirt, and jean shorts. How do rock and roll performers ensure they don't look like conservative businessmen? How does a cool independent coffee shop ensure it is not mistaken for Starbucks?

3. Take notes and freewrite: We suggest taking a lot of notes when you are observing a particular thing. Write down every little detail you observe. Don't forget to note your emotional reaction to these details. Pay attention to both the personal and cultural associations specific items carry.

4. Ask yourself one or perhaps two interesting questions, and make your essay answer that question: After observing something and taking a lot of notes, you might arrive at a question like, *What message does my campus architecture send?* Or, *Why is my suburb designed the way it is?* Or *What does my dorm room say about me?* Your essay should be the smart, detailed, convincing answer to that question.

of computers, video games, televisions, earphones, smart phones, tablets, and the list goes on and on.

In each case, the reviewer identifies a text, walks the reader through specific components of that text, like screen size or its handling around curves or the cut and length of the dress or how the building integrates into the space around it. The reviewer evaluates the pros and cons, the strengths and weaknesses, and then makes a judgment of sorts. *Is this building a contribution to the downtown area of Houston?* for example, or *Is the new iPhone worth the price increase?* In your case, you may be able to find some model reviews depending on the topic of your essay. If not, just follow the model of a good reviewer or do a close reading. Or, put another way, you make an argument about the macro by focusing on the micro. A review of a new skateboard park would include listing all the bowls, the various attractions, its location, its prices, its safety precautions (or lack thereof), as well as commentaries on the designs of the features, how they handle crowds, and so forth. You would then make an overall assessment based on your close reading of the many aspects of the park.

In other words, you can review anything. How about the commuter parking lot? The cafeteria? The classroom? Cap'n Crunch? Your school's mascot? Anything can be reviewed as long as you establish the criteria for a successful or positive review as well as a negative one.

The Close Reading

Traditionally, we think of close readings as a literary genre. Most of us have practice giving a close reading of a poem, for example. We talk about its sounds, its structure, its symbols, its possible themes. But we can also do close readings of gardens, buildings, people, neighborhoods, malls, amusement parks, highways, tourist attractions, corporate landscaping, sports arenas—you name it.

A close reading is not unlike a review in that the writer looks at and explains the various components of the text with the overall goal of demonstrating how the parts work together to contribute to the whole.

A close reading often includes either an explicit or implicit evaluation, but the evaluation is not necessarily the major component of the piece the way it might be in a review. The most important thing in the close reading is to be exhaustive, comprehensive. You really want to tease out as much as you can about the item you're writing about.

The Appreciation

We love to appreciate things, and the appreciation essay is always fun to write. Classic albums, old television shows, retiring athletes—all of these make for great appreciation essays. An appreciation is just what it sounds like. You explain why you like something and why someone else should as well. Appreciations tend to be personal and are often written in the first person, though in many ways, they share a great deal with close readings and reviews.

The best appreciations mix subjective and objective data. That is, you say what you really love about something, but you also include external information as well. Let's say you want to write about a new restaurant—your essay should be a marriage of things you love about the restaurant (food, service, location, décor, prices) and objective information such as good reviews, a Michelin star, long lines, a great Yelp rating. Essentially, your essay should be: *here is why I like this place, and here is why others like this place; therefore, you should consider liking or like this place.*

Check with your professor, but in general, an appreciation will have a slightly looser prose style and will perhaps even be a bit more chatty. Feel free to include personal stories or anecdotes in your appreciation as well. Readers always respond to those.

The Research Paper

We write about research papers throughout this book, so the advice we offer there holds true here as well. We always like to begin with this: *What question do I want my research to answer?* If you begin there and pursue that question seriously, you will be off to a great start.

Since "the world" is not a particularly narrow topic, you'll need to focus in a bit on the genre of your subject. If it's a building, you can research what else has been written about that building or other buildings like it. You might also research work by the same architect. If it is something on your campus, interview people who made decisions about it (and do any research you can). If it is a computer lab or a common room in your dorm, interview your friends, the staff, and do some research on the use of public spaces in private buildings. The key here is to have a good list of questions and ideas before starting.

We like the idea of the "researched paper" as much as we like the research paper. In a researched paper, your ideas take precedence over the ideas of others. Research enhances your own reading of a text. For example, a researched paper about your cafeteria would include your own argument about the cafeteria, but it would include some information about how universities and colleges design cafeterias. Students often think research papers mean merely recounting information, but their professors' research involves a mix of their own ideas *in conversation* with the ideas of others.

OTHER ESSAY IDEAS

When reading the world around you, literally the entire globe is your textbook, so feel free to look at things you never have before in ways that are totally new. Here are just a fraction of the options available to you.

1. Find a readable text that is part of the world around you. Ask a series of questions about it the way the authors do in the first part of this chapter. Based on the

questions and the answers to them, build a thesis and write a persuasive paper on your text.

2. Write a comparison/contrast essay on two buildings on your campus. Be sure you take into account the function of the buildings. For instance, if you write about the gym and a dorm, do not assume they serve the same purpose.

3. Take a little road trip and photograph the interesting and even not-so-interesting things you see along the way. Chronicle your journey. How do signs and space make meaning? Can you make an argument about American highway culture based on what you observe on your trip?

4. Gather photos you have taken in a day or on trip or even in a family scrapbook. Now try to write a paper that ties them together.

5. Find a text you want to explore. Instead of beginning writing right away, list at least five ways you might approach the text. Then, choose one approach to the text and begin drafting or freewriting.

6. Find an interesting area of your city or town, like an up-and-coming neighbor-hood or an historic district, or a central square or plaza. Spend a few hours walking around and taking notes. Write down everything you see, every detail, every building, every sign, every design element. Based on your descriptions, write an essay not just describing what you saw but turning those descriptions into an argument about how that space is asking to be interpreted.

7. Find two friends who dress very differently from each other. Ask them to talk about their clothing choices on that particular day. Have them explain the personal significance of specific articles of clothing or particular accessories. Are they trying to make an argument or a statement with their fashion clothes?

8. Write a comparison/contrast essay in which you read a science lab and an art studio. What are the similarities? Differences? How do the regular users of the spaces "brand" their rooms?

9. If you can, revisit one of your high school classrooms. Take some photos of it. Now write an essay comparing your high school classroom with a typical college classroom. What stays the same? What changes? Are there semiotic texts that scream "high school" or "college?" If so, what and how?

10. Write a paper on the various forms of transportation in a college parking lot. Look at cars, SUVs, bikes, motorcycles, and scooters. What does the aggregate tell you about the demographic of your school? Do we tend to associate certain types of people with specific modes of transportation? If so, why? And what are the associations?

11. Write an essay on what you think are three new or interesting fashion trends: tattoos, a haircut, a kind of jean, a hip T-shirt, or the popularity of Lululemon. Give a semiotic reading of each fashion trend and explain what message the wearer intends to send by donning that accessory.

12. Write a comparison/contrast paper in which you read your university's dining hall and your favorite local restaurant. What is similar? What's different? Does your dining hall do anything to try to approximate a restaurant?

13. Give a semiotic reading of some space in your dorm/residence hall. Maybe you read all of the material on dorm room doors on your hall; maybe you read all of the notices and ads on a bulletin board; maybe you read the main entryway; or, maybe you give a semiotic reading of a bathroom on your floor.

14. One of us used to have classes come out to the parking lot to read his car—the inside of his car. Take a stab at reading the interior of something private, like a car, a book bag, a purse, or a wallet. What can you tell about that person by these items?

RESOURCES

There are a variety of resources that can help you interpret the world. There are maps, newspapers, magazines, websites (like Google Earth), and apps (like Yelp) that give you basic data. We tend to enjoy architecture reviews in local newspapers as well as pieces on fashion, neighborhoods, and technological trends. Advances in technology have become an increasingly important part of our worlds, and publications like *Wired* do a nice job of helping us understand how we integrate technology and various devices into our personal and municipal landscapes.

Our advice for narrowing down the most useful resources will be to look for publications, apps, and websites that address your specific topic. For example, if you plan to write about the sprawl of suburbia, you should look for scholarly and popular writing about suburbia. If you want to write about a specific fashion trend, seek out fashion magazines, blogs, and other forms of appropriate scholarship.

SAMPLE ESSAY

Dean Rader, one of the authors of this book, demonstrates how signs, plants, walls, and buildings that you pass every day on your college campus can make an argument about your institution. Of course, paying attention to how other texts make arguments helps you when it comes time to make arguments of your own in your papers.

What Signs Tell Us about Campuses

DEAN RADER

Institutions of higher learning invest a great deal in their image. Like companies and corporations, colleges maintain a profound interest in branding and market recognition, although how a college develops and maintains that reputation is unique among large institutions. One of the most public sources of college image-building is its campus. It is rare to hear of a potential employee turning down a job at Yahoo! or GM because she found the building ugly, but how often do we hear students talk about the role a campus played in their decision about where to apply and attend college? Have you ever seen a college admissions brochure that did not feature its most attractive lawns and buildings?

This interest in campus aesthetic is not confined to current and prospective students. Administrators obsess about their physical plants because its main components like lawns, buildings, fountains, sculptures, statues, foliage (think: ivy), and signs all send messages about the institution. For example, why are so many buildings on campuses modeled on Greek and Roman structures? An initial response might be: Because Greek and Roman buildings look "important" or "imposing" or "learned" or "fancy" or "classical." But, then, the next step is to inquire into why a college might want to embody any of these ideals. What messages do columns, spires, fountains, gardens, gates, and walls send? How are these connected to the liberating power of education? Would a campus send a different message if its buildings resembled a western mining town from the 1800s? Similarly, what purpose does green space serve on a campus? Why have lawns and fields? Why not construct as many buildings and classrooms as possible? Why plant flowers? Why not build more labs?

One answer might be that campuses want to feel inviting both to students and to the surrounding community. However, for better or worse, colleges in the United States have not always been the most welcoming places; in fact, for many years, many older, private institutions cultivated a reputation based on exclusion—how difficult it was to be admitted or how rigorous its classes were. With the rise of public universities and the community college system, college has become more accessible; accordingly, campus architecture and design have taken on a more welcoming posture. In fact, how a campus fronts the public—how it welcomes—can often say quite a bit about how a college wants to be seen. Consider campus signage. Signs on campus may seem utterly insignificant, but, in truth, they reveal a great deal—even among campuses just a few miles from each other. The University of San Francisco (USF), the City College of San Francisco (CCSF), and San Francisco State University (SFSU) are all first-rate institutions in the same city, yet their signs and points of campus entry differ dramatically. In the case of these colleges, region has less to do with their signage than institutional history, mission, and audience, all of which get encoded in their signage.

San Francisco State University is the only four-year public university in the city of San Francisco, and it enjoys a rich history of quality education, ethnic diversity, and open, progressive policies. The campus is located in the southwest part of the city, next door to one of the more popular shopping malls in the area. Although the neighborhood is largely residential and almost suburban, the campus fronts a major north–south artery in San Francisco and a major train route on the San Francisco Municipal Transportation line, situating the university at a crossroads of train, car, and foot traffic. The main access to the university is notable for its lack of pretense. The modern sign, a basic gray monolith, blends in well with the clean modern lines of the building behind it to the left (Fig.a). Both the sign and the building are free of flourish and are almost understated in their muted colors, rectangular shapes, and unobtrusive design. Notice how the sign refrains from boasting a date, a motto, or a mascot. To the right of the sign is an open sidewalk that runs along 19th Avenue, a busy street. You can see both cars and the train within a few feet of the campus entrance. At many institutions, one

FIGURE a
A view of SFSU along 19th Avenue and its coffee and food kiosks.

FIGURE b
The main access, San Francisco State University.

would expect a large wall or imposing shrubbery delineating the campus from the fray of the street, but at SFSU no such barrier exists. In fact, Figure a reveals the openness of this part of campus. If you look closely to the right of the sign, you can make out the square umbrella-like tops of coffee and food kiosks. Here, the campus opens on to the sidewalk, the street, and the train stop, creating a sort of commons that is in concert with the university's image of an open, accessible, public university (Fig. b).

These signs seem consonant with SFSU's mission. Because San Francisco State enjoys a large enrollment of around 25,000 students of all ages and ethnicities, it's important that the institution send a message through its design that the campus is open, friendly, easily accessible, and familiar. The City College of San Francisco, one of the premiere community college systems in the country, makes similar arguments through its campus plan. Like San Francisco State, CCSF is a public institution, whose students are likely drawn to it not simply because of its quality but also because of its affordability and convenience (in fact, CCSF has eleven different sites around San Francisco). Its main campus, also in the southern part of the city, features a number of elements that stand as metaphors for the college's mission. Like State, City College's signs at its main campus are functional and free of pompous gesture. The scrolling LED sign (Fig. c) serves a practical purpose by disseminating valuable information to busy students, all of whom live off campus. This sign, like the ones in Figure d, are helpful without being intimidating. In fact, that the second sign might resemble those found at many high schools may make students who are insecure about college feel like CCSF is a less scary transition. In addition, for the many commuting students at CCSF who also hold jobs and have families, easy parking is more important than stone walls or flower beds, so this aspect of the campus's physical plant sends the important message that the college meets student needs.

FIGURE c
Sign at the front entrance of the main campus of the City College of San Francisco.

FIGURE d
Signs fronting the main parking area at CCSF.

Like those at San Francisco State, the signage and entry points encourage the public to enter the campus. As you can see, the campus features an easy ingress from the street to the stairs leading to the main building (Fig. e). Although it is not an official sign, the small sculpture of the woman with open arms, as if welcoming visitors, accentuates the campus's many inviting indicators. The main building at the University of San Francisco, a private university at the northeast corner of Golden Gate Park, is also at the top of a hill, with stairs leading up to it, but, as you will see, USF's campus planners made different decisions about how the hill and the stairs should be adorned (Fig. f).

FIGURE e
Stairway and sculpture in front of the main building at CCSF.

Students (or their parents) who are willing to pay more than $50,000 per year for a private college education likely expect more in terms of campus design than students who opt to attend a state-funded institution. The University of San Francisco, my home institution, has won awards for urban campus design and beauty, and it is a stunning place, especially from atop Lone Mountain, but some aspects of USF's campus design may reveal more about its past ambitions than its present vision. Like SFSU and CCSF, USF has many

FIGURE f
The University of San Francisco's entrance to its Lone Mountain Campus off Golden Gate Street.

points of entry, but the main sites of ingress run along Golden Gate Street, separating "lower campus" from the gate, walls, and stairs that lead to "upper campus." The upper campus, or Lone Mountain campus, used to be a Catholic women's college, which may explain the design choices here—gates, walls, and stairs constructed to keep nice girls in and bad boys out. But these choices serve other purposes. Consider all the architectural elements at work in the grand entrance to Lone Mountain. There are the Italian- and Spanish-influenced stairs (which, perhaps not coincidentally, resemble a goblet). Then, one notices the sculpted archways and the fountain (difficult to see in the photograph,

FIGURE 9
USF's shrubbery sign on the Lone Mountain hill. Note the shrubbery wall on the far right of the photo.

but just below the opening in the arch, a stream of water pours out of the mouth of a lion). Beyond all this, the stately palm trees seem to frame the arch, and behind them, the faint outline of a cross. Every detail here is intentional, from the finely wrought light on the column, to the decision to display the institution's founding date (1855), to the font of the lettering. The totality of these elements sends a clear message: This place is palatial, this place is imposing, this place is fancy, this is a place to be taken seriously. Interestingly, USF makes its sign part of the architecture of the space, advancing the argument that USF's education is as impressive as its design.

However, USF, a Jesuit university, also advances an overt mission of civic engagement and social justice, so one might argue that despite its beauty, the intimidating stairs, the walls, the columns, and the gates (that suggest separation) are at odds with key components of USF's identity as an institution of justice, engagement, and inclusion.

There is much more one could say about these signs. You can see here that even so humble an object as a sign can reveal a great deal about a university. It would be easy to devote an entire essay to decoding the semiotics of the USF stairway or the bustling, open point of entry at San Francisco State. Similar work could be done either comparatively or individually on many aspects of these campuses—and your campus too. To that end, you might ask big questions like, what are the connections between architecture, public space, and human need? Or, why doesn't my institution devote some of the money it spends on flowers, gardens, and trees to scholarships? If you don't know the answer to these questions, it may be best to start smaller. Begin with a semiotic reading of your campus and pay attention to the symbols, cues, and icons you see every day. Why do all of the buildings on my campus look alike (or different)? Does my campus combine architecture, plants, and signage to create a specific image? If so, what is it?

Without question, your campus is a rich text. Learning to look at that text through a semiotic lens enables you to see your campus and your education with a renewed interest and an informed clarity those admissions brochures can never replicate.

CHAPTER 12

READING AND WRITING ABOUT RACE AND ETHNICITY

Of all the chapter introductions we have written, this one made us feel the most uncomfortable.

Writing about people, skin color, and the relationship between appearance and attributed behavior is a minefield for any prospective author. We wanted to put our anxiety on the table right away because we believe that this anxiety mirrors the way you might feel when you are talking about race and ethnicity whether you are Hispanic, African American, Asian American, American Indian, white, or some combination of ethnicities.

As you will notice in this chapter, we are constantly hedging—saying "to a degree" or "to some extent." And there is a reason for this hesitation. When it comes to race or ethnicity, there are few if any absolutes; yet, unfortunately, racism seems to operate within a system of ignorant absolutes. Assumptions about individuals because of skin color and perceptions about ethnicities based on unexamined stereotypes lump individuals into groups where it is easy to make sweeping generalizations that never take into account individual nuances, abilities, and personalities. When these experiences occur because of perceived common characteristics, an individual experience becomes a community one. Prejudice, then, projects perceived or assumed racial characteristics on a single person or groups of people.

To an overwhelming degree, these experiences are socially constructed. Indeed, most scientists believe that race is a social, not a biological, determination. In other words, race as it was commonly perceived in the past—as a means of attributing characteristics to individuals of a common group—is not scientifically or biologically defensible. Scientists believe that perceived traits of races are a product of social experiences, despite the way we often visually identify someone of a particular race. To put it a different way, one's skin color does not determine race; factors contributing to one's race are far more complex.

We are not saying that biology does not determine the color of one's skin; clearly, biology determines skin pigmentation, as it does the color of our eyes and our hair. What we are saying (and what most scientists also argue) is that the idea that biological traits are associated with a particular skin color is false. As humans of different shades of color, we are much more alike biologically than we are different. Even if some groups do have a higher incidence of disease (African Americans with sickle-cell anemia, Jews with Tay-Sachs disease), environmental factors largely shape their existence. For example, Americans are much more likely to have heart conditions than the French. The characteristics of Americans are more alike than characteristics of people from Tibet, which is to say that the combination of biology and culture connects us in more ways than our perceptions of race might suggest.[1]

Self-perception is even more of a factor in racial or ethnic identity, as people often "switch" ethnicities or at least change their affiliation with a certain group. For instance, a recent study shows that more than one-third of respondents in a census identified themselves as a different ethnicity than when they responded to the same census only two years later. This is not to say that race is not important—it is. Race and ethnicity, even if socially constructed, guide much of our public life. By putting the burden on social constructions of race, we have to think about the way we construct race more completely rather than accept that things like skin color and racial traits are simply the way things are.

Saying a group of people is not qualified to do particular work because of how they look or the ethnicity they belong to is a clear example of prejudice. You may remember the criticism aimed at Donald Trump when, in 2016, he claimed the judge ruling on a Trump University lawsuit could not be objective because he was a "Mexican" and, therefore, biased against Trump, who wanted to build a wall between the United States and Mexico. Liberals and conservatives were highly critical of Trump for believing someone is prohibited from doing a job *solely* because of race. Trump's election comes after the election and re-election of Barack Obama, the first black president. Some saw his election as the beginning of a "post-racial" era in which racism had largely been eradicated, while others suggest that his election *caused* more racism; many observers think that question is much more complicated than either of those views.[2] What is not in dispute is that issues having to do with race and ethnicity remain at the forefront of American society; during Obama's terms in office, the killings of Trayvon Martin and Michael Brown, unarmed African American teenagers, sparked protest and led to the formation of Black Lives Matter. In 2016, Donald Trump was elected, and while people are careful not to solely explain his election on a racist backlash to Obama's presidency, there are observers that believe racism in part is one of the reasons for his success with white voters.[3]

---

1   One such source is Audrey Smedley and Brian D. Smedley, "Race as Biology Is Fiction, Racism as a Social Problem Is Real: Anthropological and Historical Perspectives of the Social Construction of Race," *American Psychologist*, vol. 60, no. 1, 2005, pp. 16–26.

2   For a good rundown of these issues, see Peniel Joseph, "Obama's Effort to Heal Racial Divisions and Uplift Black America," *Washington Post*, 22 Apr. 2016.

3   Ta-Nehisi Coates writes about the nuances of this phenomenon in "My President Was Black: A History of the First African American White House—and of What Came Next" in the January/February 2017 edition of *The Atlantic*.

In the past, people from various groups had a tendency to impose a set of values onto certain groups based simply on skin color, a tendency that has certainly diminished in the last 50 years (though we would be the last people to claim that this type of behavior is gone, and the first to acknowledge that prejudice is still very much a part of too many people's lives). Our goal in this chapter is to help you become more sensitive readers of race and ethnicity by becoming more aware of the social forces that construct the volatile texts of race and racism.

The determination that race, ethnicity, and class are socially constructed has led to new ways of thinking about our identity that carry political and social implications. Not too long ago, and for most of the history of the Western world, people made assumptions about other people based on their appearance, most notably their skin color. White people wrongly, and often tragically, assumed blacks were inferior or that American Indians were savages. For centuries, groups have enslaved other groups based on that group's race or ethnicity. In the last few decades, we have gone from the biological construction of race—one based on parentage—to one based more on social groups and associations. "Hispanic" means something different than it did twenty years ago, as does "Native American." For example, there has been a persuasive shift in identification. We tend to view Native Americans by tribe or nation, and those from Central and South America, the Caribbean, and Mexico by country of origin and nationality, rather than the catchall of ethnicity. We talk of Choctaw, Zuni, and Osage rather than Indian. We identify folks as Cuban, Columbian, or Mexican, rather than Hispanic. At the University of San Francisco, there is a resistance to Pan–Asianism among students. There are, for example, a number of different Filipino student organizations. Precise linguistic markers more accurately articulate identity, as anyone familiar with racial and cultural history can tell you.

To a degree, race and ethnicity are visually constructed, but those visual constructions are hardly without controversy. We tend to categorize people by their appearance, not by their biological background, for the most obvious reason: We have no other way of reading people. We do construct race, ethnicity, and gender, and its multiplicity of meanings and ideas, visually—not only through a person's skin but also through what they wear, how they walk, how tall or short they are. We are not trying to demonize this process as much as we are trying to draw attention to it. Like other visual constructions, it must be slowed down and digested more actively. Thus, every time we see someone and register that person's skin color, we are doing a reading of his or her ethnicity. We pick up on external codes that we think cue us into that person's racial background, but what, really, do those cues tell us? For one, even if we can determine if someone is Chinese or Russian or Kenyan or Navajo, that tells us very little about who she is as a person, what he likes to eat, what she is good at, how smart he is, what sports she plays, or what his values are.

As we indicated earlier, for centuries people in power (mostly white but not always) used skin color as a means of identifying both ethnicity and character. One of the worst and most tragic fallacies one can commit is to conflate external and internal in regard to race, to see "Asian" or "African American" and think ... something. There is a funny scene in the 1981 movie *Carbon Copy*, when George Segal (Anglo) assumes his black son (Denzel Washington), a grown man whom he has just met, is good at basketball simply because he is black. In an attempt to make money, Segal challenges a father and son who are shooting hoops to a pickup basketball game for cash. Segal's expectations, those of the other father and son, and those of the viewers, are undermined when the Denzel Washington character is terrible at basketball. Here Segal engages in a classic misreading of race. In this instance, he only lost money; however, in the case of slavery, Japanese internment, and Native removal, the consequences of racial misreading were much more significant.

To some extent, reading the "otherness" in someone's appearance makes us uncomfortable because of reasons both political and personal. We want to be—and are explicitly trained to be—democratic in the way we view others, based on the way they act toward us, not the way they look. "Don't judge a book by its cover," we say, but we are always judging books by their covers and people by their appearance, and this makes many of us very uncomfortable. This discomfort is magnified when it comes to race, ethnicity, gender, and class because we know our constructions have political, cultural, social, and personal consequences for us and for the people we are trying to read. Our democratic nature wants us to read neutrally, but our less controllable side does not, because we have been conditioned through decades and even centuries of reading values into otherness. Perhaps you have noticed or even commented on someone's ethnicity, then felt strange about it. In one classic episode of *Seinfeld*, George and Elaine muse over the ethnicity of Elaine's new boyfriend, an endeavor that makes George uncomfortable. Throughout the episode, he keeps saying, "I don't think we're supposed to be talking about this." This is because we want things that seem to be mutually exclusive—to acknowledge someone's difference but not be affected by it. Yet, how can we not be affected by something we notice and then think about?

The simple act of noticing that someone's ethnicity is different from your own creates an immediate otherness for both of you. Moreover, with this perception of otherness comes, perhaps, assumptions about that person and about yourself—that you are scarier or smarter or wealthier or poorer. In fact, in the history of America, the fact that we can and do see otherness in our fellow Americans has caused more hardship, violence, and death than we can even imagine.

Definitions of race are always changing. In the late nineteenth and early twentieth centuries and to some extent afterwards, race and ethnicity were often conflated. For instance, at the turn of the century, Jews and Italians were considered racial groups (not ethnic groups). Similarly, fewer than fifty years ago, many places in the South considered anyone to be African American if they had an African American ancestor; this was called the "one-drop" rule. Because the vast majority of Americans do not think this way now, it may seem difficult to believe that this past existed, but understanding it is crucial in understanding contemporary notions of race and race theory.[4]

Indigenous identity has become an increasingly sensitive issue. For some tribes, one must have a certain "blood quantum" level and/or be an enrolled member of a tribe. The same level of Native American ancestry that would have put someone at risk a century ago may not be enough for certain tribal memberships.

Race, like gender and class, are fluid texts, so it is important not to assume too much about individuals or groups based on what they appear to be.

Although we claim to be nondiscriminatory now, discriminatory practices in the past have influenced the present social, political, economic, and cultural structure of our country. This may seem like a highly political statement, and it is. However, the authors believe that discrimination in the past gave the white male majority a head start in this generation; race theorists call this phenomenon "white privilege." As you know, blacks, Asians, Hispanics, and Native Americans were frequently, if not regularly, denied admission to colleges, job interviews, loans, and access to restaurants and hotels and even basic medical service. Affirmative action, the idea that employers and schools should actively seek historically underrepresented individuals to fill their slots, is a response to this phenomenon by ensuring that minorities get fair consideration by employers and admission offices (for the most part, affirmative action does not involve a quota system, despite misconceptions popularly articulated). But the theory behind affirmative action, looking for ways to engage the past while living in the future in making decisions about schools and employment, is not only a government program but also a factor in admitting legacies to colleges, incorporating one's progeny into a family business, and so on. While preferential treatment may be decried as unAmerican in some quarters—after all, the Bill of Rights says all men are created equal—the fact is the past has always shaped how people are treated in the present.[5]

In addition, generations of broken promises, abuses of power, and institutional discrimination and oppression have left some members of minority communities bitter toward institutions of power and law. People are smart. They know that history repeats itself; they know that the past is always present in some form or another. Thus,

---

4 Daniel Luzer, "Primary Sources: The 1940 Census on 'White,'" *Mother Jones*, 18 Aug. 2008.
5 George Yancy, "Dear White America," *The New York Times*, 24 Dec. 2015.

the reality of slavery, the history of American Indian genocide and removal, and the memory of Asian internment constitute a legacy that still affects how members of these groups see America and its institutions, and it is a legacy that contemporary America must take seriously.

Race, ethnicity, and gender are political constructions as well as social ones. We now think of members of so-called races as political groups as well as social ones. If you read about politics, you will notice commentators talking about how a candidate was trying to "appeal to African Americans" or "appeal to women" (or more specific groupings like "soccer moms" or "the Catholic Latino vote"). The recognition that these groups have political power in one sense has empowered members of these groups and given them political power in ways they may not have had. However, of course, some people within these groups do not want to be identified as group members; it too easily reminds them of the way society constructs their identity negatively. The tendency, the need, in America to preface any such statement with the racial descriptor, goes to show how completely we see race and, perhaps, how often we cannot see past it.

What is even more important, the goals of an ethnicity as a whole may not be those of the individual. In fact, it may be impossible to state, with any certainty, what the goals of any one ethnicity may be, as all people are complex and in the process of change. Supreme Court Judge Clarence Thomas will have very different ideas about what African Americans need than will Barack Obama, even though both are intelligent, upper-class African American men. Which of the two best represents black Americans? That may depend on what group of black Americans you poll.

Stereotyping occurs as a result of our perceived view of racial or ethnic characteristics. Unless you are the rare completely neutral human being, someone we feel does not exist, you attach stereotypes to groups—even if they seem like stereotypes that are positive, such as all professors are smart, nuns are nice, textbook authors are cool, and so on.

You may also, without knowing it, hold negative stereotypes. The problem, of course, with all stereotypes is their propensity to attribute group characteristics to individuals. Believing all Jews are smart or all African Americans are athletic can have subsequent negative effects that balance out any positives.

How do we acquire our stereotypes? Some believe stereotypes are based on a grain of truth. That sort of thought makes us and others nervous, because the next logical step is thinking that traits or behaviors are inherent or natural. Researchers believe we pick up stereotypes in a variety of ways, including through popular culture and our upbringing. That is why we have stressed throughout this book the importance of looking for treatments of race and ethnicity as they appear—or do not appear—in texts.

There is also disturbing evidence that people mirror stereotyped expectations. As we discuss in the chapter on gender, mainstream American society has a tendency to punish those individuals who operate outside of the perceived norms of a certain group. Thus, stereotypes keep getting reinforced generation after generation, despite efforts from all groups to eradicate them. And many Indigenous groups are frustrated by their inability to do much about the sanctioned stereotyping of Native Americans through sports mascots and nicknames. One wonders and worries about what messages these stereotypes send to both Native and non-Native communities—especially children. Similarly, since 9/11 Arab Americans have had to face unfair suspicion and discrimination based on the radical behavior of a very, very small number of extremists.

Your view of these issues probably depends on your personal relationships as well as political affiliation. When surveying the landscape of these issues, we are likely to take our personal experiences and make them universal. If we are white and have African American friends or relatives, we more likely to be more sympathetic to black causes. If we have no friends of color, and our only exposure is through popular culture and our political affiliations, that too will shape the way we look at race and ethnicity. It is an overgeneralization to be sure, but we believe that proximity brings understanding in ways that reading about race and ethnicity can never bring. So does, we believe, actively thinking about the ways we construct race and ethnicity.

Sadly, in the United States, views on race are often influenced by financial concerns. We wonder about the number of people who are critical of immigrants from Latin American countries but whose standard of living relies on illegal immigrant labor. Similarly, in the 1800s, Asians suffered horribly from racist behavior from their employers and in their communities, but investors were eager to have them build railroads for almost no money.

Every bit of evidence suggests that racism is a learned behavior, which means that we are taught to read ethnicity. There is a famous scene on an episode of the television show *Montel*, when the children of black guests and white extremists are shown playing together in the Green Room. As this demonstrates, personal relationships can often overcome flawed teaching and empty stereotyping.

Social and economic class is a more crucial element in American life than many people think. Class also has similar connections to both self-identity and outside reality. Studies show that most Americans believe they are middle class. And because there is no set way of determining what someone's class is, a person making $200,000 a year can call himself middle class; so can someone earning $20,000 a year. Are their lives different? Absolutely. However, they may not see that. Of course, class issues run through issues of race and ethnicity, in ways both simple and complex. Some researchers believe that race and ethnicity are mostly a class problem, with the members of ethnic groups disproportionately represented among the nation's poor. There probably is some validity to this claim. However, because the nation has had a long and bloody history of clashes between ethnicities of the same class, it is hard to see class as the primary issue in racial or ethnic discrimination.[6]

On the other hand, perceptions of reality can be as strong or stronger than reality itself, and in a capitalist country that tends to link economic prosperity with personal worth, the prevailing perceptions of which groups have more can shape how we see certain people. Thus, although class may not be the primary factor in racial discrimination, it is difficult when talking about race to separate it from issues of class. When the third edition of this book went to press, the website *Stuff White People Like* was a cultural phenomenon. But as many argue, the site is more about what left-leaning yuppies like than, say, what blue-collar whites from the Deep South like. In other words, the site pretends to be about race, but it is primarily about class, and the assumptions Americans make about how class and race manifest. Films like *Get Out* and *Naturally Native*, books like *Crazy Rich Asians*, classic television shows like *The Jeffersons*, and even more recent programs like *Keeping up with the Kardashians*, complicate our ideas of race, class, and privilege.

Writing about race, ethnicity, or class can be done in a variety of ways. In the introduction, we discuss writing about popular culture through various lenses, including race and ethnicity. Practically, that means noticing how race and ethnicity manifest themselves in a television show or movie. As Michael Omi notes, writers, producers, and directors often use stereotypes when employing actors who are different from them.[7] It is also true that characters of particular backgrounds can be used as symbols rather than as fully drawn characters.

Absence of races is often a statement. Despite being on the air since 2009, the popular reality show *The Bachelor* has never had a black Bachelor, and until 2017, there had never been an African American woman Bachelorette. The number one sitcom in the country, *The Big Bang Theory*, has an Indian character, but no one else of ethnicity, or multi-ethnic or racial identity has appeared on it regularly. As we were working on a draft of this chapter in 2016, the #OscarsSoWhite movement arose to protest the absence of African American actors and actresses in the top four categories for the second year in a row. What do these facts say about the American entertainment industry? Does it reflect perceptions of the show's creators about the preferences of audiences? Or something to do more with the creators' own preferences?

---

6   Anat Shenker-Osorio, "Why Americans All Believe They Are 'Middle Class,'" *The Atlantic*, Aug. 2013.

7   Michael Omi, "In Living Color: Race and American Culture," *Cultural Politics in Contemporary America*, 1989, pp. 111–22.

Here are some things to think about when writing about race and ethnicity:

Media: How are different ethnicities portrayed in news or magazine articles? Is the author taking the "part for the whole" (talking to one member of a group as representative of all members of the group)?

Advertising: How are different ethnicities portrayed in print or broadcast ads? Is there anything that "signals" their ethnicity—is clothing used as a "sign" of their color or identity? Is the advertiser using a "rainbow effect" in the ad, appearing to be inclusive by including multiple ethnicities? Does this effect seem forced or genuine?

Television: How are different ethnicities portrayed in a particular television show? Do they conform to predictable stereotypes? Are the people of color more than merely representative? Is there a lone African American or Hispanic American on a mostly white show? One white person on an African American–dominated show? Are the members of different races allowed to date? Does their dating engage the idea of intergroup dating or ignore it?

Movies: How are different ethnicities portrayed in the movie? Do they conform to predictable stereotypes? Are the people of color the first to be targeted for death (if it's an action movie)? Are the people of color more than merely representative? Is there a lone African American or Hispanic American in a mostly white movie? One white person in a movie with a largely African American cast? Are the members of different races allowed to date? Does their dating engage the idea of intergroup dating or ignore it?

WRITING ABOUT RACE AND ETHNICITY: THE GENRES

The Analysis through a Lens

One of the most common ways of writing a paper involving race and ethnicity is to use it as a lens through which to view texts. For example, one might examine a text like *Modern Family* or *The Big Bang Theory* or *Two Broke Girls* by trying to understand how race functions in those shows. For a long time, *Friends* had no black characters, which meant that race was ignored for the most part. But that actually meant that the show was as much about privileged whiteness as it was about the absence of color. One could certainly develop an argument about what whiteness *means* in *Friends*. In a more sophisticated way, *Seinfeld* was also a show with a largely white cast, but the characters' whiteness was a subject much more than in *Friends*. More than once, the creators of *Seinfeld* engage with the politics and often awkwardness of race relations in their show. One could certainly write a paper on whether *Seinfeld* or any other show was successful in its attempts

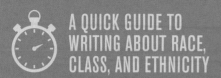

A QUICK GUIDE TO WRITING ABOUT RACE, CLASS, AND ETHNICITY

Here are a few things to think about as you begin writing:

1. Think about the question you might be trying to answer by watching the show or movie. It could be as simple as "How are people of various racial, ethnic, or class backgrounds being portrayed in the movie?" Or it could be, "What messages does the lack of diversity in a television show send to viewers?" But even more complex ideas about race, ethnicity, class, and nationality should be articulated as questions before watching, if possible.

2. Make sure you write down scenes you think might serve as evidence for the points you make. Using examples always helps illustrate a point you are trying to make. And often they serve as good introductions to the questions you are trying to answer.

3. You might also talk to friends about the show or movie you watched. Sometimes particularly controversial or complex texts benefit from deep discussion.

4. Using your own experiences, write an essay about the role race and ethnicity have played—or didn't play—in your experiences growing up.

to address race and ethnicity. Similarly, recent dramas created by Shonda Rhimes, such as *Grey's Anatomy* and *Scandal*, feature people of color in leading roles. Similarly, comedies such as *Fresh Off the Boat* and *George Lopez* have broken new ground by bringing Asian American and Latino and Chicano issues to American sitcoms. The main point here is that race and ethnicity, as well as other lenses such as gender and class, can be part of a show's theme or subtext even if *that is not the show's focus*. In other words, an episode does not have to discuss or even mention race and ethnicity to be about race and ethnicity. A great writing opportunity might be to read a certain text through the lens of race.

The Researched Paper

Writing a researched paper about race and ethnicity is an opportunity to incorporate knowledgeable sources into your paper and to take a longer or more in-depth view of your subject. There is a lot of research on race and ethnicity to draw from and there are also quite a few texts that can be studied in this manner.

One of the ways to write a researched paper is to take a text and put it in cultural context. For example one could watch the 1970s sitcom *Good Times*, and research what was happening with race relations in the 1970s, and write about the show from that point of view. Or also using *Good Times*, one could write about the forces shaping race on television in the 1970s, and place the show in that context.

As we have said, almost everything can be read through the lens of race, so you do not have to restrict yourself to shows with more prominent racial subtexts. White shows like *How I Met Your Mother*, *Friends*, and *Seinfeld*, ensemble comedies set in New York—one of the most diverse cities in the world—all deserve examination within the context of race. *30 Rock*, a similar show, deals more openly with race and, in so doing, feels more realistic and inclusive.

OTHER ESSAY IDEAS

1. Write an essay talking about ways we mark people as different through nonvisual means in popular culture. What forms of popular culture are especially guilty of this?

2. Write a short essay discussing why visual texts can communicate ideas effectively. You might compare a visual text and a written text that have similar ideas but present them differently.

3. Write about a time when you were mistaken for another group, whether ethnicity, gender, class, or age. What assumptions did the people mistaking you for someone else make?

4. Write a first-person essay in which you talk about your own identity as a text. How have people read and misread you?

5. Write an essay in which you take a stand on the issue of using Native Americans as mascots. What evidence will you use to help support your assertions? Perhaps you could examine this issue through the lens of freedom of expression and/or the lens of hate speech and civil rights.

6. Write an essay in which you analyze the rhetorical strategies of advertisements obviously aimed at certain racial demographics.

7. Trace the evolution of the portrayal of race and/or ethnicity in a particular medium—television, movies, art, public space. Has it changed in your lifetime? Why or why not? You might consider writing a comparison/contrast paper in which you read the original movie of *Uncle Buck* (starring John Candy) alongside the new sitcom *Uncle Buck* featuring an all-black cast. What is similar? Different?

8. Go to the library or the computer and do a keyword search on a particular ethnicity and a politician's name (example: "Trump" and "African American"). What comes up when you do this? Is there a trend worth writing about?

9. Do some research on the nature of prejudice. What do researchers say about its nature?

10. Get stories or novels from 75 years ago; look and see how different authors, African American, white, Italian, Jewish, and so on, portrayed people of different skin color and ethnicity. How would you characterize the treatment as a whole?

11. What are the signs that are encoded in race and ethnicity? How are they portrayed in popular culture and the media? Do a sign analysis of a particular show or media phenomenon.

12. Watch two television shows, one with a largely white cast, one with a largely African American cast. Compare how each deals with the idea of race or ethnicity. Using the same shows, notice the commercials playing—how do these construct a view of race and/or ethnicity?

13. Look at a film or films made by African American, Hispanic, or other ethnic directors. How do these directors deal with the idea of race and ethnicity, compared to white directors dealing with similar ideas? Better yet, track down movies like *Smoke Signals* or *Naturally Native*—films written, starring, and directed by American Indians. How do these films challenge easy assumptions about Native Americans?

14. Write an essay on racially questionable comments uttered by celebrities (e.g., Donald Trump, Paula Deen, Justin Bieber, Joseph Biden, Frédéric Rouzaud, Mel Gibson, and George Allen) and what these transgressions say about race, our culture, and the people who made them.

15. Write an essay on the role of race in sports. In what sense do owners, players, and fans use (or ignore) race when talking about their teams and players on their teams? The culture of sports tends to be conservative, but teams are often integrated. Explore how the culture of sports and the culture of racism coexist.

16. Read two songs or singers through the lens of race. Write a comparison/contrast paper on, say, Adele and Nicki Minaj or Blake Shelton and Kanye West. What do examinations like these tell us about genre, gender, and music?

17. Is race an issue in video games? If so, how? We have been able to find very little writing on this topic, but it could make for a fascinating essay.

18. Analyze *Master of None*, the provocative show by Aziz Ansari. How does this program address the immigrant experience in America? How does it deal with percolating anti-Muslim and anti-Middle East sentiments?

RESOURCES

On the Web

So many people write about race well and often that this can only be a partial list. Yvonne Abraham in *The Boston Globe*, Charles M. Blow in *The New York Times*, Eugene Robinson in *The Washington Post*, and Leonard Pitts Jr. in the *Miami Herald* are all columnists who write regularly, though not exclusively, about race in the United States. Ta-Nehisi Coates often writes for *The Atlantic*, and NPR's **Code Switch** is also a great program. But the truth is that more people are writing about race today than ever before, including whites; for example, the podcasts Reply All and Startup both explored race and hiring in 2016.

Books

This is only a partial list of the books that might be useful for your study of race:

Michelle Alexander, *The New Jim Crow: Mass Incarceration in the Age of Colorblindness*. This book explores the mass imprisonment of African Americans.

Ta-Nehisi Coates, *Between the World and Me*. Coates describes the world African Americans face in a letter to his son.

bell hooks, *Ain't I a Woman: Black Women and Feminism*. This classic works explores the intersections of race and gender.

Kenneth Meeks, *Driving While Black*. This book explores racial profiling, not just on the road but everywhere in public America.

Michael Omi and Howard Winant, *Racial Formation in the United States*. This work explains how race and racism was formed in the United States.

Claudia Rankine, *Citizen*. This book of poetry depicts both the subtle and overt forms of racism in society today.

Beverly Daniel Tatum, *Why Are All the Black Kids Sitting Together in the Cafeteria?* This book explores the way the world perceives race from both insider and outsider perspectives, beginning with the often-observed phenomenon described in the title.

Cornel West, *Race Matters*. This book describes the scars that racism has left on America.

SAMPLE STUDENT ESSAY

Amy Truong wrote this essay for Professor Brian Komei Dempster's Asian American Literature survey course at the University of San Francisco. Here, she reads the texts of gender, race, and family alongside Lan Samantha Chang's short story "The Unforgetting." Dempster says of Truong's essay, "I admire the synthesis of literary analysis and family history." To achieve this effect, Truong shifts back and forth between readings of Chang and her own family history.

Gender Expectations and Familial Roles Within Asian American Culture

AMY TRUONG

> In Mercy Lake he started his new job as a photocopy machine repairman ... He maintained the new Chevrolet sedan—changed the oil, followed the tune-up dates, and kept good records of all repairs ... He labored on the yard (Chang, 135–36, 140).

> She laundered Ming's new work clothes: permanent-press shirts with plastic tabs inserted in the stiff, pointed collars; bright, wide ties ... In the kitchen, Sansan learned to cook with canned and frozen foods. She made cream of tomato soup for lunch, and stored envelopes of onion soup mix for meat loaf or quick onion dip. More often ... Sansan consulted the Betty Crocker cookbook (138–39).

Are these from an episode of *Leave It to Beaver?* No. These are excerpts from Lan Samantha Chang's "The Unforgetting." Ask yourself what these excerpts mean to you. They may just simply remind some of you of an episode of *Leave It to Beaver* because these were the characteristic roles of men and women some decades ago when television sets only came in black and white—men were the breadwinners while women were the caretakers. For others, including myself, they are reminders of the life that still exists, a life that is representative of many Asian American families today.

In many Asian cultures, gender plays a role in dictating what you do. Certain members of the family are designated specific responsibilities that complement their respective gender roles much like the characters in *Leave It to Beaver*. The males support the family financially and control the household, and the women take care of the family and household chores. Lan Samantha Chang's novella *Hunger* parallels the events in my life and shows how gender roles are still very apparent in today's Asian American families. This essay seeks to capture that parallel experience of interpreting Chang's text and the texts of my own experiences.

Within Asian culture, women are raised and taught to be silent and obedient. I am a first-generation Vietnamese American and growing up, I was told, "Do not comment or speak up," whenever I wanted to voice my opinion. My opinion was considered unimportant. And for many years of my life I believed that this was true. I never spoke a word unless I was asked to speak or spoken to, until I finally became tired of being mute. As a young teenager, my parents were going through difficult times with their marriage. One night, my mother, father, grandmother, brother and I sat down to have a family meeting about the issues between my parents. My dad did all the talking while my mom sat in silence like she always did. "Your mother has committed terrible sins and has destroyed our family," he said to us sternly in our native language. Not once during the entire family meeting did anyone in the family speak other than my father. Before the meeting ended, I finally worked up the nerve to defend my mother since she refused to defend herself. "Daddy, you shouldn't speak about Mommy like that in front of us," I declared. As soon as I said it, my father slapped me hard on the back of my head and told me, "Do not ever speak unless you have been instructed to." I immediately received a scolding from my mother and grandmother as well. Ironically, it was my mind that they thought was poisoned, and they blamed America for my "rebellious" breaking of silence.

The characters in Lan Samantha Chang's *Hunger* also suffer from silence. Min, the wife, very rarely speaks a word when she does not agree with her husband. Instead, she lets him do as he pleases and remains quiet as a good Asian wife. For instance, her husband treats their youngest daughter in ways that she does not particularly agree with. Her husband places a lot of pressure on their daughter and that is not how she wants their children to grow up. Yet she remains silent, because she believes that it is her place to let her husband control their family and their daughter in the way that he wants. For example, the mother's silence is demonstrated on one occasion when her daughter and husband are screaming: "Baba, let me stop! You go ahead and cry! ... You cry all you want! ... You cry! But—play! ... As I ironed I watched Anna fiddle with the frayed towels that had once been pink but now were faded to a creamy white ... I opened my mouth but my throat was dry" (59).

She wishes to protect her daughter and attempts to speak, but chooses to refrain from doing so due to her respective roles as a woman and wife. Ironically, it is only after her death that she is able to voice her thoughts. In essence, the novella's point of view is symbolic and emphasizes how a woman's voice can be silenced due to her gender role.

Ruth, the youngest daughter, is also silenced and lets her father live vicariously through her. Though she hates it, she does not speak against his wishes. For example, her father makes her play the violin and has her practice for hours on end. She practices so much every day that it brings her to tears and causes her to resent her father, because she cannot do or say anything that will prevent him from forcing her to play. For instance, when she and her father are locked in the practice room, he tells her, "Do you understand? From now on, you work. You practice everyday ... No no no no—Her voice rose to a shriek. There was a slam as he closed the door, and they were trapped inside the room together.... He clapped and counted. She played and cried" (60). Though she cries and screams, she continues to play because this is her father's desire. Irony once again occurs. Just as Tian leaves his family to pursue his passion for music, Ruth's passionate hate for that same music drives her to leave her family as well. As a woman, she is put in an impossible position: her breaking of silence and fighting back is a form of defiance and shows a lack of respect towards the male figure, causing the destruction of this family.

In Vietnamese culture, the oldest daughter is also expected to play a major role in the house—she is expected to handle household chores and responsibilities in the absence of a mother. My mother is the oldest daughter and was only fourteen when she arrived in the United States after the Vietnam War. My mother came to this country with her older brother, Nihn (age 18), her two younger brothers, Can (10) and Toan (4), and her younger sister, Ngoc (5). "Life was very hard and unbearable sometimes," she said. My mother had to take on the difficult responsibility of taking care of all her siblings. At the tender age of fourteen, she assisted her siblings with their schoolwork, put food on the table and clothes on their backs, attended school, worked a part-time job, and attempted to learn the English language. My grandparents finally arrived in the United States (along with two more children) when my mother was 22 years old. "I thought it was over," she told me. But this was not the case. My grandparents expected more from my mother because after eight years in the United States she spoke the English language, understood how the system worked, and already seemed to have things under control. My grandparents soon developed a bad gambling habit and left my mother to take on the burden of caring for her six siblings. I ask my mother why she continued to put up with it. She responded only by saying, "I am obligated, Amy." Till this day my mother is the one who holds her family together, and one day she expects me (the oldest and only daughter) to do the same for my siblings and our family.

In *Hunger*, Anna is the oldest daughter who, like my mother, has the responsibility of taking care of the home in the absence of her mother. She hires men to work on the home, decorates it so that it will be more presentable, and even gives tours to interested buyers. Strangely, she denies bids on the house and does not move out into a beautiful loft, a comfy townhouse or spacious condominium. As much as Anna longs to sell the house in order to rid of all their unhappy memories, a part of her feels obligated to stay there. For instance, Anna's mother watches her as she lays in bed and notices, "through all this, Anna sleeps; but on some nights, as the melodies fade away, she shudders and sits up in bed ... Perhaps she has been dreaming of her greatest hope and fear—that the house is gone, that it is destroyed, and nothing more remains of it" (114). Anna's personal desire to forget her family's past conflicts with her duty to her family to keep their home. Anna stays loyal to her gender and familial role by remaining in that home, resulting in restless nights due to her split conscience.

On the other hand, men play a very different role in an Asian family. They are the primary (and often only) breadwinner in the family. My father came to the United States when he was 23. Because of his limited knowledge of English, he found it difficult to obtain good work or even go back to school. "No one would hire me because my English was very hard to understand," he explains. This affected him ten years later when he and my mother married. Because my father did not know the language well, my mother was the breadwinner in their relationship. This made my father "lose face." Not being able to contribute to the household as much as your wife was a shameful thing and made him lose a lot of his pride. "I was very embarrassed that your mother made more than me. I was too ashamed to even go out because I worried that others would see me and speak badly of me," my father states, no longer embarrassed. Not being able to provide for the family financially, my father expressed his "manliness" in other ways. Though my mother made most of the money, he decided where that money would go and how it would be distributed. He was also very strict, held strongly to Vietnamese traditions, and made sure we knew that he still wore the pants. He made sure that I was never out late, because traditionally it was not appropriate for a young lady to be out past dark. Even to this day, I am expected to be home and in bed at 10 p.m. He made sure that we never spoke English in the house so that we would remember where we came from and so that others would know that we were still very Vietnamese even though we were born American. When we spoke English, he either ignored what we said or scorned us for doing so. "You must remember your origins. This house is not a white man's house," he droned in our native language. He also made sure of this by having my mother cook traditional Vietnamese meals every day and restricted us from having things such as burgers, fries and sodas. He told us, "Vietnamese food is healthier than American food ... tastes better too. All Americans know how to do is fry their food. The Vietnamese, on the other hand, are real chefs." My father is now trying to regain his respect and honor by taking night courses and practicing his English with my mother and his children. He hopes that by doing this he will earn a better job with better money so that he can fulfill his duty as a man and father.

Tian, the father in *Hunger*, is the breadwinner and the head of his household, much like my father. He provides the only source of income and does so by first working as a music professor, then in a restaurant. He also calls all the shots and makes all the decisions for each member of his family. For example, he decides that Ruth is going to play the violin and that she is going to play it well by forcing her to practice whenever she has free time. According to the novella, "All morning during summer vacations,

plus two evenings a week, he sat in the tiny room for hours and helped her practice"
(62). Though the text indicates that he is helping Ruth, no normal teenager wants to
be locked in a room practicing a craft that he/she has no interest in. Therefore, force is
used on Tian's part to get her to do so. He also decides that she is not going to attend
the university where he once taught even after they offer her a scholarship. They have
an argument and he demands, "You're staying here. 'Let go of my arm! You're hurting
me!' You are not leaving this house as long as you are still a child. Do you hear me?
'I'm not a child!' You're my daughter and I'm your father!" (72).

It is not traditional among Asian families for a child to leave the home to attend
school. His refusal to succumb to this American tradition represents his need to control
the family.

Tian also tells his wife Min what to do. One such incident occurs after his recital.
Tian's colleagues want him to stay and have some drinks. He tells them that Min is
tired, but it is she who insists that they stay. He hushes her quickly and tells her that
they are going to go home. Min urges him,

> "It is okay." My [Min's] voice cracked against the words ... "Come on," said
> Tian. He took my arm and pulled me around the corner, to the coatrack. "I'm
> not that tired; I could have gone out with them" ... "Why did you want to leave
> so much?" ... "I want to go home" (22).

Though Min is persistent that her husband mingle with his American friends, his desire
is apparently more important than hers, displaying both his power and her silence. Tian,
like many other Asian men, including my father, is the money-earner and controller of
the family. They both support the family financially and make all the decisions pertain-
ing to each member of the family whether or not protest occurs.

Male sons also have a respected role in the Asian family. They are expected to bring
in income and help with the household expenses as well. My younger brother, Tim
(19), lives with my parents and has paid rent every month since he was seventeen and
received his first job. My parents do not like to call it rent. They prefer to term it "duty"
or "obligation." Tim is still young and would prefer to spend his money to go out and
have fun with his friends. He and my parents constantly argue about this topic but my
parents do not budge. "Tim, it is your responsibility to contribute to the needs of the
family. This is only preparing you so that one day you can handle the responsibility of
being a father, the man of the house, when it is your time," they continually insist to
him in Vietnamese. Likewise, they tell Tim that American traditions have made him
ungrateful and lazy. In due time, they will be lecturing the same thing to my other
younger brother, Will (5), as well.

In *Hunger*, all of the characters, like my brother, struggle between achieving their
individual desires and observing their respective gender and familial roles. Min wishes

to speak her thoughts, but her role as a wife prevents her from doing so. Min has other desires and yet after "Twenty-one years … I had never admitted my disappointment with him. I had not complained about a lack of money or time together. I had taken what he brought home and made it into our daily lives" (94). Min is very unhappy and though she yearns to express her disappointment and opinion, she cannot because she has to maintain her role as dutiful wife.

Tian decides to pursue his love for music but at the cost of abandoning his family and his responsibilities to them. According to Tian,

> Everyone … has things they want to do in their lives. But sometimes there is only one thing—one thing that a person must do. More than what he is told to do, more than what he is trained to do. Even more than what his family wants him to do. It is what he hungers for (28).

Unlike some members of his family, Tian chooses his own personal longing over his obligation to his respective gender and familial role, claiming that it is something that he must do, as though he has no choice.

Ruth challenges her prescribed role as a daughter so that she can live the life that she always wanted to, also at the cost of her family. She searches for freedom from her duties, saying, "'I'm quitting! I'm never going to pick up a violin again for as long as I live.' And without a pause, he cried, 'Then I don't want you! You are not my daughter! You are nothing!'" (88). After this heated exchange, Ruth "walked to the door, opened it, and stepped outside" (90). Ruth and Tian have their differences, but they are very much alike. As stated earlier, they both leave their families to pursue their dreams, disregarding their responsibilities to their family.

Anna wishes to forget all her memories by selling their home. Instead, she is true to her respected role and remains in that home even against her own wishes. For example, "One day she opened the door to a brisk young couple full of plans, the woman's belly swollen with hope like freshly risen dough … They bid, and Anna refused to sell" (107). Anna has invested much money into fixing the house so that she can begin to forget the past it holds, but her obligation to stay in that house so that her family's story can be saved keeps her from doing so.

Like my brother, the characters of *Hunger* make sacrifices in order to fulfill their roles. Likewise, those who follow their desires make huge sacrifices as well. Their personal longings and respected gender and familial roles create internal conflicts that are a part of their everyday lives just as is so with members of today's Asian American families.

It has been thirty years since my parents first arrived in the United States. Most people would expect them to assimilate to the American culture by now but they are deep-rooted in their Asian traditions and way of thinking, just as Min and Tian from *Hunger* are. They raised my brothers and me by attempting to pass on their way of thinking, hoping that we honor our roots. We are Vietnamese and were raised to understand and adhere to Vietnamese values, meaning that we are to accept our gender and familial roles as many of Chang's characters do. What my parents fail to understand is that we are also American and have been greatly immersed in and influenced by the American culture as well. My siblings and I believe that gender roles are a thing of the past ... a thing that belongs to the generation, time, and country in which my parents grew up.

In essence, my siblings and I are Anna and Ruth in *Hunger* while my parents are Min and Tian. We are a great representation of an Asian American family torn apart by our prescribed gender and familial roles. Reminiscent of the family in *Hunger*, my family is one of many Asian American families conflicted with such issues. These issues tear apart the family in Chang's story, but many Asian American families are learning to cope with these problems by finding a balance between familial responsibilities and personal desires instead of letting one or the other dictate their lives completely. For us, these issues have become an everyday part of our lives and our struggles seem to be far from over. There is much that my siblings and I need to understand about the immigrant generation and vice versa. Whether or not these conflicts will ever disappear is still a mystery and has yet to stand the test of time.

Works Cited

Chang, Lan Samantha. *Hunger: A Novella and Stories*. New York: Penguin Books, 1998.

CHAPTER 13

READING AND WRITING ABOUT PUBLIC AND PRIVATE SPACE

Whether we are in bedrooms, bathrooms, coffeehouses, classrooms, stadiums, or record stores, we are always someplace, and understanding our relationship to these places and spaces helps us better understand the world. How? By providing us tools to recognize the way the physical world influences our inner world, the way those constructing spaces might shape us, or attempt to.

In this chapter, we will talk about public and private space, architecture, and design as constructed texts as an entrée into writing about those spaces. What we mean by space is the environment created by human-made activities, including built areas, such as classrooms, stadiums, shopping malls, and dorm rooms. Architecture and design are forces that help construct these places and spaces and give them their particular personality.

In a sense, architects and designers are the authors of buildings and public spaces; they construct these texts through a series of decisions. And if you look around you, not only will you see patterns of decisions made by architects and designers, but you will also see the influence of those who pay the designers and the people who use or live in that particular space.

For example, architects may have had some leeway in designing your classroom, but their decisions about certain aspects of appearance or comfort might have been affected by construction cost, local building codes, and state educational requirements. The kind of institution you attend, whether it is a private or public university or college, probably had some impact on these decisions. The designers and architects were limited by function—putting a fireplace or a kitchen in a classroom would be inappropriate. And the designers were undoubtedly influenced by the period in which they lived; you probably can pinpoint the date within twenty years of construction based on colors, materials, and lighting. For instance, rectangular buildings built with brick or cinder blocks reflect the architectural style of the 1960s and 1970s, whereas a wooden Victorian house was probably built as much as 100 years earlier.

Such decisions also exist in corporate and retail venues. If you walk into a Starbucks, for example, you will see the results of a series of carefully made judgments: the color scheme, the décor and the lighting, the font type of the signs that describe coffee products, and where all of this is placed. It is not hard to gather from these aspects of design that Starbucks is going for both cool and familiar in its space. They want customers to feel they are not only purchasing coffee but that they are having some unexpressed secondary experience as well. Stores like Anthropologie and Urban Outfitters and restaurants like Rain Forest Café and Hard Rock Café, all use décor, design, and detail to send a message and to create an aura.

Is it one element that creates this aura? No—it is a series of details taken together. Drawing conclusions from architectural decisions and public space is not much different than making these conclusions from reading literature; each has its own grammar, symbols, and themes that we interpret to get a picture of the work as a whole.

Here are some other things to think about when writing about public space and architecture.

There is a difference between public and private spaces, but often the two interact in important ways. We should begin by saying that when we use terms like public and private we are not referring to ownership but to *use*. There are many public places (like publicly owned land) that most people cannot easily access (some federal land for example), and there are private areas that anyone can use (like stadiums and shopping malls).

The distinctions between public and private exist even on a smaller scale, though this is not what experts mean when they refer to public space exactly. We think of our homes as private, but if you share a house with one or two or three or even more people, then your private residence will have public spaces, like the living room, the kitchen, the back yard. If you share a bathroom, then that most private of places is also, in some ways, a kind of public space.

The most obvious spaces we share are places that were designed to be shared by the public like parks, quads, commons, stadiums, river walks, markets, beaches, hiking trails, campsites, libraries, and malls. These are designed to reflect our values, interests, and identities. These places are a common ground where our publicness, our civicness is expressed and even celebrated. Public spaces can and often are the social life of a community and a place where individuals connect with other individuals—the very process of which makes a public.

Depending on the space, there are going to be different rules, signs, and messages designed to communicate a variety of things for a variety of reasons. Signs and color codings on a ski slope will have one purpose, those on New York City's subway system will have another, those near the famous Cloud Gate sculpture (better known as "The Bean") in Chicago's Millennium Park yet another. A courthouse is another public space, as is the DMV, with many and perhaps many confusing signs. Our behavior in these spaces is manipulated for a reason, and we often rely on time-tested powers of deduction to help make sense of order, procedures, and locations depending where we are. Public spaces rely on semiotics and our collective abilities to decode signs and symbols to ensure safety, utility, and enjoyment.

What makes for enjoyment in a public space? According to the American Planning Association, there are eight criteria for a "Great Public Space":

1. Promotes human contact and social activities.
2. Is safe, welcoming, and accommodating for all users.
3. Has design and architectural features that are visually interesting.
4. Promotes community involvement.
5. Reflects the local culture or history.
6. Relates well to bordering uses.
7. Is well maintained.
8. Has a unique or special character.[1]

As you begin your essay on public (or private) spaces, you might want to keep a checklist of these eight items. How many does your space contain? What is missing? How does the absence of one of these affect the overall enjoyment or utility of the space?

Colors and shapes often have symbolic value. Part of the grammar we wrote about earlier (color and shape) helps architects and designers speak to the public in a language they understand, either consciously or subconsciously. Psychologists have shown that particular shapes and colors have psychological effects on their viewers. Designers and architects also draw on traditional uses of color and shape, again, as a sort of grammar of construction. Of course, homeowners may think they choose certain shapes or shades because they look "pretty," or "nice," but what they mean by "pretty" is arbitrary as well. Still, it is very unlikely that the walls in your classrooms are red or black. They are probably also not adobe, wood, or steel. We venture that they are not painted in a checkerboard style or with stripes. Rather, they are probably white or off-white, neutral in some way so as not to distract you from the process of listening and learning.

Combinations of these colors and shapes often form recognizable designs that are imitated repeatedly, especially in regard to public structures that want to suggest something beyond mere functionality. For example, arches, columns, and white picket fences often symbolize ideas that transcend their simple presence—arches and columns have often stood for power and tradition, and the white picket fence stands for tradition as well, but perhaps a different kind of tradition. The Washington Monument on the National Mall in Washington, DC, is, from a functional perspective, a poor use of space. You can't do anything in there. Its significance is symbolic; accordingly, a great deal of thought went in to selecting a design that would signify the values the government wanted. You might ask yourself what values the Washington Monument embodies: Compassion? Triumph? Ambition? Femininity? Patience? As important as the structures themselves are the spaces

---

1   "Characteristics and Guidelines of Great Public Spaces," *American Planning Association*, n.d.

surrounding the structures. A house with a white picket fence around it is a much different text than a house with a high metal security gate enclosing it.

We associate certain kinds of structures with economic and social class—brick versus mobile homes, skyscrapers versus corrugated tin buildings, strip malls versus warehouses. Buildings and spaces are rarely just buildings and spaces. When it comes to public space, almost nothing is random. So, when you begin constructing your own papers about architecture or space, we recommend that you begin by jotting down notes in your journal about your topic. If you are writing about your campus, try to get at the associations of things like "ivy," "columns," and even the word "campus." Why do colleges often rely on Greek and Roman architectural elements? Why are there so many green and open spaces on so many campuses? Are there reasons, beyond practical ones, why campuses love big buildings? What do these connote? From there, you can begin to unpack the packed world of space and design.

Cost and community preferences often contribute to the design of a public or private space. Although most designers seek to make buildings and spaces both beautiful and useful, there are other factors that often interfere with stated goals. Cost is always an issue—people can only build what they can afford, and some materials are prohibitively expensive for a given function. Design help can also cost money, as does land, construction, and so on.

The surrounding community also plays a role in design. Community standards, often in the form of zoning laws, will have an effect on what something looks like. Zoning regulations determine the use of a particular piece of property and, depending on the locale, can also determine the size and function of what is built on that property. Even politics can help determine how something is designed. For example, at the University of Texas at Austin in the 1970s, a prominent student meeting-place was significantly altered when the administration built large planters to restrict student gatherings protesting administration policies.[2] Similarly, at the State University of New York at Binghamton, a beloved and locally famous open space in the center of campus called the Peace Quad, where students gathered to read, protest, talk, eat, and listen to music, was paved over so that a large new building could be erected in its place. Issues of class and race can also affect public and private spaces. For example, there are very few upper-class communities near industrial plants, nor does one often find a poor neighborhood that has easy access to the attractive elements of a city. Think about where Mercedes dealerships are located. In the same place that you might find the best auto repair spots? Or, think about country clubs versus public golf courses. Wine bars and dive bars?

---

2   Nicole Cobler, "West Mall's History Molded through Free Speech Demonstrations," *The Daily Texan*, 24 Nov. 2013.

In some cases entire communities determine how a city can look. Santa Fe, New Mexico has a city ordinance that requires new buildings to have an adobe look.[3] Hilton Head, South Carolina prohibits certain kinds of signs. San Francisco, California has some prohibitions on large chains and franchises. Houston, Texas has almost no zoning restrictions, which makes it wildly inconsistent from block to block.[4] These communities are particularly aware that how a space looks can affect how we feel in that space.

Space can be manipulative, comforting, or both. Designers have conscious ideas about the world they construct, and they often think about how and where they want people involved with their work. If you have ever found yourself frustrated in a poorly designed building, you may have wondered what idiots designed the place. The design of casinos, for instance, is most interesting. Casinos have no windows and usually only one or two exits, and you almost always have to walk through the slot machines to get to them. Why might this be the case? Increasingly, many art museums make you exit through the gift shop when you have finished looking at an exhibition.

In your life, how do elements of design work? Think about sidewalks. Do they always take you where you want to go? What about doorways? Are they always at the most convenient place? In your own room, think about where you put your desk, your chairs, and your bed: What is your main concern in placing them—your convenience or someone else's? All of those decisions influence those who enter your room. Think too about most classrooms at your institution. What do they resemble? Do they create a certain mood? For example, is talking about a movie or a story different in a large classroom than in a café? Why or why not? Sometimes places are friendly to their visitors or inhabitants; others are less so, either through oversight by designers, or more deliberately, as in the case of the Peace Quad or student protest space at the universities mentioned before.

What is important to know is that your emotional reaction to certain spaces is intended. If you have been to a court, then you know that the heightened judicial bench inspires a bit of trepidation; if you have walked in a particularly beautiful cathedral, the sense of awe you feel is not arbitrary; if you enter the library of an old or prestigious university, you probably experienced a hushed sense of tradition that was designed to be elicited in you when it was still in blueprints. Why do so many fancy neighborhoods have signs or columns or arches or gates as you enter them? Why in early New England villages was the church always in the center of the town? Thus, writing about these issues means that you also need to understand the cultural work architectural and design elements do.

---

3   Chris Wilson, *The Myth of Santa Fe: Creating a Modern Regional Tradition* (University of New Mexico Press, 1997).
4   Fernando Ramirez, "The Weirdest Images to Come from Houston's Lack of Zoning Laws," *Houston Chronicle*, 19 Aug. 2016.

Users have ways of altering landscapes that can have personal and political implications. One of these ways is through decoration. Humans love to personalize their spaces, whether it is a cubicle, an office, a dorm room, their computer desktop, or their cars. How we inhabit space is a means of establishing identity; space is a text we are always making and remaking. Think about your own spaces. Posters lining a room, particularly in the dorm rooms and bedrooms of your contemporaries, are usually there to send a message—that the inhabitant is a man or a woman, or someone concerned with music, sports, art, fashion, beer, and/or cars. Some rooms scream that the inhabitants are trying to be cool, while others ooze sophistication.

When one gets older, it is usually time to say goodbye to the rock posters, M.C. Escher prints, and the beer ads, but what to replace them with becomes a question all of us grapple with for the rest of our lives. Some people decide they have a style they feel comfortable with and make their decisions based on that; others feel their way through the process; still others delegate their design choices to someone else. However, there are effects from these decisions, whether they are intended or unintended. The space you live in—how you decorate it, your traces within it—is a kind of text that people can (and do) read to understand something about you.

Entities as large as cities can try to influence the way its inhabitants and visitors feel. If you have visited Santa Fe, for example, you know that art is everywhere—in front of the state capitol, in parks, outside buildings, in restaurants, in courtyards, in and outside of private homes. The message this sends is not simply that Santa Fe and its residents like to decorate their landscape, but that it is a place that values art, how things look, and how art makes you feel. Salem, Massachusetts, with its gabled houses, restored wooden buildings, and American colonial feel, strives for what we might call New England charm. The abundance of art sends a message of sophistication, worldliness, and a progressiveness that is welcoming. You may not always be conscious of it, but spaces that pay close attention to design and beauty probably make you feel good.

Of course, there can also be a gap between what the occupant of the space wants to suggest and what is actually suggested—in this way, spaces can be revealing texts. Knowing about space will help you not only be better readers of someone else's space, but may also help you avoid pitfalls of constructing unwelcoming space yourself. You may think that posters of near-naked women reclining on cars are cool, or you may think black mammy figurines are quaint, or you may like photos of guns and hunting, but there will be a sizeable audience out there who might wonder about you and your values based on how you arrange and decorate your space.

Other elements can change the landscape in ways not imagined by designers. Graffiti alters the public landscape, and so does public art. Neglect can change public space, as well as new construction surrounding a previous design. How we use and design space gives some indication of our personality, among other things. Walking into someone's dorm room, office, or living room gives us a clue of who they are (and who they think they are) (and who they want you to think they are). When you walk into a business, you also receive some indication of how they view themselves. For example, compare the interior at McDonald's to a fancy restaurant, or to a TGI Fridays, Applebee's, or Chili's; the interiors and exteriors are littered with clues about what these places think they are about. Similarly, how do Mexican restaurants tell us that they serve Mexican food? How do Chinese restaurants create an "Asian" setting? Think too about the way movies and television shows set scenes; often the settings of movies give us an indication of how we're supposed to view the characters. In *Modern Family, Big Bang Theory*, or *Friends*, for example, we see the presence of couches, bright lighting, the expensive, clean homes (in the case of *Friends*, far too expensive for New Yorkers their age) as clues to how we are supposed to relate to them. If you ever watched *Roseanne* or *The King of Queens* you see an entirely different representation of private and public space.

Public spaces are especially curious in this way. Dams completely alter natural environments, flooding entire valleys. Roads paved through forests bring cars and tourists and pollution. In urban areas, for example, some public parks have become centers for both drug use and needle exchange programs—no doubt a very different use of public space than was intended. We leave our imprint everywhere. And, just as we make our rooms or cubicles our own, so, too, do we make public space our own—for better or worse.

Ultimately, the space that surrounds us says a number of things about that particular location—who inhabits that space, what the space is used for, and how we are to read that space. Additionally, we can discern a great deal about what kinds of spaces or buildings are important given the amount and kind of space devoted to them. As you read this chapter, think about how certain spaces force you to interpret the world in a certain way, and as you write your papers, work on combining your own observations about spaces with solid research so that your arguments are strengthened by two kinds of authority—subjective experience and objective data.

Technology Has Changed What We Think of as "Public Space." When we wrote the first version of this book back in 2000, we might not have thought of the internet or your laptop or a phone as public space. But the popularity and penetration of social media has changed what we think of as "public" and what we think of as "space." Facebook is now a kind of public space—as are Twitter, Snapchat, Instagram, and Tumblr. In fact, the whole notion of *posting*, is, at its core, about making things public; the term comes from the physical act of mailing or putting up posters. In this way, they make a claim for a type of spatial representation.

These spaces are also aware of design and utility. If Facebook was not easy to use, it would not be so popular. Cyberspace is all about ease, pleasure, and efficiency. We hang out online, we shop online, we look for romantic partners online, we play games online, we even have long conversations online because they are often easier than doing the physical equivalent. The internet and other social media sites have become a new commons.

But like any public space, cyberspace and the internet have their issues. There is crowding, rudeness, bullying, arrogance, and simple annoyance. Facebook has created an entirely new ethos about how we communicate, share information, and divulge information. People now announce divorces over Facebook, as well as new jobs, harassment, eating disorders, suicidal thoughts, sexual desires, outrage, dissent, and fear. As many of you have experienced, people seem more willing to express themselves publicly in a cyberspace like Facebook than in an actual physical setting like a car or a restaurant or a café.

How people choose to represent themselves—both in written language and in visual language (emojis, photos, stickers)—can say a lot about them but also, perhaps, what they think of you. In our chapters on fashion and gender we talk about the composition of the self, and this extends to the space of the internet. Indeed, reading others in cyberspace is itself a complex process of decoding, and writing about how cyberspace and public space interact and intersect will prove one of the most intriguing activities over the next several decades.

THINGS TO CONSIDER WHEN WRITING ABOUT PUBLIC SPACE

Features: How does the space integrate with building design, scale, architecture, and proportionality to create interesting visual experiences, views, or interaction? Does it facilitate multiple uses? Is it accessible via walking, biking, or public transit?

Design and accessibility: Does the space reflect the community's local character and personality? Does it foster social engagement and create a sense of community? Does it encourage interaction among a diverse cross section of the public? Is it safe? Is it well signed? Is it fun?

Shapes: What are some of the dominant shapes you see in a public space or building? Do they symbolize anything to you? Are they supposed to? Do they remind you of other shapes in other spaces? How do the shapes relate to the space's use?

Colors: What are the dominant colors? What emotions do they evoke? Why? How would the space or architecture change if the color changed? How does the color relate to the space's use?

Size: How big is this place? How does this affect the way you view it, and the feelings it inspires? Is there a way to change the size to evoke different feelings? In what ways do the space's or architecture's size relate to its use?

Use: What is the use of this particular space or architecture? How do we know from the elements you see? Do you see unintended uses that might result from this construction? Do you see an emphasis on practicality or ornament in this space?

Interaction between architecture and space: How do the two work together? What elements in the architecture affect the way the space is constructed? Are there ways of changing this interaction?

Overall beauty: What is your general view of the place's beauty? What standards or criteria do you find yourself relying on?

Emotional response: What is your overall emotional response to this place? Why? What elements contribute to this response? What elements could you change that might provoke a different response?

Overall statement: What do you think this space or architecture says? What is it trying to say? How might any gap between what it says and is trying to say be bridged?

PUBLIC SPACE: THE GENRES

Personal Narrative

Relationships to space can be personal. In fact, Yi-Fu Tuan, a geography scholar, believes that relationships make space into place; in his view, spaces become places when they become imbued with meaning.[5] So one possibility is to write an essay on how a space that seemed abstract to you became someplace familiar.

First choose your place and write about how you encountered it.

Then write about how you experience it now.

A QUICK GUIDE TO WRITING ABOUT PUBLIC SPACE

A few things you might think about as you write your paper:

1. Define your space: Figure out exactly where you are writing about.

2. Note materials and colors: Writing about public space is often focused on the details, and these details often give some insight on the intentions of the designers.

3. Observe how people use the space: Observing and thinking about the ways people use a space—perhaps in unintended ways—can help us to understand whether the space works or in what ways it works.

4. Brainstorm/freewrite about the space either at the space or soon after visiting.

5. Getting your impressions down early makes it easier to write.

6. Think of a thesis and paragraph ideas before starting to write. It will make the first draft easier.

---

5   Yi-Fu Tuan, *Space and Place: The Perspective of Experience* (U of Minnesota P, 1997).

To make it an essay that has a wider audience, you have to explain why people might care about what you have found. You can do this through a number of ways, including writing about how your relationship with a place might relate to others by their affiliations.

Photo Essay

One of the great things about having phones with cameras is the ability to take photos as you encounter worthy subjects. Using cameraphones to document a place as a means to writing about it can be useful.

Photo essays can be about one place—a classroom, a university building, a restaurant, a bedroom, a car—or they can be about a series of places—stops on a road trip, gyms or fitness centers, supermarkets, convenience stores. They help document a place, but such documentation also needs your interpretations; good photo essays have an argument.

In a photo essay, you need 1) a subject, 2) different images of the same place or images of a variety of places, 3) text to accompany photos, and 4) an argument.

1. When taking photos, make sure you take many versions of the same place. Professional photographers take hundreds of photos of their subjects; a dozen or so for each of your subjects will work.
2. Make sure you keep notes about *when* and *where* you took the photo, as well as *what* the subject is.
3. Privacy law is very forgiving to photographers in the United States; photographers can take a photo of almost any subject as long as they or it are in public view, including private buildings as long as they are visible from a public perspective.[6] So don't worry about the *legality* of taking photos. Instead think about the ethics around doing so, which centers around one large question: does this person want her or his photograph taken? Does the person know he or she is being photographed? Will they be harmed if the photo is public?
4. You can use Microsoft Word or PowerPoint or the web to make a photo essay. The web also has a number of services that allow you to easily construct a photo essay.
5. The most important thing in a photo essay is that it has a definitive point or argument that an audience can understand. The thesis can be subtle or broad, but it definitely has to exist.

Space/Building Analysis

When architects and designers make buildings, they want them to say something. Sometimes this message is visible boldly as in a skyscraper or more subtly in the shapes of rooms or the amount and content of windows or the types of sinks in a bathroom.

Both architectural critics and casual observers may have opinions on what the architectural message is or whether the architect has achieved her aims. You can also

---

6   Bert P. Krages II, "The Photographer's Right," *Bert P. Krages II*, http://www.krages.com/phoright.htm.

perform this work by making an argument about a building or space based on 1) what you think it is trying to say and 2) what it actually says.

People differ on how important authorial intent is when analyzing a text; some think it's important to figure out what an author says, while others think that the text itself and what it says is more important. Like many critics, we think that *both* are worth considering: a space or building contains elements that its author or authors may not have considered, including developments after a building was planned or constructed, nearby spaces and/or places, unexpected uses for the space/place and so on.

To write about a building or space, first take notes. What does the building look like? What part of the space are you writing about? What colors and shapes are most prominent? Are the ceilings tall? What architectural details stand out? This notetaking has two purposes—one is to construct evidence for your paper, and the other is to help you actually come up with an argument.

Once you take notes, see if there is an argument to make or at least a question to ask of the building (beyond "what is this building trying to say?"). Then begin writing. Once you are a draft in, think about your argument again, and revise your paragraphs according to the argument.

Researched Paper

Writing about a space or place through research is similar to the process of analysis—finding a space or place or building, taking notes on it, and coming up with an argument. The difference is finding a research lens or angle (see pp. 35–36) to examine the space. Some angles could include race, class, and gender; others might include sustainability; further research might be on the type of space/place/building, for example on universities, convenience stores, and so on.

Once you have figured out the research angle and the text, focus on making sure readers can see the building or space through your description, that the research angle is well defined, and that you relate the text to the research angle. If you were to write about your cafeteria for example, and chose postmodern architecture as your angle, then you write a paper that first describes the cafeteria, explains what postmodernism is, and then shows how the cafeteria fits into this category. Or using the same text, the cafeteria, you could research what designers are taking into account when designing them, and see if your cafeteria fits in that category. Or you could write about gender and race, and whether the cafeteria has aspects that seem particularly male or white.

In all of these cases, description is really important; you should be careful to show as much as or more than you tell.

OTHER ESSAY IDEAS

1. Building as Analogy

Find a building you want to write about. Does it remind you of something besides a building in 1) its physical construction; 2) the emotional response it encourages; 3) its purpose; or 4) its structure? In what way are these disparate elements alike? Different? What does the analogy in general say about commonalities of texts generally?

2. Emotional Response

Walk around a building or a public area such as a mall or your school's common area. What do you feel? What about the place makes you feel such an emotion? Are these effects intended or unintended?

3. Commercial versus Artistic

What dominates this particular building or space—its artistic aspects or commercial ones? Or do the two work together?

4. Your Favorite Place

If possible, analyze a place you feel close to and figure out why you feel that way. Is there a theme attached to this place? How would you describe the décor? The architecture? Do you feel that your attachment to this place—or places like it—is unique?

5. Does This Building or Space "Work"?

Find a place—do you think it succeeds on its own terms? What are its terms—what criteria is it trying to fulfill? Does is succeed? Why or why not?

6. The Person from the Space

Go to an office or a dorm room or car, or some place that "belongs" to someone. What can you tell about this person from the space? How did you arrive at your judgments? Are there other ways to interpret the information?

7. The Common Element

Compare similar spaces. What makes them similar? What are their differences? What do their differences or similarities say about this type of space?

8. Your Campus

Your campus is probably a compelling public space. If it is a public institution, then it is both a public space and a space for the public. Walk around your campus, paying attention to its entrances, its signs, its means and manner of communication. What messages does it send? Does your campus make an argument?

9. Cyberspace

Take the instructions we gave you for reading built public space and apply those to cyberspace. Offer a semiotic reading of Facebook or Tumblr or Instagram. Or a chat area of a video game. How does a website try to be a public space? What does it do to invite you in and make you feel at home?

Additional Essays

1. Write an essay on your favorite (or least favorite) building in the town where you live. What values does the building have?

2. Write a paper in which you compare an older building (built before 1920) with a building built more recently (after 1960). How do the two buildings create values? How do they send messages about their contexts?

3. Write a paper in which you examine two very different spaces, like a town square and a college campus, or a playground and a bar. How do the spaces compare? How do they differ?

4. Take some photographs of areas you think are particularly rural. Now give close readings of the photos in which you demonstrate how and why these images evince ruralness.

5. Write a comparison/contrast essay in which you decode some of the images from this essay with some of the images of street art and urban landscapes. How are urban and rural vistas different? Are there any similarities?

6. Find some old representations of rural landscapes—paintings, drawings, photographs—and write an essay in which you unpack the associations you have with the iconography of rural areas.

7. Find an environment where gender and space interact. What about the space you describe makes it connect to the particular gender?

8. Think about other public spaces or buildings where separation of people into genders, races, or classes is built into the design. (Hint: Think of places where people spend more or less money to sit in different places.) Write a paper that addresses this question.

9. Look at several dorm rooms or apartments of friends both male and female. Write a short paper that discusses which elements in particular define these spaces as particularly male or female.

10. Look at other things that are gendered, such as advertisements, clothing, and cars. How do these gendered texts compare to the gendered spaces you described earlier? What elements do designers of any text use to designate gender? Write a paper that ties gendered space to another gendered text.

11. Take some photographs, but as you are doing so, document what you are thinking about while you take them. Write about this experience.

12. Give a semiotic reading of your campus. You can either read the campus as a whole—making an argument that it sends a specific kind of message—or, you can read a specific part as a microcosm (a small thing that functions as a symbol or encapsulation of something larger).

13. Write an essay on how the commercial and the educational merge at your institution.

14. Does your campus have commercial enterprises run by outside vendors? Are there advertisements in rooms, in dorms or on campus elsewhere? In what ways does that affect the campus atmosphere, if at all? Does it detract from the stated mission of your university?

15. Find some aspect of your campus that seems nontraditional in its construction or use and give a reading of that space. You might consider off-campus housing, a virtual classroom, a space that merges with the community, or even a new dorm. What makes this place nontraditional?

16. Write about the college campus as a public place. What makes a campus public? Should a private university be a public place?

RESOURCES

There are a lot of resources about public space and architecture online, but there may be a divide between organizations that regularly cover these subjects, which include the *New York Times*, *Slate*, the *Los Angeles Times*, and many other outlets, and advocacy organizations or practicing architects or planners. This division may make sorting out information that is useful for a writing project a bit more challenging. Two sites, the *Atlantic*'s City Lab and Citiscope, both cover urban architecture and public space regularly.

Books

These are books that you might find useful for research or just for expanding your knowledge about public space and architecture.

Christopher Alexander, Sara Ishikawa, Murray Silverstein, *A Pattern Language: Towns, Buildings, Construction*. This book explains the concept of grammar as it applies to building.

Robert Caro, *The Power Broker: Robert Moses and the Fall of New York*. This book explains how a government administrator can not only have an enormous impact on the public space and architecture of a city but also on its people.

Grady Clay, *Close Up: How to Read the American City*. The book talks about some of the things you need to know in order read and interpret the city.

Richard Florida, *The Rise of the Creative Class and How It's Transforming Work, Leisure, Community and Everyday Life*. Florida is an often-cited expert on the move back to cities by young professionals.

Dolores Hayden, *Redesigning the American Dream: The Future of Housing, Work, and Family Life*. This book explores gender and housing.

Kenneth T. Jackson, *Crabgrass Frontier: The Suburbanization of the United States*. This book explores the history of suburbia in the United States.

Jane Jacobs, *The Death and Life of Great American Cities*. Jacobs's book is a classic—many of her observations about city life in the 1950s and 1960s have been shown to be true.

Peter Katz et al., *The New Urbanism: Toward an Architecture of Community*. This book was one of the first to talk about ways of revitalizing housing and community in the city in the post-1970s downturn in urban living.

Setha M. Low and Neil Smith, eds., *The Politics of Public Space*. This collection explores the politics of public space.

Robert Venturi, Denise Scott-Brown, Steven Izenour, *Learning from Las Vegas*. This is one of the first books to celebrate non-classical architecture as interesting, relevant, and good on its own terms.

SAMPLE ESSAY

Consider the Moon Pie: Reading and Writing about the Road

JONATHAN SILVERMAN

American popular culture is obsessed with the road, as witnessed by the enormous output of writers and movie-makers across time and place. Such works range from the Jack Kerouac classic *On the Road* to Cormac McCarthy's Pulitzer-Prize winning novel *The Road* to movies like *Thelma and Louise* and *Easy Rider* and the Bob Hope–Bing Crosby road movies (e.g., *The Road to Rio, The Road to Morocco*), not to mention John Ford's adaptation of John Steinbeck's *The Grapes of Wrath*. Earlier works that focus on movement could also be classified as road narratives; they include diaries by those crossing the Oregon Trail, letters by African American migrants from the South to the North, and accounts by Native Americans regarding the Trail of Tears; even many narratives by the Puritans have elements of later conceptions of the road in them. When reading these accounts, we often get a sense of both identity and continuity that mark movement in the United States.

As these examples illustrate, the road in American culture is well traveled. Accordingly, in writing about such a familiar and mythic place, one might feel insecure about the ability to say anything new—such a feeling applies not only to the road—but also other familiar topics as well. One way to approach such a subject is to simply discuss what we see; taking what we observe and analyzing it rather than worrying about trying to understand all of a subject is a way around this issue. It does not mean ignoring context, but it does mean relying on one's power of observation as the *primary* source of content. In other words, we can write our own road stories.

In the summer of 2007, I drove from Connecticut, where my parents live, to Santa Fe, New Mexico, making several stops along the way. I took photographs at every stop I made in an attempt to document what kinds of messages we encounter as we drive across the country. Following are some examples of photographs that make some statements about the road, my encounter with it, and perhaps some larger truths associated with travel as well. I should note here that these photos are just a few of the hundred or so I took, and that my goal in writing about the road was to combine my photography with analysis; such an approach requires *choosing*. Had I been required to write about all my photos and all my stops, there is no guarantee that I would have been able to come up with a coherent narrative.

My approach also reflects a particular way of traveling across the country. Some like to move slowly, stopping at tourist destinations along the way, or pacing themselves by traveling only a short way each day. Some like to motor down the interstate in RVs, whereas others stick to the "Blue Highways," the national and state highways that preceded the Interstate, as termed by William Least Heat-Moon. And some like to travel like I did this time, at a hectic pace, marked by stops to visit friends, but with very little interaction with the culture beyond the road itself. Regardless of whether one stops to get to know a people or a place, signs, buildings, towns, people, and even the landscape seem to want to be looked at. Indeed, why would anything constructed near or along a road want to be *ignored*? Because traveling along a road presents a myriad of semiotic moments, traveling by road is always accompanied by a perpetual act of reading. In making this journey I found that I was reminded how much consumption was part of travel, how variable and dominant the landscape is on the road, and how signs marked the landscape in a variety of ways. But I also found that my interpretations seem unstable in that they seemed to come from this particular trip (and reading of such).

CONSUMPTION

Food is an essential part of travel. Westward travelers used to have to pack supplies in order to make the journey, though very quickly markets were created to cater to travelers. Now, we have convenience stores and travel stops. For many travelers, the accessibility of food of both good nutrition or less so is an enjoyable part of venturing across the country. Consider the (Fig. a) Moon Pie. It is not a national brand; you can find it mostly in the Midwest and the South, and so a hardy traveler venturing forth is buoyed by the find of this delectable mix of

FIGURE a

banana-flavor coating, cakelike filling, and marshmallow. (It is funny, too, that it bills itself as "The Only One On The Planet!" given the fact that one chooses one Moon Pie among a display of many.) I also like the universality of the moon in the Moon Pie—the sky is one constant in traveling, and often a way of marking one's progress across the country is by the different views we have of the sky and the horizon.

Although it is often home to the delectable Moon Pie, the travel center itself (Fig. b) goes beyond the convenience and corner store in that it is also a center of symbolic

FIGURE b

consumption. Until recently, most were associated with one gasoline brand and that's it. But here we see the trend of collaborating with other national brands, in this case, Dairy Queen. This particular center is devoted to nostalgia—note the Route 66 sign, which refers to the most romantic of former roads that was consonant with the first wave of pleasure road trips out west, as well as the path for migrants from Oklahoma to California during the Dust Bowl. Originally cutting a path from Chicago to Los Angeles, Route 66 has been replaced by I-40. You cannot see it well, but Phillips 66 is behind the 1950s-inspired sign. This particular sign intentionally evokes the romanticized image of Route 66 that writers like Lisa Mahar document. (Note, too, the faux space-age arrow seemingly straight out of the 1950s, an arrow that was supposed to signify progress. Now it points back to itself; it's a symbol of the future that harks back to the past.)

The travel stop is also a monument to American commercialism. Here, more than 100 bottles of electrolyte drink are displayed in a scene that seems a form of deliberately constructed commercial beauty. My own view here is mediated by the photographs of Andres Gursky, particularly his *99 Cent*, a photograph of a convenience store in Los Angeles. The bigger question is: can anyone be *that* thirsty? But the prominence of these drinks also might signal the transition to the Desert Southwest, where people worry about dehydration.

To me, the Moon Pie, Route 66, and Gatorade drinks in figures a–c form a triptych of road consumption, symbolizing the plenty one can find on the road, as well as the way images speak to us in unexpected—and sometimes unexpectedly beautiful—ways.

FIGURE c

LANDSCAPE

Roads frame landscapes by guiding travelers through a particular area; they then become part of what they frame, as the associated parts—guardrails, medians, exit signs, and others, not to mention the podlike businesses that surround the exits— become part of the landscape itself. In other words, the discussion about landscape actually began in the previous section. The road's landscape is also framed, however, by the response of its travelers. For some, highways are anonymous, empty routes that exist only as means of travel to one's destination. For others, seeing unfamiliar land- scapes, even if they bracket a long, relatively unchanged road, is part of the exploration of travel.

A familiar landscape to one traveler might be exotic to another. Witness my own traveling through the mid-section of the country. For those who grow up on the coasts, the sheer flatness and vision of the land can be both breathtaking and, in the case of weather, a little frightening. Shown are two shots taken from the road—the first (Fig. d) driving north in Arkansas, and the second (Fig. e) on I-70 in Kansas.

For me, someone who grew up in Connecticut, where the horizon is hidden by trees, the big sky and flat plains are fascinating and beautiful. They suggest the openness so commonly associated with the West and westward expansion, a hypnosis-inducing means of crossing the country. But to others, they are just the background of daily living. When I was in graduate school in Texas, I took my first journey across West Texas on my way to Colorado to visit a friend. I was buoyed by the beauty of land- scape throughout my travel, but I thought the cotton fields outside of Lubbock were

FIGURES
d & e

particularly beautiful. I expressed this thought to a clerk at a convenience store, who demanded to know where I was from.

"Connecticut," I said.

She responded by saying something to the effect of "It's beautiful there. This is ugly."

SIGNS

Signs are literal markers on a highway, telling its travelers what to do (drive a speed limit, slow down, change lanes) or where to go (St. Louis, Exit 287, north). But signs are also signs of a different sort—they can be unpacked to show some of the idiosyncrasies of road travel. Fig. f, taken off I-70 in Utah, illustrates the many possibilities one might choose to view the landscape. Standing in the rest area, an arbitrary location carved out in this case to view the scenery, there is no possibility that one will go the wrong way. So when looking backward, I was struck by the repetition of a sign that seems superfluous in contrast to a "beautiful landscape."

FIGURE f

FIGURES
g, h & i

For those who find direct religious expression difficult to process, landscape combined with religious signage sends several coded messages. Is the sign in Fig. g referring to the afterlife, or this particular place? Is Hell an emotional state, or a destination? Maybe this sign is also about travel of a different sort.

And then we have signs that reveal much about the country we live in, such as the Homeland Security sign taken in a rest stop in Richfield, Utah (Fig. h). Such a sign could reveal the political leanings of the owner—not necessarily a statement of risk.

The signs in Fig. i suggest a great deal of options traveling across the country, a mix of various routes, subroutes, and in the case of Route 66, historic or even nostalgic routes. When approaching this intersection, knowing how (and not only where) one is going seems imperative.

FIGURES
j & k

And then we have these signs marking a bathroom in Utah (Fig. j), signaling the sort of universality of highway travel—bathrooms where distinction is both signified by inclusion of all three possible restroom symbols (and certainly a throwback—the symbol for the women does not reflect any sort of standard of female dress in the twenty-first century).

Although this is not actually a street sign (Fig. k), the bear and the hedges do reveal through a close reading some of the concerns of this rest stop in Grand Junction, Colorado. The bear is native to the area, but also a symbol of wildness and, more important, of nature itself. In a way, so are the hedges next to the bear, on top of a constructed stone wall, in front of manicured grass. But taken together, they suggest a manicured nature, perhaps the nature that travelers prefer to encounter. Taken as a whole, this photograph also reminds the traveler of his or her own home as well as the pull of nature.

Another trip down another road might engender an entirely different semiotic experience and a different interpretation. The cultural and visual rhetoric of the road is always active, although because it is stationary, it may feel passive. However, we are the ones for whom the road and its many texts are designed. Paying attention to the various associations bears, signs and products carry may help us understand how the road tries to determine its own interpretation.

CHAPTER 14

READING AND WRITING ABOUT NATURE AND THE ENVIRONMENT

In this section, we are going to talk about writing about nature and the environment, which are similar terms but with different meanings and, more importantly, different functions in the ways we think about encountering our world. The etymology of "environment" comes from the French term *environ*, which means to circle, to travel around, to circumnavigate. So, our environment is that thing which is circling around us, surrounding us. The term "environment" enjoys at least two related meanings. The most common is the healthiness of the air, water, and land on and in which people, animals, and other beings live. A secondary definition might be the conditions that you work or live in, as in, "A crowded football stadium might not be the best working environment for writing papers."

While the environment is something we are worried about improving and maintaining, nature is a more general concept about a type of land. A basic working definition of nature is the physical world of Earth—plants, animals, water, and the phenomena of these things. Synonyms include "Mother Earth" or "the Natural World" or even "Mother Nature." We think of nature as elements we can see and things we can go into (caves, water, forests), on (hills and mountains), eat and drink (food, berries, animals, water), and enjoy (all of the above). We tend to distinguish between nature and civilization—one is full of buildings, roads, the electrical grid, and people, while the other is *not*. However, as the world gets smaller and its population gets bigger, the line between nature and civilization is increasingly hazy—what is car camping, after all but a mixing of the "natural" and the "civilized"? If humans were not on earth, there would not necessarily be nature—just "land." One way of thinking about the differences between nature and the environment is the way we encounter them. We might say, "I'm tired of being inside this office building; I need to go experience nature." On the other hand, we would not say, "I need to experience the environment." We might say that we are trying to protect it, though, and the environment we are trying to protect might include land set aside to remain undeveloped—in other words, nature.

We also want to encourage you to think about the associations you have with terms like nature and environment. Let's consider a well-maintained, meticulous garden either behind someone's house or as part of a public park or museum. If you are in the park, are you *in nature*? Both of the authors of this book like to play golf—is riding a golf cart around to hit a little ball being in nature? Are golf courses good for the environment? Are they good for nature? Can we experience nature in a setting that is harmful for the environment? Is going to a park or going on a hike more of an engagement with nature than, say, sitting in your backyard? Or going to a soccer field? Or playing disc golf? Or going for a ride on a jet ski? We have found that pretty much everyone we know has ideas about what "nature" is, what "the natural" might be, and what constitutes "the environment," but these don't always agree with each other.

The differences between concepts carry over into the ways we write about them. Writing about the environment is similar to but perhaps different than writing about nature, and especially so-called nature writing. When we think of nature writing, we tend to imagine writing that praises the beauty of trees or wonders at the majesty of mountains, whereas writing about the environment might focus on the way human development and interactions have changed our relationship to air, land, or water, and this writing is often more explicitly political than nature writing. Writing about nature and the environment can be rewarding and compelling, but it requires some forethought and preparation. Here are some things to consider.

We can read nature as a text. Nature is a text we have been taught to read—especially in America. Early settlers were often in awe of nature and its unpredictability.[1] In the work of writers like Emily Dickinson, Henry David Thoreau, Nathaniel Hawthorne, and Ralph Waldo Emerson, there is a distinction between the tamed and the wild, the known and the unknown. Thoreau, in particular, believed people could find their best selves in nature, that it was restorative and, well, just "natural." Understanding nature is part of understanding our environment. And, understanding our environment necessitates an understanding of nature.

Thoreau's *Walden; or, a Life in the Woods* is one of the first books to examine nature as something to be *read*. Thoreau would never have used that language, but in his chapter "Reading," he makes implicit and explicit connections among books and the natural world. Thoreau finds himself engrossed in nature, as he might be in a good book—the natural world as foreign to him as a place of residence as any foreign land he might read about. "It is something to be able to paint a particular picture," Thoreau writes, "or to carve a statue and so to make a few objects beautiful; but it is far more glorious to carve and paint the very atmosphere and medium through which we look."[2] By this, Thoreau means, among other things, that by looking at nature or landscape, we

---

1   Roderick Nash, *Wilderness and the American Mind* (Yale UP, 1967).
2   Henry David Thoreau, *Walden* and *Resistance to Civil Government* 2nd ed. edited by William Rossi (Norton, 1992), 61.

make it, we participate in it, we take it into our beings and make sense of it. In other words, we *read* and ingest nature.

Regardless of your religious beliefs, you can also think of nature as something authored. If you believe in evolution, then nature is its own author that has been writing (and revising) itself for billions of years. If you believe in a god that created the universe, then that god is the author of nature and has placed it here for us to enjoy, respect, and make sense of. People are the pesky editors who keep taking away this and that or spilling things on its leaves. Indeed, over the last several years a somewhat unlikely alliance has developed between liberal environmentalists and conservative Old Testament fundamentalists, both of whom believe nature is sacred and should be saved.[3] Either way, thinking about yourself in relation to nature is an important issue worth your consideration and reflection. How do we *interpret* nature or the natural world? In what ways do we make sense of nature the way we would a novel or a film?

The environment has associated symbols. Just think about what the image of a tree has come to represent. Or the color green. Or the image of a drop of water. Over time, we have loaded up aspects of the environment with a host of associations. These associations extend to a word like "environmentalist," which, depending on your political leanings, could be a positive or a negative term. Similarly, everyone knows the recycling symbol. We all know what people mean when they use the term "tree hugger." We have come to believe that composting is "good" for the environment. But why?

Writing about the environment is tricky because of the politics associated with it. What is interesting about the environment is that no one is really *against* its health. No one wants to ruin the environment—well, not many people—but we all have varying degrees of interest in protecting it. We also don't always know precisely what we mean when we say we are pro-environment or that we want to preserve the environment. Do we mean cutting down fewer trees? Limiting carbon monoxide pollution? Cutting back on water usage? Reversing polar ice-cap melt? Few people think pumping more pollutants into the atmosphere is a good idea, but large chemical companies, auto manufacturers, families with two working parents who commute, and cities which have to power their grids may not want to be the ones to cut back. In this sense, "the environment" has become something of an idea or a concept—perhaps an abstract one—rather than a concrete, knowable entity.

When writing about the environment, which can be an abstract but also a hot-button issue, you need to be precise with your facts. Writing an argumentative paper about why protecting the environment is a good thing is far less useful (and harder to prove) than writing a paper calling for your university to reduce its reliance on fossil fuels. In

---

3   Chris Berdik, "Christian. Conservative. Treehugger," *Politico*, 6 Dec. 2015.

the former, it is impossible to know who the audience for your essay is. However, in the latter example, the audience is fellow students and the university administration. You are calling for specific people to alter a specific behavior.

One of the best pieces of advice we can offer when writing about environmental issues is to think about solutions—don't just provide criticism. It is easy to be critical of a company's behavior or a city's energy policy. It is another thing altogether to offer actual reasonable solutions, such as new policies, community action, legal options, and benefits to the common good. If you offer sound, reasonable solutions, backed up with smart, objective data to support your claims, your essay will gain credibility.

There are many environments—some of which do not include nature. When we talk about the environment, we usually mean the health of the natural world, but there are environments that do not include the natural world. We live in human environments, we work in office environments, we live, increasingly, in a technological environment. Obviously, all of these environments can be read as texts, in part because they have more obviously human authors. Here, built environments overlap with issues of public and private space—we suggest you take a look at that chapter if these kinds of environments are more interesting to you.

Interesting places to consider are hotels, restaurants, and gift shops that are inside national parks. Or actual living forests that are inside museums. Greenhouses. Meticulously planted orchards. Hydroponics. Flowerbeds and gardens in cities. In these instances, where does nature begin and civilization end? How many different environments can be contained in one space? Is an indoor forest nature? In *The Martian*, the main character grows potatoes inside his temporary living quarters on Mars. Is that nature? Environment? Mother Mars?

Can you write about the environment without being an environmentalist? The answer is yes. That question is a bit like asking if you can write about football without being a sports fan. Or, can you write about art if you are not an artist? The answer to both is yes. Our point is that we don't want students to shy away from a topic because of labels attached to the topic. Increasingly, Americans are wary of labels—this is proving especially true of younger generations. Fewer and fewer college-aged students identify as Republican or Democrat; they don't want to be pigeonholed or restrictively categorized. We understand that. We also understand wanting to be independent and not beholden to a creed or a way of thinking.

Indeed, writing about the environment can carry some potentially thorny political issues. For example, as we were writing the first draft of this essay, the United States Senate voted 98–1 that climate change is real and not a hoax. However, just one year earlier, back in 2015, the same Senate voted 50–49 that humans are *not* the cause of climate change or global warming. And, as we were preparing the final version, President

Trump had just announced that the United States was pulling out of the Paris Climate Accord. So, the earth is getting warmer, but there is disagreement about the causes and even further disagreement about what can and should be done.

As it stands, there seems to be very little wiggle room for someone to write about the environment without taking a stand one way or the other. This makes for great essay options! For example, much of what we think of as nature, like parks, hiking trails, beaches, and landscape, have been either built or constructed for public *use*. We put use in italics because it is a tricky word. We are expected and even encouraged to *use* nature but not *abuse* or *misuse* it. But even this is complicated. Very likely trees are cut down in order to build hiking trails. Or natural grasses and plants are plowed under to build new parks.

In Edward Abbey's great essay "A Walk in the Park" (1972), the author explores the interplay between nature, environment, technology, and crowds as he writes about the many complicating factors surrounding a proposed highway to a scenic overlook. More people will get to see nature if the highway goes through but perhaps at the expense of nature. One of the more comical areas of state and national parks is the signs that tell people where to take photographs, as if the park is itself a text helping you to capture another text.

Climate change is an example of how altering the environment affects nature. There is a scientific consensus that human activity is causing the world's temperature to rise. While there are some who disagree about how quickly the temperature is going up and the effects humans are having, climatologists are virtually certain that this is now occurring. The debate is a *political* one, because the consequences facing the world if this is true are significant, and they require actions that include forms of sacrifice that may impact our daily lives today.

Nature is always affected by climate. If the world is warmer, some areas, for example, can have longer growing seasons, while others might be more prone to flooding because of the effects a warmer climate has on weather. If there is more rain in the desert, things bloom more readily. If there is warm air in the polar regions, ice sheets melt. Climate changes affect all living things, something which is true even without the concept of global warming.[4]

Researching nature and the environment often involves multiple types of sources from a variety of disciplines. Writing about nature and the environment involves science, data, and often the law. If you want to write about "the destruction of the rain forest," research specific rain forests. If you want to call for better recycling programs,

---

4   For a rundown of the effects, see "Global Warming" on the Union of Concerned Scientists website, www.ucsusa.org/global-warming. Accessed 7 Dec. 2017.

find out which ones work and which ones do not. Even simply offering a reading of a wilderness area, a beach, or a park can often be augmented by some research about that park.

Researching nature and the environment is part of a rich tradition. People like Thoreau and Emerson tended to describe and praise nature. John Muir, George Perkins Marsh, and Al Gore have all argued that we have a moral and spiritual responsibility to preserve land and use it responsibly. Other writers from Rachel Carson to Joan Didion to Michael Pollan to Wendell Barry to Linda Hogan have written extensively about the problems (and necessity) of living harmoniously with nature. On the other side, conservative politicians like Jim Inhofe from Oklahoma, have written about how God rather than humans is controlling climate change.

Here are some things to think about as you *write* about nature and the environment. Writing about nature and the environment uses many of the same interpretive and decoding strategies you use when reading things like movies, fashion, public and private space, and architecture. As you do with many texts, think about not only what you see but what you *feel*. Many subjects, too, will benefit from additional research.

Description: The natural world is one of the first and oldest and best topics of writing. But you need to be specific. Be sure to describe nature concretely, using vivid, precise, descriptive terminology when possible. Do not rely on clichés or platitudes. Do not say something is "beautiful"—show that it is through description.

Location: Describe where you are (or where you are writing about). Are you writing about a desert? A forest? A mountain? What defines those places as those types of places—in other words, what makes a forest a forest? A desert, a desert? Make the reader see the place you are writing about.

Context: What do we need to know? Is there history, legal policy, controversy surrounding your topic? If so, let your reader know what it is.

Tensions and conflicts: What are the main conflicts of the text you are writing about? What issues are at stake? Is there tension between the self and society in the text? How? Why?

Technology: How does technology affect your reading of nature and the environment? Did you use a car or a bus to get to your locale? Are you writing about it with a computer or a pen? Is there a relationship between how you encounter the place and the place itself? For example, does it matter that you can drive through Golden Gate Park in San Francisco and Central Park in New York City?

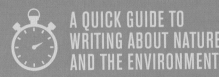

A QUICK GUIDE TO WRITING ABOUT NATURE AND THE ENVIRONMENT

1. Take notes: Make sure if you are going to a park or wilderness area that you take a notebook or pad. Carefully note the names of the plants, trees, animals, insects, the air. If you take interpretive information from the locale, write down the source. If you do not know the source, write down as much as you can.

2. Document: If you can take a photo-graph of the location/topic do so. If not, outline the work on your pad.

3. Feel: Note your initial and final emotional responses to the text. Nature often hits us emotionally before we register it intellectually.

4. Look around you: If you are writing about something in nature, note the sur-roundings. Are you in a park surrounded by a city? Are you in a national park? Are there roads and buildings, trails and guide signs? Where does nature end and the non-nature begin?

5. Communicate: Think about what you would tell a friend about your topic or journey to and from the place, or what happened while you were there. What is the most interesting thing you see? Think about audience too. Many outdoor parks, nature preserves, oceans, mountains, and woodland areas have brochures and other interpretive texts. How are you being asked to *read* certain spaces?

6. Culture within culture/nature within nature: As with anything, you should con-sider the social, political, and economic issues surrounding your topic. Both the envi-ronment and nature are loaded political (and historical) (and religious) texts. They often come with important cultural associations.

WRITING ABOUT NATURE: THE GENRES

Close Reading/Analysis

In a close reading you give a detailed reading of an individual text analyzing all its parts with a particular focus on its formal and thematic elements. If you are giving a close reading of a mountain, for example, you must give as much detail as possible about the mountain—its name, history, size, height, climate, relationship to indigenous groups, wildlife, flora, fauna, and number of visitors.

In literary studies, this is called an "explication," and it's a popular assignment for unpacking a poem. In an explication, the writer explains the poem line by line, paying attention to rhythm, sound, symbolism, tone, and so on. Natural texts have a similar kind of grammar.

When writing about nature, you do something similar—you read and analyze. What do we mean by "read" and "analyze"? You might start by describing the text at hand, performing an inventory of sorts. Then think about what these elements say about the text. What colors do you see? What kinds of trees? Flowers? Bugs? Birds? Are there paths? Telephone lines? Hikers? Snow? Rocks? Does the mountain feel more constructed than natural? Or vice versa?

To some degree, writing about these topics is like explaining a poem—there are no right answers, just good arguments. Make a good argument and support it with your observations.

Comparison/Contrast

One of our favorite kinds of essays to assign our own students is the comparison/ contrast. We like this because it lets the writer focus on two texts and explain one by way of the other. In terms of the natural world, you could compare a city park with a natural wildlife area. Or you could contrast a beach with a field. You can also compare and contrast differing environmental groups or policies. You could compare Greenpeace and the Sierra Club, for example. Or the Environmental Protection Agency (EPA) in America with the equivalent agency in a different country. Another interesting essay would be to compare/contrast two differing pieces of environmental writing—something by Rachel Carson and Edward Abbey for example.

As with many of the topics in this book, people's ideas about the environment have changed over the years. Now, most universities have Environmental Science or Environmental Studies programs. We have become more aware of environmental issues—and of threats to the natural world—and are altering our cars, machines, factories, and cities. Taking advantage of these changes could make for a fascinating essay. A particularly interesting approach might be to compare some sort of environmental policy from the 1970s with something from today.

The Review

In a review, writers tell readers whether they think something is of sufficient quality to see, play, visit, or consider and then give the reason for their opinions. Reviewers of natural or environmental texts face a few specific challenges, such as the familiarity a reader has with the text or genre. But there are always ways to mediate that. Here are some basic tips on writing a review.

You can review almost anything as long as you understand the specific thing you are reviewing, and you establish the criteria. For example, Cottonwood Canyon State Park in Oregon and Staunton State Park in Colorado just opened in 2013. A review of either park might include amenities, trails, interpretive signs, vistas, unusual flora and fauna—even a ranger station and gift shop. Is taxpayer money going to a good cause? Or, you could revisit a classic like the Grand Canyon, or hike the Appalachian Trail, or camp in Big Sur. You could write a review of the trip—did it meet your expectations? What were the high and low points? What, exactly, was the experience like?

Reviews often begin with detail from the text and move to an indication about how the reviewer feels about the text—the quality of the text (in this case a new beach or classic hike. A good reviewer gives context and basic information about the text itself, and then moves on to what one might call an extended reading of the text or texts.

The Persuasive/Argumentative Essay

We figure that most of your essays on this topic will be either appreciation essays (I love this meadow!) or persuasive essays (I hate that factory polluting our river!). The two are quite different but share a love and appreciation for some aspect of the natural world.

Persuasive essays are essays that try to persuade the reader to consider the writer's point of view. As writers, we may, in our heart of hearts, want to change people's minds, but it is very rare that reading one essay will change anyone's mind. However, we may be able to get them to consider our perspective, and in so doing, knock over the first domino. The best persuasive essays are those that offer a mix of ethos, pathos, and logos. Many writers make the mistake of only going for the logos (here are three reasons we must keep this tree) or the pathos (cutting down this tree will bring every child in our town to tears and also kill many beautiful birds). Somewhere in there is a mix of reason and emotion. Throw in some common sense for good measure.

OTHER ESSAY IDEAS

1. Write a paper in which you define nature. Then show why a place readers may not expect to be "nature" actually is.

2. Write a poem about your favorite place in nature and then write an essay about the process of writing a poem about the image.

3. What is the relationship between nature and civilization? What associations do we have with each term? What is the relationship between nature and wilderness?

4. In what way is how we see the world affected by what we believe or what we know? How do our background, our beliefs, our interests, and our personality affect how we see nature and the environment? How does the political climate of our society affect how we see the environment?

5. Is it ever just to break the law to save some aspect of nature? Not long ago, students at the University of California at Berkeley staged a sit-in to protest cutting down an oak grove on campus to make way for an athletic training facility. Edward Abbey and groups like the Earth Liberation Front advocate eco-terrorism, such as tree-

spiking and arson to debilitate machines and agencies charged with what they see as
environmental destruction. Can natural law ever transcend civic law?

6. Write an essay in which you make an argument for nature as art.

7. Write an essay in which you demonstrate and explain how something in nature
    is worth saving. Or worth destroying.

8. Do you believe the EPA does enough or too much? Write an essay in which you
    critique or highlight two or three policies that are important to you.

9. Write a paper (using photos if possible) about the everyday beauty of a place
    familiar to you.

10. Write an argumentative essay in which you lay out and argue for a new environ-
    mental policy in your town or city. Should there be more recycling? Better water
    protection? More protected green space? No cars on smog days?

11. Write an essay about the relationship between nature and environment on your
    campus. How does your campus create different environments? How does your
    campus use nature to market its brand and create a sense of peace and tranquility?

RESOURCES

The resources for writing about nature and the environment are as diverse as—if not
more so than—the field itself. The best places to start are with Google searches and
with the reference desk of your libraries. If there is a professor at your institution who
teaches classes on your topic, ask him or her for advice on the best way to get started
or on what sources to consult. Experts in the field are always the best resource.

For websites that cover the environment, check out *Grist* and *Treehugger*; *Wired*
magazine often covers the technological impact on the environment.

Books

Here are a few books that might be useful in beginning your research (or for furthering
your interest in the topic).

Edward Abbey, *Desert Solitaire*. This classic explores the desert southwest and human
    impact on it.

Rachel Carson, *Silent Spring*. Probably the most famous of environmental books, *Silent Spring* details the negative effect of pesticides in the United States.

Mike Davis, *City of Quartz*. This book explores Los Angeles as an environment.

Elizabeth Kolbert, *Field Notes from a Catastrophe: Man, Nature, and Climate Change*. The reporter for the *New Yorker* explores climate change from a reporter's perspective.

Bill McKibben, *The End of Nature*. This book explores global warming and its effect on the environment.

Bill McKibben, ed., *American Earth: Environmental Writing Since Thoreau*. This anthology is a great collection of works written about the environment.

Michael Pollan, *The Botany of Desire: A Plant's-Eye View of the World*. This book explores a few plants, including the apple, and explains the intricacies of nature.

CHAPTER 15

READING AND WRITING ABOUT GENDER

"How could someone possibly *read* gender?" you might be asking. Isn't gender obvious? If you are looking at this introduction for the first time, we suspect this is what a lot of you are thinking right now. For many of you, details of gender are cut and dried, black and white, male and female. This chapter addresses gender as a text, and, as you will soon see, there are many other reasons why one might be interested in reading gender in a sophisticated way—as something *authored* or *constructed*.

Without question, gender has become one of the most hotly contested subjects in recent American culture, most recently with the #MeToo movement, but this issue is not new. The gender wars have been at the forefront of public debate for centuries. Ancient poets like Sappho and Greek plays like Aristophanes's *Lysistrata* explored issues of inequality between the genders long before Gloria Steinem, Hillary Clinton, Beyoncé, or Lena Dunham. More recently than Sappho or Aristophanes, an amazing Mexican nun named Sor Juana de la Cruz wrote poems and letters extolling the virtues of education for women, citing Biblical passages as examples for equality. And more than 200 years before Susan Faludi's *Backlash* (a controversial book appearing in 1992 that posited a backlash against feminist advances), Mary Wollstonecraft wrote an important and influential book entitled *A Vindication of the Rights of Woman*, in which she called for a recognition of women as "rational creatures" capable of the same intellectual and emotional proficiency as men. So while certain aspects of this chapter may feel new to you, in truth, people have been reading (and writing about) gender for centuries.

Still, perhaps it would be beneficial to talk about what we mean by the term "gender." When we use gender we refer to socially constructed behaviors and identity tags, such as "feminine" and "masculine." Gender should not be confused with "sex," which speaks only to biological differences between males and females. Sex, then, refers to biology, whereas gender refers to culture and society.

If you have read the chapters on movies or television, then you know that having the experience of reading a certain text is not the same as reading it well. Similarly, many of you have significant experience reading genders, but you may not have written about gender. This chapter in particular (and college in general) is designed to remedy that. On one hand, reading gender implies a kind of superficial determination of another person's sex. In some cultures, that used to be easier than it is now; in fact, it can be somewhat difficult to tell if a person is a man, a woman, or neither. One of the authors of this book regularly has students ask to be referred to using gender-neutral pronouns like "they."

Those of you with a soft spot for classic rock may remember a line from the long-haired Bob Seger who, in his song "On the Road Again," adopts the persona of someone making a critical remark about his own long hair: "Same old cliché / Is it a woman or a man?" This statement and the simple fact that we assume that we can tell if a person is male or female suggests that there are traits or cues that might tip us off about gender.

Using or reading these codes or behaviors is called "doing gender," and we all do gender at some point. Doing gender means participating in any behavior associated with a certain gender such as painting your nails, growing a beard, wearing high heels, earrings, makeup, neckties, and sports jerseys. In each of the previous examples, every one of you associated a certain trait with a certain gender. Did you link painting nails with men or wearing neckties with women? Probably not, but it is likely that most of you have seen a man sporting painted nails or a woman wearing a necktie. These people are playing with typical expectations of gender, and to some degree, we all do that a little bit. In fact, if, like us, you have lived in New York or San Francisco, where gender diversity is more common and more accepted, then you have likely encountered women sporting facial hair and men donning heels.

If there are external traits in a culture, then it is probable that there are assumed internal gender traits in a culture as well. Although these external indicators may seem minor, ultimately, as you have probably noticed by now, doing gender often translates into men doing dominance, and women doing submission. For instance, in America, most people tend to associate nurturing behavior with women and aggressive behavior with men. Similarly, women are assumed to be "dainty" while men are "rough"; women are "refined," whereas men are "brutish." But is this always the case? As you read this, you are probably thinking of some dainty guys you know and some brutish women. What's more, you should be able to identify specific moments in your own lives and in the lives of your parents, siblings, and close friends when they have, even for an instant, done something that you associated with another gender. The point is that we carry so many assumptions—many of them dangerous—about genders that we may discover that we have already interpreted gender before we have read and thought deeply about gender and genders.

Our goal in this chapter is to encourage you to rethink any preconceptions about and expectations of gender. Why do we expect women to be "emotional"? Why do we expect men to be "responsible"? Why is there societal pressure on women to be thin? Why are men not expected to wear makeup and shave their legs? Why is there no male equivalent for "slut"? Why are women not taught to see marriage as the end of a certain kind of independence the same way men are? Why are all of our presidents men?

Why are most kindergarten teachers women? Why are behaviors read as being "bossy" okay for men but culturally problematic for women? Why is there "mansplaining" and not "womansplaining"? Why is it uncommon for boys to play "groom" the way girls regularly play pretend wedding? These are puzzling phenomena that raise more questions than answers; however, what we do know is that learning to read gender as a text will help you make sense of the world and respect each other.

As we were finalizing copy edits for this chapter, the troubling news about Harvey Weinstein, Louis C.K., and other male celebrities harassing, groping, and objectifying women was a major news story. We seem to be entering a new era in which women feel more comfortable speaking out against men who abuse power. While this chapter cannot stop or even prevent inappropriate behavior, it can help educate readers about why respecting people of different genders is in everyone's best interest.

Social scientists remind us that gender is socially constructed, and therefore, in a way, we are recruited to gender. Consequently, society tends to punish those who don't conform to its gender roles. The goal of this chapter is to help you read the various means of recruitment; we want you to become savvy readers of the texts that encourage you to do gender.

While one's sex may be determined by biology, gender is constructed. What we mean by "constructed" is that gender is built, invented, created. Of course, while some gender traits might seem to be related to one's biological make-up, gender can still be constructed or "performed." We can think of these traits in both external and internal terms. For instance, our culture assigns certain behaviors or characteristics to maleness. These may include strength, rationality, virility, affluence, and stability. To send out cues that he possesses all these things, a man may bulk up, he may wear designer clothes and drive a sports car, he may watch and play a lot of sports, he may date a lot of women or men. However, what if the values our culture assigned to maleness were grace, refinement, monogamy, and nurturing? What if these traits were the most male traits? Would men still bulk up, watch football, go hunting, watch Rambo movies, and drive pick-ups? Some might, but most would not. Why? Because they would be ostracized and stigmatized, not seen as "real" men, according to society's expectations of masculine behavior.

Men who adhere to socially constructed codes of gender behavior have read the texts of maleness and America well—they know how to fit in. Just as external elements connote gender, so do internal elements. For instance, what if mainstream heterosexual female behavior were characterized by aggression, dominance, sexual assertiveness, and independence? Would women still wait for men to make the first move? Would women still link their sense of identity with men? Would women think of marriage in the same way? Would women feel differently about their bodies? Would women be afraid to beat their dates in bowling, or fear appearing smarter than their male partners? Maybe, but maybe not.

Without even knowing it, you are probably performing or doing gender in various aspects of your lives. There is not necessarily anything wrong with this; however, you should be aware that there can be negative implications, and we would encourage you to read your own gender and the genders of others with increased care and sensitivity.

Though we have talked mostly about gender in heterosexual terms, doing gender is not reserved for straight folks. Chances are, you are familiar with terms like "butch," "femme," and "queen." That these terms exist suggests how important gender constructs are to our identities, and they reveal how, even in same-sex relationships, we do gender. What's more, as many gay men and lesbians will confirm, gender is not tied to biology. Some gays and lesbians would argue that genders are, in fact, fluid. For many, having a penis does not prohibit someone from being or living as a woman, just as having breasts and a vagina does not prohibit many people from living as a man. Here, the distinction between "sex" and "gender" is critical. You may have your own assumptions about how gay men and women do gender, how trans and bi people do gender, just as you have expectations about how straight men and women do gender.

Our perceptions of gender can be influenced by a number of factors, including stereotypes, tradition, popular culture, and family. We are all aware of stereotypes surrounding gender: Women are better communicators, men are stronger; men like power tools, women like fashion. Without realizing it, you may make gendered assumptions about traits of women all the time. For instance, if you are in a grocery store, and you want to know the ingredients for a cake, who are you most likely to ask: a woman or a man? If someone tells you they have a wonderful new doctor, are you more likely to assume the physician is a man or a woman? If you hear that someone went on a shooting spree in a school, are you most likely to assume that person was male or female? Stereotypes are amazingly powerful, and we may not realize the degree to which our thoughts, beliefs, and actions are shaped by them.

Similarly, cultural and family traditions continue to affect how we see ourselves and other genders. We have a number of female and male friends who complain about how, after every holiday dinner, the men adjourn to the living room to watch football, while the women clear the tables and do the dishes. At that same dinner, it is likely that the father or grandfather carves the turkey or ham and leads the prayer. One might say that these are roles that both genders silently agree to; yet others might say that these behaviors reflect and inscribe a pattern suggesting that the important duties are reserved for men, while the menial tasks remain "women's work." Thus, we grow up not merely ascribing values to genders but linking the importance of specific genders to the importance our society places on the kind of duties we think of as female and male.

Equally persuasive is popular culture. How many of our preconceptions about gender come from billboards, television shows, advertisements, movies, and commercials? Research indicates that is it a significant proportion. For instance, psychologists and advertisers suggest that the average viewer believes about one in eight commercials she or he watches. That may not seem like a great deal, but over the course of eighteen or nineteen years, you have seen (and probably internalized) thousands of commercials, many of which have, no doubt, influenced your own views of gender. From rock and country music lyrics to commercials for cleaning products to NFL pregame shows to advertisements for jeans and tequila to television sitcoms to the infamous beer commercials, images of men and women doing gender flood us from all sides. Because of this, pop culture can fuse into stereotype, and tradition can meld into popular culture; at times, we may not know which comes from which. So many people conform to the expectations of gender roles that these roles appear natural or innate. We urge you to stop and think for a moment before assuming anything about gender.

Oddly, perhaps the most influential source for our gender roles comes from our own families. Before we are even aware of it, we see our mothers be feminine, and we see our fathers enact maleness. In fact, most agree that our early caretakers—whether it is our mothers, grandmothers, nannies, fathers, uncles, or siblings—provide for us the foundations of gender roles. What we see our fathers do, we think is what most men do, and more importantly, what men are supposed to do. As you get older, you will be shocked at how easily you slip into the same gender roles and gendered duties you observed your family engaging in for eighteen years. What's more, over time, these behaviors get coded, recoded, and coded again. Every time you see your father turn on the TV and not help clear the table, it sends messages about what men and women do and do not do. Similarly, every time you do see your father change a diaper or your mom fix a car, it sends other messages about what men and women can do. Most importantly, these behaviors can send subtle but powerful messages about what you can do. So, as you think about gender roles in your own life, consider how gender in your family is a complex but powerful text.

Feminism (or feminisms) can and should be supported by both men and women. Often we ask our students if they believe that women should be paid the same as men. They say yes. We ask them if they think men are inherently smarter than women. They say no—usually an emphatic no. We ask them if they believe that women should be afforded the same opportunities for employment as men. They all say yes. We ask them if they think that there should be equality between men and women. All claim there should. Yet, when we ask how many are feminists, virtually none raise their hands. This reality continues to be perplexing and frustrating. The authors of this book are straight men, and both of us identify as feminists—so why the resistance among students?

One reason may be the word "feminism," which is itself a text—a loaded text for that matter. There are any number of definitions of feminism, ranging from very open definitions (if you think men and women should be treated equally, then you are a feminist) to more forceful definitions, such as Barbara Smith's ("Feminism is the political theory and practice that struggles to free all women: women of color, working-class women, poor women, Jewish women, disabled women, lesbians, old women—as well as white, economically privileged, heterosexual women").[1] Some people think that a definition of feminism must be religiously conceived, since much discrimination has ties to religious conservatism (a feminist is a person who supports the theory that God the Mother is equal to God the Father). Though neither of the authors are women, both of us lean toward a definition of feminism that is broad enough to take in all interested parties. For us, feminism is the understanding that there has been an imbalance between how men and women have been treated, and that balance between genders must be restored. We also tend to believe that feminism implies more than a passing interest in bringing about this change; feminists must, on some level, act in a way that helps facilitate a more equitable balance. These actions might be as small as refraining from using sexist language or as large as protesting in front of the Capitol. Thus, we prefer the term "feminisms" because it acknowledges the fact that feminism is as individual as each individual.

For some reason, many students associate feminism with hating men, refusing to shave legs, being "bitchy," being militant, being strident, and, in general, being unlikable. None of these traits has ever been part of the mission of feminism. Rather, feminism as an idea, as an ideology, has always been about equality. In fact, there remains no single feminism but, as we've suggested, inclusive and intriguing feminisms. Instead of thinking of feminisms as exclusionary, it is more helpful and more accurate to think of feminisms as inclusive. And, like any text, feminism is always open to revision.

There is a double standard in America regarding men and women. You do not need a textbook to tell you this—most of you already know it. In fact, the 2016 presidential campaign and election brought many of these issues to the forefront, including sexual harassment and male privilege. In fact, at no time in American history were issues of gender and gender difference/discrimination more a part of the fabric of everyday life.

The double standard we saw during the campaign is one that we experience and live all the time. Most women would acknowledge that they feel a palpable pressure to be thin, sexually restrained, and well mannered, whereas American culture not only allows but also encourages males to be physically comfortable, sexually adventurous, and crass. That the concept of "manspreading" is only now getting talked about is a testament to this. Similarly, women who work in the corporate world have argued for decades that female behavior characterized as "bitchy," "cold," and calculating when enacted by women is praised and considered commanding, rational, and strategic when carried out by men. On the other hand, both men and women have suggested recently that cultural pressure on men to never be seen as vulnerable, to always be in control, in charge, and emotionally cool leaves little room for personal growth and fulfillment.

---

1   Rory Dicker, "How Do Barbara Smith and bell hooks Define Feminism? It's Not Just about Equality," *Alternet*, 22 Feb. 2016.

Even though America has evolved immensely in terms of gender equity, there remain dozens of unwritten or even unspoken codes that both men and women feel compelled to adhere to. Thus, how people of different genders act in the world has everything to do with cultural expectations placed on their genders. Moreover, when men and women do gender "properly"—that is, as society dictates they should—they make gender seem invariable and inevitable, which then seems to justify structural inequalities such as the pay gap, the lack of elected female politicians, or even good roles for women in theater, film, and television.

In short, issues of gender involve more than leaving the toilet seat up; they arise out of personal, public, private, and cultural worlds. We hope that this chapter will make you a more engaged reader of how gender gets enacted in each of these worlds.

Here are some things to think about as you transition from *reading* and reading about gender to *writing* about gender. Writing about gender utilizes many of the same interpretive and decoding strategies you use when reading things like movies, fashion, public and private space, and visual art. You are required to pay attention to what you notice but also, and perhaps more importantly, you are required to pay attention to what you think about and feel when you notice something.

- **Media:** How are men and women portrayed in television shows, movies, video games, and music videos? Do the media try to set the criteria for what is "male" and what is "female"? How do they do this? *Meet the Parents* gets a lot of mileage out of the Ben Stiller character being a male nurse named Gaylord Fokker. Even today, being a male nurse can be a source of humor (and yet the presence of Adam Scott as a nurse in *Knocked Up* gets no comment at all). Is that belittling to men or women or both? If you add his profession to the character's name, perhaps the end result is that a number of groups are being ridiculed.
- **Advertising:** How are women and men portrayed in magazine ads? Do advertisers tend to associate certain products or tasks with a specific gender? How do ads influence how we read gender roles?
- **Television:** Is there much variance in how men are portrayed on television? What kinds of shows are geared toward men? What about women? What kinds of activities do we see women engage in on television? Are gender roles related to stereotypes about race, class, and geography?
- **Movies:** Many actors and actresses bemoan the lack of good movie roles for women. Why is this the case? Can you think of many movies in which a younger man falls for an older woman? How often do women rescue men in movies? Why is male nudity so rare and female nudity so fetishized? How often are older women lead characters in Hollywood movies?

- Public space: How do we know that a place is geared toward men or women? What visual clues do we see?

- Fashion: Fashion includes clothes and shoes but also makeup, hair styles, jewelry, accessories (purses, briefcases, luggage), gadgets, and even tattoos. Oftentimes, a person might prefer gender-neutral clothing and shoes but opt for more traditionally feminine or masculine accessories. Why might this be?

- Music: This is a great era for women in music. M.I.A., Adele, Lady Gaga, Beyoncé, Nicki Minaj, Gwen Stefani, Taylor Swift, Pink, Rihanna, and even the controversial Miley Cyrus. What makes all of these singers interesting is how they work gender into their music. Each of these has been "read" through the lens of gender or sexuality or feminism. You might also consider gender in music by men. We all know about the history of misogyny in some rap and hip hop lyrics, but are there other lenses for writing about men and gender within the music industry?

- Workplace: In the last few years, pay inequity between men and women has been a major topic in the news. In 2010, for the first time in United States history, women outnumbered men on US payrolls. Yet there are very few women CEOs of major companies and, by comparison, fewer female vice-presidents in large companies. There are also disturbing trends of women not getting promoted because they are "bossy" or "hard to get along with"—two traits that have never held men back from getting promoted. Do we still expect different things from men and women at work?

- Education: Think about your professors. Do you have different expectations of your female and male professors? Traditionally, students have given female teachers and professors they find unattractive lower teaching evaluations in a way they do not for male teachers and professors they find unattractive. Similarly, students tend to complain more about female teachers who are demanding than about men. Why is this?

WRITING ABOUT GENDER: THE GENRES

The Idea/Observational Paper

In this kind of essay, you write about a phenomenon or trend you notice or are curious about. This might be anything from the growing tendency for culture to notice that females engage in upspeak and vocal fry to the (largely male) obsession with video games to the pressure for teenage girls and boys to sext or to a particular fashion trend among men or women. The idea/observational essay begins with your idea, and you back up your thesis both with observational data (what you see, the notes you take, what people tell you in interviews) and published research on the phenomenon. In this essay you not only document that something is happening, but you try to show *why* it is happening and what it *means*.

A QUICK GUIDE TO WRITING ABOUT GENDER

1. Ask questions: Our associations with gender are deep. Before starting, think of a question related to gender—do not just use gender as your lens. Locate it in time or within a particular part of culture. For example, if you are writing about gender in science fiction movies do not ask only "how is gender portrayed in science fiction movies?" Perhaps ask, "What does the way gender is portrayed in science fiction movies say about the way we visually construct gender in movies?" or "How does the way gender is portrayed in science fiction movies reflect current attitudes about gender?"

2. Take notes: Before you start writing your essay, you might take some notes in a journal or just talk into your phone. Our personal stances on gender can also be wildly contradictory. We might be totally cool with a female president but not cool at all with a female boss. Similarly, when watching a television show or movie or looking at advertisements, think about the associations we have with men, women, bodies, and brains. What do we expect of men's and women's brains? Bodies?

3. Do research: Writing about gender affords you a great opportunity to combine your own observations with objective research. Let's say you want to write about fashion trends on your campus. You not only can take notes about what you see students wearing, you can also look up statistics about who buys what, what kinds of styles are trending, and what kinds of comments about clothes you hear (or overhear).

For a more serious topic, you can also rely on research to help you explore a topic like date rape on college campuses or hate crimes against gay men or lesbians.

If you are a student on a campus with fraternities and sororities, those can often provide useful situations to document extreme behaviors at both gender poles. And, of course, there is a lot of research done on male and female behaviors in Greek organizations.

4. Think about definitions: If the paper is more observational or personal, think of how you are defining gender. Are you focusing on behavior? Attitudes? Is your paper more about biology or culture? Consider using a specialized dictionary or a textbook (rather than an online or traditional dictionary) to define it further.

5. Confront your fears: Writing about gender can force us to confront some uncomfortable ideas we hold very dear—ideas that are often rooted in religious beliefs. Good writing results from being fearless. Be willing to take on notions that might feel scary to you (or your parents).

Do not be afraid to write about feminism if your teacher wants a persuasive essay. But feminism has both simple and complex definitions, so it's best to define what you mean by feminism when you are writing about it.

6. Consider issues of race: Questions of gender don't always involve issues of race, but often they do. According to a 2013 report by the Center for American Progress, Latinas hold only 7.4 percent of college degrees earned by women, though they make up 16 percent of the female population.[2] Is this random? Probably not. Similarly, any careful reading of hip-hop music and culture must take into account gender roles and the representation of women in hip-hop songs. This also applies if you are studying country and western culture and music.

We talk more about this sensitive topic in the chapter on race, but it is fascinating to explore how gender roles are enforced, rewarded, and punished within racial and ethnic groups.

For example, we recently came across a fascinating article on how difficult it is for a man to get a job as a nurse. Why might this be? In 2015, two women graduated from the Army Ranger course for the first time. Why might this be?

The Reading-a-text Essay

This is the kind of essay most of us are used to writing. Here you might write about female characters in a novel, the representation of women in a movie or TV show, how women are portrayed in magazines like *Maxim* and *Men's Health*. Here, your focus is on a specific text, and you not only describe the features of the text but you make an argument about that text. For example, you may want to write about the new trend of strong women in prime-time television dramas like *Orange Is the New Black*, *Empire*, *The Good Wife*, *Scandal*, and *How to Get Away with Murder*. Or, perhaps you want to compare Daenerys Targaryen and Cersei Lannister from *Game of Thrones* (or Melisandre of Asshai and Brienne of Tarth). Or, let's say you are interested in writing about the representation of girls in teen movies. You might choose to do a comparison/ contrast of *Clueless* and *Mean Girls* or *G.B.F.* and *Dope*. Another interesting essay idea would be to *read* the images of men and women by a famous photographer like Herb Ritts, Annie Leibovitz, or Robert Mapplethorpe. Are there ways these images reinforce or undermine gender stereotypes?

A simple but fun exercise is to watch or read a recap of the red carpet part of a major award show like the Emmys, Oscars, or Grammys. Write down all of the nasty and nice comments about bodies, clothes, men and women. What do you notice?

Lastly, consider writing a detailed analysis of one text, like the Beyoncé video for "Lemonade" or "Formation." Talk about the lyrics, the images, the themes, the sound of the music, the fashion, the gender politics. Perhaps you can argue why it is an important feminist text.

The Personal Essay

A personal essay is a first-person account of something that has happened to you, a series of experiences, or an insight (or recurring insights) you have about a topic.

---

2   "Fact Sheet: The State of Latinas in the United States," *Center for American Progress*, www. americanprogress.org. Accessed 7 Dec. 2017.

Perhaps you were a cheerleader in high school, and you experienced a number of comments, behaviors, and interactions because of this. Your essay on a year of being a cheerleader would include specific details about events that led you to some sort of larger understanding about gender roles. The key thing is that your essay can't just be you recounting stories—it has to show some sort of transformation in your ideas about something. If you are a guy, you might write about the difficulties of always having to appear masculine or athletic when all you want to do is play *Dungeons & Dragons* or watch *Mythbusters*. We know several men who played sports in high school even though they didn't like sports but felt, as males, that they had to in order to be accepted.

Or, let's say you want to write about being male and gay but closeted. Perhaps you could write about all the ways you tried to perform traditional straight masculinity in order not to be found out. The key to these essays is to be specific and candid. You must also let your audience know what you learned along the way.

Another possibility is to write a personal essay about a text. For many women, the show *Girls* has been transformative. If this is the case for you, perhaps you could write a personal essay in which you give two or three examples of how the show has helped (and continues to help) you.

OTHER ESSAY IDEAS

1. Write a paper in which you examine and debunk three stereotypes about gender.

2. Few female celebrities are more in demand right now than Amy Schumer. Write an essay about how her show or stand-up routine takes on issues of gender.

3. Write a personal essay in which you examine three ways in which you "do gender." What do your means of doing gender say about you?

4. Write an argumentative essay about certain texts that you think are harmful in terms of how they perpetuate gender stereotypes.

5. Read a magazine that is aimed at another gender. If you are a woman, read *Maxim, Sports Illustrated, GQ, Details, Men's Health,* or *Field and Stream*; if you are a man, read *Cosmopolitan, Shape, Redbook, Ladies' Home Journal, Martha Stewart Living, Ms.,* or *Working Woman*. Write a paper in which you give a semiotic analysis of the magazine.

6. Write a paper on daytime television. What messages do the commercials and the programming send to women (and men) about women (and men)?

7. As this book goes to press, there is a proliferation of pro-anorexia sites on the internet. Write a paper that is a reading of anorexia and/or bulimia. Why does this disease affect mostly middle-class white women? Why do men rarely suffer from these ailments?

8. Give a semiotic reading of male/female dating. What roles are men and women supposed to play early in the dating process? What behavior is okay? What is forbidden? How do we know these rules?

9. Go to the room or the apartment of a friend of yours of a different gender. Give a semiotic reading of that person's room. How is it different from yours? How does your friend's room reflect his or her gender?

10. Give a reading of the gender dynamics in your household. What gender roles do your parents or stepparents fall into? Your siblings?

11. Write an essay in which you define masculinity. Who are contemporary role models for *your* brand of masculinity?

RESOURCES

Thankfully, the resources for exploring issues of gender are infinite. Your college or university will have statistics about male and female applications, graduation rates, distributions in majors, and perhaps even rates of employment and graduate school acceptance. Local non-profits will also have resources as will public libraries and even city halls. In fact, for some of you, there will be so much information in so many different places, you may not know where to begin.

A good place is the reference desk of your local or university library. They can almost always help get you started with the right databases, journals, books, and websites. You should also talk to your professor. She or he has done a lot of research to prepare for teaching this class, and it is possible they have some good ideas about how you can find sources to help support your essay.

We have found that popular magazines like *Cosmopolitan, Maxim, GQ, Women's Health, Style, O!, Men's Health, Entertainment Weekly, Rolling Stone, Us, Martha Stewart Living,* and *Ms.* are often good places to start. They can give you ideas and examples. Next will probably be more academic journals like *Signs, Personality and Social Psychology, American Journal of Sociology, Gender Issues, Journal of Social Issues, Journal of Cultural Diversity,* and many others.

CHAPTER 16

READING AND WRITING ABOUT FASHION

True or false: One of the authors of this book was voted "Best Dressed" during his senior year of high school.

If you guessed false, you would be incorrect. One of us was, in fact, named "Best Dressed." But what did (and does) that mean? Is dressing a competition? What were the criteria? Some people care about being perceived as dressing well, and others do not. And dressing well is so dependent on time and context; would the co-author win best dressed *now* with that garb from Oklahoma in the 1980s?

The way trends change over time and the expectations our potential audiences might have shape every interaction we have with fashion. In fact, if you had trouble deciding what to wear this morning, that frustrating process might just lead to a great essay. To be sure, when we think about putting on clothes—when we stare at the closet or imagine wearing a certain shirt with a certain pair of pants—we are *composing* ourselves as a text. We hesitate, we imagine, we compose and recompose ourselves. We try things on (a form of revising?), we embellish, we adjust our fashion grammar. We do this because we understand that we are going to be *read* by others. People will make judgments about us; they may even critique us. When we choose our fashion, we are, in a sense, authoring ourselves. A fascinating 2012 study conducted at Northwestern University revealed that the judgments we assign to clothes and professions send just as powerful messages to the wearer as to the audience.[1] Participants in this study were given the same white lab coats. One group was told they wore a painter's smock; another was told they were wearing a doctor's coat. Researchers found those wearing a doctor's coat paid more attention to detail and sustained longer focus. Thus, clothes can certainly say something *about* you, but according to this study, they can say things *to* you as well.

The term "fashion" has its roots in composition. "Fashion" comes from the Latin word *facere*, which means "to make." We use fashion as a verb in this sense, as in, "Medieval warriors would fashion weapons out of wood and metal." Here, "fashion"

---

1   Hajo Adam and Adam D. Galinsky, "Enclothed Cognition," *Journal of Experimental Social Psychology*, vol. 48, no. 4, July 2012, pp. 918–25.

means to make or build or put together. Over time, the verb form of the word morphed into a noun. Now, fashion is a word we use to "make" ourselves, to "put ourselves together." So the idea of writing about or interpreting fashion should feel fairly easy. Its own roots acknowledge the degree to which it is a genre of making.

For the purposes of this chapter, when we use the term fashion, we mean the prevailing style of clothing and other accessories. In terms of personal fashion, it is the habitual or distinctive way one dresses, wears makeup, styles one's hair, and wears jewelry. We are interested in fashion as a text—as something that sends messages that can be decoded—and therefore written about.

You can control what you wear, but you can't control how you are read. Clothes go beyond merely keeping us warm or covering us up. They are one of the ways we create identity. What's more, fashion is a way we communicate aspects of our identity to the public without having to say anything. For many, though, fashion is more than mere clothing or even mere communication; it is a form of status. If you've ever watched the red carpet component of the Oscars or Emmys, you know how important the fashion statements can be. Commentators ask who Beyoncé is wearing or who designed Jennifer Lawrence's necklace. Recently, the Carolina Panthers quarterback Cam Newton made headlines for wearing $850 Versace zebra print pants when he exited the plane in San Francisco for Super Bowl 50. Why do we care what a professional athlete wears when he travels? What are the pants supposed to say about Newton? Football players? African American men?

These questions then lead us to other questions. What do we wear on a first date? What do we wear to a fancy dinner? What kinds of jeans or dresses send the "wrong" messages? What *are* the wrong messages? Why do country clubs not allow jeans? What is at stake if I wear a hoodie?

Clothes say something about us, whether we like it or not. The problem with fashion is that the wearer of the clothes might have one thing in mind, and people sitting next to you on the bus or in class might have a very different idea about what you are wearing and what it means. In other words, you can try to dress "neutrally," but neutrally does not read the same to everyone.

Throughout this book, we talk about the power of semiotics. In case you have not read Chapter 1, semiotics is the study of signs, and signs have two main components— the signifier and the signified. The *signifier* is the sign itself, like a stop sign; or in the case of fashion, an article of clothing like Cam Newton's pants. The *signified* is the message sent by the sign.

Now, here is where things get tricky in regard to semiotics and fashion. We all know the signified of a stop sign. It means "stop." We all know the signified of the recycling logo or the McDonald's golden arches. We know what these things mean because there is a direct connection between the signified and the signifier. In other words, we know the *intention* of the sign. With fashion, there is often a gap between the intention of the fashion object and the reception of the fashion object. By reception we mean how the object is received or interpreted. For example, Cam Newton's pants were described as "insane" by *GQ* and interpreted by many to be a sign of confidence, but others thought the pants sent the opposite message because they suggested that Newton was trying too hard. Who knows what Newton's intent was—perhaps he just wanted some attention. What is interesting is how his signifiers (the pants) led to two utterly different signifieds (the message they sent). Fashion can communicate our social status (successfully or not), our political affiliations, our religious beliefs, our education levels, and even our cultural preferences. We might make very different assumptions about the same fashion item in two separate contexts.

For example, let's consider a John Deere trucker hat. That hat on a 25-year-old white farmer in rural Kansas will send a different message than the same hat on a 25-year-old white barista in San Francisco. We see this all the time. Cowboy boots at a fancy restaurant in downtown Dallas send a different message than cowboy boots at a hipster bar in Brooklyn. A woman wearing an army uniform on a military base might communicate one thing; the same woman wearing an army uniform at a party might communicate another. Someone wearing a Washington Redskins shirt at a pro football game might communicate one thing; someone wearing the same shirt on the Navajo reservation might be communicating another. A college woman who wears a T-shirt bearing the Greek letters of her sorority might be communicating dozens of different messages based on individual associations with that sorority. The sorority can control what their image embodies to a certain degree but not entirely—people have opinions about sororities outside of the control of the woman wearing the shirt—or, for that matter, the sorority itself.

No doubt you have experienced this yourself. How often have you experimented with different clothes than you normally wear in hopes of eliciting a certain kind of reaction, when in fact you sparked something totally different than you intended. Perhaps by wearing a pair of Chuck Taylors you thought you were being cool, when in fact some read your choice of tennis shoes as sloppy or underdressed. Perhaps there was a time when you wore a sleek dress and pearls to an event so people would see you as sophisticated, when in fact folks read your clothes and thought you were trying to be snobbish. There are few more uncomfortable feelings than being overdressed or underdressed. Our clothes often indicate to others how well we know and understand ourselves, our surroundings, and our contexts. They can also serve as an indication of how seriously we take an event at hand. Would the president wear a flannel shirt and jeans to a state dinner? Would Hillary Clinton hit the campaign trail wearing Juicy Couture sweatpants? Would you show up to a funeral in shorts and flip-flops? Maybe. But probably not.

Ultimately, fashion is a way for us to both express individuality *and* to fit in. It may seem a paradox to expect fashion to do both, but clothes have a rare function of being a necessity and a luxury. You need clothes to exist in a civilized society. To go into stores, attend class, do your job, visit a church, or swing by the DMV, you need to be wearing clothes. However, we don't have to all wear the same clothes all the time. Even if you have a uniform for school or work, at times you get to express yourself by way of your clothes. Problems can arise, though, based on different assumptions about fashion, gender, class, race, and politics.

Men and women both wear clothes, but for women fashion can be particularly complicated. Many women we know love clothes. They love shopping for clothes, they love trying on clothes, they love getting dressed up. We also know many women who hate shopping, hate dressing up, hate wearing uncomfortable garments, and simply want nothing to do with fashion or the fashion industry. In many areas, women in the latter group can be judged more harshly both by other women and by men. Despite our advances in gender equity, there is still a double standard when it comes to women and fashion. For example, there is no male equivalent for "dressing like a slut" or even "dressing like a prude"—terms we hear all too often.

Popular culture may have a lot to do with this double standard. We rarely see fathers in sitcoms or romantic comedies tell their sons who are about to go out on a date, "You are not leaving this house dressed like *that*!" But such exchanges are common for parents and daughters. Similarly, there are no fairy tales where young men are made to feel bad because they don't have nice clothes for the ball. On the other hand, we are bombarded by commercials where women fawn over shoes and purses. An astonishing percentage of the pages in major women's magazines like *Vogue* and *Cosmopolitan* are devoted to women's fashion (and, in fact, readers often treat those advertisements as content). Readers of publications like *People* and *Us* are asked in many issues which female celebrity wears an outfit best. Are Seth Rogen and Jonah Hill judged in this way? George Clooney and Brad Pitt? Even women whose position is outside of fashion like Hillary Clinton and Sarah Palin face constant scrutiny for their fashion. Recently, both Ivanka Trump and Melania Trump were critiqued and praised for the dresses they wore and the headscarves they did not wear when they visited the Middle East. Did Mike Pence receive such scrutiny? We doubt it.

In addition, the expectation for women to look sexy or thin or feminine puts a great deal of pressure on women to make fashion choices. You might find yourself making quick unconscious assumptions about someone based on what she is wearing. Our question would be—do you make similar assumptions about or judgments of men based on their clothes? Perhaps, but those assumptions tend to be economic or professional as opposed to moral. For example, in *Pretty Woman*, the Julia Roberts character suffers intense humiliation when trying to buy clothes at an exclusive Beverly Hills salon, despite the fact that she has a great deal of money to spend on clothes. Later in the movie, when she returns to the same boutique dressed like a Hollywood socialite, she gets to enact revenge on the women who refused to help her. It is a great moment in film where fashion = moral triumph.

Of course, there are fashion issues for males. Men can wear clothes that unintentionally make them look—to some—like a "thug" or a "gangster," but those connotations carry different value systems, which we will turn to now.

Fashion is also bound up with questions of race. If you think that fashion has no bearing on men, think about the loaded cultural significance at this moment in American history of the hoodie, especially African American males and the hoodie. In fact, Hillary Clinton said as much in 2015, "If we're honest, for a lot of well-meaning, open-minded, white people, the sight of a young black man in a hoodie, still evokes a twinge of fear." Clinton was not necessarily speaking about herself but was trying to capture a national anxiety about the semiotics of one article of clothing; nevertheless it is an astonishing statement in part because it suggests the power of fashion to be a symbol for racial bias.

But the hoodie is not the only incendiary item when it comes to race. Back in 2002, Abercrombie & Fitch had to recall thousands of T-shirts bearing a logo of a fake Chinese laundry company whose logo was "Two Wongs Can Make It White." If that were not problematic enough, the T-shirt also included racist representations of two Asians. Similarly, a disturbing trend has emerged recently where young white women are posting photos of themselves wearing Native American headdresses. For some reason, this gesture appears to be tied to music and music festivals, most notoriously by singer Ellie Goulding as well as singer Christina Fallin (who happens to be the daughter of Oklahoma governor Mary Fallin). Both women suffered intense criticism for appropriating something sacred for the purpose of fashion statement. Recently, during her halftime performance at Super Bowl 50, Beyoncé's decision to celebrate the fashion of female Black Panthers caused a firestorm of controversy. Of course, these are rather dramatic instances of the intersection of fashion and race, but smaller and less visible examples happen daily. T-shirts with confederate flags invite one reading; a woman wearing a burka invites another; a man wearing a Sikh turban invites yet another; a nun in a habit still another. While the wearers of these items may or may not be asking to have their fashion read through a particular lens, our culture and our own personal biases have endowed certain items of dress with cultural, religious, and racial significance. It all comes down to the signifier and the signified.

Brands can say a great deal about us. In contemporary fashion culture, few signifieds have more power than brands. Many of us know the logos for Polo, Lacoste, Prada, Louis Vuitton, Rolex, Hermes, and Seven for All Mankind. We also recognize the logo for brands from Target, The Gap, Old Navy, Dickies, Carhartt, and Levi's. While it is possible we gravitate toward these brands because we believe in their quality, research shows we choose our brands based on our interest in being affiliated with the values associated with those brands. Someone who wears Dickies and Ben Sherman work shirts is asking to be read differently than someone wearing Palace and Stone Island. Though Apple does not do fashion, someone wearing a T-shirt with the Apple logo is making a statement about his or her affiliation, and we might assume something different about that person than if we saw someone quite similar in a Microsoft T-shirt. The same holds true is you saw three people walking toward you, one of whom was wearing a Golden State Warriors jacket, the other a Los Pollos Hermanos shirt (from the television show *Breaking Bad*) and another a "Make America Great Again" hat. Which of the three would you be most likely to have something in common with? Let's turn the tables: would you be more likely to wear: a Céline Dion T-shirt, a Taylor Swift T-shirt, or a Sleater-Kinney shirt? If your blind date showed up wearing one of these, what would you assume? What if the person wearing the shirt was male?

Recently, brands have become particularly relevant for shoes. Just think about the associations you attach to Adidas, Birkenstock, Air Jordan, New Balance, Puma, Chuck Taylor, Toms, SAS, Manolo Blahnik, Doc Martens, or Tony Lama. Shoes are often more easily identifiable by way of brand than other articles of clothing. Choosing to wear Chuck Taylors with a suit or a dress sends some kind of message about you and your values. One would argue that you *want* to send that message by choosing to wear Chuck Taylors with your dress or Doc Martens with your tux. The nuances of that message will differ, perhaps, based on who is looking at and interpreting your wardrobe selection, but to be sure, brands and their symbology are increasingly powerful signifiers.

The logo—that small symbol a brand uses to indicate its identity—is one of the more interesting semiotic devices. The Izod alligator, the Dolce Gabana DG, the Polo man and horse, the Nike swoosh, the Louis Vuitton LV and little stars, the three Adidas leaves, the interlaced C's of Chanel, the forward and backward G's of Gucci, the red, white and blue rectangle of Tommy Hilfiger, Rolex's R and crown. These logos represent semiotics in its purest form. The LV of Louis Vuitton is the signifier, and the many associations or values that symbol evokes is the signified. Louis Vuitton relies on a fairly universal signified for their brand: luxury, quality, exclusiveness, affluence, good taste. Of course for others, luxury logos carry a different signified: exclusionary, capitalist, bourgeois, snobbish, a disregard for the poor, a greater interest in products than in helping others. Those associations may be fair or they may be unfair, but they are impossible to control completely. As we say throughout this book, signifiers float. They are not wholly stable. But that is what makes them (and their relation to fashion) so interesting to interpret.

Here are some things to think about as you write about fashion. Writing about fashion can be a lot like writing about literature. It has genres and characters and themes and style. Paying attention to details—how the micro feeds into the macro—is always important. Part of being a convincing writer about fashion is being able to use the terminology of the industry. Being aware of these terms and knowing how to use them will make your papers more specific, more authoritative, and more professional.

Function: What is the purpose of what the person is wearing? Is it supposed to keep the wearer warm or cool? Is it supposed to make the person look cool?

Form: What is the piece of clothing? What shape does it have?

Fabric: What is it made of? Does it make a difference when it comes to form or function?

Demographic: Is this item geared toward an age, gender, class, or race/ethnicity? How do you know?

Price: Is this item expensive? Is it supposed to look expensive? Inexpensive?

WRITING ABOUT FASHION: THE GENRES

There are a variety of genres in writing about fashion, including the review, the appreciation, the recap, and the overview, as well as more generic forms such as the analysis and the research paper. Over the years, fashion criticism has emerged as a popular form of writing in popular magazines like *Us* and *People*, but more scholarly forms of fashion research and writing are starting to take hold in universities and fashion/design circles. Like literary criticism, fashion criticism uses a combination of writerly observation, research, philosophical inquiry, and sociology to make sophisticated claims about fashion, directors, and genres. On the other end of the spectrum is the live blog and/or tweeting. Many celebrities have recently begun fashion blogs as a way to write about important trends. Sometimes, people write personal essays about fashion as well; photo essays and even video essays are very popular when it comes to writing about fashion.

The Review

In a review, writers tell readers whether they think something is of sufficient quality to buy and then give the reason for their opinions. Fashion is interesting in this regard because the costs involved can be significant. If you don't like a movie, a book, an album, or a burger, you've probably only paid $5 or $10. You might be cranky, but

A QUICK GUIDE TO WRITING ABOUT FASHION

1. Start where you are: One of the best ways to begin is to look at the fashion choices of your classmates or people on your hall or your friends on your team or in your fraternity or sorority. Do you notice fashion trends—or uniformities—at your college? What are they? Why do you think they have emerged? Sometimes the most revealing texts are those closest to you.

2. Ask questions: Before you take pen to paper or fingers to keyboard, make sure you are trying to answer a question by considering fashion. For example, if you are writing about shoes, narrow things down. Do you want to learn about athletic shoes? High heels? Boots? Once you land on a more specific topic, see if your essay can answer questions about that topic. Who wears boots? What do boots convey when worn by men? Women? What kinds of boots exist? You might also survey friends and classmates to see what they say about your topic.

3. Take notes: If you are writing about a fashion trend, it is good to have a mix of observation and research. Go to a cafe and write down what people who enter are wearing. Common public spaces like cafes, airports, the DMV, sporting events, church, and the mall are great places to take notes on fashion. Events like parties, dances, fancy dinners, weddings, and graduations are also great places because, chances are, people will choose specific clothes that are appropriate for that event. Do certain events tend to inspire certain kinds of clothes? Would you wear the same clothes to church and a party? Maybe, depending on the party, but maybe not. Why do you think this is?

Clothes in movies, television shows, music videos, interviews, and performances also can be wildly entertaining. Take good, detailed notes when you read fashion on television.

4. Brainstorm for a thesis: Even if you do not use your original thesis, it helps when writing a draft. Again, we like it when students use their essays to answer a question. Why are Uggs so popular with young women but not men? Why aren't there as many fashion options for men? Why do we wear clothes or shoes that are uncomfortable? Fifty years ago, everyone dressed up to travel; now it seems as though people dress down. Why? Why does fashion change? Why do things go out of style but then come back in?

5. Organize ideas by paragraph: If you have a first draft with definable paragraphs, the draft will be stronger and easier to revise. You can also use transitions to help connect your paragraphs and ideas.

the monetary loss is relatively minor. However, if you pay $200 for shoes or a purse or a sweater, and it's not good or is uncomfortable or falls apart or unravels, you may be downright angry. Also, people are different sizes and shapes, and sizing can vary depending on clothing manufacturers. Thus, fashion reviewers face a few specific challenges. Here are some tips to mediate those.

HOW TO START

Pick a fashion item or trend that bears visiting and revisiting. Read as much as you can and do surveys or interviews to get input from a variety of people. Everyone has an opinion about some aspect of fashion. Since your essay is probably, in some way, about semiotics, your paper will benefit from getting as many signifieds as you can.

HOW TO WRITE

Reviews often begin with a description of the item or the trend then move into an analysis. So, let's say you want to review the dress and shoe choices for the Best Actress nominees at the Oscars, you would start by describing what each nominee is wearing, and then, perhaps, include quotes from what others have said about the fashion choices before offering your own analysis and evaluation. Two things to remember: 1) include pictures and 2) include your reasons why a fashion choice is successful or unsuccessful.

If you are doing a very different kind of review, say, reviewing five new running shoes, then you have a different task. You must describe the pros and cons of each, how each feels, and weigh the benefits versus the cost. Here's what readers want to know from a review:

1. Whether an item is worth buying (or copying!).
2. What the review's definition of "good" or "successful" is.
3. Why does the shoe or purse or hat or fashion item succeed or fail? We want specifics.
4. Will readers like it?
5. What other fashion item yours resembles.

So a structure of a review might look like this:

1. Opening anecdote
2. Context of review
3. Backstory of item
4. Analysis of item with particular descriptions of important details
5. Comparisons to other similar items
6. Why or why not the reviewer thinks the item is worth seeking out in some way

Reviewers not only need to be competent in evaluating the work in question, but they also need to be entertaining. If you are not a funny writer, then be a concise and concrete one.

The Research Paper

Researching fashion requires context. One can do research on particular fashion items, but unless the dress or shoe or watch has been around a long time, there probably is not much writing about it and likely no scholarly work done on it. Therefore, researching fashion requires a context related to what you are studying *or* research on a general subject regarding fashion. An example of the first type of research might be reading an outfit through the lens of gender—say, expected work attire for women in business settings.

An example of the second type would be an article on feminism in 1970s fashion. The first focuses on understanding a particular context or setting; the second focuses on broader social issues, using fashion as cultural marker. In this example, you might write more broadly about four, five, six, or even seven fashion choices or icons. In other words, the first uses fashion as its primary text, while in the second feminism is as much under discussion as fashion.

Writing a research paper about fashion means you will have to come up with an angle or a lens; researching your topic without one will lead to a paper without an argument and likely without scholarly sources. But how do you come up with a lens? Let's dig down into the process. Let's say you want to write a paper on the history of the necktie. You would need to do a lot of research on how and why and where the tie began. You would need to provide many images showing the evolution of the tie. You might also interview people and ask them to talk about what a tie signifies and where and when a tie is most and least appropriate. We can imagine you compiling research, interviews, and your own observations into your essay.

Another research lens would be on the influence of a specific designer, say, Coco Chanel. Let's say the question you want your essay to answer is: "What are the major contributions Coco Chanel made to contemporary fashion?" How would you go about answering those questions? Well, there are no doubt books on Chanel, essays on her importance, perhaps even museum exhibitions. You might also interview designers, professors, and people who work in fashion, either in retail or otherwise. You might research what the governing trends were in that period; there has been scholarly work done on fashion trends over time.

Lastly, you might consider the lens of culture. A provocative and potentially important essay might be on a topic we mentioned earlier—the hoodie. What has the hoodie come to symbolize? It is certainly a loaded signifier with a number of different (but related) signifieds. Similarly, you might also write about fashion and representation, for example, the constant scrutiny of the fashion choices of women in politics, such as Michelle Obama and Hillary Clinton.

The Appreciation

The appreciation engages with why one likes a particular fashion item or icon. It reads the person or object, but in a way that stresses quality and uses criticism as a form of positive engagement. It might use as evidence awards won, the importance in popular culture, and the influence on later fashion. This form has been increasingly popular online, most notably in articles like "10 Fashion Tips You *Must* Try!" or "The Essential Items All Men Need" or "If You Buy Only One Pair of Shoes This Year...."

Live blogging/tweeting

A form of instant reviewing, live blogging or tweeting has become increasingly popular in fashion circles. This type of writing you are unlikely to do for a grade in class, but it might make for some good practice. You might blog or live tweet your response to fashion choices at the Grammys or on *The Bachelor*. You might try tweeting funny, snarky, or heartfelt reactions to what contestants wear on *The Voice* or certain runway shows.

The Personal Essay and Comparison/Contrast

The personal essay is written in the first person and basically explains in great detail why a certain topic is important to the writer. This kind of essay relies less on research and close reading of the text and more on the emotions, reactions, and impressions of the writer. Where an appreciation essay might focus on why *you* or *society* should consider a specific fashion topic, a personal essay is concerned with why the *writer* has a soft spot for something fashion-related.

What makes these sorts of essays interesting is three things: 1) a detailed description of meaningful elements of the object or the contributions, history and influence of a specific designer; 2) an approach and voice that is candid and relatable; and 3) very good writing. Let's say you absolutely love a leather jacket of yours, and you want to write about it. Its place as a fashion icon is less important than what it means to you, how it makes you feel, compliments you get, or the various things you've done while wearing it. In other words, the jacket is a window into *you*.

Another quite different approach is the comparison/contrast essay. In this type of essay, the author compares and/or contrasts two seemingly similar fashion trends, items, or designers. For example, you could compare and contrast the clothes of Donna Karan and Donatella Versace. Who are the designers creating for? How much do their clothes cost? Who buys them? What kinds of items do they make, specifically? Another option would be to compare/contrast the semiotics of similar items like Adidas and Nike. Who wears Adidas? What is their brand? Who wears Nike? You could also write about competing trends, like the popular but seemingly incompatible trends for men of the hipster and the lumberjack.

OTHER ESSAY IDEAS

1. The General Fashion Assignment

In this paper, read a fashion trend and write a paper analyzing some aspect of it. What do we mean by "read" and "analyze"? You might start by describing the trend, performing an inventory of sorts. Then think about what these elements say about the trend—say, chunky glasses. What conclusions can you draw about the work from the observations you have made? A fashion item has traditional elements of texts such as a narrative and symbolic language of one sort or another, as well as visual elements that contribute to fashion's meaning. A purse definitely has a form, style, structure, and even a message. Issues of utility, weight, usability, and convenience also some into play.

2. Look at Fashion

For this paper, notice the way the characters dress in a particular film or TV show. From what you know about fashion, what are the creators of the film trying to convey with their choices of fashion for their characters? *Hunger Games* is a good example, as is the original *Star Wars*. Are the film makers hoping to tie into prevailing opinions about the way certain groups (e.g., those of color, class, gender, and age) dress in providing clues on how we're supposed to understand these characters? What about something like *Game of Thrones*? Fashion is an important if strange element of the show's characters. Taken together, what conclusions can we draw from the fashion choices of the creators? The series *Empire* has received a great deal of attention for its focus on fashion. A great essay would be to read the various characters in the show through the lens of their clothes.

3. Analyze the Publications

Unlike many other aspects of American culture, fashion is still very much dependent on print publications. Big glossy magazines like *Vogue*, *Cosmopolitan*, *GQ*, *Elle*, *Harper's Bazaar*, *Marie Claire*, *Style Watch*, *Glamour*, and *InStyle*. An interesting essay would be to compare and contrast three different publications. Or pick two or three photo layouts in the magazine and write about what work the ads, the clothes, the models—the whole spread—are actually doing and communicating.

4. The Unintended vs. the Intended

Sometimes when people make fashion choices they are explicit about what they are trying to convey, like when they wear a tuxedo or their pajamas. Sometimes, however, we send messages with our clothing choices without knowing it. In the book, *You Are What You Wear: What Your Clothes Reveal About You*, psychologist Jennifer Baumgartner argues that our "external selves" (i.e., clothing choices) reflect our "internal selves." However, the values you attach to certain clothes might not be what others do. Your Chuck Taylors might, to you, signify "cool," "hip," "retro," and "comfort," but to someone else they could suggest "sloppy" or "too casual." But those are relatively minor. More serious issues arise when men wrongly assume something about women based on their clothes. These assumptions, of course, are based on larger stereotypes and double standards women face but men do not. All of this simply reinforces what we have been arguing throughout this chapter—clothes send messages.

5. Fashion and Economic Class

Anyone who has seen *Pretty Woman*, *Empire*, *Real Housewives of Beverly Hills*, *Sex in the City*, *Gossip Girl*, *The Bachelor*, or *The Bachelorette* knows that fashion is often an indicator of social and economic class. Sometimes, characters in these shows use brands as weapons against each other, as though a better bag or cooler jeans suggest more affluence, and by extension, more sophistication and class. If this topic interests you, we encourage you to explore this rich connection between fashion, branding, and class. You will be able to find psychological sources, examples in media and popular culture, articles in magazines, and personal anecdotes to help support your arguments.

6. Fashion and Religion

Recently, a Sikh man in a suburb of Chicago was beaten and called a terrorist—all because he was wearing a turban or *dastar*. Sikhs, who are not Muslims, wear turbans, ironically, as a symbol of justice and solidarity for the oppressed. However, post 9/11, the signifier of "turban" has, for some, taken on an entirely new signified. We all have associations with the collars of priests, the habits of nuns, the robes of preachers and bishops, and the garb of monks. We recognize yarmulkes, burkas, bindis, and crosses. While we don't think of religion and fashion as intertwined, it is interesting to reflect on how much religion relies on fashion to carry its value systems and communicate its existence. Classrooms—especially those at public colleges and universities—can sometimes be awkward places to have conversations about religion, but that might make writing about these issues even more rewarding.

7. Understand the Audience

Creators of fashion often target their lines to particular audiences—or their advertisers do—in order to see a greater return on their investment. Look at ads as well as the placement of stores, the font in the name, and even where they advertise, and see if you can determine what demographic they are appealing to. What do you think are some of the problems inherent in targeting a particular demographic?

8. Race and Ethnicity

For a long time, race and ethnicity have been an issue in fashion. Reading fashion through the lens of race can be a complicated process, but, we think, a rewarding one. Talk with your instructor about proceeding, and by all means avoid any trafficking in stereotypes, but do not be afraid to ask important questions about the ways fashion and race intersect.

9. Honor the Fashion Object

Write an essay on why you feel a specific fashion item like a shirt or a watch or a hat or a dress is "good." Your first step, of course, is defining what you mean by good." Does good mean comfortable, durable, sexy, professional, classy, washable? Be specific.

10. Disparage the Fashion Object

Write an essay on why you feel a certain object or trend is "bad," going through the same process as you did when you defined what "good" meant. A useful exercise is to write both positive and negative reviews. We tend to prefer terms like "successful" and "unsuccessful" rather than good or bad, as those tend to be easier to prove. In fashion, you often see terms like "fashion mistakes" or "fashion faux pas." This is a very popular genre, and you should have NO trouble finding plenty of material—maybe even from your own closet!

11. Follow the Character

Is there a celebrity or athlete or politician who you think makes excellent fashion choices? Write an essay in which you give examples of why this person is a fashion role model for you.

12. Media Journal

We want you to follow a fashion phenomenon you see in the media for the length of the course. A brief (two- or three-sentence) summary is fine but should not dominate the entry.

Additional Essays

1. What is the greatest fashion item ever created? Justify your choice.

2. Why are T-shirts with funny/obscene/provocative sayings so popular in America? Write an essay on T-shirts as personal philosophy.

3. Write about the relationship between fashion and music. What if Blake Shelton and Jay-Z swapped clothes for a concert? Lady Gaga and Adele? How do musicians communicate their values and aesthetics via fashion?

4. Write about sports uniforms. The Golden State Warriors have some really cool uniforms, including new ones with Chinese characters for Chinese New Year. How does fashion enter into the sports arena?

5. Write about fashion and gender identity. LGBTQ issues and the semiotics of fashion have a long and fascinating history. What does it mean to "cross dress"? What is threatened when people wear the "wrong" clothes?

6. Write a personal essay about a time when you wore something that made you *really* uncomfortable and totally *not* yourself. What was it? Why? Why can something as simple as different clothes so completely alter how you feel about yourself?

7. Write about a time when you had some sort of clothing disaster.

8. Write a comparison/contrast essay about fashion and national identity. How can clothes reflect national values?

9. Write an essay about fashion trends in different parts of the country—or even different parts of your city.

RESOURCES

Probably the best resources for fashion writing are the magazines we mention above. There are also a number of scholarly publications that include articles on fashion, like *Journal of Fashion Marketing and Management*, *Psychology and Marketing*, *International Journal of Consumer Studies*, *Journal of Retailing*, *Dress*, and *Fashion Theory*. There is also a helpful book called *Writing for the Fashion Business* by Kristen Swanson and Judith Everett, but it is, as its title suggests, primarily for people already in the fashion business. Some books to consider include *The Rise of Fashion: A Reader*, ed. Daniel Leonhand Purdy; Daniel Dellis Hill, *As Seen in Vogue: A Century of American Fashion in Advertising*; and Fred Davis, *Fashion, Culture, and Identity*.

CHAPTER 17

READING AND WRITING ABOUT VISUAL CULTURE

Let's begin with a quick overview of what we mean by visual culture. When we refer to visual culture we tend to mean any kind of text that is first and foremost *visual*. Primarily, visual culture comprises what we think of as art—paintings, sculpture, and photographs, though items like artistic installations or collages go in as well. In addition, there is public or street art, which tends to use walls or the sides of buildings rather than traditional canvases, like murals and graffiti. But the enormous umbrella of visual culture also covers video games, advertising, T-shirt designs, comics, YouTube, and even the visual component of smart phones and apps. In short, any medium that is primarily *visual* in its concept and design can be considered visual culture.

Traditionally, these texts make meaning through visual signs—colors, shapes, shadings, and lines—as opposed to making meaning with words or music. Like everything else we talk about in this book, visual culture is full of complex texts that you are encouraged and invited not simply to look at but to read. And, as we say elsewhere, the act of writing is fundamentally linked to the act of reading. Writing comes out of the process of interpretation; so even if you are not literally taking notes when you look at visual culture, the very process of trying to figure it out is (or can be) the beginning of writing.

Visual culture begins (but does not end) with art. In this chapter, we will talk a lot about art, as it remains one of the most important aspects of visual culture and the field you are most likely to talk about in college. When writing about art, keep in mind its universality and longevity. Long before there were written languages, there were visual ones. Ever since human beings could hold sticks and daub them in mud, there has been art. In caves in France, on cliffs in Utah, on tablets in the Middle East, on paper in the Orient, and on tombs in Egypt, men and women have been drawing pictures. If you have visited any of these places and seen these texts, you get a sense of the artist's overwhelming urge to represent the world—that is to represent or remake the world. That is really all art of any kind is—an individual's way of presenting the world in a new way. Vincent Van Gogh's sunflowers, Claude Monet's water lilies, Pablo Picasso's musicians, Georgia O'Keeffe's flowers, El Greco's Jesus, even Jackson Pollock's splatterings are attempts to make us experience some aspect of the world in a way we had not before.

For a variety of reasons, art resonates with us in ways other media do not and perhaps cannot. For one, we are visual creatures. We see millions of things every day and in so doing rely heavily on our sight. Visual artists take our enormous practice of seeing the world and use it to make us see something new. So in some regard, there is very little to learn. Artists use what you already use. All you have to do is get an idea of the few tools they use to make their art do what they want it to.

Test your first reactions, both emotionally and intellectually. Painting, photography, and street art often have definite advantages over poetry and fiction in that when you look at a piece of art, you don't immediately ask yourself what a certain tree symbolizes or what the blue rectangle is a metaphor for. Accordingly, you can approach reading visual culture in different ways. Instead of trying to figure out what an image means, try to pay attention to what the image evokes. What sort of reaction or response does the piece elicit? Is there a mood or tone? Does the painting or its colors create any particular emotion? Does the ad of the well-designed super-modern house create a sense of desire? You might also ask yourself how the image works with notions of beauty. Is the text conventional in its use of beauty, or does its creator challenge typical ideas of beauty?

If Hieronymus Bosch's *Garden of Earthly Delights* makes you uncomfortable, then the painting has succeeded as a rhetorical and semiotic text. If you thought Shepard Fairey's prints of Barack Obama were cool, then you got what he was going for. If you find Georgia O'Keeffe's paintings of flowers, pistils, and stamens strangely erotic, then you are probably experiencing the kind of reaction that she intended. Works like Picasso's *Guernica* might affect you emotionally first, then begin to move you on an intellectual level—or vice versa. Either way, artists use shapes, colors, scale, and tone to make you feel a certain way. Thus, you may be reading the text of the artwork on a subconscious level and not even know it.

Pay attention to the grammar or syntax of visual culture. Like written language, visual media has its own set of rules and structures. You don't have to know many of these terms or ideas to enjoy or understand art, but knowing some does help to decode individual artistic texts. For instance, let's look at the notion of composition. Chances are that you are in a composition course right now, and while artistic composition is slightly different, there are similarities. To compose means to put together or assemble. It comes from two Latin words: *com-*, which means "together," and *ponere*, which means to "place or to put down." Accordingly, composition means to place together. In this way, the composition of a photograph or advertisement resembles the composition of your essays: both are texts that have been assembled from various components (a word with the same origin).

So the composition of a work of art is the plan or placement of the various elements of the piece. Most of the time, a painting's composition is related to the principles of design, such as balance, color, rhythm, texture, emphasis, and proportion. The same can often be said of a particularly smart advertisement or web page. Murals and street art often rely on compositional rules to help images communicate with each other as well as with the surrounding buildings.

Let's say you are looking at Leonardo da Vinci's masterpiece *The Last Supper*. You might notice the symmetry or balance of the painting, how the table and the men are perfectly framed by the walls of the building, and how Jesus is framed in the very center of the piece by the open doorway. Placing Jesus in this position, lighting him from the back, gives him a certain emphasis the disciples lack. His red robe and his blue sash add to his stature, as does his posture. He looks as though he is offering a blessing, a gesture that underscores da Vinci's interpretation of Christ as a giver and a healer. Thus, how the artist places his subject (at the center) and how he depicts him (as offering both thanks and blessing) and how his subject is contrasted against the rest of the painting (in red and almost radiating light, power, and glory) is a kind of argument or thesis to the painting, just as you will create an argument or thesis for your own composition.

Taken all together, then, the various components of a painting or a photograph contribute to the piece's effect. This is true even for visual texts that may not seem like art. Look, for example, at the web page for Four Barrel Coffee in San Francisco (four-barrelcoffee.com) or Dot Zero Design out of Portland (dotzerodesign.com). In both instances, these sites play with very simple notions of composition for a dramatic effect. You might also pay close attention to how your favorite video games make arguments through their visuals, how ads and graphics evoke coolness, and even what effect the icons of your iPhone apps have on you.

How we see, evaluate, interpret, and write about visual culture is influenced by a number of forces. For a long time, there has been a rift between "high" and "low" art, and in that conflict a concept like visual culture arose. Some people believe that artists like Picasso, Claude Monet, Édouard Manet, Vincent van Gogh, Leonardo da Vinci, Michelangelo, Francisco Goya, Edgar Degas, and the like produce high art, whereas, say, Nagel prints, photos of cars, most outdoor murals, much folk or "primitive" art, digital images, cartoons, Hummel figurines, Precious Moments statuettes, and any mass-produced design is seen by many as "low" or populist art. For instance, we love the Dogs Playing Poker series (see Fig. 17a), but you are unlikely to see any of these paintings (despite how funny they are) in the Louvre, the Metropolitan Museum of Modern Art, or the Chicago Art Institute because they are considered blue collar or pedestrian or unsophisticated. That said, William Wegman's photos of dogs (Fig. 17b) *are* considered art. You can find calendars and postcards in the gift shops of most museums and the photos themselves on the walls.

FIGURE 17a: C.M. Coolidge, *A Friend In Need* (1903)

FIGURE 17b: William Wegman, *Jack Sprat* (1996)

Still, the question of why one is art and one is tacky remains. Both are color images of dogs at tables. What makes the Wegman piece art? (One reason might be that the Wegman dogs in a way are mocking the dogs playing poker. Of course, the dogs playing poker might be themselves mocking something else.) These kinds of questions are at the heart of the art world and continue to serve as cultural markers of education, sophistication, social class, and good taste. There are many, many people who would judge your sense of taste depending on which of these two images you think is the best art. Now, if you like the poker dogs better than the eating dogs, that's one thing, but if you argue that the poker dogs are better *art*, that is another matter altogether.

These issues come into play in provocative ways when we consider larger questions about visual culture, most notably issues of public art and street art. For some, graffiti is not art, but for others, it is a form of social communication. A tattooed body, a tagged building, a painted van can all be seen as artistic texts—as forms of visual culture—but they may not be taken seriously as art by certain members of the cultural elite and can even be seen as examples of defacement. Why are murals by Diego Rivera or Rigo 23 considered art but not André the Giant posters? Why are YouTube videos not taken as seriously as short films? Why are graphic novels rarely taught in universities the same way "regular" novels are?

Visual culture, as its name suggests, gives us insight into how our culture is thinking about visual texts. Like music, literature, and film, visual culture tells us about an era. It should come as no surprise that during the Middle Ages and the Renaissance, when the Catholic Church dominated the religious and political landscape of Europe, most of the paintings reflected Biblical themes. Similarly, during the Romantic period, large, dark, brooding, tumultuous paintings tended to mimic romantic characteristics that worked their way into both architecture and fiction. Even the earliest cave paintings and rock art focuses on themes important to the artists of the time—hunting, fishing, keeping warm, and invoking the gods. The belief that visual documents reflect the world in which they exist is called mimesis. Some people may argue that artistic movements such as Surrealism and Cubism were movements away from mimetic art because people like Marcel Duchamp, Georges Braque, Picasso, and Salvador Dali distorted reality in their work. However, if we consider that, at this time, most artists, writers, and thinkers found the early twentieth century to be a time of chaos, dis-order, violence, alienation, and fragmentation, then one can make a compelling argument that Picasso's and Braque's fissured pictorial landscapes reflected a fissured cultural and political landscape.

Currently, as our culture becomes more politically conscious, so too do visual texts. Andres Serrano has become famous for his photographs of guns, murdered corpses, and Ku Klux Klan members; Native American artist Jaune Quick-to-See Smith assembles journalism articles about violence toward American Indians, sports mascots from teams whose mascots are Indians, and icons of Indigenous stereotyping such as toy tomahawks and moccasins to call attention to Native representation; photographer Cindy Sherman did a series of disturbing photographs of mutilated female mannequins as a commentary on the violence toward and objectification of women; and Michael Ray Charles, an African American painter, has made a career out of augmenting representations of Sambo, a disturbing stereotype used to mock African Americans. Banksy, perhaps one of the most famous living artists, combines street art, messages about corporate culture, and the commodification of art in his pieces. In each of these situations, art crosses over from the aesthetic world and into the world of ethics, becoming not just artistic statements but political statements.

Who is Shigeru Miyamoto? For one group of readers, that name will draw a huge blank. For others, he is as important and influential as the Beatles, Martin Scorsese, Michael Jordan, Michael Jackson, or Steve Jobs. Miyamoto is arguably the most significant figure in video game design, having been responsible for *Donkey Kong, The Legend of Zelda, Mario, F-Zero, Star Fox*, a ton of Wii games and the basic design of aspects of Nintendo and Wii itself. In 2014, US sales of video games alone topped $15 billion, while box office receipts for movies hit around $10 billion domestically.[1] And yet, a name like Miyamoto is not nearly as well known as a similar artist or director or creator in a different field, probably because gaming is considered low or pop culture, which gatekeepers do not take as seriously as high art.

An interesting figure somewhere in the middle might be an influential fashion designer like Donna Karan, Vera Wang, or Coco Chanel. They are people who have designed items that have had huge impacts in fashion and have changed how women (and men) think about clothes, bodies, elegance, and utility. Are they artists? Designers? Capitalists? It is difficult to tease these distinctions out—clothes are culture, and we see them all day every day. One could argue that Calvin Klein or Ralph Lauren has impacted visual culture as much as any painter—maybe more.

We mentioned Fairey above because his posters of Barack Obama became national icons during the presidential campaign. It was a rare moment when someone with a street art background successfully entered into the world of high art and political culture, and it is worth asking how and why these images of this man struck a chord. When you write your paper, do not be afraid to consider all of the non-art forces that have shaped attitudes about your topic.

Often there is a gap between those who create art and visual culture and the society for which it is created. It is somewhat of a cliché by now, but what an artist finds appealing is not always what the public finds appealing. In 1989, three

---

[1]   Brian Schmidt, "Video Games Bigger Than the Movies? Don't Be So Certain ...," *GameSound.com*, 14 June 2015.

men—Jesse Helms (a Republican senator from North Carolina), the conservative politician and commentator Patrick Buchanan, and art critic Hilton Kramer—launched an all-out attack on *The Perfect Moment*, a traveling exhibit of photographs by Robert Mapplethorpe that was funded by the National Endowment for the Arts (which gets some of its money from tax dollars). Some of Mapplethorpe's photographs crossed the line of decency, according to those critics and others, because of their explicit homo-erotic themes and because two photographs were of naked children. What resulted was a long legal and cultural battle over pornography, public funding for the arts, morality, and artistic freedom.

Similarly, Andres Serrano's wildly controversial photograph *Piss Christ* nearly got the NEA shut down for good. The 1987 photograph of a crucifix dropped in urine angered so many people that it brought about the most thorough scrutiny of public financial support for the arts in American history.[2] But America is not the only battleground for art and culture. To this day, if you visit Picasso's famous painting *Guernica* in Madrid, you will likely be accosted by locals who will want to give you a revisionist reading of the painting, which still remains behind glass to protect it from vandalism.

Photography tends to draw more fire than other art forms because people do not always see photographs as texts but as a reflection of the actual world. Along these same lines, think about how public art can be. Paintings and photos hang on walls of hotels and libraries, and grace the walls of museums. We encourage our children to go to museums to get "enlightened." If what parents find at the museum disturbs them, then the public role of art often gets called into question.

Now, do we ever encourage our children to turn to video games to be enlightened? What about advertisements? One of the authors of this book lives in San Francisco, and his nine-year-old son is somewhat obsessed with determining the difference between "murals" and "graffiti." One approach is to try to figure out what the differences are; another is to figure out why it matters.

As readers of the world, be aware of the various forces that determine how we see art and how we see art's role in forging a vision of contemporary culture. In the case of public art (painting or sculpture that is in an outdoor public space as opposed to a private residence or museum), community standards can affect how a visual text is received. Public art like murals, memorials, and sculptures on public land are often funded by local taxpayer dollars. If residents do not agree either with the political message or the aesthetic design of art funded with their tax dollars, there can be big problems. However, this also happens on smaller scales. Most of you can think of an over-the-top Christmas decoration, a controversial poster, a questionable advertisement, an offensive sign, or a religiously divisive installation from your hometown that

---

2   Travis M. Andrews, "Behind the Right's Loathing of the NEA: Two 'Despicable' Exhibits Almost 30 Years Ago," *Washington Post*, 20 Mar. 2017.

got people all worked up. Good paper topics are those that enable you to write not just about the formal aspects of visual culture but social and political aspects as well.

We have probably all seen images, videos, postings, advertisements, and even T-shirts that cross the line of good taste. In fact, in an increasingly visual world, we are bombarded by visual texts. Our job as good readers is to tease out the signified from the signifier.

Contemporary visual culture deserves your attention. If you are like most people, you are totally confused by a great deal of contemporary art, which often seems like images that do not create meaning, but you are probably okay with contemporary design, graphics, and advertising. Why do you think this is?

What is important to recognize about recent visual culture is the audience's role in constructing the text. While artists and designers do create work that may reflect their perspective and their culture, they also rely on the viewer to bring to their work an idea about what the text is and how visual texts function. Frequently, viewers of modern art complain that they could have done the work themselves; they focus on craftsmanship. But the artist might argue that the conception of art and the discussion of what art is and what it means is what makes modern art so compelling, and being a good reader of modern and contemporary art can give you valuable insights into recent social, political, and artistic moments.

Consider how so-called high art and texts of popular and visual culture are similar. Increasingly, art museums are including things like furniture, fashion, blueprints, graphic design, industrial design, and street art in their collections. The distinction between art and not-art is becoming less and less important. Pieces like Claes Oldenburg's big funny sculptures of clothespins and erasers, Andy Goldsworthy's works made out of leaves, sticks, and his own saliva, and the street art of people like Jean-Michel Basquiat, Keith Haring, and Lee Quinones have radically altered even modern ideas about what art is. Street art in particular has exploded in the past ten years. For example, in 2001 IBM hired people in San Francisco and Chicago to paint the Linux symbol (a penguin) and a peace sign on sidewalks around town to promote Linux computer systems. Sony launched similar campaigns to draw attention to its PSP gaming system, and clothing designer Marc Ecko has praised street art as a valid form of creative expression. For your own assignments, think about what you think art should do and be. What is art? Such a definition essay may work well in addressing modern art.

Reproductions and technology have changed the role and impact of visual culture. One of our favorite books is *Ways of Seeing* by British writer John Berger. Based on a BBC television series, *Ways of Seeing* walks the reader through various ways we see the world. Berger's analysis ranges from looking at landscape to art to advertisements to fashion. For example, Berger makes a compelling argument about how women are posed and presented in modern ads. According to Berger, these seductive images are a reproduction of the way male artists would position the ideal woman in Renaissance and Enlightenment paintings. Notice, for example, how many early nude paintings feature women in unnatural and uncomfortable poses and how, quite often, they look directly at the viewer (assumed, at the time, to be male). Contemporary artist Cindy Sherman plays with this tradition in many of her photographs.

Another of Berger's more enduring observations involves what happens to a work of art when it is reproduced over and over and over again. For Berger, the ability to reproduce art—to put the *Mona Lisa* on T-shirts, to place Van Gogh paintings on coffee mugs, to make huge blow-up dolls of Edvard Munch's *The Scream*, to be able to hang a poster of Gustav Klimt's *The Kiss* in every residence hall in the United States—translates into the ability to change the meaning of that art based on how it is used.

For example, one of the most famous American paintings—perhaps the most famous American painting—is Grant Wood's *American Gothic* (Fig. 17c). You have likely seen an image of the painting hundreds of times, though you probably have never stood before the actual work of art. Indeed, even though the original hangs in the Chicago Art Institute, you don't have to travel to the Windy City to see *American Gothic*—you can just search the web.

But is double-clicking on a photo of *American Gothic* on Google really seeing *American Gothic*? You might be seeing a copy of the painting, but you're not seeing the *actual painting*. What is the painting made of? What are its dimensions? Thousands of people visit Chicago to see it every year; however, by the time they get there, they have probably been exposed to reproductions and alterations of the painting hundreds of times over the course of their lives. These issues make some wonder about the specialness or uniqueness of a work of art in the age of reproduction.

The famous German thinker Walter Benjamin first posed these questions in a remarkably influential essay called "The Work of Art in the Age of Mechanical Reproduction" (1936). According to Benjamin, even the best, most perfect reproduction lacks the original work's "presence in time and space, its unique existence at the place where it happens to be." For Benjamin, this raises important questions about authenticity, particularly in regard to photography's ability to print images over and over again. Can a photograph be a unique, original work of "art" if you can print hundreds of them? On the other hand, in the case of the OBEY images by Shepherd Fairey, their value, their commodity, relies on being reproduced over and over again.

One of Benjamin's most enduring arguments is that the mass reproduction of art changes how the masses respond to art. Or, put another way, the ability to reproduce famous paintings can turn high culture into popular culture. For instance, people who wear American Gothic ties might be honoring the painting, or they might see it as an ironic gesture. Twenty years ago, Gustav Klimt was a sort of fringe artist, but the proliferation of *The Kiss* has transformed him into another Monet or Degas or Picasso—

FIGURE 17c: Grant Wood, *American Gothic* (1930)

not because thousands were wowed by the painting while visiting the Österreichische Galerie Belvedere in Vienna—but because folks have been wowed by the reproduction of the painting they have seen on cards and posters around the world. In fact, the great irony is that most who love the image have never seen the original painting.

On one hand, this is great for art, artists, and museums. On the other hand, however, Berger and Benjamin argue that these instances of reproduction strip the original of its power (what Benjamin calls aura). For example, how does it change your regard for the "authentic" *American Gothic* when you see the images on the next page?

A quick Google image search for *American Gothic* returns dozens of hits for crazy versions of this classic image. Neither Berger nor Benjamin could have predicted the proliferation and alteration of artistic images in the digital age. What's more, computer programs like Photoshop make it easy to take Wood's painting in all sorts of directions. What makes these images funny is that they not only play on the original painting, they also play on the overuse of the original painting—proving Berger's and Benjamin's points. The repetitive use and overexposure of *American Gothic* has altered the meaning of the original painting, transforming it into a kind of icon to be parodied.

Even the images you see in this chapter are reproductions; in fact, they are reproductions of reproductions. And yet, the ability of our publisher, Broadview Press, to print these images relatively cheaply means you get to see dogs playing poker from the comfort of your dorm room, library, or favorite coffee shop.

Reading visual culture helps you see the world in new ways. When thinking about art, look at the perspective of the pieces in question. Has the artist made you see the world or nature or a person or an object differently? If so, how? Ask yourself how the artist has represented the world, that is, how has he or she re-presented the world? Why might an artist be interested in altering your perception of something? Perhaps because if you learn to see the world in a new way fairly often, then looking at the world will be a way of creating your own art.

AMERICAN GOTH

FIGURE 17d

FIGURE 17e

FIGURE 17f

FIGURE 17g

Often this is deliberate. While artists paints, sculpt, take photos, write, and so on for their own reasons, many if not most of them are trying to engage with the world as they see it. How they translate their internal visions of external ideas can have a profound effect on viewers. Even artists who paint abstract work (think paintings of squares, like Mark Rothko's) have this impulse. In fact, their impulse is often to have viewers do *more* work than representational painters, whose work resembles recognizable subjects.

Here are some things to think about as you write about visual culture. Writing about visual culture utilizes many of the same interpretive and decoding strategies you use when reading things like movies, fashion, public and private space, and architecture. You are required to pay attention to what you notice, but also, and perhaps more importantly, you are required to pay attention to what you think about and feel when you notice something.

- Theme: What are the major themes of the work? What is the artist trying to suggest?
- Technique: What techniques do the artist or designer use to get his or her message across? Why *these* techniques? Does a mural do different work than graphic design? If so, then perhaps the techniques are also appropriately different.
- Characters: What are we to make of the characters in the painting or photograph? What is their function? What is their race? Their social class? Are they like you? How?
- Setting: Where does the text take place? When is it set?
- Tensions and conflicts: What are the main conflicts of the text? What issues are at stake? What kinds of issues of identity is the artist working on in the text? Is there tension between the self and society in the text? How? Why? What is the agenda of the artist? Why does she or he want me to think a certain way?
- Market: Is the text you're examining designed first and foremost to make money or to incite action? Is it to be purchased or merely seen? This might distinguish a very expensive Michael Kors bag from a piece of street art.
- Technology: How does technology affect visual culture? Do we not take video game design seriously because it is a game to be played as opposed to a painting to be appreciated or a dress to be admired? With the proliferation of texting, even emojis have become important components of visual culture. What can and do they communicate?

WRITING ABOUT VISUAL CULTURE: THE GENRES

One of the many good things about writing essays on visual culture is the incredible diversity of types of papers you can write. One of the bad things is the incredible diver-

A QUICK GUIDE TO WRITING ABOUT VISUAL CULTURE

1. Take notes: Make sure if you are going to a museum that you take a notebook or pad. Carefully note the name of the work and the artist. If you take interpretive information from the artwork, write down the source. If you do not know the source, write down the name of the museum.

2. Document: If you can take a photograph of the text, do so (many museums do not allow photographs, but some do—ask). If not, outline the work on your pad. If it is a mural, poster, article of clothing or game, you should be able to take a photo with no problem.

3. Feel: Note your initial and final emotional responses to the text. Visual culture often hits us emotionally before we register it intellectually.

4. Consider but don't rely too heavily on intention: When we talk about intention, we refer to what the author, painter, or designer *intends* to do—what her aim for the text is. Think about this and write down, at least in key words, what work you think the artist is doing. We authors think there is a relationship between what audience members see and what artists intend, and that understanding both is a good way of thinking about art of all kinds.

5. Look around you: If you are writing about public art, note the surroundings. Does the text fit with the surroundings? And vice versa? If you are looking at an ad in a magazine, what magazine is it?

6. Communicate: Think about what you would tell a friend about the piece of work you just viewed. Sometimes the most important thing jumps out when storytelling.

7. Culture within culture: As with anything, you should consider the social, political, and economic issues surrounding your topic. The hoodie has become a very controversial article of clothing and as such a major text in visual culture. So have images of guns. So have altered images of Rosie the Riveter.

sity of types of papers you can write. Sometimes, students get so overwhelmed by all of the possibilities not only of topics but of paper possibilities they freeze up. Don't let that happen to you! Here are some likely forms of essays you might be expected to write.

Close Reading/Analysis

A close reading is pretty much what it sounds like. You give a detailed, specific reading of an individual text analyzing all its parts with a particular focus on its formal and thematic elements. If you are giving a close reading of an advertisement, say, as we do in our discussion of the Geico ad earlier in this book, you would explain the various aspects of the ad but also make claims for what argument the ad itself is trying to make.

A common assignment is to give a reading of a work of art like a painting or a sculpture or a mural. Again, you would write about formal details like the brushstrokes or colors of a painting, the materials and scale of a sculpture, the angles, swishes, and designs of a mural. You would then talk about how all of the formal details help contribute to the piece's overall theme. Any close reading combines the formal and the thematic.

In literary studies, this is called an explication, and it's a popular assignment for looking at a poem, where, traditionally, the writer explains the poem line-by-line, paying attention to rhythm, sound, symbolism, tone, and so on. Visual texts also have a kind of grammar, like a poem, and are often incredibly rich texts for close readings.

For a visual culture text, you do something similar—you read and analyze. What do we mean by "read" and "analyze"? You might start by describing the text at hand, performing an inventory of sorts. Then think about what these elements say about the text. What conclusions can you draw about the work from the observations you have made? A painting has traditional elements such as color, composition, and scale as well as something like a message or theme. A video game is often judged by its realism and the quality of the graphics as well as how complex it becomes as users get more fluent. Similarly, fashion has its own terms as rubrics. Whatever your text, pay close attention to how it is put together and to what gives your text its specialness.

Comparison/Contrast

One of our favorite kinds of essays to assign our own students is the comparison/contrast. We like this because it lets the writer focus on two texts and explain one by way of the other. Often, if we are writing about one image, like the André the Giant OBEY image, we don't always know what to compare it to or what exactly to say about it. But if we have a partner image, like the Fairey Obama image, then we have a *specific* and known point of comparison. We can say X does this and Y does this. We can consider the artist's intention, the reason behind the making of the image, where and how the image was originally revealed, and even cite what experts have said about the image.

Another interesting topic along these lines would be to compare street art with graffiti. What makes one art and another graffiti? Or perhaps you could compare/contrast logos from past and present presidential candidates. Maybe you could write about the logos/mascots of three major sports teams—especially ones that are controversial, like the Redskins, Braves, and Indians. Lastly, a great topic would be to compare the fashion choices of first ladies from the 1960s, 1980s, and 2000s, noting the differences but also how the differences reflected changes in society.

The Review

In a review, writers tell readers whether they think something is of sufficient quality to see, play, visit, or consider and then give the reason for their opinions. Reviewers of visual culture texts face a few specific challenges, like the degree of familiarity a reader has with the text or genre. But there are always ways to mediate that.

First, you choose your text—pick a video game, a fashion piece, or a work of art you can look at more than once. Then figure out your criteria: what makes a good video game (fashion piece, and so on)? Then engage the text. Take notes—sometimes impressions will be enough. If you are in a museum, write down what you see and hear. If you are outside writing about street art do the same and also describe your surroundings. If you are reviewing a game, what are your friends saying about it also?

Reviews often begin with detail from the text and move to an indication about how the reviewer feels about the text—the quality of the technique, the quality of the graphics and design, the creativity of the composition. A good reviewer gives context and basic information about the text itself, and then moves on to what one might call an extended reading of the text or texts.

OTHER ESSAY IDEAS

1. Write a paper in which you define art. Then show why three paintings, photographs, murals, graphics, or sculptures meet your definition of art.

2. Write a poem about a cool image or fashion piece, and then write an essay about the process of writing a poem about the image.

3. What is the relationship between gender and art? Many of the most famous paintings, photographs, and sculptures are of nude women. How has art altered how men and women see the female body?

4. In what way is how we see the world affected by what we believe or what we know? How does our background, our beliefs, our interests, and our personality affect how we see art? How does the political climate of our society affect how we see art?

5. Google Diane Arbus and look at her photographs. Compare an Arbus photograph with a classic portrait like *Mona Lisa* or a Goya painting. How do they differ? Now look at some photos by Sally Mann and Andres Serrano. Is their work art? Why or why not?

6. Write an essay in which you make an argument for video games as a form of art.

7. Write an essay in which you demonstrate and explain how a work of art makes a political statement.

8. Do you believe that public funding for the arts should be cut if the public finds the art objectionable? Can the public, if it supports an exhibit with its tax dollars, censor a work of art?

9. Write an essay on the artistic situation for one of the texts. What cultural or societal forces may influence what or how an artist creates?

10. Write about a visual culture text through the lens of politics. Can a mural be political? Can clothes, fashion, or tattoos make social commentary?

11. Write an essay using old family photos as a point of departure. How hard is it to read texts from the past through the lens of the present?

12. Go to a local diner and take some photographs—candid photographs if possible. What stands out in the subjects?

13. Go to a library and look at some books of art and photography. How many of the photographs and paintings focus on everyday life? When does this become more prevalent? Why do you think that is so?

14. Write a paper (using photos if possible) about the everyday beauty of a place familiar to you.

15. Write a comparison/contrast essay in which you examine video games from the 1980s with some from today. What has changed?

RESOURCES

The resources for visual culture are as diverse—if not more so—as the field itself. To learn more about fashion, read popular and scholarly publications like *Elle*, *Fashion Theory*, *Fashion Digest*, *Menswear*, and *Vogue*. There are similar publications for art, video games, graphic design, technology, and advertising. The best places to start are with Google searches and with the reference desks of your libraries. If there is a professor at your institution who teaches classes on your topic, ask him or her for advice on the best way to get started or on what sources to consult. Experts in the field are always the best resource. There is also the Timeline of Art History sponsored by the Metropolitan Museum of Art.

Books

Sylvan Barnet, *A Short Guide to Writing about Art*. This classic helps us navigate the difficulties behind writing about visual art.

John Berger, *Ways of Seeing*. This is a book that focuses on understanding visual culture.

E.H. Gombrich, *The Story of Art*. This is one of the most well-known books about art history.

Scott McCloud, *Understanding Comics*. This book explains how comics work, for sure, but also is good at helping us understand how art is constructed more generally.

SAMPLE STUDENT ESSAY

Theresa George argues for reading graffiti through an inclusive lens in her essay for Professor Devon Holmes's Rhetoric and Composition class at the University of San Francisco.

The Multifaceted Nature of Street Art

THERESA GEORGE

"THESE MYSTERIOUS HEROES of wild communication, these spontaneous artists whose signs were volatile and abrupt, tough and angry, vehement and vital, created a great fresco ... irreverent and complicit, committed and contrary, implicated and distant, sentimental and caustic." Here, Lea Vergine, author of *Art on the Cutting Edge: A Guide to Contemporary Movements*, speaks of graffiti, a passionate form of art and expression that is rarely regarded as such. This unique art form provides a feeling of social belonging, literacy practice, and political and educational outreach for many of its creators. Unfortunately, a great number of city planners and criminologists have worked together in efforts to try to eliminate street art and in effect the stigmas that allegedly go along with it. The problem we must face is not how to control these spontaneous, and many times planned, events of artistic ability but how to approach each of these works as authentic and meaningful as they relate to their creators and their environments.

Just like many other socially accepted phenomena, street art can and does take many different forms, from innocent public displays of individuality to upscale alternative art. It takes on names of "tagging," "graffiti," and even "writing," all of which will be used synonymously in this paper to refer to street art for the sake of discussion. As Lea Vergine describes, graffiti includes "graphic-isms, graphemes, scratches, clashes, grazes, twistings and lacerations of the world or the surface on which they are applied" (215). She passionately declares that they are the "grapho-spasms of love" (215). Regrettably, the majority of graffiti's onlookers do not regard it with the same respect and admiration. What Vergine believes is "the painting of desire or wild communication" (215) is seen as "symbolic of the collapse of the [societal] system" (qtd. in Gladwell 183) by New York City subway director David Gunn. His remark surfaced amidst a citywide effort to eliminate graffiti from the subway stations and cars. Graffiti was believed to be a significant contributor to the high crime rate in New York City at the time. Criminologists James Q. Wilson and George Kelling advance the "Broken Windows theory":

> If a window is broken and left unrepaired, people walking by will conclude that no one cares and no one is in charge. Soon, more windows will be broken, and the sense of anarchy will spread ... relatively minor problems like graffiti ... are ... the equivalent of broken windows (Gladwell 182).

And with the birth of this sociological theory came swift yet diligent action to rid New York City of street art. Subway cars with graffiti were labeled "dirty cars" while those lacking any signs of life were clean cars (Gladwell 183). In effect, indication of any creativity or interpersonal memos from city dwellers was associated with filth and the undesirable. This is not, however, the correct representation street artists would like their art to be identified with. In photographing and assessing the street art in New York City, David Robinson states in the introduction of his book, *SoHo Walls: Beyond Graffiti*:

> Whereas the city establishment sponsored or at least tolerated community murals, it viewed graffiti as defacement and vandalism. For the writers themselves ... the graffiti created points of beauty and something positive amid the pervasive decay, desolation and brutal ugliness of their neighborhoods (6).

It is crucial for onlookers to understand that street art does not serve just one purpose or create only one reaction. It does more than merely exist on a wall for visual pleasure or disgust. Not only does graffiti create beauty for those living in hostile environments, it can be a source of educational outreach for those same inhabitants. Laurie MacGillivray, author of "Tagging as a Social Literacy Practice," explains,

> In vilifying the practice of tagging, society too easily overlooks its evolving symbol system and the complexities of the phenomenon. The public's misunderstanding is particularly relevant for ... teens from working-class backgrounds because of their historical academic underachievement.... (354)

The inaccessibility to canvases for artistic expression and other activities that middle- and upper-class adolescents usually have leads lower-class adolescents to the streets to utilize "public canvases" of walls and sidewalks. In this sense, graffiti holds special significance for their creators and their creators' communities. Many associate graffiti with gang communities since many violent gangs mark their territory with types of graffiti. But MacGillivray clarifies that there is a well-defined difference between gangs who tag to inform other gangs of their territory and those who tag because of the innocent desire to tag: "Taggers are not gang members ... tagging is a social practice. Tagging has its own rules and codes, it is a literacy practice imbued with intent and meaning" (354). This statement may be a shock to those who generally see street art as random, undisciplined, and meaningless. However random acts of graffiti may be, they are surely not undisciplined, as MacGillivray discovers when researching and interviewing taggers.

Just as subway directors and criminologists see graffiti as undesirable, street artists see poor and meaningless art or tags as extremely unwanted as well. It is of great significance to the street art community that every piece of writing on walls, sidewalks, or subways possesses meaning and signs of talent. In interviewing taggers educated on the subject, MacGillivray finds, "While anyone can participate in tagging, it is only those who display talent that are valued in the tagging culture" (363). She cites that one tagger even stated, "if individuals are not talented, they should not engage in tagging" (363). MacGillivray continues on with this idea: "Most of our participants talked with disdain of those who tag poorly and explained that it hurts the reputation of taggers as artists" (363). This attitude towards their way of life illustrates the "social responsibility and non-elitism advocated by most graffiti artists" that Robinson experienced while photographing their work (Robinson 8). In assessing the artists' system of tagging MacGillivray expands on this idea of responsibility within their community: "In choosing the nature of their message and deciding on placement, taggers displayed sophisticated decision making which parallels the values of conventional writers" (367). This recognition of street artists as comparable to "conventional writers" qualifies them for a place in society far beyond what the average onlooker would imagine. Perhaps if more people were aware and understanding of the codes of conduct that exist within the graffiti community, as does exist with mural communities, then street art might be more welcomed and perhaps respected.

There are many similarities between murals—communal art completed on public spaces by a group of people with permission—and graffiti. Malcolm Miles, author of *Art, Space and the City: Public Art and Urban Futures*, even categorized graffiti as "unofficial street murals" (206). Of his observations, Robinson adds, "The motives of graffiti writers seem to have been similar to those of the community muralists: self-assertion, pride and self-expression" (6). These comments are quite foreign to the paradigm of public art that Jane Golden, author of *Philadelphia Murals and the Stories They Tell* and an active member of the Philadelphia Anti-Graffiti Network, accepts. Her value of murals stands high above her regard for graffiti and tagging. She has the following admirable remarks to say about murals in the preface of her book: "Murals work on a symbolic level, providing opportunities for communities to express important concerns, values, and aspirations ..." (2). In the foreword of Golden's book, Timothy W. Drescher states that "murals express community, but they also help create it ... sometimes designing and producing a local mural begins a process of social connections and political activism that previously did not exist" (8–9). However distinct Golden and Drescher may find their observations of murals to be from that of graffiti, let's recall and compare comments made by Laurie MacGillivray in assessing the purposes and consequences of tagging:

> Tagging ... can be conceived of as a local literacy practice and as an avenue into the construction of youth identity and group affiliation ... [it is able] to sustain social relationships; it is a form of dialogue and conversation.... Another purpose of tagging can be to provide commentary on larger social issues (355, 360, 362).

The word use of Golden and Drescher ("community," "values," "concerns," and "social connections") to describe murals closely identifies with that of MacGillivray in regard to graffiti ("identity," "group affiliation," "social issues," and "social relationships"). Most appropriately in this sense and for the respect of varying ways of expression in our culture, the two should be regarded with similar, if not the same, value. It appears here that street art provides just as much community building and strengthening as does mural creation. Onlookers, sociologists, and criminologists must not forget the crucial value that street art holds for those who have little if nothing else in their lives.

As stated above, graffiti can be a means of expressing views on larger social issues when no other means is available, especially to young adults with low-income and undereducated backgrounds. Graffiti is the result of "an individual event [that] takes place in response to the social relationships with the expectations and norms of others" (MacGillivray 367). This unique style of communication between people of limiting backgrounds developed from "a need to express shared urban experiences" (MacGillivray 357) as well as to educate each other on social and world events. Images that MacGillivray came across in her observations included genuine reactions to political occurrences such as the recent bombings in Iraq and the "negative effects of corporate-sponsored deforestation on the environment" (362). It is an amazing ability of young urban dwellers to communicate such information to each other and to the public when the common means of obtaining it are generally inaccessible to them. Joe Austin, author of *Taking the Train: How Graffiti Art Became an Urban Crisis in New York City*, believes graffiti's development follows one of several pathways by which young people's political education became transformed ... demonstrating some of the ways that youth cultures have continued to create and appropriate cultural and physical spaces of relative autonomy (270).

Rather than seeing graffiti as dirty and representative of a lack of education and discipline, it should be viewed as the collective experiences, desires, and desperation for communication between city dwellers and their peers. Whether or not these progressive feelings towards graffiti infiltrate the mainstream way of thought, graffiti will remain active: "In all likelihood the ... effort will continue, undertaken by individual artists outside the mainstream who want to express themselves, make a point and provoke others while claiming their own freedom" (Robinson 15). The freedom to express oneself or one's experiences in an artistic way is highly respected in the United States; it is only just that this freedom be granted to persons of all ages, education level, and socioeconomic backgrounds.

Among the profound purposes of street art such as political and education outreach lies an aesthetic purpose—the expression of the organic nature of art. While David Robinson photographed the art-covered walls of SoHo, New York City, he discovered an intense nature possessed by graffiti that he had not expected:

> Art was in the SoHo air, its energy palpable, spilling out of the lofts onto the streets—and onto the walls.... I found the "public galleries," out on the streets, just as compelling as the art displayed indoors ... the art ... was organic, not restricted to white walls and neutral space (8, 5).

His experiences with the art in New York City were so powerful that he compared the essence of the art on the walls to that of Abstract Expressionism. There are even many art critics who see graffiti as a form of modern art, hence its presence in numerous galleries around the world, including the famous Museum of Modern Art in New York City.

If the great importance of graffiti art to the art community can be recognized by the prestigious taste of famous galleries, then the public too can recognize its societal, educational, and political importance to the communities that create it. From literacy practice to social belonging, street art serves multiple essential purposes to its creators and their surrounding environments. Whether the public chooses to accept the messages that artists display on walls and subway cars or continues to refute their art as legitimate, street art will not relinquish its existence. And as David Robinson so vehemently declares, "Their voices cannot be silenced, their creativity cannot be erased" (15).

Works Cited

Austin, Joe. *Taking the Train: How Graffiti Art Became an Urban Crisis in New York City.* New York: Columbia University Press, 2001.

Gladwell, Malcolm. "The Power of Context." *The Tipping Point: How Little Things Can Make a Big Difference.* N.p.: n.p., 2000. Rpt. in *The New Humanities Reader.* Ed. Richard E. Miller and Kurt Spellmeyer. 2nd ed. Boston: Houghton Mifflin Company, 2006. 178–195.

Golden, Jane, Robin Rice, and Monica Yant Kinney. *Philadelphia Murals and the Stories They Tell.* Philadelphia: Temple University Press, 2002.

MacGillivray, Laurie, and Margaret Sauceda Curwen. "Tagging as a Social Literacy Practice." *Journal of Adolescent and Adult Literacy* 50.5 (Feb. 2007): 354–369.

Miles, Malcolm. *Art, Space and the City: Public Art and Urban Futures.* New York: Routledge, 1997.

Robinson, David. *Soho Walls: Beyond Graffiti.* New York: Thames and Hudson Inc., 1990. 5–15.

Vergine, Lea. *Art on the Cutting Edge: A Guide to Contemporary Movements.* Milan: Skira, 1996.

CHAPTER 18

READING AND WRITING
ABOUT MOVIES

The contemporary American poet Louis Simpson writes in one of his poems: "Every American is a film critic."[1] He is probably right. Just about everyone we know loves movies, and as much as we love movies, we love talking about them. We freely disagree with movie reviewers and each other. André Maurois once quipped that in literature as in love, we are astonished by what others choose. That may be doubly so for movies. This makes writing about movies even more fun—you get to commit your good ideas and strong opinions to print.

Despite our familiarity with movies and our apparent willingness to serve as movie critics, we sometimes resist taking a more analytical approach to them. For many of us, movies are an escape from school or critical thinking. After a long day, many of us want to sit in front of a big screen and veg out for a couple of hours with a movie like *The Hunger Games* or *Twilight* or one of the X-Men flicks. Your authors confess that we have been known to veg out too, so we are not knocking the idea of losing oneself in front of a seemingly mindless action flick. However, we do want you to be aware of the fact that movies are never just mindless action flicks. They are always cultural texts, loaded with ideas about a particular culture, either consciously or unintentionally expressed.

For instance, some film and cultural critics have argued that despite the futuristic special effects, the original *Star Wars* created a sense of nostalgia for the value systems of the 1950s; values that by today's standards may seem racist, sexist, and blindly patriotic.[2] The diversity of the main characters of *The Force Awakens* and *Rogue One* might be attempts to correct these oversights for contemporary audiences. For others, the 1990s favorite *Fatal Attraction* is more than a suspenseful movie about a crazed psycho-killer boiling a bunny. Some see the film as an allegory on AIDS claiming the film reinforces the central fear of AIDS: If you sleep around, you risk death.[3] Still oth-

---

1   Laurence Goldstein, *The American Poet at the Movies: A Critical History* (U of Michigan P, 1994).
2   Chris Pandolfo, "Star Wars and Conservatism," *Conservative Review*, 6 Nov. 2015.
3   James Jasinski, *Sourcebook on Rhetoric* (Sage Publications, 2001) 7.

ers see the film as a document that confirms the backlash against women during the conservatism of the Reagan years.

In a much different vein, cultural critics and film historians have argued that genre movies like comedies, family melodramas, and gangster flicks tell stories about and support mainstream American values—the centrality of parenting, traditional hetero-sexual marriage, the necessity of law enforcement, and the security of suburbia. In fact, some film and cultural critics like Thomas Schatz and André Bazin have argued that classic Westerns like *The Searchers, Red River,* and *Broken Arrow* reflect an era's views on race, justice, and "American values."[4] In a smart review of *The Dark Knight,* Greg Barnhisel, a professor at Duquesne University, argues that the film essentially supported the mass surveillance of Americans as practiced by the Bush Administration. Many people disliked *Avatar* because they saw it as shameless propaganda for the environ-mentalist movement. Some African American and American Indian scholars have argued recently that America's obsession with zombie movies reflects our country's fear of being overtaken by "the other"—i.e., minorities. Could movies about alien invasions really be about our fear of being "invaded" by undocumented "aliens" from other countries? You may disagree with these particular readings, but they show how movies can be a rich source for cultural exploration and debate.

However, there are obstacles when writing about movies from a purely cultural perspective. In some ways, our familiarity with movies becomes a liability when trying to analyze them. Because you have seen so many movies, you may believe that you already know how to read them. In some ways, you do. As informal movie critics, you are geared toward analyzing the plot of a movie or determining whether a film text is realistic or funny or appropriately sad. And if asked about music, fashion, setting, and dialogue, you would likely be able to talk about these aspects of filmmaking. But when reading literature, you prepare your brain for a more intense act of analysis than you do when you watch *Sausage Party.* You probably have not been taught to look through the plot and dialogue of movies to see the film as a cultural text. Though at times difficult, the process is often rewarding.

For instance, pay attention to how many Arab Americans or Native Americans you see in contemporary movies and how they are represented. Watch for roles for strong, confident women. Look for movies in which poor or blue-collar people are treated not as a culture but as interesting individuals. See how many films are directed by women or minorities. Pay attention to product placements (that is, brand products such as soda cans, cereal, kinds of cars, or computers) in movies. Work on seeing cinematic texts as products, documents, and pieces of evidence from a culture. Rather than diminishing your enjoyment of movies, this added component of movie watching should enhance

---

4   For example, see Thomas Schatz, *Hollywood Genres: Formulas, Filmmaking, and the Studio System* (McGraw-Hill, 1981).

not only the actual film experience but also your understanding and appreciation of movies as produced, constructed texts. This approach is also absolutely critical when you begin to freewrite, outline, and construct your papers.

So, when writing about movies, try to keep a few of the following things in mind:

Like literature and music, movies are comprised of genres. Movies, perhaps even more than literature and music, rely on genres, such as Westerns, science fiction, comedy, drama, adventure, horror, documentaries, and romance. You may not think about film genres that often, but you probably prepare yourself for certain movies depending on the genre of that particular film. You come to comedies prepared to laugh; you arrive at horror movies prepared to be scared; you go to chick flicks expecting romance, passion, a video montage, and a happy ending. If you don't get these things in your movie experience, you will likely feel disappointed, as though the film didn't hold up its end of the bargain. Though they should be familiar with genre, many critics insist on reviewing all movies as if they are supposed to be as earnest and dramatic as *Manchester by the Sea* or *Titanic*, when movies like *Ghostbusters* or *Napoleon Dynamite* clearly try to do different things.

The idea of genre in movies is as old as film itself. In the early days of Hollywood, the studio system thrived on genre movies, and in fact, genre films were pretty much all that came out of Hollywood for several decades. Even today, blockbuster movies are most often genre pieces that adhere to the criteria of a particular genre. *Divergent* is not *Old School*; *The Fault in Our Stars* is not *It Follows*. Different genres evoke different emotions, and they comment on (and reinforce) different values.

Being aware of genres and their conventions will help you when it comes time to write a paper on movies. When you read a film, think about how it fits into a particular genre. Taking into account formal, thematic, and cultural forces (the Cold War, civil rights, Vietnam, feminism, the Great Depression, the economic pressure to turn a profit, and even the recent wars in Iran and Afghanistan, or the world after 9/11) will allow you to see movie production as a dynamic process of exchange between the movie industry and its audience. In your papers, be mindful of why we like certain genres and what these genres tell us about our culture and ourselves. The fact that some writers and critics distinguish between "movies" (cinema for popular consumption) and "films" (cinema that tries to transcend or explode popular genre formulations) suggests the degree to which genres influence how we write about movies.

Movies are a powerful cultural tool. A hundred years ago, people satisfied their cravings for action, suspense, and character development by reading books and serials; today, we go to the movies, or, more and more frequently, avoid the communal experience of the theater for the private experience of watching at home. Innovations like Netflix, TiVo, On Demand, and Amazon Prime have made watching movies at home (and writing about them!) even easier. And we are living in a visual age. In America, video and visual cultures have become the dominant modes of expression and communication, and learning to "read" these media with the same care, creativity, and critical acumen with which we read written texts is crucial for being a savvy viewer and writer. To better understand the phenomenon of movies, we need to contextualize the movie experience within American culture, asking in particular how thoroughly American movies affect (and reflect) American culture.

In addition, movies are not just indicators for American culture—they determine culture itself. Fashion, songs, modes of behavior, social and political views and gender and racial values are all underscored by movies. For instance, *Wayne's World* made Queen's "Bohemian Rhapsody" and phrases like "schwiing!" and "Party on, Garth" part of everyday American life. On a more complex level, many critics claim the 1967 movie *Guess Who's Coming to Dinner*, in which a wealthy white woman brings home her black fiancé, went a long way toward softening racial tensions in the 1960s and perhaps even helped make interracial marriage acceptable.[5]

We even define eras, movements, and emotions by movies—the 1960s is often symbolized by *Easy Rider*; the 1970s by *Saturday Night Fever* and *Star Wars*; the 1980s by movies like *Fast Times at Ridgemont High* and *Do the Right Thing*; the 1990s by *Titanic*, *Pulp Fiction* and *Forrest Gump*; the 2000s by the *Lord of the Rings* and Judd Apatow movies; the 2010s by *Hunger Games*, films of Marvel and DC Comics heroes, and perhaps *Black Panther*. Because more people see movies than read books, one could argue that the best documents of American popular culture are movies. Thus we tend to link the values and trends of certain eras with movies from those eras. Movies help us understand culture because they embody culture.

Movies also guide our behavior. In contemporary society, we often learn how to dress, how to talk, and even how to court and kiss someone, from the cinema. In fact, for many young people, their model for a date, a spouse, and a romantic moment all come from what they have seen in movies. In other words, influential models of behavior, aspects of their hopes and dreams, come not from life but from movies. So, as you read the following pieces, as you watch movies, and as you write your papers, ask yourself if you desire the things you desire because movies have planted those seeds in your heads.

The advertising and marketing of a movie affect how we view the film itself and how the studio views itself (and us). Next time you watch trailers, pay attention to how the film being advertised is presented to you. Be aware of how movies are

---

5   Glen Harris and Robert Brent Toplin, "*Guess Who's Coming to Dinner?* A Clash of Interpretations Regarding Stanley Kramer's Film on the Subject of Interracial Marriage," *Journal of Popular Culture*, vol. 40, no. 4, 2007, pp. 700–13.

packaged, how they are marketed, how actors talk about them in interviews. Whether you know it or not, you are being prepped for viewing the movie by all of these texts. Even independent films market themselves as similar to other (popular) independent movies. Marketing is selling, and studios fund, market, and release movies not so much to make the world a better place but primarily to make money (though directors and actors may have different motivations). Also, unlike a book publisher, a studio has likely paid tens of millions of dollars to make a movie, so it needs a lot of us to go see it. We might ask ourselves how these considerations affect not only the advertising but also the movie itself.

In addition, Hollywood studios rarely have your best interests at heart. This is not to say that studios want to make you an evil person, but moviemakers have only rarely seen themselves as educators. For instance, few studios fund documentaries—and the controversy over Disney/Miramax refusing to distribute Michael Moore's incendiary 2004 documentary *Fahrenheit 9/11* is a testament to this fact. Few studios seem eager to make movies about poets, painters, composers, or philosophers because they know that not many people will go to see them. Movie studios began as a financial enterprise; studios and the film industry grew as America and American capitalist ideals grew. Nowadays, the topics and subjects of movies have been largely market tested just like any other consumer product such as toys, soft drinks, and shoes.

Movies use various techniques to manipulate audiences. Manipulation is not necessarily a negative term when we talk about the manipulation of everyday objects, but when we move into the realm of emotions, manipulative texts become problematic. Film is such a wonderful medium because directors have so many tools at their disposal; however, it is relatively easy to use those tools to manipulate audiences. Directors employ music, lighting, special effects, and clever editing to help make their movies more power-ful. Music reinforces feelings of excitement (*Lord of the Rings*), fear (*Jaws*), romance (*Titanic*), tension (*Mad Max: Fury Road*), quirkiness (*Juno*), and mystery (*Arrival*). In the 40s and 50s, moviemakers often used lighting and filters to make women *appear* especially delicate or fragile. The famous film star from the 1930s and 1940s, Marlene Dietrich, would only be shot from one side and insisted on being illuminated with overhead lights. The first several minutes of *Citizen Kane*, widely considered the best American film ever made, are shot largely in the dark to help drive home the sense that the reporters are "in the dark" about media mogul Charles Foster Kane.

In movies like *Avatar*, *The Martian*, *Gravity*, *Arrival*, and *Inception*, special effects make the story we are watching seem less like light and shadow and more like reality. Even how a filmmaker places a camera affects how we view the film. The close-up, spookily lit shots of Anthony Hopkins's face in *Silence of the Lambs* make us feel as though Hannibal Lecter might eat *our* liver with some fava beans and a nice Chianti. Similarly, in many Westerns, the camera is placed at knee level, so that we are always looking up at the cowboy, reinforcing his stature as a hero. Director Orson Welles uses similar techniques in *Citizen Kane*. Alfred Hitchcock was a master of placing the camera in manipulative places. From *Psycho* to *Rear Window* to *Rope*, we see exactly what he wants us to see and how he wants us to see it. We see nothing more than what the camera films for us.

There are other forms of manipulation as well. Many people feel that Steven Spielberg's movies end with overly manipulative scenes that pluck at the heartstrings of the audience, forcing overdetermined emotions and over-the-top melodrama.[6] Such accusations are often leveled at teen romance flicks and so-called biopics because they make a person's life seem more maudlin, more heart-wrenching than it could possibly be.

Costumes, colors, sounds and sound effects, editing, and set design all contribute to how the movie comes to us. Sound and music are particularly effective. In *Star Wars*, for instance, each character has a specific musical profile—a kind of theme song—whose tone mirrors how you are supposed to feel about that character. You probably all remember the dark, deep foreboding music that always accompanies Darth Vader. Like music, the clothes a character wears tell us how to feel about that person. The clothes of Ryan Gosling or Will Smith in various movies probably reinforce gender expectations, as do those of Jennifer Lawrence and Scarlett Johansson. How a spaceship or a dark scary warehouse looks puts us in the mood so that the plot and action can move us. Savvy viewers of movies will be aware of the ways in which films try to manipulate them because, in so doing, they will be better able to read other forms of manipulation in their lives.

The best writers about movies—Anthony Lane, Ann Hornaday, David Denby, Stephanie Zacharek, Wesley Morris, and David Edelstein—always pay attention to these issues in their reviews. Lane in particular always reads movies on his own terms. He sees them as he wants to—never as the studio or the director tries to present them. Great movie writing comes from great movie reading.

Movies are not just about ideas and action, they are also about values. Next time you watch a Hollywood movie, consider the value system the movie supports. By "value system," we mean the values, priorities, and principles a movie advocates. For instance, although we liked the first *Legally Blonde* movie, we were shocked by how traditional the movie's ending was. While the entire movie demonstrates the ways in which the underappreciated female character gets the best of boys, law school colleagues, and professors—even her enemies in the courtroom—all of these very important successes take a back seat to the fact that, ultimately, she lands the hunky guy. It is as though all

6   Robert Dogherty, "The Legend of Steven Spielberg's 'Soft' Endings," *TheMovieNetwork.com*, 14 Oct. 2015.

of her accomplishments were important so that she could win the cute boy in the end. The ultimate message, then, is that what women accomplish on their own is fine, if that is of interest, but the real victory, the real triumph, is snagging the cute guy.

Similarly, many Hollywood movies advocate the importance of social class, as Michael Parenti points out in his now famous essay "Class and Virtue." Movies like *Maid in Manhattan*, *Pretty Woman*, *Trading Places*, *Clueless*, and *Project X* spend most of their energy figuring out ways for their characters to make a jump in social class. Even a movie like *Hunger Games* explores this theme. It is worth asking how many truly popular Hollywood movies are truly radical versus how many reinforce traditional, mainstream middle-class values. We are not suggesting traditional middle-class values are bad; rather, we urge you to consider the value system advocated by the most powerful cultural machinery in the country. For example, we have enjoyed recent movies like *Wonder Woman*, *Moana*, *Star Wars: Rogue One*, *The Force Awakens*, *Black Panther*, and the new *Ghostbusters*. We are also happy that *Moonlight* won the Academy Award for Best Picture in 2017. The controversy surrounding the botched announcement of the film at the ceremony, coupled with the lack of African American nominees over the past several years (see #OscarsSoWhite), underscores the importance of paying attention to values in film.

Our contention here is that a studio's or a country's value system directly affects the movies you see, the stars acting in the movie, the plot structures, and the ultimate messages these movies send. They also affect how you see your own life, as you may find yourself, without knowing it, comparing your own life to that of a movie character. Again, paying attention to these issues will make you a smarter watcher of movies and a better writer about them as well.

Here are some things to think about as you write about movies. Writing about movies can be a lot like writing about literature. They have genres and characters and themes and style. Paying attention to details—how the micro feeds into the macro—is always important. Part of being a convincing writer about movies is being able to use the terminology of film. Being aware of these terms and knowing how to use them will make your papers more specific, more authoritative, and more professional.

- **Camera angles and positioning:** How is the camera placed? Is it high, low, to the side? And how does it move? Is it a handheld camera, or is it stationary? How does it determine how you see the movie?
- **Lighting:** Light and shading are very important to movies. Are there shadows? Is the film shot during the day or mostly at night? How do shadows and light affect the movie and your experience of it?

- **Color and framing:** Often, directors try to give certain scenes an artistic feel. Is the shot framed similar to a painting or photograph? Does the movie use color to elicit emotions? How does the movie frame or represent nature?
- **Genre:** What genre are we watching? How do the writers let us know this? Music is often key here, as is lighting.
- **Characters:** Who are the characters? Do they represent something beyond actors in a plot? How do the writers want us to perceive them, and why? How would changing the characters change the film?
- **Setting:** What are the settings? What do they say about the movie? What do the writers want us to think about the setting? Could the film take place somewhere else and remain the same?
- **Plot:** What happens? Is the plot important to understanding/enjoying the movie?
- **Themes:** What do the movie's writers think about the issues/ideas/subjects they present? (Themes are what writers believe about issues, ideas, and subjects, *not* the ideas and issues themselves.)
- **Figurative language:** What symbols, metaphors, and motifs present themselves? What effect does their repetition have?
- **Visual constructions:** How do the writers make us see (or hear) what they want us to hear?
- **Absences:** What is missing? What real-world notions are not represented?
- **Conventional/nonconventional:** In what ways is the movie typical of its genre? Atypical?
- **Race/ethnicity/gender/class:** How are movies—intentionally or not—about issues of race, class, or gender? How do issues of race, class, and gender coincide with other categories we have mentioned, such as character, setting, plot, and theme?
- **Reality:** In what way does what is depicted in a particular movie or in general reflect the world as you normally experience it? What is different? Does this matter?
- **Tie-ins:** Increasingly, promotional tie-ins at McDonalds, Walmart, Target, and Starbucks are part of the movie experience. In what ways are movies commodities? Springboards to get you to spend even more money?

WRITING ABOUT MOVIES: THE GENRES

There are a variety of genres in writing about movies, including the review, the appreciation, the recap, the overview, as well as more generic forms such as the analysis and the research paper. Over the years, film criticism has emerged as an important and popular form of scholarly inquiry. Like literary criticism, film criticism and film theory uses a combination of writerly observation, research, philosophical inquiry, and sociology to make sophisticated claims about movies, directors, and genres. At the other end

A QUICK GUIDE TO WRITING ABOUT MOVIES

1. Ask questions: Before beginning to watch the movie, make sure you are trying to answer a question by watching the movie. For example, if you are watching *Twilight*, you might think not only about what vampires are but what they mean. In other words, the question you might be trying to answer is what do vampires say about American culture? Or what do they say about class, race, or gender in American culture?

2. Take notes: If you are writing about a movie in a theater, make sure you bring a notepad and paper. Even if you take minimal notes in the screening, sit a few minutes, perhaps when the credits are rolling, and write down some ideas or images that struck you during the movie. If you are writing by watching the movie through your computer or television, make sure you pause every five or ten minutes, particularly if you have watched the movie before. For easier review, look at the controller time to see when key scenes take place. Once you have watched the movie, quickly try to answer the question you posed. If you come up with a few answers, think about the scenes that best illustrate the points you are making.

3. Brainstorm for a thesis: Even if you do not use your original thesis, it helps when writing a draft.

4. Organize ideas by paragraph: If you have a first draft with definable paragraphs, the draft will be stronger and easier to revise.

of the spectrum is the **live blog** and/or **tweeting**. And sometimes, people write **personal essays** about movies as well.

The Review

In a review, writers tell readers whether they think something is of sufficient quality to watch and then give the reason for their opinions. Movie reviewers face a few specific challenges.

Here's what readers want to know from a review:

1. Whether a film is good.
2. What the reviewer's definition of good is.
3. Why does the movie succeed or fail? We want specifics.
4. Will they like it?
5. What other movies this particular movie resembles

Here are some tips to help with these questions.

HOW TO START

Pick a movie or movies you can watch more than once. Watch with a notebook and the ability to pause the recording. Take notes—sometimes impressions will be enough. Listen for good quotes. Above all, make watching an active process rather than a passive one.

HOW TO WRITE

Reviews often begin with a scene from the film and move to an indication about how the reviewer feels about the movie, the quality of the acting, the strength of the screenplay, and the creativity of the direction. A good reviewer gives context and basic information about the film itself, and then moves on to what one might call an extended reading of the movie.

So a structure of a review might look like this:

1. Opening anecdote
2. Context of review
3. Backstory of movie/director/actors
4. Analysis of movie with particular descriptions of important scenes
5. Comparisons to other movies
6. Why or why not the reviewer thinks the film is worth watching

Reviewers not only need to be competent in evaluating the work in question, but they also need to be entertaining. If you are not a funny writer, then be a concise and concrete one. Give just enough material about the movie to whet people's appetites for the movie itself. Lastly, consider whether or not you should include spoilers—if you do, signal their inclusion!

The Research Paper

Researching movies requires context. One can do work on particular films, but unless the film has been around a long time, there probably is not much scholarly work done on it. Therefore, researching movies requires a related context to the film you are studying or a general subject regarding movies. An example of the first type of research might be reading a film through the lens of feminism or race. Let's say you want to write about race in the *Star Wars* movies, you might begin with a question like how is *The Force Awakens* more racially progressive than, say, *Star Wars II: Attack of the Clones*, which features the disturbing Jar Jar Binks?

An example of the second type would be an article on feminism in 1970s movies. The first focuses on understanding a particular film; the second focuses on broader social issues, using movies as the evidence. In this example, you might write more broadly about a number of movies. In other words, the first uses movies as its primary text, while in the second feminism is as much under discussion as the films are.

Writing a research paper about a film means you will have to come up with an angle or a lens; researching the film without one will lead to a paper without an argument and likely without scholarly sources. But how do you come up with a lens? Let's dig down into the process. Let's say you want to write a paper on the representation of women in James Bond movies. Older movies are legendary for their sexist portrayals of women, but the recent versions with Daniel Craig have made attempts to remedy that issue. The fact that others have written about the film should *help* you write an informed essay rather than hinder you. In working on research papers, reading what others have written about the text you are examining helps you clarify your own thinking. So even if others have done feminist readings on the same topic, you can as well because your conclusions will be different.

You might also write about larger issues in Bond films. How have the villains changed over the years? Do the changing villains reflect our culture's changing stance in regard to "foreign enemies"? What about Bond himself? The Daniel Craig Bond is more troubled and brooding and has less swagger than the Sean Connery Bond. Does this tell us anything about our ideas about men? Heroes?

You might also consider researching a specific genre, like Civil War films or movies about the fashion industry. If you trace this kind of film over two or three decades, it can lend a historical sweep to your project.

Examining a film to figure out how to approach it might seem difficult at first, but thinking about all the different categories a film fits in will help.

The Appreciation

The appreciation engages why one likes a particular movie. It reads the film but in a way that stresses the film's quality and uses criticism as a form of positive engagement. It might use as evidence awards the movie has won, its importance in popular culture, and its influence on later movies. This form has been increasingly popular online, most notably in articles like "10 Movies You Must See before You Die" or "The Best Movie No One Has Seen." These kinds of essays use various sources of evidence to argue why you should not only see but also *appreciate* a certain movie.

Live Blogging/Tweeting

A form of instant reviewing, live blogging or tweeting has become increasingly popular. This type of writing you are unlikely to do for a grade in class, but it might make for some good practice. As you watch a movie like *Step Brothers* or *The Notebook*, you might try tweeting funny, snarky, or heartfelt reactions to certain scenes.

The Personal Essay and Comparison/Contrast

The personal essay is written in the first person and basically explains in great detail why a certain movie is important to the writer. This kind of essay relies less on research and close reading of the text and more on the emotions, reactions, and impressions of the writer. Where an appreciation essay might focus on why *you* or *society* should consider a specific movie, a personal essay is concerned with why the *writer* has a soft spot for the movie.

What makes these sorts of essays interesting is three things: 1) a detailed description of meaningful scenes, acting, and directing; 2) an approach and voice that is candid and relatable; and 3) very good writing. Let's say you absolutely love *The Hunger Games*, and you want to write about why. You will need to be as specific as possible about the ways individual scenes or performances affected you.

Another quite different approach is the comparison/contrast essay. In this type, the author compares and/or contrasts two seemingly similar films. Writing a paper about the various ways *Twelve Years a Slave* and *Mean Girls* are different is rather pointless, but writing a paper comparing and contrasting Katniss Everdeen and Bella Swan might be interesting. Along the same lines, you might consider writing about movies that take different approaches to similar topics like *Boyhood* and *Boyz n the Hood*. Or if Westerns are making a comeback, reading a classic Western like *The Searchers* against a more recent Western like *Dead Man* or *Django Unchained* could be fascinating. Since we brought up Quentin Tarantino, a paper on *Django Unchained* and *Inglourious Basterds* and how each takes on institutions of racism (the Holocaust and slavery) could be really good. Or, read across eras and genres. Consider a comparison/contrast essay in which you read *Black Panther* against a so-called blacksploitation film from the 1970s.

OTHER ESSAY IDEAS

1. The General Movies Assignment

In this paper, read a movie and write a paper analyzing some aspect of it. What do we mean by "read" and "analyze"? You might start by describing the text at hand, performing an inventory of sorts. Then think about what these elements say about the text. What conclusions can you draw about the work from the observations you have made? A movie has traditional elements of texts such as a narrative and symbolic language of one sort or another, as well as visual elements that contribute to the film's meaning.

2. Look at the Fashion

For this paper, notice the way the characters dress in a particular film. From what you know about fashion, what are the creators of the film trying to convey with their choices of fashion for their characters? *Hunger Games* is a good example, as is the original *Star Wars*. Are the filmmakers hoping to tie into prevailing opinions about the way certain groups (e.g., those of color, class, gender, and age) dress in providing clues on how we're supposed to understand these characters? Taken together, what conclusions can we draw from the fashion choices of the creators?

3. Analyze the Theme

In most romantic comedies and dramas, there is an explicit moral of the story, something that the authors of the movie think the audience should learn. For example, what is the message of *Bridesmaids*? *Maleficent*? *How to Lose a Guy in 10 Days*? *28 Days Later*? Do you think the studios or screenwriters think these morals are important? If so, do they present an honest attempt to educate the audience, or are they a vehicle for laughs? Do you know any films that do not have a clear message to impart? How would you compare them to the films that do have easy messages or themes?

4. The Unintended vs. the Intended

Sometimes movies are explicit about what they are trying to convey. Sometimes, however, what is not present in a film says as much about the film as what is there. For example, *Boyhood* was criticized by some groups for showing twelve years of a boy growing up in Texas and encountering no Chicanos or Latinos except for the manual laborers his mother hires then helps. Similarly, have you ever wondered why there are almost never any Native Americans in movies except Westerns? Writing about what is *not* in a film or film series can be illuminating.

5. Real vs. Unreal

Many people may say that they watch movies to escape reality. In what ways do the producers of films try to be "real"? In what ways do they ignore reality? You may already have noticed that we tend to watch characters in action with other characters, and that basic human functions like bathing, eating, sleeping, and going to the bathroom are ignored. On a more philosophical level, you may also notice that the problems these characters face are resolved relatively quickly, and the communication between characters is highly evolved. For this paper, you might discuss what overall effect the inclusion of reality might have on the audience.

6. Understand the Audience

Creators of movies often target their films to particular audiences—or their advertisers do—in order to see a greater return on their investment. Watch a film, or several, and see if you can determine what demographic the studios are appealing to or what kind of film their advertisers feel they are. Are the two audiences different? Is one more broad than the next? What do you think are some of the problems inherent in targeting a particular demographic?

Another fun exercise can be comparing the trailers that are shown before a romantic comedy as opposed those shown before a violent crime thriller.

7. Race and Ethnicity

For a long time, race and ethnicity have been an issue in movies. Watch a film through the lens of race, paying close attention to how the film addresses (or does not address) the issue of race. Do members of a particular race play a particular role on the film? Do you notice a pattern about what kinds of characters tend to be black? White? Asian? Latino? Do these roles embrace or reject previous stereotypes? Consider how often film villains are of Middle Eastern descent. Does this pattern further racist attitudes toward people assumed to be Arabic or Muslim?

8. Honor the Film

Write an essay on why you feel a film is "good." Your first step, of course, is defining what you mean by good. Does good mean writing that is funny, realistic, philosophical, or a combination of these factors or others? Is good defined by the quality of the actors? Can you define what a good movie is without constructing the criteria from the film you like? What other films fit into the definition you constructed?

9. Disparage the Film

Write an essay on why you feel a film is "bad," going through the same process as you did when you defined what good meant. A useful exercise is to write both positive and negative reviews. We tend to prefer terms like "successful" and "unsuccessful" rather than good or bad, as those tend to be easier to prove.

10. Follow the Character

What single character in a film do you most identify with? Why? Does this identification make you at all uncomfortable? What does this identification say about you and the movie's character?

Additional Ideas

1. What is the greatest movie you've seen? Write an essay in which you argue why your choice is the greatest, but be sure to establish criteria for "greatness."

2. Chances are, you have seen *Avatar* or *Star Wars*. Write your own analytical review of one of these films. Feel free to reference one of the reviews you have read. Perhaps you will agree or disagree with one (or many) of the reviewers. Be sure to analyze the film; do not simply write a plot summary.

3. As we were working on this edition, *Moonlight* won the 2017 Academy Award for Best Picture after an awkward mistake during the televised ceremonies. If you have seen the film, write an essay comparing that movie to other Oscar winners or to one or two other movies nominated, like *La La Land* or *Hell or High Water*. Why do you think *Moonlight* won?

4. Write an essay on a director's body of work. Directors like Steven Spielberg, Woody Allen, Quentin Tarantino, Paul Thomas Anderson, Kathryn Bigelow, Judd Apatow, Sophia Coppola, J.J. Abrams, or David O. Russell have directed a number of different movies. Consider writing an essay in which you compare two or three of their movies. How have they contributed to film history? To American culture?

5. Write an essay in which you explore issues of gender in one or two recent movies. Perhaps you can pick a movie directed by a woman and one directed by a man. How are women represented? How are women's bodies presented or framed? Male bodies? Do the women have strong roles, or are they limited, stereotypical roles? Do the women date or love men their own age, or are the men much older? Do the women have good jobs and healthy lifestyles?

6. Write an essay in which you explore issues of race. As in gender, how are issues of race and power represented in the film? What kind of music runs through the film? Are minority characters filmed or framed differently than white characters? There is an old joke that the one black character in a horror film is one of the first to die. Is this still the case? While there are a number of wonderful movies by people of color (*Do the Right Thing, Smoke Signals, The Joy Luck Club, Twelve Years a Slave, Spy Kids, Moonlight*), you might also consider how minorities are represented in movies made by whites.

7. Explore notions of class in American cinema. How often are poor people in movies? While there may be women and people of color in Hollywood and in the studio system, how well does Hollywood understand low-income America? Are there realistic film portrayals of working-class or low-income families? Some would say that America is more classist than racist: Is this theory proved or refuted by Hollywood?

8. Write an essay in which you offer a reading of a film based solely on the film techniques: sound, lighting, camera angles, music, framing, and editing. How can technique determine meaning?

RESOURCES

Probably the best resources for regular film reviews are the online databases *Rotten Tomatoes* and *Metacritic*. Each one lets you read reviews by non-professionals as well as reviews by the top movie reviewers in the country. The Internet Movie Database (IMDB) is another great online resource because it gives all sorts of background information about the film, the cast, the director, the ticket sales, the special effects, the filming locations, and the movie's reception.

Your university's library will also very likely have books of film criticism as well as popular journals and magazines. Some general magazines you should be able to access online like *Cineaste*, *Film Journal*, *Film Comment*, *Films in Review*, *Hollywood Reporter*, *MovieMaker*, and *Preview*. More scholarly academic journals include *Film Quarterly*, *Quarterly Review of Film and Video*, *Camera Obscura*, *New Cinemas*, and *Framework*.

Books

There are a number of very important books on film as well:

Carol Clover, *Men, Women, and Chainsaws: Gender in the Modern Horror Film*. Princeton: Princeton UP, 1993.

Joshua Clover, *The Matrix*. London: BFI, 2004.

bell hooks, *Reel to Real: Race, Sex, and Class at the Movies*, new edition. New York: Routledge, 2008.

Robert Kolker, *A Cinema of Loneliness: Penn, Stone, Kubrick, Scorsese, Altman*. New York: Oxford UP, 2000.

Sidney Lumet, *Making Movies*. New York: Vintage, 1996.

Michael Ryan and Douglas Kellner, *Camera Politica: The Politics and Ideology of Contemporary Hollywood Film*. Bloomington: Indiana UP, 1988.

Susan Sontag, "Notes on Camp"; "Against Interpretation"; "Jack Smith's Flaming Creatures," in *Against Interpretation, and Other Essays*. New York: Dell, 1964.

SAMPLE STUDENT ESSAY

Whitney Black wrote this essay while a student at the University of San Francisco in 2003. In her short persuasive essay, she takes what is perhaps to most readers an unpopular stance. Black reads *Star Wars* through the lens of a classic American Western, arguing that the film essentially replicates the standard formula of Hollywood Westerns—even the good guys wear white and the bad guys, black. As you work through her essay, you might ask if Black reads too much into the film. Or does she pick up on deep-seated American values that many people are reluctant to question? Finally, is it possible to identify problematic aspects of a movie but still love it?

Star Wars and America

WHITNEY BLACK

Though *Star Wars* takes place in the far-off frontier of space, and is less concerned with recreating America's past than it is with imagining the future, the film is still a classic American Western, right down to the requisite good versus evil, us against them dualities. Like all formulaic Westerns, *Star Wars* is about opposition and the promotion of good old-fashioned American values. The environment is the unfamiliar galaxy, but the underlying message is pure Americana; *Star Wars* subverts patriotism within the rebel forces and religious "force," and establishes the rebellion's struggle against the tyrannical Empire as a pro-American ideological battle. The rebel forces, with their pared down attire and allegiance to the old "force" religiosity, are the antithesis to the techno-driven, machine heavy homogeneity of the Evil Empire; similar to how the American identity, with its commitment to traditional democratic values, differed from the oppressive threat of communism. Communism, during both the Red Scare and the Vietnam War, served as both a threat to American ideals and as a way to glorify those ideals by contrast. The un-American construct of the Empire, like the un-American Communist mentality, function as the perfect counter-parts; both are outsider systems, whose differences illuminate America's "greatness," and generate a need to preserve that "greatness." The Rebellion is obligated to defend a way of life, a sense of individual freedom, from the Empire.

Like the Western's struggle between cowboy and Indian, civilization and savagery, *Star Wars* simply modernizes the conflict, replacing cowboys with Jedi and Indians with evil empire affiliates. Though the characters have changed, the implicit Western message of expelling a threatening "other" remains. Both *Star Wars* and the classic Western are filmic homage to an American ideal; while the classic Western rewrites the past to stabilize and reassure the present, *Star Wars* acts as a cautionary tale against what an absence of those ideals means for the future. The "us against them" duality is less about racial differences than it is about America's ideological system. It is glorious democracy against a "bad" counter-government. Though *Star Wars* does not directly ally itself with America's geography, location is inconsequential; the rebels are as American as Indians killing cowboys, symbols of a filmic tradition advocating American values by setting them against an external threat.

Star Wars succeeds at its "Western-ness" because of its dependence on opposition. Nothing solidifies the righteousness of "good" as much as the presence of a contrasting evil. The Evil Empire justifies the Rebellion (obviously a force is necessary to confront the manifestation of evil) while divulging the danger of sacrificing the rebel cause to the empire. The Empire is the ominous threat and represents everything opposing the rebel value system, persona, and way of life. The result is audience approval of the rebel cause; audiences, whether aware of it or not, identify with the rebels as individual heroes fighting against a different, and thus threatening, authority. While the Rebellion, and its association to the Imperial Senate, most certainly symbolizes the people's voice, the Empire is ignorant of the wants of the common people, and is a realization of abused power, and a warning against forces opposed to American democracy. While America, with its own structured Senate, associates its ideals with a "power to the people" mentality, the Empire is in obvious contrast, determined to exploit technology (the Death Star) and become an ultimate power and oppressive regime.

Not only does *Star Wars* link technology to tyranny and oppression, but it also creates another opposition of technology versus nature, with nature encompassing the rural American identity of honor, duty, and goodness while technology embodies the age-old fear of change. Clearly, the Death Star is both an example of misused power, and a warning against change. The machine, because of its relation to the Evil Empire, is a digression away from humanity; technology threatens the existence of individual power and becomes an instrument for proliferating evil. The protagonist Luke Skywalker succeeds against the Empire by relying on the power of his subconscious, turning off his computerized tracking system to respond on instinct. He uses his faith in the force, a religion of nature, and old fashioned and unquestioned belief; the outcome of his success, his ability to defeat the Empire, perpetuates yet another American notion. Believe in its value systems and justice will be restored.

The film's message is clear: Hold fast to our present way of life and the future will be saved. Like any Western, *Star Wars* is a cinematic love letter to Americana, and the country's perpetual fear of confrontation. Westerns deal in oppositions, because the rebel in space or in the west is always sacrificing their own safety to salvage a community. Community salvation mirrors American salvation, and the protagonist's determination and commitment to deep-rooted American rightness serves as the best possible form of American patriotism and duty. The Western always needs a hero willing to die for the cause, ready to save America from the threat of change. Westerns contend that America is the "best and only way," oppositions are the worst imagined evil; both feared and destroyed and ultimately never tolerated.

Works Cited

Lev, Peter. *American Films of the 70s: Conflicting Visions*. Austin: U of Texas P, 2000.

You ... bout *reading* television as
oppo... btedly know the structure
of sit... know about the probable
audie... mething about plot devices
and l... out and time commercials.
You p... ically in the last few years.
Thanl... y watch television without
a tele... evision shows has changed
somev... ns, things are pretty much
the sa...

Th... ing is more help than hin-
drance... ncept of "television." But
watchi... hing is passive; reading is
active. ... such as a poem or a short
story. ... ext is put together, what
the au... ues are. We read complex
passag... nge words as well as more
general... taught to think about what
literatu... nce beyond mere plot. Yet when we
watch t... ns. We have been watching television
since w... idance. Our parents, friends, newspapers, a... should watch, but once we get in front
of the te... , we tend to let the show dictate our response without our interaction.
To understand television, we have to learn to question the structure and content of
television shows as well as the presence and absence of ideas, people, and places. And
so when watching and writing about television, we should consider a number of things:

The structure of television encourages passive viewing. When we read a book or
magazine or website, the text is in our hands (or in our lap or on our desk). We can
start and stop reading whenever we want to; we can reread at our convenience. We can

underline these texts and make notes on them. We can, of course, take this particular text with us on the bus, to the bathroom, or to the coffee shop. However, when we watch television, we are already physically disconnected from the text. Thanks to recent technology, we can start and stop shows, which is great, but we can't mark them up. But even when we watch online or with the remote control, there is often a laugh track telling us not only when but how to laugh, commercial interruptions telling us to wait, and familiar plot conventions telling us to respond in predictable ways.

Various aspects of modern life also contribute to a consumption of television that is not particularly critical. For instance, it's likely that your home lends itself to passive television watching. Most people arrange their dens or family rooms so that the TV is center stage, the main focal point of the room. And, after a long day of work (or school), there is often something comforting about settling down in front of the television for an episode of *American Horror Story*, a baseball game, or a movie. Our architecture, our work, and our home lives facilitate watching television as an act of disengagement.

Are networks and television producers conspiring to have us watch this way? Some of television's harsher critics would say yes, but others might view television as a form of escape from the realities of modern life, or even as something educational. In either case, we can better understand television by watching with critical engagement, taking notes, and if possible, replaying the program before sitting down to write about it.

Unlike works of literature, television shows have no recognizable author. When we pick up a book, we know who has written it—the name of the author is usually displayed as prominently as the title. Once we know who has authored a book, we can use this information accordingly. Traditionally, when scholars study written texts, they often focus on the words on the page, the symbols, the themes, and the plot contained within, but many also use the life of the author, and the author's other texts, to gain deeper understanding. Though modern scholars have diminished the power of authorial intent, the author, even if less important to scholars, still exists and may exist most profoundly for readers.

Who authors less traditional texts is not always clear. In movies, for example, we have two, and sometimes three people, to whom to attach authorship: the screenwriter, the director, and sometimes either the producer or cinematographer; in architecture, sometimes an entire firm serves as the author of a building. In television, even more so than movies, there is no discernable author. We might consider the show's writers the authors, but as you well know, writing is only a small part of a visual text. There are the various settings, the clothing the actors wear, and the angles cameras use. In addition, we never know quite who has composed a particular show. There are writers listed, but there are often show runners who sort of oversee the scripts but don't always pen them. We also hear stories about actors writing their own lines, as well as the presence of ad-libbed material. In addition, unlike authors of their own works who are responsible for virtually all of the production of the text (except of course for the book itself), the producers of a television show do not have the same direct connection to the texts they construct. They often play defining roles in shaping elements of the text that we can also make use of—the casting, the setting, the themes, even who technically writes the show—but do not do the writing, the set construction or the casting themselves.

So the question is, how do we or can we refer to a show's author when writing about it? One way is to refer to the show's *authors*, and use as a possibility for discussion what the presence of group authorship means to a particular text as opposed to discussing a single author. Recently, we have become more aware of show runners—main authors who create and write the main arc of television shows. In any case, the question of authorship is one large difference between television and more traditional texts. What's important to consider when writing about television is that even reality shows and televised basketball games are *made* events. They are *filmed (videotaped)*, *directed*, *edited*, and *produced*. They don't just exist on their own. They have been created, essentially, by a conglomerate for you to consume. Your job as a writer is to look beyond, behind, under, and around television production to get at the real cultural work TV programming does.

Television shows are character-driven, genre-based, and plot-oriented. Television shows are much more genre-driven than the traditional texts we read. While literature contains a number of different types of forms, many of which do not fit into a particular genre, television shows operate almost exclusively within genres. A genre is a type of a medium with established and expected formulas and devices. Romances and Westerns are prime examples of novel genres. Most works of fiction that critics consider literary do not fit into a particular category of novel such as romances, Westerns, and science fiction, and it's rare that a literature class will discuss works from these categories since scholars and professors often consider them to be formulaic, with easily predicted plots. In recent years, critics have begun to study these works more carefully, but their interest in these texts has probably not often made it into your classroom.

Television, on the other hand, is all about genre. Dramas, comedies, action shows, reality shows, or various hybrids like dramedies, all have recognizable components. There is a great supercut on YouTube, for example, that merely splices together characters on reality shows saying, "I'm not here to make friends." Traditional texts have these components as well, but in television shows, they are often omnipresent. We know what to expect from sitcoms, gritty police dramas, and shows about families. The fact that shows about hospitals, lawyers, and the police comprise almost 80 percent of the hour-long dramas on prime-time network television speaks to the ubiquity of genre. One reason innovative programs like *Arrested Development*, *Northern Exposure*, *Twin Peaks*, *Freaks and Geeks*, and *Wonderfalls* had short lives on television was because they could not be placed in any particular genre. Viewers didn't know how to watch them because they didn't know what to expect from them. Television shows tend to be neglected as a field of study in the college classroom because they are genre-oriented.

So in writing about television, we have to understand that in large part shows fall into a particular category. We may want to ask whether an individual program "transcends" the normal fare of that genre, as well as what conventions of that genre a particular show follows. Once we start thinking about genre, we might also think about how this might affect the audience's viewing experience.

The audience pays for its free television. On its surface, network television would appear to be free; however, upon closer scrutiny, it turns out that we do pay for TV in a number of ways. First of all, we buy (and keep buying) more and more expensive television sets. Secondly, most Americans get their programming through monthly cable or satellite subscriptions that add up to between $300 and $1500 per year. More and more people are subscribing to streaming services like Netflix, Hulu, and Amazon, which also cost money. Contrast the price of a TV set and cable with the fee of a library card, which is free, and TV may not seem like such a bargain.

While some people are figuring out ways around this via YouTube and other streaming options, there are still often ads to contend with, which is an indirect way we pay for television. Instead of charging viewers to watch, television networks present commercials, paid for by advertisers. Advertisers, in turn, choose shows in which to advertise. Then, the price for those ads likely gets passed onto you in the purchase price of the items you buy.

But we pay for television in another way as well, and that is with our time and attention. If you watch a commercial, then you are essentially paying for that program with your time. Advertisers know this and plan accordingly. You can often tell what audience an advertiser thinks is watching by paying attention to its commercials. Because they in part are responsible for paying for a show, advertisers do play a role in what makes it to television, although the networks play a much larger role. If a show's content is considered controversial, advertisers may shy away, with the idea that it may lose potential customers who attach the advertisers to the show's content. If advertisers do not want to advertise with a show, the show may not survive.

The size of an audience may also play a factor in how we view a particular program. We might think about how a show geared toward appealing to millions differs from a novel, which often has a more limited appeal. Television is entertainment for the masses, and its direct connection to commerce is another factor we have to look at when writing about it.

What is not there is often as important as what is. What is not in a show is often as important as what is in it. For example, as Oprah Winfrey pointed out when the cast of *Friends* came on her show, there was no black "friend." Winfrey's observation raises another: what does the absence of minorities of any kind in a city of incredible diversity say about the creators of a show? We can make the same comments about any number of sitcoms: see *The Big Bang Theory, Two and a Half Men, Will and Grace, How I Met Your Mother,* and *Seinfeld* (although *Seinfeld* is smart enough to talk about its relative whiteness). The ethnicity of the casts may send a message about the target audience for the show but also what kind of family, relationship, or group is considered normal or cool. Unlike 30 years ago, there are now a number of programs that feature people of color that are, in fact, written and perhaps even directed by people of color, like *Black-ish.* Despite this notable improvement, many American groups get little or no representation on TV. For instance, as this book goes to press, there is no show that looks at Chicano/Latino or Native American families, relationships, or culture on prime-time television. While there are a few shows attempting to reflect the diversity of America (*Fresh Off the Boat* addresses Asian American concerns, and Aziz Ansari's *Master of None* takes on Arab American issues, but the latter is on Netflix and accessible only to those who subscribe), most of our programs feature white and black actors. Whether it is people of a certain age, particular areas of the country or world, or specific jobs, many aspects of modern life do not appear on television. For example, early in the first season of the NBC drama *Quantico,* there is a scene where a Muslim FBI trainee, who wears a hijab, is shown swimming in a burkini. For many Muslim and Muslim American women, this was a radical moment as it was the first time something like this had been seen—and seen positively—on prime-time American TV. The new program *This Is Us* takes on the issue of mixed-race adoption.

When writing about sitcoms or other television shows, also note the presence or absence of traditional gender roles, realistic dialogue, and typical, real-time events. Looking for absence rather than presence is difficult but rewarding; trying to understand what is missing often helps us understand the flaws of a show (or any text for that matter). It relates to the idea of writing about text through a lens, which we discuss in the introduction.

Visual media have specific concerns. Television is a decidedly more visual medium than traditional texts such as short stories and poems. Thus we have to take into account how a show looks as well as sounds. The visual presence comes most obviously in its setting. In some shows, the setting is crucial. *Scandal* is all about Washington, DC. In *Big Bang Theory,* a university drives a great deal of the plot. In *The Simpsons,* the Midwestern averageness of Springfield often determines the issues the show addresses, sometimes explaining a character's actions. Part of *Breaking Bad*'s appeal is its use of New Mexico as a setting and backdrop. *Grey's Anatomy* is set in Seattle, but how much really is Seattle a "character" in the show? We also might look at other settings—the foreign cities of *Homeland,* the offices of *Mad Men,* the sets of *The Bachelor* and *The*

Bachelorette, the kitchen of *Black-ish*, the loft of *New Girl*, etc. None of these settings are random—they are all fabricated to make some sort of argument about the characters or to create an aura that reinforces what we want to see.

You might also ask how the clothing of each cast member contributes to the audience member's idea of who and what the character is supposed to represent. On shows like *Keeping Up with the Kardashians, Empire, House of Cards, The Big Bang Theory, The Bachelor, Game of Thrones*, and even *Ellen*, clothing plays a crucial role in what the audience is supposed to understand about the show's characters, or in the case of *Ellen*, the host. Finally, you might ask how cameras are used and the colors that dominate the broadcast. Shows like CSI and *Quantico* use handheld cameras, ostensibly for a more realistic look. A soap opera uses close-ups held for a number of seconds before cutting away to another scene or commercial.

Because settings and clothing are visual and present in every show, and are a result of choices the show's authors make, they are often useful subjects for writing. Papers about the relationships between the characters and the places they live or work can be the basis of a paper about the implicit values of a show. What do these techniques say about the shows in which they are used? Overall, the visual elements are crucial to understanding some of the show's intended and unintended messages, and its distinction from more traditional texts.

Finding themes is easy, but finding meaningful ones is difficult. Themes are often the intended meanings that authors give their works. For example, a theme of Harper Lee's *To Kill a Mockingbird* would be that racism can interfere with justice, and this interference is highly destructive to a society's fabric. CSI essentially had the same theme in every episode—criminals always leave traces, and deviancy is common. *Modern Family*'s theme changes from episode to episode, but the message remains consistent—contemporary families have new rules and have to be their own models. Every text has a theme, and whether we know it or not, we pick up on a text's thematics.

Of all the elements involved with watching television, the theme is the most easily discerned and often the least interesting. Most often, any television theme revolves around tolerance and patience and above all, the problematic nature of jumping to conclusions. Although many critics sometimes justifiably complain about the violence of television shows, most shows favor right over wrong, happiness over sadness, lessons learned over lessons forgotten. Shows like *The Sopranos, Game of Thrones*, and *Adult Swim* play with these traditions, which is one reason critics tend to praise them. All in all, looking for a theme is often the easiest task a television reader has.

What's more difficult is trying to understand whether the television author(s) handled these lessons too simplistically or offensively, or at the expense of the quality of the show? In other words, does the theme take away from the show's other elements? In watching sitcoms, finding the theme is easy, but one must be careful. *The Simpsons*, for example, has a traditional television sitcom theme and structure in many of its shows but often brutally satirizes American culture. So which message is more important? Clearly, what happens during the show matters more than what happens in their conclusions, which often tie up the loose ends of an episode in a manner similar to more traditional sitcoms, often as a way of criticizing the conventions of television itself.

Overall, the medium of television has a number of general concerns that play into our enjoyment as well as our critical stance. As a writer, you do not have to take into account all of the above, but thinking about them is a good way of breaking free of your traditional relationship to television. There are also more specific ways of analyzing a television show. Immediately below is a list of questions you can ask of a television show when you are getting ready to write about it.

Here are some general things to think about when writing about television:

Genre: What genre are we watching? How do the writers let us know this? (Visually, orally, by way of music, laugh track?)

Characters: Who are the characters? Do they represent something beyond actors in a plot? How do the writers want us to perceive them, and why? How would changing the characters change the show?

Setting: What are the settings? What do they say about the show? What do the writers want us to think about the setting? Could the show take place somewhere else and remain the same?

Plot: What happens? Is the plot important to understanding/enjoying the show?

Themes: What do the show's writers think about the issues/ideas/subjects they present? (Themes are what writers believe about issues, ideas, and subjects, not the ideas and issues themselves.)

Figurative language: What symbols, metaphors, and motifs present themselves in the show? What effect does their repetition have?

Visual constructions: How do the writers make us see (or hear) the show?

Absences: What is missing? What real-world notions are not represented in the show?

Conventional/nonconventional: In what ways is the show typical of its genre? Atypical?

Race/ethnicity/gender/class: How do the writers talk (or not talk) about these issues? How do these issues show up in other categories we have mentioned, such as character, setting, plot, and theme?

Reality: In what way does what is depicted in a particular television show or in general reflect the world as you normally experience it? What is different? Does this matter?

WRITING ABOUT TELEVISION: THE GENRES

There are a variety of genres in writing about television, including the review, the appreciation, the recap, the overview, as well as more generic forms such as the analysis and the research paper. There is also the live blog and/or tweeting. And sometimes, people write personal essays about television as well.

The Review

In a review, writers tell readers whether they think something is of sufficient quality to watch and then give the reason for their opinions. Television reviewers face a few specific challenges. Television shows have multiple episodes, and some reviewers may not have access to all the episodes.

HOW TO START

Pick a television show you have access to more than one episode of. Watch with a notebook and the ability to pause the recording. Take notes—sometimes impressions will be enough. Listen for good quotes. Above all, make watching an active process rather than a passive one.

HOW TO WRITE

Reviews often begin with a scene from the show, move to an indication about how the reviewer feels about the show, gives context and basic information about the show itself, and then moves on to what one might call an extended reading of the show. Here's what readers want to know from a review:

1. Whether a show is good.
2. What the review's definition of good is.
3. Will they like it?

They also might want to know why the reviewer likes it, as well as what other shows the reviewer thinks the show is like. So a structure of a review might look like this:

1. Opening anecdote
2. Context of review
3. Backstory of show
4. Analysis of show
5. Comparisons to other shows
6. Why or why not the reviewer thinks the show is worth watching

Reviewers not only need to be competent in evaluating the work in question, but they also need to be entertaining. If you are not a funny writer, then be a concise and concrete one. Give just enough material about the show to whet people's appetites for the show itself.

The Researched Paper

Researching television requires context. One can do work on particular shows, but unless the show has been around a long time, there has probably not been much scholarly work done on it. Therefore, researching television requires a related context to the show you are studying *or* a general subject regarding television. An example of the first type of research would be a feminist reading of a particular television show. An example of the second type would be an article on feminism in 1970s television. The first focuses on understanding a particular show; the second focuses on broader social issues, using television as the evidence. In other words, the first uses television as its primary text, while in the second feminism is as much under discussion as the television shows are. In both cases, these are *researched papers* rather than research papers; you are not just putting information into a paper. You are supplementing your analysis with information gleaned from research.

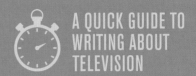

A QUICK GUIDE TO WRITING ABOUT TELEVISION

1. Be prepared to start and stop the program: You need to make what is a passive activity, active. If you watch mostly on your computer, keep a notebook handy to jot down ideas and observations or be ready to toggle between watching the show and writing about it.

2. Ask a question about your subject before beginning your viewing: Writing about and watching a show becomes more focused if you have a question you are trying to answer.

3. Take notes extensively: One reason is to remember the text better, but the more important one is to gather information.

4. Brainstorm for a thesis: Even if you do not use your original thesis, it helps when writing a draft.

5. Organize ideas by paragraph: If you have a first draft with definable paragraphs, the draft will be stronger and easier to revise.

Writing a paper about a television show means you will have to come up with an angle or a lens; researching the show without one will lead to a paper without an argument and likely without scholarly sources. But how do you come up with a lens? Let's dig down into the process. Let's say you want to write a paper on *The Big*

Bang Theory, as of 2016 the most popular show on television. The show features four scientists and, in later years, their significant others. The show has generated a decent amount of criticism, some of it based on its portrayal of scientists, women, race and ethnicity, and class. The fact that others have written about the show should *help* you write a paper rather than hinder you. In working on research papers, having others write about the text you are examining helps you clarify your own thinking. So even if others have done feminist readings of *The Big Bang Theory*, you can still do a feminist reading. Your conclusions will be different. If others have argued that the show is anti-woman because of the Penny character, you might counter with a discussion of Amy Farrah Fowler and Bernadette. Or you might argue that Penny is a feminist character. You could also write a paper on masculinity and *The Big Bang Theory*; in what ways do the characters straddle traditional gender roles?

You might also argue bigger issues about *The Big Bang Theory*. You could try to understand what it means about our attitudes about science that a show that features physicists is our number one show, and survey other shows that have featured scientists. You might discuss the place of this particular sitcom in the pantheon of other number one shows. You might discuss the specific nerdiness of the settings: Sheldon and Leonard's apartment; the labs, offices, and cafeteria at the university; the comic book shop; Howard's bedroom in his childhood home. Note that some of these topics don't *need* research, but a research angle would enhance the argument. Many people have written about sets on television shows, what makes a show popular, and the presence of particular types of characters on a show.

Examining a show to figure out how to approach it might seem difficult at first, but thinking about all the different categories a show fits into will help.

OTHER ESSAY IDEAS

1. The Appreciation

The appreciation engages with why one likes a particular television show. It reads the show, but in a way that stresses the show's quality and uses criticism as a form of positive engagement. This form has been increasingly popular online, even as people bemoan the negativity of discourse on the web. People like to write about what they like, because sharing their view often leads to a sense of community; we often forge our strongest ties when we agree on the things we like.

The key to writing a good appreciation is to make an argument about why you like the show and use evidence from the show as well as contexts.

2. The General Television Assignment

In this paper, read an episode of a television show and write a paper analyzing some aspect of it. What do we mean by "read" and "analyze"? You might start by describing the text at hand, performing an inventory of sorts. Then think about what these elements say about the text. What conclusions can you draw about the work from the observations you have made? A television show has traditional elements of texts, such as a narrative and symbolic language of one sort or another, as well as visual elements that contribute to the show's meaning.

3. Look at the Fashion

For this paper, notice the way the characters dress on a particular television show. From what you know about fashion, what are the creators of the show trying to convey with their choices of fashion for their characters? Are they hoping to tie into prevailing opinions about the way certain groups (e.g., those of color, class, gender, and age) dress in providing clues on how we're supposed to understand these characters? Taken together, what conclusions can we draw from the fashion choices of the creators?

4. Analyze the Theme

In most sitcoms and many dramas, there is an explicit moral of the story that those who script the episode attach to the ending. Taking one such show, a night of shows on a particular network, or an accumulation of episodes of the same show, what sorts of morals are presented to the audience? Do you think the creators think these morals are important? If so, do they present an honest attempt to educate the audience, or are they a vehicle for laughs? Do you know any shows that do not have a moral of the story? How would you compare them to the shows that do have morals?

5. The Unintended vs. the Intended

Sometimes television shows are explicit about what they are trying to convey. Sometimes, however, what is not present in a show says as much about the show as what is there. For example: Oprah Winfrey made a comment to the cast of *Friends* on her show: "Why isn't there a black 'friend' on your show?" Look at a popular sitcom and try to determine what may or may not be missing on a show. You might focus on the racial make-up of the characters or their gender, class, or age.

6. Real vs. Unreal

Many people may say that they watch television to escape reality. In what ways do the producers of shows try to be real? In what ways do they ignore reality? You may already have noticed that we tend to watch characters in action with other characters, and that basic human functions like bathing, eating, sleeping, and going to the bathroom are ignored. On a more philosophical level, you may also notice that the problems these characters face are resolved relatively quickly, and the communication between characters is highly evolved. For this paper, you might discuss what overall effect the inclusion of reality might have on the audience.

7. Understand the Audience

Creators of television shows often target their shows to particular audiences—or their advertisers do—in order to see a greater return on their investment. Watch a television show, or several, and see if you can determine what demographic they are appealing to or what show their advertisers feel they are. Are the two audiences different? Is one more broad than the next? What do you think are some of the problems inherent in targeting a particular demographic?

8. Race and Ethnicity

For a long time, race and ethnicity has been an issue on television. Watch a show and see what it says and does not say about questions of race and ethnicity. Do members of a particular race play a particular role on the show? Do these roles embrace or reject previous stereotypes? For example, consider the characters of Darryl and Stanley from *The Office* or Kelly Kapoor. How often does race become part of their character? Olivia Pope on *Scandal*? In *Modern Family*, Gloria's accent is a source of jokes in many episodes. Is this racist?

9. Honor the Show

Write an essay on why you feel a show is "good." Your first step, of course, is defining what you mean by good. Does good mean writing that is funny, realistic, philosophical, or a combination of these factors or others? Is good defined by the quality of the actors? Can you define what a good television show is without constructing the criteria from the show you like? What other shows fit into the definition you constructed?

10. LGBTQ

Television has made great strides in representing gay, lesbian, and now, with *Transparent*, transgender issues. Write an essay in which you chart the evolution of gay or lesbian characters on television. A young Billy Crystal played a gay character on the sitcom *Soap*, which aired in the late 1970s and early 1980s—probably the first openly gay character on American TV. How have things changed?

11. Disparage the Show

Write an essay on why you feel a show is "bad," going through the same process as you did when you defined what good meant. A useful exercise is to write both positive and negative reviews. We tend to prefer terms like "successful" or "unsuccessful," but either way, be sure to define your criteria.

12. Follow the Character

What single character on a television show do you most identify with? Why? Does this identification make you at all uncomfortable? What does this identification say about you and the television character?

13. Comparison/Contrast

Look at a few episodes of a sitcom from the 1970s and compare it to a sitcom of similar theme and structure from today. You could write about *Three's Company* and *Two and Half Men* or *Good Times* and *Black-ish* or *All in the Family* and *Modern Family*. What has changed? What hasn't? Similarly, with YouTube and Netflix, programs from other countries have become hugely popular. Compare a very popular show like *Borgen* with *Scandal* or *The Bridge* with its Swedish/Danish inspiration, *Bron.*

14. Social and Economic Class

Consider the role of economic class on American TV. In the 1960s and 1970s with shows like *The Waltons*, *Little House on the Prairie*, *Good Times*, *Sanford and Son*, and *All in the Family*, poverty or near poverty was a major theme. We see that less now. Almost every character on television seems to be doing pretty well. *Roseanne* was groundbreaking in this regard, and *King of Queens* broached the topic somewhat, as did *Breaking Bad*. Write an essay in which you pay close attention to poverty, wealth, and class on television.

15. Media Journal

In this assignment, you follow a phenomenon for the length of the course. It could be a television show or a continuing event (such as a sport). Each journal entry should provide some sort of commentary on the phenomenon, moving beyond general plot concerns. A brief (two- or three-sentence) summary is fine but should not dominate the entry.

RESOURCES

On the Web

There is a lot of writing about television on the internet; almost every major news and culture site has a television writer. Some of the ones to read include Eric Deggens, the TV critic at NPR; Linda Holmes, host of NPR's *Pop Culture Happy Hour*; James Poniewozik, with the *New York Times*; Emily Nussbaum, who recently won a Pulitzer Prize for her writing for *The New Yorker*; Alan Sepinwall, the critic at Hitfix.com; Mo Ryan, the critic at *Variety*; Todd VanDerWerff, at Vox.com; Willa Paskin, the critic at *Slate*, and Matt Zoller Seitz, the critic at *New York* magazine. All of these writers have a strong Twitter presence.

Books

Here are a few books that might be useful in studying television:

Herman Gray, *Watching Race: Television and the Struggle for "Blackness."* This book explores African American portrayals on television.

Elyce Rae Helford, *Fantasy Girls: Gender in the New Universe of Science Fiction and Fantasy Television.* This book explores the 1990s trend of including strong, feminine heroes like Buffy and Xena in the fantasy genre, and where feminism fits into this development.

Susan Murray and Laurie Ouellette, eds., *Reality TV: Remaking Television Culture.* This collection explores reality television.

Horace Newcomb, *Television: The Critical View.* This book is a collection of critical essays about television.

Neil Postman, *Amusing Ourselves to Death.* This book explores the corrosive effect of television on culture.

SAMPLE STUDENT ESSAY

Lara Hayhurst's essay comes from a Pace University class on feminism and visual culture. Professor Patricia Pender taught a class called "Girls on Film" at Pace University in which students engage films about and by women through various theoretical lenses. Here is a section from Dr. Pender's syllabus that explains the class's focus:

> This class explores the phenomenon of "girl culture" as it has been represented in recent mainstream cinema in the United States. It examines the unlikely feminist heroines of twentieth and twenty-first century popular film; Alicia Silverstone's Cher in the classic "chick flick" *Clueless*, Reese Witherspoon's rampaging Vanessa in the explosive *Freeway*, and Michelle Rodriguez's feisty Diana in Karyn Kusama's *Girlfight*. Paying particular attention to issues of race, class, ethnicity, education, sexuality, psychology, and geography, the class will attempt to interrogate and destabilize mainstream media representations of female adolescence as predominantly white, heterosexual, and upper-middle class. We will examine recent cinematic representations of African American (*Just Another Girl on the* IRT), Latina (*Girlfight*), queer (*All Over Me*), and transgender (*Boys*

Don't Cry) adolescents, and employ a variety of methodologies: anthropological, cinematic, psychological, and economic.

As part of the course, Dr. Pender requires a significant research component that culminates in a research paper that also involves an active reading of a text associated with the class. Here were the more specific requirements:

- Focus on representations of GIRLS (not women) on FILM (including TV).
- Make sure your film is MADE and SET sometime between 1980 and now (unless you have talked it over with me already).
- Make explicit connections to Third Wave Feminism—either in terms of your film's representation of girls, its subject matter (the issues it addresses), its narrative, its aims, its intended audience, its reception in popular media, or a combination of the above.

Putting the "Me" Back in Medical Drama: *Grey's Anatomy's* Adventures in McFeminism

LARA HAYHURST

Feminism's third wave longs to use popular culture and the media as a weapon of empowerment for women rather than an obstacle hindering their progression. The Third Wave propagates itself as not just a compromise between strident Second Wave ideals and the gutted superficiality of the Girlie Feminism movement, but as its own, progressive breed of feminism that is integrated, inclusive, open-minded, and tangible to all females. With this in mind, analyzing specific cultural productions that should ideally be serving as Weapons of Female Empowerment is an important exercise. Television holds an important place in our contemporary media, and by analyzing a television show with a large female viewership, such as *Grey's Anatomy*, that also quietly promotes itself as a progressive and feminist piece of pop culture, we can determine if this part of contemporary media and television is beneficial or detrimental to the ideals of the Third Wave.

   When perusing critical responses to *Grey's Anatomy*, one encounters conflicting critiques that alternately brush the series off as daytime drama or consider it a dynamic, culturally progressive piece of television. This leads me to believe that while *Grey's Anatomy* has certainly taken the female fantasy narrative made so popular by *Sex and the City* much further on the feminist radar by including a multiracial cast and professional, yet flawed, women, the series also misrepresents itself as a progressive piece of

VIT, or Very Important Television. It seems that *Grey's Anatomy* merely satisfies the appetite of cultural norms with a suggestive gloss of progressive feminism and color-blind casting. It cannot be denied, however, that this formula, and *Grey's Anatomy*'s operation within it, certainly appeals to the sensibilities of today's average female viewer, which *Grey's Anatomy* identifies as its primary fan base: young women between the ages of 18–49 with generally upper levels of income (Lisotta 1). These women, whose ideas and writing can be read in a number of online *Grey's Anatomy* blogs and fansites, also seem to be self-identifying feminists interested in the series' portrayal of "strong, successful women" ("Feminism Friday").

Although *Grey's Anatomy* is now in its third season of prime-time television on the ABC network, the program was initially a mid-season replacement that occupied a strategic time placement after the network's fantastical juggernaut, *Desperate Housewives*. However, *Grey's* soon developed enough of a fan base and high enough ratings to move into a night of its own (Gilbert 1). Set in the fantasy world of Seattle Grace Hospital, the series features a gaggle of surgical interns just beginning their residencies, and we experience their lives and loves as narrated by Meredith Grey, our protagonist. Though sometimes denigrated and brushed off as "nighttime soap opera with scalpels and condoms" (Gilbert 1), it cannot be denied that the series has momentum, significance, and a fiercely loyal and far-reaching fan base.

Ellen Pompeo, who portrays lead intern Meredith Grey on the series, claims that the girls of *Grey's* are more evolved and different from the "flawed bimbo" female stereotype that consistently appears on television (Freydkin and Keck 1), which is exactly what creator Shonda Rhimes had in mind when she began writing *Grey's Anatomy*. Rhimes, who must be credited as the first African American woman to create and produce a top-10 network series (McDowell 2), found TV drama's leading ladies existing "purely in relation to the men in their lives," and then decided that she wanted to see more women on TV like those she knew—women who were "competitive and a little snarky ... complex, ambitious, clever, confused women" (McDowell 2). The inaccurate representation of women on TV is nothing new; "although popular TV dramas ... appear to present characters and plotlines that defy gender stereotypes, [Susan] Douglas still finds telltale signs of cultural bias against women in such programs" (Maasik and Solomon 270). Susan Douglas, in her essay "Signs of Intelligent Life on TV," reiterates the point that modern television strives "to suck in those women [middle and upper-income folks between the ages of 18–49] whose lives have been transformed by the women's movement while keeping guys from grabbing the remote" (272). This is exactly what *Grey's Anatomy* is striving to do; it appeases and appeals to first-world feminists, but hidden contradictions abound in their devotion to both the series and Third Wave Feminism.

One extensive feminist blog on the series, *The Thinking Girl*, praises the number of female characters on *Grey's Anatomy*, and how they are portrayed as "dedicated and deserving"(2), but it later admits that the men continually have the upper hand of the girls within the show. Dr. McDreamy (a.k.a. Derek Shepard), an attending surgeon involved in a complicated relationship with Meredith, is obviously superior to her because, as the site writes:

> He holds all the cards in his *marriage* because his wife cheated on him, and he feels that gives him a moral superiority that allows him to be an asshole to her. And [Meredith] has to deal with accusations of sleeping her way to the best surgeries, and claims of favoritism, while [McDreamy's] morality is never questioned in any way. But, he's just so darn dreamy! With that floppy hair and dimples, he is oh-so-hard to resist! (2)

Although many find McDreamy hard to resist, viewers also cheered Meredith during season two of the series when she issued a verbal diatribe to her boss, and former lover, after he decided to return to his aforementioned wife. Meredith begins dating and pursuing one-night stands after the break-up, and McDreamy, now devoid of the "moral superiority" that *The Thinking Girl* awarded him earlier, becomes jealous that he no longer holds Meredith and Addison in the palm of his hand. Now known colloquially among fans as the "Whore Speech" (Freydkin and Keck 6), Meredith rants:

> You don't get to call me a whore. When I met you, I thought I had found the person I was going to spend the rest of my life with. I was done. So all the boys, and all the bars, and all the obvious Daddy issues—who cared? Because I was done. *You* left me. *You* chose Addison. I'm all glued back together now. I make no apologies for how I chose to repair what *you* broke (Greysanatomyinsider.com 1).

This seems like a feminist message; girl talks back to man who did her wrong and unapologetically pursues her own sexual interests in his absence. It's smatterings of occurrences like this that provides *Grey's* with a feminist vibe. But what becomes of this exchange? McDreamy storms off, later recants and dumps the wife, and we are left with a simpering Meredith pleading to His Floppy-Hairedness; "Pick me ... choose me ... love me" (Greysanatomyinsider.com 1).

More examples of feminist contradiction occur when one fan/blogger later compliments the "smart dialogue" and "good friendships" (Greysanatomyinsider.com 1) within the series, and then a few pages later rants, "wouldn't it be incredible if some writer out there could damn well come up with some real compelling female conversation?" (Greysanatomyinsider.com 7), because she feels that the girls, although important and professional, limit their conversations amongst themselves to that suitable to a gaggle of high school girls. But my thought is: would *Grey's Anatomy* be as successful as it is if they didn't? When fans are saying things like, "The setting, the medical emergencies—that's all secondary—in the end, I'm tuning in every week to watch [the girls] find love ... and hope they get loved in return" (Freydkin and Keck 5), and, "My favorite is Callie. She's real. She rocks a size-12 body and she's Hispanic, which is awesome ... and she's got the best lip gloss" (8), it appears that "feminist" women may long for a more stereotypical, culturally cookie-cutter life and romance than they may let on, and they may not be interested in the altruistic somberness of *Grey's Anatomy*'s older siblings such as ER and even *House, MD*.

Because *Grey's* fan base is over 68% women, and it is ranked number two in female viewership (second to *Desperate Housewives*), it is clear that women are buying what *Grey's Anatomy* is selling to them, a brand of McFeminism that makes them feel like progressive peers of the ladies of Seattle Grace. In reality, however, this McFeminism is merely a dressed up version of the same old thing; girls that need the leveling weakness of a messy love life, existential angst, and unflattering blue scrubs in order to make them culturally tolerable (Stanley 1). The men of *Grey's Anatomy*, who consistently have the upper hand in their female interns' lives, also happen to be a giant McSelling Point for the female viewers. Creator Wilson herself has said of *Grey's* men, "They were my fantasy men ... they got to say and do things I wish men would say and do" (McDowell 2). So, these "fantasy men" are doing what their creator wished all men would say and do: punishing their respective intern's sexual/romantic mistakes by assigning them inferior duties at the hospital. Countless times in the series, if Meredith or Christina are acting inappropriately to their lovers, Drs. McDreamy and Burke, they will be denied access to surgeries by their respective attending, so the doctors' control over the interns extends past the romantic and into the educational as well.

To the credit of *Grey's Anatomy*, however, it does present us with a more utopian view of humanity that varies from TV dramas of the past where, as Susan Douglas puts it:

> ... female friendships are nonexistent or venomous ... Asian and Latina women are rarely seen, and African American women are generally absent except as prostitutes, bad welfare moms, and unidentified nurses. In the ER emergency room, the black women who are the conscience and much-needed drill sergeants of the show don't get top billing, and are rarely addressed by name (273).

Rhimes explains the racial diversity of her cast by saying, "If you have a show in which there's only one character of color—which is what most shows do—then you have a weird obligation to make that person slightly saintly because they are representing all the people of color ... But if you have all different races, people get to be good or bad, flawed, selfish, and competitive" (Ogunnaike 3). These advances help make *Grey's Anatomy* more progressive than some of its earlier counterparts, and the series is also sometimes credited for the defibrillation of medical dramas like ER and the success of medical comedies like *Scrubs*, although fans of both shows have sometimes looked down upon *Grey's* for being short on altruism and long on "Hospital High School" drama (Gilbert 2), like when Addison Shepard (McDreamy's wife) finds Meredith's panties in her husband's operating room and posts them on the hospital callboard under a sign that says "Lost and Found." Instances like these humanize the serious world of the hospital, which viewers find appealing, but some critics think that it creates mere cartoons of characters that would be better served in a more austere medical drama (Gilbert 2).

What all of this information and critique boils down to, however, is that *Grey's Anatomy*, much like its fan base, is complicated and contradictory (an interesting thought, as the show's original working title was *Complications*). These are girls and women that want professional careers, personal control, and success; all the things that the femmes of *Grey's Anatomy* seem to have, but deep down inside they, and the surgeons, may just really want dysfunctional romance and some great lip gloss. With this brand of Diet Third Wave Feminism, we have upper-middle class females that don't identify with the commercial "girls-can-do" attitude of Girlie Feminism per se, but neither do they relate to the rigidness of the Second Wave. Are these women who can become active enough to actually do something and join the ranks of what Third Wave Feminism is all about? Or do they just want to put on the glossy veneer of a Very Important Feminist, much like *Grey's Anatomy* is Very Important Television?

Grey's Anatomy may actually be fostering a generation of young females who aren't, and don't want to be, blind to the issues of race, gender, class, and socioeconomic hardship, but nor do they want to mess up their aforementioned lip gloss. This is a generation that isn't quite as self-centered or issue-blind as the Ally McBeals of yesteryear, but neither are they the great, altruistic humanitarians of today ... and *Grey's Anatomy* seems to be catering to those McFeminists just fine.

Works Cited

Albiniak, Paige. "Why '*Grey*' Seems So Bright." *Broadcasting & Cable* 30 May 2005. *Business Source Premier Database*.

Douglas, Susan. *Where the Girls Are: Growing Up Female with the Mass Media*. New York: Three Rivers Press, 2005.

"Feminism Friday; *Grey's Anatomy*." *The Thinking Girl*. 10 Nov. 2006. http://www.thinkinggirl.wordpress.com/2006/11/10/feminism-friday-greys-anatomy.htm>.

Freydkin, Donna, and William Keck. "*Grey's* Ladies: Hospital Show's Appeal Lies with Its Strong, but Flawed, Women." *USA Today* 21 Sept. 2006.

Gilbert, Matthew. "*Anatomy* of a Hit: It Doesn't Want to Save the World. And That's Why We Love It." *The Boston Globe* 7 May 2006.

Grey's Anatomy Insider Fansite. 26 Feb. 2007. http://www.greysanatomyinsider.com.

Grey's Anatomy. Internet Movie Database 26 Feb. 2007. http://www.imdb.com/title/tt0413573.

"Grey's Anatomy." *Wikipedia*. 26 Feb. 2007. http://www.en.wikipedia.org/wiki/
  Grey's_Anatomy.

Lisotta, Christopher. "Upscale Young Viewers Go for *Anatomy*." *Television Week* 2
  Oct. 2006. *Business Source Premier Database*.

Maasik, Sonia, and Jack Solomon. *Signs of Life in the USA: Readings on Popular
  Culture for Writers*. New York: Bedford/St. Martins, 2006.

McDowell, Jeanne. "A Woman and Her *Anatomy*." *Time* 22 May 2006.

Ogunnaike, Lola. "*Grey's Anatomy* Creator Finds Success in Surgery." *The New York
  Times* 28 Sept. 2006.

Stanley, Alessandra. "Television Review: Male Misery Just Loves Female Company."
  The New York Times 3 Jan. 2007.

How I Wrote This: An Interview with Lara Hayhurst

Why did you write this piece—what was the assignment or motivation for writing?
This piece was an assignment given as a final paper for a course I took my senior year
at Pace University; "Girls on Film: Cultural Studies in New Wave Feminism."

What did you do when you decided to write?
The course focused around distinguishing the different waves of feminism; the second
wave of the sixties, "Girlie" feminism, and how they all influenced the current third
wave of feminism, which strives to use pop culture and media as a tool to advance
women. When asked to write an extensive paper on a facet of media or pop culture
relevant to women and the third wave of feminism, I had to choose a topic that I felt
extremely familiar with, so as not to make the task too daunting. I was already a big
fan of *Grey's Anatomy*, and felt that the way it treated its female characters was complex and interesting.

How did you begin?
I was already up-to-date with the current season of *Grey's* as far as knowledge and
observation went, but I rewatched some favorite episodes and those that I remembered
dealing specifically with the women or women's issues. I also waded through a lot of
blogs, fansites, and the like to get a feel for how real women in the show's primary
demographic felt about the characters, what they liked and disliked about certain episodes, and what they were drawn to discussing.

Describe the process of writing the first draft.
It was a few years ago, so I don't remember fine details, but I remember spreading all
my research out in front of me and highlighting the sections that dealt with my different points of discussion in different colors. I made an outline and then filed in my

bibliographic support as I went, taking it paragraph by paragraph. Going back and revisiting the paper, I find the beginning sections a little hard to read, the flow isn't as smooth and the quotations don't come naturally all the time, but around the middle of the paper I pick up speed and I quite like the way I ended it!

Did you write a draft all the way through?
Yes, I always prefer to write that way. Even if it becomes stream of consciousness rambling, it's always helpful to me to see where my mind goes and then relate back to my references for support.

How much editing did you do as you wrote?
Not a lot. I did my big edit after I submitted my first draft and got feedback from my professor.

How did you do your research?
I did most of my research beforehand. Because my topic was so contemporary, a lot of internet searching and wading through blogs and fansites took up my time, but I also used textbook and reading materials we had been given in class, just to make sure I was relating my thesis back to the overall objective of the course. Looking back on my bibliography, it's a mix of easily accessible sites like Wikipedia, blogs, and print articles (USA Today, Entertainment Weekly, etc), and more broad resources such as Where The Girls Are and Signs of Intelligent Life in the USA. I'm hoping this made the paper topical and on-point, but also accessible.

How long would you say the process took?
We were given the assignment at the beginning of the semester, and I think I chose my topic right away. I collected research and began watching episodes for a few months, and then the actual writing probably took a week.

How did you edit the draft?
I did my edit mostly based on my professor's suggestions. I was working for a grade, after all. I also always like to read my work out loud and make sure it flows easily. I made a few changes that way, and I also read it aloud to my husband to make sure it was understandable off the page as well as on. He gave me some ideas and help that I appreciated from a layman uninvolved with my course or the project itself.

What was the response when you turned in your essay?
Favorable! I remember sending the draft to my Dad, an author, and he thought it was strong. I received a good grade on the paper, and was thrilled when my professor suggested I submit the essay to Dr. Silverman for his upcoming textbook.

Are you satisfied now with what you wrote? Would you make any changes?
This was the first time I had revisited the essay since we edited it for publication, and
I think I mention above, that I found the first few pages a little jumbled and my thesis
a little unclear. I think towards the middle I really settled in and it becomes clear that
my thesis is really one of exploration and contradiction, not a black and white opinion.
I think if I had made it more clear at the onset that my paper was about "Diet Third
Wave Feminism" and the upper-middle class "McFeminists" that subscribe to it using
shows like *Grey's*, the paper would be more clear.

   Just on a side note; I've actually fallen off the *Grey's Anatomy* wagon and haven't
seen any of the past two seasons. Snippets of the episodes I've caught on TV kind of
annoy me, and I think the show has lost its edge. I think it has become a little more of
a nighttime soap opera in recent years, and I think other viewers agree. It has spawned
its own little sub genre of television, however, which I think is interesting. Shows concerning the gaggle of new interns that arrive at the hospital/law office/university and
succeed/fail/love say snarky dialogue is prevalent, but none of the shows seem to be
doing particularly well with ratings. My personal TV preference now lies with *Mad
Men*, *Dexter*, and *Damages*; all shows that could have their own critiques of third wave
feminism, in my opinion.

CHAPTER 20

READING AND WRITING ABOUT SPORTS

Sports as a category is so large that we could pair every chapter in the book with sports—a book about sports movies, a study of sports and its relationship to the environment, sports and music, sports and fashion, and in particular, sports and gender. But even though sports engage all those other types of texts, it also has its own culture that is important to reckon with on its own.

To us, this begins with the fact that Americans care about sports. Not all Americans, and not all sports, but the most-watched program on TV every year is the Super Bowl; Super Bowl Sunday is essentially a national holiday.[1] People get together and watch the game, the half-time show, and the commercials, even if they do not have rooting interest in the game. In other words, the setting for the commercials and the music is *sports*.

But it's not just the Super Bowl that has cultural impact. Indeed, almost every sporting event has a type of cultural connection either explicit or implicit. For example, the NCAA men's and women's basketball tournaments has spawned a national mania in picking the results, which in recent years included live picks by President Obama on ESPN.[2] ESPN, which originally stood for Entertainment and Sports Programming Network, has six channels and a well-read website. There are often multiple radio stations in a city devoted to sports, and sports at the high school level is often a gathering place for a community, supplementing or sometimes surpassing political and religious institutions. Many big cities have sports cable devoted to local teams. And increasingly, sports fans participate in fantasy sports, in which they pretend to own teams that they draft. This itself has spawned its own enormous media.

Many people do not care about sports (including some professors), but even those people would concede that sports matter. Unlike life, sports has definitive outcomes, even if we second guess decisions by their participants, and we think people might be comforted by these concrete outcomes. We would argue too that people love sport because it allows them to connect to something larger than themselves. Finally, games

---

1   Catherine Taibi, "Super Bowl XLIX Was Most-Watched Show in U.S. Television History," *The Huffington Post*, 2 Feb. 2015.

2   Alex Wall, "All the President's Picks: See His 2015 NCAA Tournament Brackets," *The White House*, 20 Mar. 2015.

can be very entertaining, and they have their own built-in tension; no one knows what is going to happen until the game or match is played. Unlike most other media, and very much like life itself, games are unpredictable. Unlike life, games have definitive outcomes, which itself can be comforting.

Various sports also appeal to us because they involve activities that many of us do or have done. We can relate to the athletes we watch compete. That notion of competition is also an important component of sports. We like it when there are good guys and bad guys. Oftentimes, we locate identity (college, community, city) in our sports teams. We like cheering and supporting those who represent us and compete on our behalf. We also like spectacle, and we love drama. In a Venn diagram, then, there would be enormous overlap between American sports and American values.

People are worried about the importance of sports in American culture. Because sports are so prevalent on television, the internet, and the radio, because so many resources on high-school and college campuses are devoted to sports, and because athletes and teams often receive preferential treatment, commentators, teachers, and scholars have leveled a number of critiques at sports. They are worried that sports have supplanted other forms of culture that they feel are more enriching. They worry that the passion people have for teams is too fervent and leads to bad behavior. They worry about the gambling associated with the sports. They also are concerned with the health of athletes, including fears of concussions in football players, and they are also worried that players in local, high-school, and college sports focus on sports rather than education. For example, H.G. Bissinger's fabulous book, *Friday Night Lights* (and resulting television series and movie) is a classic example of the damage that can be caused when a school and a town privileges sport over education and equality.

People who love sports have responses to all these concerns, but often not to the satisfaction of those making these criticisms. So many people choose to live with contradictions of sports as they do with other forms of culture: television shows that are insufficiently diverse, movies that are predictable, music that is derivative. Being critically engaged does not, in our opinion, mean a wholesale rejection of a form of culture, but an acknowledgment that all genres and even all texts within them have their own weaknesses. So while the authors acknowledge all the ills of sports, we follow sports, sometimes with a critical distance but also with interest.

Sports are a business. Sports and its associated business are billion-dollar industries. People spend money to attend games, buy sports-related apparel, purchase their own sporting equipment, pay for cable television, pay dues for fantasy sports, and so on. During the final game of the 2016 NBA finals, when the Cleveland Cavaliers played the Golden State Warriors, two courtside tickets were sold for $50,000 each. That is

$100,000 for two people to attend a game of basketball. That is more money than 95 percent of Americans make in a year.

Teams spend money to pay players and employees, build stadiums, and pay taxes. Governments often help fund stadiums. Colleges, universities, and high schools spend money on equipment and scholarships. Companies buy advertising with networks to advertise during games. Networks spend money on equipment and employees. But is someone making a business decision when purchasing a tennis racket or a New York Yankees cap? Are universities making purely business decisions when they decide to subsidize their college sports teams? We would say no. Even owners of professional sports franchises, who now do very well, often purchase sports teams as a manifestation of their own desires. These business and money connections are complex financially *and* emotionally.

Endorsements play an increasingly large role in sports and can be a fascinating bridge between sports and the aims of this book. For example, what associations do you have for the Nike swoosh? The Adidas leaf (officially known as the "trefoil")? The Puma puma? The Under Armour symbol? The New Balance N? But endorsements go beyond athletic gear; they also now encompass cars and jewelry and even websites. These companies want you to link the abilities of their endorsees (Tiger Woods for Rolex and Nike; Steph Curry for Under Armour; Serena Williams for Nike, Gatorade, and Wilson) with the values and abilities of their products. So strong are the ties between player and endorsement, it can even affect things at the national level. In 1992, the United States Olympic basketball team (the Dream Team as it was called) won the gold medal in basketball. The uniforms and warm-ups were made by Reebok and had a Reebok logo on the shoulder; however, many of the players on the US team, including Michael Jordan and Charles Barkley, had big endorsement deals with Nike. At the medal ceremony, the Nike players unzipped their jackets so that the lapel flopped over and hid the logo. Jordan, Barkley, and Magic Johnson actually covered up the Reebok patch with the American flag to ensure they not be associated with Reebok.

One thing that gets people thinking about the relationship between sports and capitalism is their own experiences playing sports, which they see as innocent and capitalism-free (even though a local insurance agency probably sponsored their little league team). They project themselves into a world in which capitalism and free enterprise seems outside of or even contradictory to the idea of sport, which we consider play. But we can (and have to) think about both business and play at the same time, even if we believe we would value our experiences differently than the players and teams we root for.

Sports have built-in stories. Every game has a story built into it—it has a beginning, middle, and end, and to some degree, protagonists and antagonists, especially if you have a rooting interest in the game. There are also external stories built into sports;

every athlete has a story about how he or she became an athlete, and often cities themselves have stories attached to them. Some of these stories are predictable. The authors wrote the first draft of this chapter a day before the 2016 Super Bowl; there were predictable stories about the Denver Broncos quarterback Peyton Manning—about his legacy, impending retirement, and so on. There were familiar discussions on whether one team's excellent defense can stop another team's excellent offense. There were features on players who grew up in or near San Francisco because that's where the game is being played.

We worked on a subsequent draft the day after the Cleveland Cavaliers defeated the Golden State Warriors in the NBA championship, and Dustin Johnson won the US Open Golf tournament and his first major. Both of these events had huge stories surrounding them: Steph Curry versus LeBron James; the record-breaking year of the Warriors; the repeated meltdowns of Dustin Johnson. Sports rely on drama, on the importance of the narrative. A day before that, at the COPA soccer match in California, Chile handed Mexico its worst loss in soccer in over 50 years. It was a national scandal in Mexico! And just a few weeks before that, Serena Williams lost in the finals of the French Open, which would have been a record win for her. Today it's Switzerland versus Poland in the first game of the knockout stage of EURO 2016, the European soccer (football if you are outside of the United States and Canada) championships.

We worked on the final version during the 2017 Stanley Cup finals, the NBA finals, the College World Series for both men and women, and the NCAA track and field national championships. Which of these contains the best stories? The most intriguing personal profiles? Most human interest?

What is important to remember is that sports rely on drama, and drama is created by stories. Writing about sports without acknowledging the swirl of noise around them is to miss much of the aura, power, and culture of sports.

Sports reflect the values of the surrounding culture. In a sense, almost all cultural expression, whether literature, movies, art, politics, or sports, has some connection to the culture around it. The most obvious connection is the money attached to sports, which compares to movie box office or television ratings or poll numbers or prices at auction for an artwork—we like to talk about how much things cost and what they are worth.

But there are other cultural connections worth exploring besides economic ones. People ask questions about why women's sports, for example, do not get the same type of viewership as men's sports. Women athletes make much less money than men. Sometimes colleges try to cut women's sports to make room for more high-profile male sports. Often women's practice facilities are much smaller and less advanced than their male counterparts. You might think about what is at stake when women's sports are not taken as seriously as men's, or when the complaints of young female gymnasts about an abusive doctor are ignored for years.

People also talk about the racial make-up of various sports, and less prominently, class make-up of players and coaches. There are some who wonder whether sports teams mimic the feudality of historical battles. For example, football is largely military in its design and terminology. It is primarily about the acquisition of land. The uniforms include guards and helmets (like knights and soldiers); a quarterback is referred to as a "field general"; we use terms like "attack" and "surrender" and "flank." A quarterback throws "bombs" and "fires missiles." A big fullback is described as a "tank." Even mascots are bellicose—Raiders, Buccaneers, Pirates, Warriors, Cowboys. Can you imagine the Denver Samaritans? Or the Chicago Kitties? The Brooklyn Nurses? America is a nation with a history of warfare, and we tend to idolize military heroes. So one could argue that football is a metaphor for war and certainly for battle; therefore it is not surprising that it is more popular in the United States than in a country like Switzerland or Luxembourg.

There are also connections between America's urban and rural settings. We tend to think of basketball as being a notably urban sport, whereas baseball tends to be more rural or suburban. We associate golf and tennis with elite demographics; NASCAR with blue-collar ones. These associations are not always accurate, but they play into the larger cultural associations with sports. *Friday Night Lights* demonstrates how the values of the town of Odessa, Texas were invested almost completely—at the expense of everything else—in its high-school football team. As you think about sports and culture, consider how many people, institutions, cities, and even countries make sports part of their identities. When looking at sports through this lens, you will often be surprised. For example, when Oklahoma City landed the NBA franchise formerly in Seattle, it completely changed the city. People who thought they were University of Oklahoma Sooners fans found themselves watching basketball religiously, and a state known for its problematic relationship to African Americans suddenly embraced a team comprised of many African American players as heroes.

Sports are a visual text. While we might listen to and read about sports, much of how we experience sport is through our eyes. Commentators have sometimes remarked how beautiful good sports are, an aesthetic judgment about visual quality. But their visual nature goes beyond their beauty. What to make of the way we adorn our athletes in numbers, mascot names, and the name of their geographic location? Why do managers of baseball teams wear team uniforms, and football and basketball coaches wear something else (sweatshirts with a team logo, suits or sport coats, and so on)? Athletes' bodies are also texts, as are stadiums, websites, scoreboards, and fan wear. By looking at these elements, we can learn about what sports values. For example, why have the

Washington Redskins not changed their racist mascot? Why are the Oakland Raiders black and silver (instead of, say, pink and turquoise)?

We talk often in this book about the grammar of a visual text. Sports also have a grammar—both in terms of their vocabularies but also their optics. Tennis courts have lines and rules. Gymnastics has a grammar of poise, athleticism, and balance. Ice skating has a series of hierarchized criteria. And adding to this the varied and often gendered uniforms athletes wear (skirts in women's field hockey and tennis, helmets with facemasks and pads in football, for example), sports seems more and more like a spectacle to be beheld than an exhibition for appreciation.

Think about how sports ask to be *seen* and *watched*. What is the significance of apparatuses, accouterments, and other equipment? Uniforms and colors?

Sports have symbols. This point overlaps with the others before it, but it bears repeating that the individual elements of sports are themselves symbols. A primary example of this is the Washington professional football team. The Redskins have a racist name and a racist mascot; it is for many Native Americans and non-Natives deeply offensive. But it also symbolizes the deeper insularity of the Washington franchise, whose owner seems determined to keep it despite these objections.[3] For those who want to preserve the mascot, the opposition symbolizes a type of political correctness. Supporters also view the name as a form of free speech. For those who favor getting rid of the name, its racist history overrides freedom of speech concerns. The fact that Washington is in the name is also symbolic because it represents the city and perhaps the man behind it, as well as the irony that the team plays in Maryland, not DC. For some who violently oppose the nickname, the fact that a team with a racist name and logo are housed in the nation's capital is particularly hurtful because it seems to suggest that our government condones colonialism and the negative representation of Indigenous Americans.

But besides this obviously complicated symbol, even common items such as base-balls and basketballs are symbols, and so are other parts of the sports landscape. Why are there so many sticks and balls in sports? And to what extent is sports clothing representative of roles one has in society? What does the presence of headphones in football mean? Why don't basketball players have a dugout? Why do women wear skirts while playing golf and tennis? Why does NASCAR insist on having their racecars look like cars we can buy? These are questions about symbols and the meanings we attach to them.

In events like the Olympics, the games not only traffic in international symbols, but the deployment of flags, medals, and podiums makes strong connections between national and athletic greatness and dominance. Countries do not have mascots in the Olympics, but they do often use flags in place of mascots, as though national pride is

---

3   Scott Allen, "Daniel Snyder on the Redskins Name Controversy: 'The Truth Is on Our Side'," *Washington Post*, 3 Sept. 2014.

on the line, as though the performance of a young person in a pool or on a track or on a mat has something to say about a country's strength and even its virtue.

What's more, athletes have themselves come to symbolize certain values. You probably have attached associations to many if not all of the following figures: Simone Biles, Draymond Green, Tom Brady, Ronda Rousey, Buster Posey, Tiger Woods, or Maria Sharapova. In fact, as we were working on the final version of this chapter, Serena Williams was getting a great deal of press for posing (nearly) naked and pregnant for *Vanity Fair*. To be sure, Williams is functioning as a symbol—a number of symbols in fact—but her image is a classic example of how sports figures transcend mere sport.

When writing about sports, think about how often we infuse values into the act of competition. In a country like America, where free enterprise and capitalist competition are part of our ontology and our epistemology, the action and business of sport aligns particularly well with our national identity.

Chances are, sports are very important to your college. If you go to a major research university—a NCAA division 1 institution—it is likely that sports are part of the identity of the institution. It is possible that the football stadium is the largest and most central structure on your campus, outsizing academic buildings and the library. Some professors find this annoying, but we have found that students often love having sports as part of their college experience. And sports can benefit an institution in a number of ways. For example, at many institutions, the grade point averages (GPAs) for female athletes are higher than those of the student body at large. In some instances, like the recent controversies surrounding rapes committed by student athletes at Stanford and Baylor, athletes and coaches can bring shame to what should be a joyful part of being a student. At schools like Notre Dame or Duke, football and basketball are as important to campus culture as academics. In fact, one of the authors of this book was able to publish a beautiful book with the University of Texas Press because when the UT football team won the national championship, the university's press received an influx of cash. So, in this instance, scholarship benefitted from athletics, but this is not always the case.

Sports in America are often extensions of our national attitudes toward race and gender. Earlier we wrote about the cultural relationships sports engenders, and their relationships to race, class, and gender. But we think race and gender and sports have components that are important to discuss beyond cultural relationships. Many of us know about Jesse Owens, an African American track star in the 1930s, who won four gold medals at the 1936 Berlin Olympics (the subject of the 2016 movie *Race*), and Jackie Robinson, the African American baseball player responsible for breaking the color barrier in major league sports (and the subject of the 2013 movie 42), but the matrix of sports and race goes beyond integration. If we start with the idea that many people want the same things for themselves and their children—a future where their children are self-sufficient and happy—then we begin to understand a little about why race and gender and sports are so contentious; discrimination associated with it reduces our common humanity at the cost of stereotype and prejudice. In other words, society sometimes reads people into roles that may or may not fit them. Think of your own assumptions about people different from yourself and what sports they do—or even should—play. Do you think that there are sports that particular societal or ethnic groups are more suited for? Now imagine, you are a member of one of those groups who wants to play a sport not associated with your group or you are a member of a group associated with a sport and don't want to play that sport. While most if not all legal barriers to participation in sport have been eliminated in the United States—something that is not true in a number of other countries—cultural barriers still remain. The recent furor over athletes kneeling for the national anthem was so incendiary, it garnered the attention (and the criticism) of the president of the United States.

Similarly, America's ongoing debates about gender and gender equality have now fully entered the arena of sports. Indeed, we noted previously that female athletes tend to get paid much less than male athletes; nowhere is this fact more overt than in professional soccer. In 2016, six members of the US Women's National Soccer team filed a lawsuit due to the fact that women soccer players were paid roughly 25% less than male soccer players, despite the fact that the women's team generated nearly $20 million more in revenue in 2015 than the U.S. Men's National team.[4]

This issue goes beyond pay and into the realms of culture and representation, including the ongoing sexualization of female athletes—which is itself a form of coverage. For example, even though 40% of all sports participants (and 43% of all scholarship athletes) are women, women's sports still receive only 2 to 4% of all sports coverage.[5] And, even when there is coverage on television, for example, the events are usually relegated to niche networks, like the Golf Channel, whereas men's golf tournaments are typically broadcast on major networks like CBS. Even more disturbing is how female athletes are portrayed and written about. Dr. Mary Jo Kane, a professor of sport sociology at the University of Minnesota, notes that women tend to receive a different kind of coverage than men when it comes to sports: "[F]emale athletes are more likely to be portrayed off the court, out of uniform and in highly sexualized poses where the emphasis is on their femininity and their physical attractiveness rather than their athletic competence." So, it is not just the amount of coverage but the mode and quality of coverage that matters. In sports, in the media, and in the boardroom, women deserve the same opportunities to be taken seriously as men.

---

4   Jasneel Chaddha, "Discrimination in the Marketing and Compensation of Female Athletes in the Age of Trump," *Huffington Post,* 9 Jan. 2017.
5   Mary Jo Kane, "Progress and Inequality: Women's Sports and the Gender Gap," *Improving Lives: CEHD Vision 2020 Blog,* 27 Jan. 2017.

A good reader and writer of sports is aware of the many external factors that affect the game—not just the scoreboard. Here are some things to think about when writing about sports:

Sport: What sport are we watching? What makes this sport distinct?

Players: Who are the players? What do they look like? What is similar about them? What is different? How do they compare to other sports?

Field/stadium/court: What is the setting for the game—field, stadium, or court? What does the setting look like? How do the players interact with it? How do the fans? What is distinct about this place? How is the field or court similar to other places within and without sports (for example, how is a stadium like a mall? A theater? A school?)? How do the sport's organizers want us to think about the sport?

Story: What happens in the game? To what degree is the game predictable? To what degree is in unpredictable? Would you say it is more or less predictable than a movie or television show?

Themes: Are there themes involved in the sports? (Themes are what writers believe about issues, ideas, and subjects, *not* the ideas and issues themselves.) For example, is one team a favorite and the other an underdog? How do these roles of teams or players affect the way we view it? In what way is violence a theme in sports? Why is winning so important?

Figurative language: What symbols, metaphors, and motifs present themselves in the sport? What effect does their repetition have?

Absences: What is missing in watching a chosen sporting event?

Race/ethnicity/gender/class: How do these issues present themselves in the event itself and the way it's covered both during and after the game? Race is a crucially important issue in sports. At some institutions, racial diversity happens mostly because of sports. Why do you think this is the case? Is this good or bad?

Reality: In what way does a sporting event reflect the world as you normally experience it? What is different? Does this matter?

Gender: Sports is one of the areas in American culture that remains divided by gender. Men and women work together, live together, even serve together in the military, but

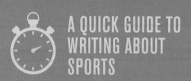

A QUICK GUIDE TO WRITING ABOUT SPORTS

1. Be able to start and stop a program when watching: If you can, try to record a sports event if you are going to write about it. You need to make what is a passive activity, active.

2. Ask a question about your subject before beginning your viewing: Writing about and watching a sporting event becomes more focused if you have a question you are trying to answer.

3. Take notes extensively: One reason is to remember the text better, but the more important one is to gather information.

4. Brainstorm for a thesis: Even if you do not use your original thesis, it helps when writing a draft.

5. Organize ideas by paragraph: If you have a first draft with definable paragraphs, the draft will be stronger and easier to revise.

they play in different leagues in team sports, have different divisions in races, and have entirely different associations in golf and tennis. There are also inequities in pay, viewership, and attention in the media. Why is this the case? A great paper would be to explore funding and resources for men's and women's sports at your college. Also, consider issues of age and gender. The harmful abuse of girl gymnasts by a male doctor, despite dozens of complaints raises so many questions about gender and power, it is hard to know where to begin.

WRITING ABOUT SPORTS: THE GENRES

Writing about sports consists of a variety of established genres: the game story, the profile, the column, the feature story, the problem story, the related literature, and the research paper.

So much of writing about sports is in magazine or newspaper journalism, though there is a large body of work on sports in research as well. Three of the most common forms of sports writing—the **game story**, the **profile**, and the **column**—appear daily in newspapers and on news and sports websites. Others appear in magazines or in research journals.

But sports have long been the site for more in-depth examination not only through journalism but also through scholarship. One can write an **analysis** of symbols associated with sports, produce a **researched paper**, examine a phenomenon through the lenses of race, gender, and class, and even use theoretical lenses such as narrative theory. You can also use sports to write about income, demographics, and even politics. Do Republicans favor NASCAR and football? Do Democrats skew toward tennis and basketball? Why might this be the case?

Sports Analysis

There are a few types of analyses of sports one can do. One is to explore the symbols of sports in a paper. For example, one might do a paper about sports nicknames, mascots, the field of play, uniforms, or sponsors. In writing a paper about sponsors, you might compare the type of sponsors for two sports commonly viewed on a Sunday afternoon—NASCAR and professional golf. Both sets of athletes often adorn themselves with their sponsors' products. Golfers tend to represent products geared toward wealthier consumers, like Rolex watches and Lexus automobiles, while NASCAR drivers often represent products that are ever-present in everyday life such as Coca-Cola and Coors Lite. Or one could write a paper on the differences between uniforms in various sports and what they represent; why do women wear skirts while playing tennis and golf?

To begin writing a paper like this, think of the question you want to ask. For example, how does sport sponsorship reflect the audience of a sport? Putting the paper topic into a question will force you to come up with an arguable thesis, which in this case would begin something like this: "Sport sponsorship reflects the audience of NASCAR and professional golf in x, y, and z ways." Then your paper would be set up with paragraphs in each of the ways you describe below.

The Researched Paper

Writing a researched paper—a paper whose research supplements what is an argumentative paper—about sports starts with coming up with a question you want to answer about sports, and coming up with an angle or a lens. Researching the question without one will lead to a paper without an argument and likely without scholarly sources. But how do you come up with a lens? Let's dig down into the process.

Let's say you want to write a paper about sports stadiums and what they say about American culture. The first thing to do would be to narrow the topic to a more specific question. Maybe you want to write about their architectural styles; maybe you want to write about the way the fans are seated in relationship to the players; perhaps you want to write about the concessions; maybe you want to write about the relationship between a geographical location and stadiums. All of these are potentially good questions to ask, and all of them would have sufficient material to draw on.

Let's think about the last question, which could go a few ways. Do you want to write about the relationship between a particular stadium and its locale, like Fenway Park and Boston? Or do you want to write more about the trends of constructing or renovating stadiums in urban areas more generally? Actually, you might want to do a little of both. It would be good to know something about bigger trends in stadium construction as you approach Fenway Park. You could begin by approaching Google Scholar (scholar.google.com) or one of your university's databases that you would find on your library website. Some keywords you might begin with are "stadium," "renovation," "cities," and see what you get. When you find a few articles or books you think are relevant, it's time to step back and see what you have.

What you are going to do next is figure out what writers agree and disagree on when it comes to stadium renovation. Academic papers are better when they include previous work; it gives you something to work with when forming your argument, and it also shows you are working on something while knowing its context.

The final step is to look at a primary text, in this case, a stadium, and make your own argument about it. Think about what messages its design sends, and how that compares to the work you have already read. Then combine this with an introduction, your literature review, and a conclusion and you have an essay.

Sports Journalism

Game stories cover what happens in a game. They have the elements of typical journalism stories—a lede, which is the opening of the story, a nut graf, or contextual paragraph, and the story of the game.[6] To write a game story, you go to the game, watch the game while taking notes, perhaps interview players and coaches, and write about what happened.

To write a profile, you decide on a subject, interview the subject, ask the subject for additional sources. Begin with an anecdote, describe her or his current status, circle back to his or her upbringing, and then talk about his or her current life and why we should care about him or her.

To write a column, you decide on a sports-related subject about which you have an opinion and expand on it.

The classes associated with this book will likely not be journalistic classes, so it is more than likely these assignments may not be appropriate for your course. However, they are a crucial part of the ecosystem of sports, so it is important to understand them even if you don't use them.

OTHER ESSAY IDEAS

1. Uniform: Write a paper about what your college or university sports uniforms say about your school.

2. Shape of the field: Choose a sport or sports and write a paper examining the shape of the field, and what it says about the sport (and perhaps society).

3. Ball: Write a paper examining to what extent the shape of the ball (or puck) is arbitrary and necessary for the sport. For example, basketballs could be different sizes and so could baseballs and footballs (which could be a different shape).

---

6   Lede and graf are specific journalism terms. Lede was coined to avoid being confused with "lead," which referred to the typesetting process. Graf has similar origins. Merrill Perlman, "Leading Questions," *Columbia Journalism Review*, 1 Nov. 2010.

4. Gender: In general, women's sports are less popular than men's sports, and in both golf and tennis the matches are actually shorter. At the same time, sports are seen as one way women can challenge traditional gender roles. Explain the contradictions involved in these ideas. You might consider writing about a film like *Bend It Like Beckham* or *Battle of the Sexes* that take on these issues.

5. Television: Most of us primarily watch our sports on television, and so examining sports and how they are portrayed is a useful topic. Some papers you might write include an examination of graphics on television and what they say about the games they portrayed; the language of commentary from play-by-play and color commentators; what slow-motion replays show us about sports; the perceived audiences for sports through their commercials; and so on.

6. Race: Race and ethnicity are one of most discussed social and cultural aspects of sports. As is the case now with the many protests among professional athletes during the national anthem, there are questions about whether sports has a beneficial influence on race relations. There are even questions about the roles members of minority groups play in sports (in football, general managers, coaches, and quarterbacks are still underrepresented according to many commentators), and so on.

RESOURCES

On the internet there are innumerable resources for sports fans, among them ESPN, *Sports Illustrated*, Yahoo! Sports, Bleacher Report, and the SB Nation universe of websites devoted to teams and sports (one author's alma mater, the University of Texas, has *two* of these sites). For researchers, you might consult the website Sports in American History, which is a great resource.

Books

Sports books are one of the most popular types of books, and there are many books about individual sports, teams, and athletes. The books listed here include some of those and some academic books as well.

H.G. Bissinger, *Friday Night Lights*. Nominally about a season of football in Texas, it is also about race, class, and sports.

Yago Colás, *Ball Don't Lie: Myth, Genealogy, and Invention in the Cultures of Basketball.* This book explores the history and culture of basketball.

Franklin Foer, *How Soccer Explains the World: An Unlikely Theory of Globalization.* This book explains how soccer (football) is a lens, window, and metaphor for the world.

Laura Hillenbrand, *Seabiscuit.* This is the book about the famous racehorse of the 1930s; it is also about how class interacts with sports.

Michael Lewis, *Moneyball.* This book explores how one team used statistics to remake its team.

Lindsay Parks Pieper, *Sex Testing: Gender Policing in Women's Sports.* This book explores the way the International Olympic Committee used testing to exclude women from the Olympics, in effect punishing women who were deemed too strong to be considered a woman.

George Plimpton, *Paper Lion.* In this book, Plimpton went through the training camp of the Detroit Lions; it's an inside look at what it means to be a professional athlete.

William C. Rhoden, *Forty Million Dollar Slaves: The Rise, Fall, and Redemption of the Black Athlete.* This book explores the history and culture of black athletes in the United States.

Lissa Smith, *Nike Is a Goddess: The History of Women in Sports.* This is a history of women in sports.

Welch Suggs, *A Place on the Team: The Triumph and Tragedy of Title IX.* This book explores the history of Title IX, which, among other things, forces universities and colleges to provide equal access to athletics for men and women.

CHAPTER 21

READING AND WRITING ABOUT THE MEDIA AND ADVERTISING

As we were working on a draft of this chapter in 2016, Hillary Clinton and Donald Trump emerged as the presumptive nominees for president. We did a round of proof-reading in May and June of 2017, when various scandals about President Trump and his White House saturated the news. Final edits happened in late 2017 as ongoing concerns about Trump and Russia were top stories. Both Trump and Clinton have or have had a rocky relationship with the media, and both, especially Mr. Trump, enjoy critiquing the media. But what is "the media"? When candidates or athletes criticize the media, we think we know what they mean, but are we correct? In the past twenty years, the word media has become almost an obscenity, particularly to those who are caught in its gaze. Such a sticky word demands a definition.

Media is a wildly complicated term. Anything from a book to a magazine to a news program to a radio show to a film to a website is technically a medium (*media* is the plural of *medium*). For the purposes of this chapter, we will define the media as organizations or companies that deliver information—this includes journalism, advertising, and social media. In terms of journalism, we refer to those outlets that seek to cover any kind of news in whatever form. Probably the most technically correct way to refer to news organizations would be just that—news organizations—but because media is itself a word that is used often and carelessly, we want to engage it here. This introduction may seem one of our more political ones, but there is a reason for that: everyone, from liberals to conservatives, from the rich to the poor, from young to old, have strong opinions about the media, their role in American culture, and their perceived biases. Our purpose in asking you to read "the media" in a sophisticated way is designed to help you broaden and complicate your view of this increasingly important but beguiling concept.

"The media" has become an easy term for an industry or series of industries that deliver messages, encourage social interactions, and transmit data. Everyone seems to think the media are too intrusive. And yet ... we watch and we read. If we did not watch or read, the media would change because the media are not one entity but many, which are always changing. For instance, there was no cable television when the authors of this book were born, and thus no CNN. When we were in graduate school, the internet was only a military communications system, hardly the consuming force it is today.

In the past few years, the term "social media" has become its own concept, and it too appears to be intruding on all aspects of our lives. For example, have you checked your Snapchat or Instagram since you began reading this chapter? The need to be updated and in touch can be overwhelming. And whatever we write and think about the media now is destined to change for better or worse as our world changes and technology advances.

You might be wondering why we have decided to combine advertising, journalism, and the media in one chapter, when each could be its own chapter or its own book. For better or worse, the distinctions between media, advertising, and journalism are fuzzy at best. Is a post on Facebook by Fox News journalism or advocacy? On the CNN. com website, one could find a news story about America's favorite cities to visit within eyeshot of an ad for Orbitz—is this coincidence? In the 2016 election, the concept of fake news made this intersection of news, media, advertisements, and technology even more salient. Even beyond these instances, the texts of journalism and advertising and the media are so interdependent, that it seems responsible to link them semiotically.

Even though the media are diverse in nature, they share a number of concerns that connect them. Almost all forms of media struggle to balance various interests: public interest versus profit, fairness and objectivity versus bias, national coverage versus local, depth of coverage versus breadth of coverage, the need to report quickly versus the imperative to report accurately. Some newer forms of media, particularly partisan blogs, are deliberately biased in their role in both advocating positions and criticizing more traditional media. All the conflicts sometimes lead to our sense that there is something wrong with the media, that something is not working right. Still, media organizations perform a crucial role in American life and American culture. This introduction will begin to explain some of the difficulties and misconceptions attached to the media so that you might be better able to craft smart essays.

In terms of writing about the media, one of the things that the internet has fostered is a vibrant media criticism, a type of writing you could undertake as well. If you choose to write about the media, you could critique how various media cover news, or even the semiotics of a particular form of media. But you are probably more likely to write about advertising. Advertisements use a lot of symbols, and they often telegraph who their intended audience is through these symbols. And they are good candidates to be analyzed with some of the lenses we wrote about in Chapter 5, such as race, gender, and class. Following are some things to consider about the media.

The media are businesses, not (only) a public service. Although the media are in the business of selling newspapers or garnering ratings points, they also have obligations to the public. Some argue that because of the advantages given to television and radio networks by the government—exclusive use of broadcast frequencies for radio stations and various broadcast advantages to the big four broadcast television networks (NBC, CBS, ABC, and FOX)—media outlets have further obligations to the public interest.

And yet, the media are business organizations. As a way of trying to maintain some distance between the business side and the editorial (news) side, media organizations often try to separate the two divisions: the editorial side covers the news; the business side gets advertising and does accounting work. Those businesses that try to intimidate the editorial side by threatening to withdraw advertising are likely to get frosty receptions from both the editorial side *and* the business side. Part of that has to do with the newspapers having the reputation that their coverage cannot be bought or sold as part of their credibility.

However, the business and editorial sides often do have connections. Special sections in magazines and in newspapers in which coverage is devoted to a particular event or phenomenon are the most obvious examples, but when we watch television some decisions seem motivated by the business component; local coverage of a business opening or prominently mentioning sponsorship of local events are examples of this interchange. Even the editorial side of large newspapers like the *New York Times* and the *Washington Post* may have unconscious motivations toward the business end; a newspaper is generally designed to highlight the most important stories, a tactic that "sells" the newspaper to the patron. Small-town papers may make even less of a distinction between the editorial and business sides. In smaller communities, the publisher, who either represents the owner or is the owner, does often influence editorial decisions, especially in the editorials of a paper.

Given the fact that the basic structures of media organizations are unlikely to change, the most important thing to do is to watch or read news with an active, sometimes skeptical eye, looking for links between business interests and media outlets. Even more importantly, read news widely. Look at alternative papers or read media criticism. Taking such steps will help you become a better reader of the media.

The media are made up of a variety of people. Do you think Megyn Kelly and the local newspaper's columnist have similar roles in the media? Of course not—but the latter is as much a media member as the former. When columnists, politicians, or sports figures refer to "the media," whom, specifically, do they mean? Miss Manners? ESPN? National Public Radio? The folks at the History Channel? Twitter? The obituary writer of your hometown newspaper? Probably they are thinking of the very public media outlets like the major television networks, the overly aggressive talk radio personalities, and perhaps some writers for national newspapers and magazines. However, most members of the media are regular, virtually anonymous people who try to bring you information.

Although many members of the media have similar aims, their format and their audience shape their content. Radio news can only read a few paragraphs of a traditional newspaper story in its allotted time and has to rely on taped interviews to enhance it. A television news report has to focus on visual material, and national newspapers have different expectations attached to them than does the local weekly or a magazine like the *New Yorker*. Newspapers analyze long-term events better than television does, and magazines do it even better. But in covering house fires and the weather, and showing sports highlights, television is more effective. Overall, the media have different elements that make various organizations better suited to do one job rather than another.

In addition, there are very few absolutes when it comes to the media. Some newspapers and television stations are civic-minded organizations dedicated to upholding the public trust. Sometimes newspapers seem motivated more by financial concerns. Some ads are very entertaining. Some are offensive. Some media outlets try to present the news in the most balanced, most objective way they can. Other sources make no bones about being biased. The *Daily Kos*, a liberal website, has a wholly different aim than *Red State*, a conservative site, but neither are objective. It is important that you be able to tell the difference between the purposes of the *Daily Kos* and CNN or the *New York Times* and *Red State*. The crucial thing is to be able to view the media generally, and advertising and the news specifically, with a critical eye. Being able to distinguish between data and rhetoric is key to being a good reader of the media.

Despite what your favorite conservative radio or television talk show host says, the media are not particularly liberal. You may not be familiar with the ongoing controversy of the supposed liberal bias of the media, but if you spend any time watching or reading columnists—both from the left (liberal) and right (conservative)—you will encounter claims of a liberal media. Actually, the fact that someone points out that there is a liberal bias itself undermines the idea of one. If there is such a liberal bias, then how have we heard about it? Through the conservative media.

You may think we exhibit a so-called liberal bias in taking this stance, but the business element that often shapes editorial content, especially in small communities and perhaps the networks as well, tends to be more sympathetic to conservative political ideals. In addition, the fact that most media outlets recognize many conservative commentators probably shows how baseless this idea of a liberal media really is. Most publications also do not foreground information that is of concern to liberals or liberal organizations. For instance, do you know of any major news publication with a "Labor" section? How about a section entitled "Feminism"? Or, for that matter, "Racial Equality"? Does your local radio station give an environmental awareness update? Probably not (though with the growing concern about global warming, perhaps that may change). However, every major paper devotes a great deal of time to its business section, and just about every radio station gives some kind of market news or stock report. Many sportswriters, owners of sports franchises, and many athletes themselves tend to be both politically and socially conservative, and sports is a major aspect of any media outlet. Finally, simple coverage of events can reflect bias. In the September 2002 issue of *Harper's Magazine*, for example, the Harper's index lists the number of appearances made by corporate representatives on US nightly newscasts in 2001 at 995, while the number of appearances of labor representatives was 31.

On the other hand, it may be unfair to accuse the media of leaning too far to the right. Most actors, filmmakers, and singers find affinity with left-leaning causes and, as you know, entertainment always makes the news. Both liberal and conservative groups assail the media for bias, which probably indicates that the media's bias falls somewhere in the middle. The media's political bias may or may not be of concern to you now, but it is one aspect of the media you will continually hear about as they play a larger and larger role in public discourse.

The media is not objective, but its members try to be fair. Reporters and editors are human beings with political, social, and cultural preferences that they hope to acknowledge and put away when reporting. Reporters quickly learn they have to ask both (or many) sides of questions when it comes to an issue. News stories often have this "she said, he said" quality. Does that mean the media always do a good job of being objective or fair? Definitely not, but they generally aim to do so. Those outlets with a specific political agenda are usually responsible enough to make that orientation clear in their editorial page or early in the publication or program. It is also worth noting that editorial writers and columnists are under no obligation to be fair or objective; their object is to deliver their opinion for better or worse. Calls for their objectivity miss the point of what an editorial is supposed to do—deliver opinions.

Questions of objectivity and fairness are not only important when talking about the media but also in your own work. As writers and researchers, we hope we are being objective when we undertake a subject, but we naturally come to any subject with a viewpoint that is shaped by our experiences and the ideas that come from them. That is why we may disagree with each other over whether we liked a movie or a book, or over which candidate we support in an election (or even who we find attractive or not). In fact, one of the reasons we discuss the idea of lenses so insistently throughout this book is that a lens, whether it be liberal, conservative, about race, class, or gender, or through a particular geography, allows us to acknowledge a particular point of view.

Though reporters come to the news with biases, they generally understand their obligations to report fairly and generally serve the public interest, just as editorial writers and columnists understand their mission to seek to influence public opinion. The bigger point here is that critics who claim a lack of objectivity from the media are uninformed about the reality of the media (sometimes deliberately so). The media often deserve the criticism they get from both liberals and conservatives, but an imperfect media is to be expected in any system—in particular, one whose primary focus is business. Understanding these concerns will help you understand the media in a more inclusive and a more informed way.

Advertisers reflect consumers' desires as well as business's desire to sell to them. Separate but related elements of the media are advertisers and marketers who have a crucial financial relationship with newspapers, magazines, web pages, television news, social media sites, and television shows. In essence, advertising pays for our free television and subsidizes our purchase of magazines and newspapers. Without ads, we would pay for broadcast television (which is why premium channels like HBO cost money) and pay a lot more for newspapers and magazines. What do advertisers get in return for their ads? The simple answer is public exposure for their products or services. The more complicated (and perhaps unintended) one is an influence in public life. Although some critics object to the very existence of advertising in public life, most everyone acknowledges that advertising is the price we pay for living in a capitalist society. What is most criticized about advertising is the way advertising seeks to sell us products through manipulation and base appeals—its use of implicit and often inflated promises of various forms of happiness (sexual gratification, satiation of hunger, thinness, coolness) with the purchase of advertised items. When we consider these issues plus the sheer proximity of where and how ads and other media appear, it makes sense to think of these two entities as two sides of the same coin. While advertisers are not what people automatically think of as the media, their influence and importance in American society and their impact on various media outlets cannot be denied.

There is a long-standing belief that advertising is manipulative and somehow unsavory. While we will not argue fully with those ideas, we believe it is important to think about what exactly advertising does. For one, we do think that advertising generally tries to sell us things we want (even if we "should not" want them). Advertising items that consumers do not want is not a particularly effective use of advertisers' dollars. If you look at the majority of what advertisers sell, they consist of consumer items such as food, cars, clothing, electronics, and services—things that people want, though again the issue of how many of these things we should have or want is another question. Advertising can only influence a consumer so much—if a new snack food tastes like soap or broccoli, endorsements by every celebrity will still fail to sell it. Accordingly, some advertising experts believe that the greatest influence happens in choosing a brand at the point of sale, not in actually choosing to buy the product itself. Most of the marketing research that businesses do is not geared toward learning how to manipulate but learning what consumers will buy.

Yet the question of how far advertisers go in changing our attitudes about our world and what we should want is an open question that researchers continue to try to answer.

We think that blaming advertisers for the perceived shallowness of human desire oversimplifies the role advertisers and consumers play in deciding what they want.

In addition, both of us have been confronted in the classroom with the idea that the public is not very smart compared to the students themselves. This kind of thinking on the part of students probably underestimates the intelligence of the public. If you assume the public is as savvy as you are, you will avoid many pitfalls.

Advertising and graphic design can be considered artistic. Artistic components abound in advertising. Advertisers and directors of commercials compose their ads so that they are both aesthetically pleasing and effective at getting us to buy. Advertisers often use the same principles as artists by seeking tension, drama, comedy, and beauty in their work. And sometimes directors and artists do both commercial and more artistic work. For instance, film directors such as David Lynch and the Coen brothers have all done television commercials, and many artists do graphic design (including those involved in the Absolut Vodka campaign). What complicates graphic design and television commercials as art is their associations with commercial interests. Americans like to separate art from commerce; we would rather have our artists make their money from selling their art to the community, not to companies. However, increasingly, the two worlds are merging.

What do we do when we see a funny or clever commercial or a piece of advertising that is particularly striking? Perhaps we feel at war with ourselves in trying to place within a context what is clearly artistic expression and yet is trying to sell us something. Can we enjoy the art of advertising while decrying its influence? It is a difficult question. There are a lot of creative advertisements and interesting graphic designs out there; to make a false distinction between high art and commercialism is to ignore how the texts of advertising and the texts of art work.

Advertisers appeal to us through common images whose meanings we have already learned. Advertisers appeal to us through images that are iconic—standing directly in for something—or symbolic, meaning they have associated meanings. Diamond manufacturers do not have to tell us that diamonds serve as an icon for sophistication and wealth—we already know that. Thus, the diamond ring has become an icon for luxury, as has a spacious car with a leather interior and adjustable seats. We have learned what manicured lawns, Bermuda shorts, and gold jewelry mean by association. We know what it means to see a beach, golf clubs, a city, or any number of settings in a commercial. Because advertisers communicate through images as much as they do words, and these images seem to convey what they want without too much effort, looking at the visual language they use can tell us more about the role these images play in American culture.

Researchers disagree about advertising's effects on consumers. Many researchers believe there is a connection between advertisements and harmful behavior. Jean Kilbourne for example, suggests that ads influence our children in harmful ways, particularly young women.[1] William Lutz argues that the way in which advertisers alter the meaning of words can have a harmful effect on language and how we use it.[2] Others are not so sure.

The authors are not convinced in one particular way, with this caveat. We believe the relationship between humans and any form of culture is complicated. We are not denying that there is a relationship between advertising and behavior—we are just not convinced about how direct it is. Similarly, we are not making any specific claims about the relationship between the media and advertising except to say that the two are increasingly intimately related and that we urge you to continue to be literate readers of both.

Social media has changed the media landscape in innumerable ways. Many people now get the bulk of their news from posts that friends and family put up on Facebook, Twitter, Tumblr, and personal blogs. What is important to remember is that all of these posts are curated and even filtered—probably by people you like and agree with. Even the term social media implies community over objectivity. Facebook, Twitter, and Snapchat are forms of media that are designed to increase our social networks, not necessarily our knowledge of current events or global awareness. This is not a bad thing—in fact it can be great—but, as in the case of advertising, mixing friends and news and family and politics can be compromising. For example, both authors have friends and colleagues who have decided to unfriend (or at least unfollow) people on Facebook because of posts they consider offensive or insensitive.

So what does it mean that so many of us get news via social media? We aren't sure. But we are intrigued; in part we are curious about the form and immediacy of social media. For example, one of the authors was teaching a summer class on 29 June 2012, when the cell phone of nearly every student in class started going off. The students were receiving texts and alerts informing them of Michael Jackson's death. On one hand, it was disturbing to have class interrupted in this manner, but on another, it provided an unusually communal moment to mourn, reflect, and share.

We want you to be able to distinguish between social media and news media. This may seem obvious, but pretty much every news outlet posts news items on Twitter and Facebook. So, what's "social" and what's "news?" If your mom sends you a link to a story in the *Washington Post*, is that a social act or an informational one? Is the

---

1   Jean Kilbourne, *Deadly Persuasion: Why Women and Girls Must Fight the Addictive Power of Advertising* (Free Press, 1999).
2   William Lutz, *Doublespeak: From "Revenue Enhancement" to "Terminal Living": How Government, Business, Advertisers, and Others Use Language to Deceive You* (Harper & Row, 1989).

distinction important? Maybe. Maybe not. But one of the things we've noticed is that news is often shared on social media to reaffirm beliefs already held rather than complicate viewpoints. The increasing popularity of podcasts adds yet another layer to this issue; people can now listen to content they approve of instead of radio. We encourage you once again to pay attention to the source of information you might be getting on social media.

As many of you know, the notion of fake news became an important component of the 2016 presidential campaign and election. Individuals from the United States and Russia fabricated entire stories and posted them on Facebook or other partisan (or invented) websites in order to foment doubt about some of the candidates, in particular Hillary Clinton. In one famous case, Cameron Hughes, a recent college graduate, created a website called ChristianTimesNewspaper.com and concocted a totally bogus story about "tens of thousands of fraudulent Clinton votes" in an Ohio warehouse. Hughes illustrated this story with a photo of a man wheeling out huge cubes marked "ballot boxes." The only problem is that the photo was actually from Birmingham, England. But, no one really bothered to check out the story, and it went viral and may have, in some instances, swayed voters. Thus it is increasingly important to check sources and verify information.

As the worlds of advertising, media, journalism, and social media converge, the ability to read, discern, and evaluate information is going to be among the single most important skills on the planet.

Here are some things to think about when writing about media:

Journalism

Medium: What form of media are you watching or reading? How does form contribute to coverage? Is reading a blog the same as reading the *Boston Globe* online? Is listening to Rush Limbaugh on the radio or via podcast the same as watching Sean Hannity on television?

Bias: What point of view does the story seem to have? Are there some key words that indicate this? Do all the same stories seem to have the same viewpoint? If there is a bias, is the story still "fair"—does the reporter seek multiple perspectives?

Message: How does an advertisement deliver its message? How are ads rhetorical? Also, websites often include extra information not included in the print versions. Does the medium alter the message? The great media scholar Marshall McLuhan claimed that the medium *is* the message. Is he correct?

Signs: When watching a newscast, how does the program communicate in image (video, photograph, graphic)? What symbols does it use? Are there any unintended meanings? How does the clothing of the reporters and anchors contribute to what we take from the newscast?

Audience: To what audience does the news article or news report appeal? How can you tell? Will others outside the target audience feel alienated by the report or article? What are news organizations assuming about their audience in a particular piece or the newscast, magazine, website, or newspaper as a whole?

Reality: Do the images and ideas match your idea of reality? Are they supposed to? Do they (the people reporting and presenting the news) see the world the way you do?

Race, ethnicity, gender, class: How are images of any or all of these groups presented? Can you tell the bias of the reporter or news organization from their presentation?

Commerce: How does media negotiate the awkwardness of advertising and other forms of funding? In 2016, the *New York Times* ran an article on the influence of big money on journalism, citing, for example, claims that Sheldon Adelson, owner of the *Las Vegas Review-Journal*, tried to keep negative articles about him out of the paper he owns.

Sources: Is your source a blog? The website of a major newspaper? A partisan publication? An advertisement disguised as a news story? Pay attention to where you get your information.

Advertising

Signs: How does the advertisement speak to you through images? What do the images symbolize? Are there unintended meanings attached to the symbols? Can you classify the symbols into types? What do advertisers assume about the connections you will make between the signs presented and what researchers call the point of purchase?

Audience: What is the target audience of this advertisement? How do you know? What assumptions are advertisers making about their audience?

Social Media

Networks: What does your network of "friends" say about you and your views? Do you get a majority of your news from sources posted by friends? How does social media try to merge the social and the informational?

Objectivity/subjectivity: Social media is really just a series of outlets rather than a network, program, or publication. Does social media blur boundaries between objective and subjective messages?

WRITING ABOUT MEDIA AND ADVERTISING: THE GENRES

The Rhetorical Analysis

One of the easiest ways of analyzing an advertisement is by using Aristotle's three appeals (ethos, pathos, and logos); the appeals provide a natural organization of the paper.

ETHOS—APPEAL TO AUTHORITY

An advertisement or other visual text uses the trustworthiness and credibility of the author to make its appeal. The ethos many times is the brand name itself—a brand we are familiar with may bring credibility. Or the advertiser may use someone famous or with expertise to present the advertisement. Politicians often use endorsements to provide credibility. Many times the ethical appeal is the weakest in an advertisement, however.

PATHOS—APPEAL TO EMOTIONS

This appeal tries to get the reader to feel a particular emotion through the use of images or words, or both. An advertisement typically wants us to be motivated to purchase the particular item. The copywriters may do this by presenting images, colors, people, letters, or a combination of the above to evoke feelings of intrigue, happiness, or pleasure in some form. The images are often aimed at reminding us of other ideas or images. The appeal to emotions is often the strongest in an advertisement.

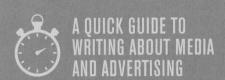

A QUICK GUIDE TO WRITING ABOUT MEDIA AND ADVERTISING

1. Think about audience: Advertising and media makers are often highly aware of who they are writing to, whether it's by region, age, race or ethnicity, gender, education.

2. Look for symbols/signs: Advertising usually has textual material, but it often communicates through its symbols, whether they are traditional (good-looking models) or offbeat (lizards).

3. Note the medium: Is the maker trying to communicate through television or YouTube or print? Ask yourself how the medium affects the way the message is presented.

4. Be aware of persuasion: Is your source trying to present information without bias? Or is it a persuasive text? How can you tell if a video or story or report is merely communication or a form of persuasion?

5. Consider the complicated role of social media: With the advent of Facebook, Twitter, Tumblr, and Snapchat, the media has expanded its scope. Though these social media platforms are not traditional media outlets or traditional forms of advertising, they can serve as delivery mechanisms for both.

LOGOS—APPEAL TO REASON OR LOGIC

Advertisements often try to present a logical appeal, using facts of one sort or another. For example, an advertisement might use claims that its product is the most popular brand or has won the most awards. It might claim that the time to purchase the item is sooner rather than later because of the discounts its manufacturer is providing.

THE TARGET AUDIENCE

When talking about visual texts, you might also talk about who its target audience is—how old or young, how rich or poor, where they are from, and so on.

In writing the rhetorical analysis, you focus on showing *how* an advertiser uses the three appeals (the advertiser is the author of the ad). Here might be the outline of a typical paper:

An introduction talking about advertising.
A thesis statement describing the argument you are making about the ad.
A paragraph providing an organized general description of the ad.
Three or more paragraphs about the strengths and weaknesses of the three appeals.
A paragraph that talks about the target audience.
A concluding paragraph that explains why one appeal is stronger than the other.

The Researched Paper

There are several ways that one could do a researched paper about media and advertising. One might be an extended rhetorical analysis, but with research about the genre of advertising or medium added to make a more in-depth argument about the way advertisements work. Another might be a paper about the way a particular periodical works in serving its readership. The underlying structure is this: choose a text or question, find a research angle, research what has been said about this topic, and read the text or answer the question in the rest of the paper.

OTHER ESSAY IDEAS

1. Watch *The Daily Show* one night and critique the presentation of news.

2. Compare *The Onion* to *The Daily Show*. What functions do each perform?

3. Watch *The Daily Show* and a network news evening broadcast. In what ways do they differ in their presentation? Where does *The Daily Show* borrow from network news? Which show informs you better?

4. Perform a sign analysis using an advertisement that uses another familiar place (a front lawn, an office, sports field, etc.). What about the place's familiarity is part of the appeal?

5. Write a paper discussing the presence of fantasy and familiarity in a typical advertisement. What types of ads rely more on fantasy? Which on familiarity?

6. Examine the types of intimate relationships portrayed in advertisements. Write a paper examining how advertisers use those relationships to appeal to their target audience.

7. Write a comparison/contrast essay in which you analyze an ad you find particularly manipulative and one you find reasonable and straightforward. Give specific analytic examples of how the two ads differ from each other.

8. Write a short paper comparing the front pages of an electronic version of a newspaper with its print equivalent.

9. Spend an afternoon taking notes on a newspaper site that updates. In what ways is the newspaper taking advantage of new technology? Is it undermining or enhancing the newspaper? Read a few bloggers linked on the newspaper page and some other bloggers. Write about the differences and similarities in tone.

10. Write a paper on someone famous through their top 25 Google links. Where do the links lead you? What does this say about the subject? Google?

11. Google search your name or someone close to you and write about what you find there.

12. Take a research subject such as the first amendment and Google it and do a more formal research subject. How do the results compare from Google, the research database, and books?

13. Read a week of editorial pages from a local newspaper. What are some things you notice? How do columnists use particular words? What do they stand for?

14. Using the rhetorical triangle assignment at the beginning of the book, write an analysis of an advertisement.

15. Put yourself in the shoes of an advertiser for a particular product. Write an ad campaign for that product taking into account target audience, signs, and the medium you would use to advertise it.

16. What issues on campus could be covered better (or at all) by the local media? Why do you think they are not covered now?

17. Write an essay in which you analyze the five most recent posts on your Twitter or Facebook feed that contain news items or links to news stories. What do they say about you and your network?

18. Write about the odd trinity of social media, advertising, and journalism. How and where do they intersect?

RESOURCES

Websites

Mashable does a good job of covering social media: http://mashable.com/category/social-media/.

The *Guardian*, a British paper, also covers it well: http://www.theguardian.com/media/socialnetworking.

Adweek does a good job covering advertising and the media.

The Pew Research Center has very good coverage of the media: http://www.pewresearch.org/topics/state-of-the-news-media/

Books

There are quite a few books on the media, particularly in the field of communication, or on the history of particular institutions, like the *New York Times*. Here are some more general, idea-driven books.

Nicholas Carr, *The Shallows: What the Internet Is Doing to Our Brains*. Carr explores what he thinks the internet is doing to our brains.

Susan J. Douglas, *Where the Girls Are: Growing Up Female with the Mass Media*. This book explores the nature of the media's affect on women.

Henry Jenkins, *Convergence Culture*. This explores the nature of converging (combining) medias.

Bill Kovach and Tom Rosensteil, *The Elements of Journalism*. Kovach and Rosenteil explore what audiences really want from journalists.

Andrew Rojecki and Robert Entman, *The Black Image in the White Mind*. This book explores how the media contributes to our ideas about race.

Michael Schudson, *Advertising, the Uneasy Persuasion*. Schudson questions the influence of advertising.

Clay Shirky, *Here Comes Everybody*. Shirky explains the new powers of social media.

Sherry Turkle, *Alone Together: Why We Expect More from Technology and Less from Each Other*. Turkle explores what it means to be in this digital age.

Siva Vaidhyanathan, *The Googlization of Everything (and Why We Should Worry)*. Vaidhyanathan explains the influence of Google beyond being a search engine.

SAMPLE STUDENT ESSAY

Brittany Gray was a freshman at Virginia Commonwealth University in Richmond when she wrote this analysis of a "Hanes Her Way" ad in 2001. In her analysis of an ad piece, Gray reads her ad through the lens of the familiar vs. fantasy.

Hanes Her Way

BRITTANY GRAY

IT KNOWS WHO YOU ARE. It knows what you want. It gets into your psyche, and then—onto your television, your computer screen, your newspapers and your magazines. It is an advertisement, folks, and it's studying every little move you make, be it in the grocery store or the outlet mall. These advertisement executives know just what the consumer needs to hear to convince him or her to buy the product. Grocery stores even consult such advertisement firms on matters such as just how to set up the store in order to maximize consumer purchase. It has been watching, and it knows just what mood to set to get into the head of the consumer, and just how to set the scene.

This particular scene is a mild, relaxed morning. The sun streams in through the windows. The lighting is a tranquil yellow, and the background music is "Fade Into You" by Mazzy Star, a soft and haunting ballad which perfectly complements the temperate setting. Through a doorway a man watches a woman who is wearing a white t-shirt and white cotton underwear as she makes a bed, snapping a sheet into the air and watching it drift back down onto the bed in slow motion. Then a voiceover begins. The man talks over the music about how when they were dating, his girlfriend used to wear such tiny, sexy underwear. Then he says that now that they are married she just wears old worn cotton underwear by Hanes. He goes on to say that there is something comforting about the cotton underwear. He says he loves when he opens the laundry hamper and sees the worn out underwear in there waiting to go into the wash, because it reminds him of his mother and his childhood. The commercial then fades out on the Hanes trademark.

The ethical appeal in this commercial is particularly strong. For starters, the brand name of Hanes goes back a long way and has been trusted for years. There is nothing more comforting about buying a product than knowing that millions of people aside from oneself also trust the product. Also, the people in the ad seem to trust the product. It seems that trust and stability are the qualities that Hanes wants the customer to attribute to their underwear.

The pathos in this commercial was the strongest of all the appeals. The fact that, first of all, the couple is married, and also that the man seems to love and accept his wife so openly plays a part in the emotional appeal. It is not often that couples on television are married anymore, and when they are, their lives and marital stress are often the topic of comedy. This couple is not only happily married, but obviously has been married for a while as well, given the fact that the wife has had time to change her style of underwear and the fact that her Hanes Her Way cotton briefs are well worn.

Another aspect of the pathos is the setting of the scene. The tranquility of the lighting, the airy atmosphere consisting of so much white cotton and linen, and the relaxing background music all play a role in the manipulation of emotion. The way the man stands there with such a nostalgic look on his face, watching his wife and speaking about her so wistfully is meant to really touch something inside—and it does. Not only that, but the man still finds his wife beautiful, even after so many years, and even after the underwear that he initially found so attractive is gone. The entire ad evokes a sense of tranquility and comfort, seeming to say, "our product will fulfill you just the way these people are fulfilled."

The appeal to logic in this ad was for the most part absent, aside from one thing. After all, there is no real logic to a man liking his wife's underwear, nor is there any rhyme or reason behind the comfort that seeing the underwear lying in the hamper brings him, reminding him of his childhood and his mother. Hanes underwear does not make the sun come out in the morning, and it certainly won't find someone a spouse. The logic of the commercial, as well as the fact of the matter, is that Hanes underwear is comfortable—especially Hanes Her Way white cotton briefs.

The audience targeted in this commercial was without question middle-class women, probably aged 12 and up. Most men do not get misty-eyed hearing pretty music, and they are not particularly struck watching a man speak so fondly of his wife. However, women thrive on such things. Every woman loves to see a man talk about his wife as though she were the only woman on the earth, because it is such a rare occurrence.

That is not the only aspect of the ad directed at women, however. The lighting in the commercial, paired with the beautiful sunny morning, as well as the crisp white linens shown throughout the commercial, are all aimed at women in middle-class families. Women love to see that level of comfort and cleanliness within a home, as it all touches on a woman's romantic, idealistic side. Also, the fact that the couple and their home is so completely average shows that Hanes is for average, normal people. Everyone wants to feel that what they do is normal and accepted, especially women trying to run a home. It is one less thing to worry about, one less thing that can be criticized when it comes to a woman's running of her home. It also shows that the happiness of the couple is not out of reach—they are just like every other working class American couple.

These audience clinchers are not entirely in opposition to the ones used in men's underwear commercials. Many men's underwear commercials portray scenes containing rumpled beds in the morning, and fresh white linen. Underwear commercials in general seem to abound in their portrayal of morning sunrises and beautiful people making beds. In men's commercials, though, it seems that there is always that bittersweet touch of masculinity. There is constantly some muscular role model, doing the types of things that strong, ideal men should do. The man in the commercial always seems to do the same stereotyped things. He gives the dog a bath, he plays with the kids. He does the dishes with a smile, pausing to toss a handful of bubbles at his adoring wife. He goes jogging in the morning before his coffee. He shows his son how to throw a baseball just right, and of course he doesn't neglect his daughter—he tosses her into the air, and playfully dodges her blows during a pillow fight. And of course, he feels perfectly comfortable sitting around in nothing but his white cotton briefs.

Women on the other hand don't need examples of femininity. They know how to be women, and showing what the typical woman does in a day would be cheesy and clichéd. Just show a woman a good old-fashioned love scene and most likely she's sold. This commercial probably shouldn't appeal to me so strongly. It is exactly like most other commercials for women's underwear I have seen. They all have the same basic elements: white linen, sunny mornings, happy families, and beautiful, smiling people. I'm not sure if I can place my finger on exactly what made this commercial stand out for me. I think it was the combination of the music and the couple. I've never heard music like that in an underwear commercial. The music used is normally that sunny, get-up-and-go type of music, but this commercial utilized the softer sound of Mazzy Star. The voiceover and the utilization of romance really struck me too. Though the ad was not particularly original, I still felt that it was a beautifully done commercial.

The ethos of this commercial was definitely strong. The name of Hanes is one of the most trusted in underwear, and the advertisers used the stability of the marital relationship to illustrate this. However, the pathos was the most outstanding of the appeals in this ad. The fact that the underwear was made by Hanes was made known, as well as the reasons why Hanes should be trusted. However, the vivid sensory imagery in this commercial which made it so pleasing to the eye and such a joy to watch rules over the ethical appeal. A sunny morning means much more to me personally than the comfort of knowing that I'm wearing sturdy underwear, which is a comfort that is forgotten soon after putting the underwear on. A morning as beautiful as the one on TV is not commonly seen, nor is a couple more obviously in love. It is simple joys such as these that the commercial strikes at, and the joys seem to overpower the main ethical and logical appeal—that Hanes makes good underwear.

CHAPTER 22

READING AND WRITING ABOUT MUSIC

We cannot escape music. Almost any place we go music is playing—in the supermarket, at Starbucks, in the car, and on television. In fact, as we write this, we're listening to The Both and The Clientele, with a little bit of De La Soul, Glenn Gould, Simone Dinnerstein, and Elvis Costello thrown in. Accordingly, music often serves as the soundtrack for our lives; we attach memories to particular songs, and those song–memory attachments tend to be long lasting.

Music too is one medium we are at once reading actively and passively as we emotionally connect to the sounds and tones—we do not think so much about the mood a song evokes as much as how it makes us feel. Accordingly, we actively read music, if we read it at all, by focusing on its lyrics—after all, the content of what's sung in a song is the easiest element to interpret. In addition, we have the tools for interpreting words already: we know how to read and make sense of language or literature. And such tools can be useful in understanding music.

Still, writing about music has its difficulties. Of all the texts in this book, music may be the most emotionally powerful. We can argue about books and movies and television shows, but discussions about music—favorite artists, what albums you would take to a desert island, who is better, the Beatles or the Stones—elicit the most passionate responses. And we often put that passion to good use. We turn to music to put us in a romantic mood, to celebrate events, to announce the arrival of the bride, to begin graduation ceremonies, to initiate all sporting events. Our lives are framed by music—it may be the text we are the most unable to live without, which is why it is particularly important to be a good reader of it. And in the case of your courses, be a good writer about it.

But we have any number of other considerations to decipher a song's intentional meanings, as well as some of its unintentional ones. Here are some to keep in mind when listening to and writing about music.

Music is made up of genres. Both professional and amateur listeners often classify a song's type in trying to understand or enjoy it. There are many genres of music—classical, rhythm and blues, rock and roll, rap, country, jazz, and "pop," as well as numerous subgenres within these groups (alternative, emo, trip-hop, fusion, etc.). Bands often combine genres, transcend genres, or even comment on them as they play within them. Sometimes, for example in the case of rap music, the commentary is part of the music itself. Some people place an enormous amount of importance on genres when deciding to listen to particular music—they want ways to understand what experience is ahead of them, and whether, based on past experience, they will like a particular song or band.

Of the genres we have listed, the one hardest to qualify is "pop" music (which is why we place it in quotes). For many, the term has negative connotations since it stands for "popular," which in some circles means "unsophisticated" or that it panders to a popular sensibility instead of artistic integrity. For the authors, pop music is an umbrella that often covers parts or wholes of entire genres at one time or another—classical music was the pop music of its day, as was early jazz or swing. Even much of classic rock was once popular. Having said that, what is popular oftentimes is worth studying for what it may tell us about our contemporary world.

Still, musical genres are not value free. We tend to associate certain traits with particular genres. If we see a number of country and western CDs in someone's car, we may (often incorrectly) assume something about them or their socioeconomic class. The same might be said for a collection of Mozart and Bach albums. Genres are themselves complex texts whose significations change over time as culture, tastes, and people change.

One of the most straightforward papers you can write is one about whether a song, album, or artist fits into a particular genre. This lends itself to an arguable thesis. One thing you likely should think about when doing this type of paper is defining the characteristics of the genre. In other words, you might ask yourself what musical characteristics such as guitar, rhythm, and other instruments define a particular genre. Or do its lyrics define the genre? When it comes to country music and rap music, for example, they are often easily defined by recognized characteristics such as steel guitar and straightforward lyrics in country music, and sampled music and more explicit lyrics in rap. But often artists write and perform music that has some characteristics of a genre and not others; this instability can often lead to a productive writing situation.

Music is (or is not) a reflection of the culture that surrounds it. Music is often of a time and place and can offer clues to the society in which it is written. For example, much of Bob Dylan's work in the turbulent 1960s directly reflects the world around it; his songs frequently engage the protest movements of the time. Gangsta rap also seemingly helps tell stories from disadvantaged areas with its focus on the dilemmas of living in such areas. These forms of music can bring a broader understanding of various social ailments to the "average" listener. By a bizarre coincidence, Ryan Adams's catchy tribute to New York City, "New York, New York," was just gaining popularity when the events of September 11, 2001, occurred. The song became an unintended anthem and tribute that has, for many, come to symbolize the hope and sacrifice that New Yorkers felt after the attacks.

But making automatic leaps from music to culture and vice versa can be problematic. Songwriters sometimes have social aims that go along with their music, and
sometimes they do not. Even if they do, there can be unintended messages that flow
from their music; music may unintentionally reflect society as well. For example, some
people believe that disco music, with its programmed beats and the sexual innuendo
in many of its lyrics, reflected the so-called shallow values of the 1970s, though those
writing the music probably did not intend their music to have this effect (and we
disagree). Similarly, since Kurt Cobain's suicide, some critics have associated the entire
grunge sound with nihilism—something Cobain likely never would have wanted. More
recently, Beyoncé has taken on race, gender politics, and traditional notions of power—
all important questions at the forefront of public discussion in the 2010s.

On a purely musical level, we can also listen to a song and place it in a particular era
because of certain musical conventions of the period—identifiable instruments or sounds
in general often give this away. Can you think of some conventions used today? Some
we associate with a previous era? Think not only of songs but also of commercials. Do
you remember when rap beats became a big part of commercials? It was not always so.

Finally, sometimes musicians write songs that seem not to be of a time and place.
Gillian Welch's popular album *Revival* sounds as though it is a relic from early twenti-
eth-century Appalachia, yet Welch, a Californian with classical music training, recorded
the album in 1995. Smash Mouth could fool some into believing they were around
in the early 1960s. Amy Winehouse evoked sounds of a previous era, as does Sturgill
Simpson. What qualities do these artists convey in their songs? What do they avoid?

**The packaging of music reflects the aims of the bands, or the record compa-
nies, or both, and it has an effect on the way we view the music.** The packaging
of music involves a variety of things that sit outside of the actual music itself, such as
promotional videos, album covers, song titles and lyrics, and even advertising. As you
know, how musicians present themselves can be crucial to how we perceive them and
probably how we perceive their music. For example, how would we view the music of
Taylor Swift coming from Kendrick Lamar, and vice versa? Would One Direction be as
popular if they looked like Joe Biden? The persona of each of these artists contributes
to the way we perceive them and their work.

Often we read performers not only from the packaging of an album but also visually through photographs in rock magazines, reports on entertainment shows, live
concerts, and videos. In particular, the handlers of the musician or the musician himself
or herself use the music video to provide another way of determining how potential
consumers see the artist. Websites do similar work but may offer different portrayals
of the performer depending on whether the artist, a fanatical listener, or the record
company sponsors the site.

Sometimes the packaging of an artist helps us understand what musicians think
they are doing; other times the package is a wall that interferes with our experiencing

music honestly or directly. Accordingly, we have to recognize that packaging comes as a part of listening to the music, and we can do with that information what we will. For example, many fans of musicians assume that these musicians "sell out" when they sign a record deal with a large corporation, often looking for evidence of such behavior in the music, as did the fans of the band R.E.M. in the 1990s when they moved from the independent label I.R.S. to the mega-label Warner Brothers. Others just listen to the music with little regard to packaging, marketing, or in some instances, lyrics.

Packaging also can reflect the times—if we see an image of a band from a different decade we may understand a more complex relationship between the band and its era. But in reading packaging of bands from past eras we have to take into account the same factors we do in evaluating packaging from our own era.

When writing about the many nonmusical things surrounding music, describing the materials is an important step, similar to the steps needed when writing about the songs or albums themselves. A detailed visual description of what the cover looks like as well as a shot-by-shot description of the video is useful. While not all of this might make it into the paper, writing about the materials will likely help you understand it.

While the music we like may reflect personal tastes, it may also reflect cultural tastes. How many of you have heard of Toni Price? The Derailers? The Gourds? Dale Watson? Texan students may recognize these names, as all of these performers are hugely popular in the Austin, Texas area, selling out concerts and receiving considerable airtime on local radio stations. Yet few people outside of Austin and even fewer outside of Texas know this music, despite the fact that Austin enjoys a reputation as a progressive musical city. And, even though we now have access to a truly stunning array of music via iTunes, Spotify, Pandora, and other global services, our listening preferences tend to be influenced by the local rather than the global. What your parents, siblings, and friends listen to tends to shape what you will listen to—simply by way of exposure.

In addition, for many people, what they encounter on television, the internet, and in print determines their musical tastes. If bands do not make videos or are not featured in popular magazines, we may never know they exist. Many forms of alternative music never make it onto the airwaves; accordingly, potential listeners never find music outside of the mainstream. American trends toward playing and replaying market-tested music like pop, rock, country, and rap tend to reinforce listening tastes and habits. In short, you may like the music you like simply because that's all you have been exposed to. Thus, our tastes may depend less on comparison shopping or eclectic listening than the demands of the marketplace.

Some of your professors might be amenable to you writing about the evolution of your musical taste as a type of personal essay. If you write this type of essay, you should still think about the traditional aspects of essay writing—an argument, evidence, and focus.

The music itself contains readable elements that contribute to the listener's experience. Music creates moods as well as meaning. It is often hard to isolate the aspects of songs that make us feel a particular way. Often, performers intend the pace of a song, its intensity, or the sounds of the notes to affect listeners in specific ways. Hard-driving punk, smooth jazz, rap with samples and scratches, and string concertos with a lot of violins spark conscious and subconscious reactions. Sometimes, these reactions are strong and mysterious; other times, we know all too well why we feel what we do. Music functions much like poetry in that it evokes as much as it overtly states.

We can often tell by the pace of a song what the mood is—a fast song means something different than a slow song. The instruments in a song indicate/signify something (for example, the presence of trumpets or violins tells the listener something about the intentions of the artist). They are there to make the song sound better, but the way they sound better is often indicative of something else as well. Similarly, how the lyrics are sung may indicate how we are to read the song. For instance, Lady Gaga's voice demands a kind of response that Céline Dion's does not; how we read Johnny Cash's voice will differ from how we read Aretha Franklin's. Blake Shelton might make you feel one way, Prince another. Mary J. Blige is not P.J. Harvey.

Smartphones, iPods, and streaming music have completely altered our relationship to music and public space. And so have services like Spotify, which take our preferences, give us what we like, and then add new music that it thinks we might like. One of the authors is a power user of Shazam, constantly tracking music overheard on shows, in cafes, and even in Ubers. On the bus, the subway, while walking down the street or across campus, we see people bobbing their heads in giddy oblivion, and until we see the headphones protruding from their ears, we may think they are suffering some kind of seizure. But these compact players, mostly in the form of smartphones these days, have increased our ability to add soundtracks to our days. In fact, psychologists have argued that listening to music this way actually makes people happier—and if you listen in the morning, it can dramatically affect your mood for the entire day.

In writing about music, separating the emotional response from the intellectual one can be difficult. And we are not sure you have to—by describing the way music makes you feel, you get at the heart of one of the crucial aspects of interpreting music. Even professional writers about music sometimes describe the emotional aspects of music when writing about it.

Making an argument about music can be as simple as defending a song, album, or artist or as complicated as analysis through musicology. The key is remembering to be concrete in describing the music and above all to make an argument.

The listeners create the music. What we as listeners make of this sound, the packaging, and lyrics is largely up to us. We can choose to ignore the packaging, the lyrics, or the music, or a combination of the above, and arrive at one kind of interpretation. We can read biographies of musicians, watch their videos, or read the lyric sheets on Genius to get at a more complete reading of a musician or band. We can choose to listen to music on an expensive system that enhances the effects of a vinyl record, or listen to it on a car stereo or an iPhone and have that transform our understanding of the song. Or we can get in the car, turn on the radio or Sirius/XM, and find the first song that we like.

THINGS TO CONSIDER WHEN WRITING ABOUT MUSIC

Lyrics

Theme: What are some of the themes of the song (themes are generally what the author thinks of the subject)? Are there both intentional and unintentional themes?

Plot: Is there a plot to the song? Does the song tell a story or convey a narrative?

Literary devices: Do you notice any devices such as the use of figurative language (metaphor, simile) or repetition or rhyme? Are there notable symbols? Are these devices effective? Do they add to your enjoyment?

"Literariness": Do you think the lyrics have a literary quality? Would the lyrics stand alone as a poem? Why or why not?

Music

The instruments: What instruments does the band use? Does it use them effectively? Does their use symbolize anything outside of normal use?

Mood: What is the mood of the song? How does the music reflect this—through the make-up of its instruments, its speed, its tone (minor or major), or a combination of factors?

Technology: Are there technological aspects in the song? What are they? What effects do they have on the song?

Sound: Writing about sound is hard. How do you describe the guitar solo at the beginning of "Give Me Shelter" or the repeating "trouble trouble trouble" from Taylor Swift? Finding the right descriptive expression can augment the effect and precision of your writing.

The Whole Package

Genre: How would you classify this song by genre? Would you do so by the lyrics or music? Why? Are there ways that songs resist classification? If so, in what ways?

Effectiveness: Does this song "work"? Why or why not? Is there an element of the song that's stronger than the others?

How and where it's played: Unlike a poem, you can hear songs in the car, in a dance club, in the elevator, on a date, in the doctor's office, and at church. How does setting influence how you hear a song?

WRITING ABOUT MUSIC: THE GENRES

There is a variety of established genres of writing about music, including the album review, the concert review, the appreciation, the profile, and the research paper. We have also listed a variety of other types of assignments you might undertake or your professor might assign.

The Album Review

The key to writing an album review is to find a way of communicating your opinion in a way that makes clear your own musical preferences and how they might match up with your audience's preferences. While it's important to form an opinion about the album and give evidence for that opinion, useful record reviews also contextualize the review in such a way as to make listeners understand whether or not they would like the album.

In order to write a good review, you will have to listen to the album at least three times. First listen to it

A QUICK GUIDE TO WRITING ABOUT MUSIC

1. Make sure you have a place to write down notes. Sketch out some preliminary questions you want to answer when listening.

2. Listen to the album or song all the way through. Listen to it again, this time taking notes. If you think there is a particularly important part of the song or album, note the time of that part.

3. Read over your notes. Highlight or bold parts you think are useful. See if you have an argument.

4. Think about the way the paper might be split into paragraphs. Try to connect the notes to the paragraphs.

5. Alternatively, write an entire draft after listening to the song. And *then* go through and take some of these steps.

6. Researching information on music will often require using a mix of academic or scholarly sources, magazines and newspapers, online forums, and encyclopedias. You will have to be extra careful about researching music because you may have to use or at least evaluate some sources that may not be reliable.

7. We prefer engaging the primary text before doing research; we like writing our thoughts down before we search out information. It often allows us to focus the research process and avoid the inclusion of random bits of information. Research should help an argument you are making; seldom do your professors want you just to do research. Research and supporting material can help you make arguments and perhaps widen your vocabulary.

without doing much writing, if any, and with as much concentration as you can muster. Or go for a walk listening to it on your headphones. Then listen to it again with a notepad, and start taking notes as you listen. Notice the tempo of each song. Notice the lyrics that strike you. Notice your *emotional* response to the album, because often we form our ideas about music emotionally before we do so intellectually.

The Concert Review

A concert in essence is a story that has a beginning, middle, and end. It often begins with the crowd waiting with anticipation, listening to music curated by the venue or artist, and ends with the crowd leaving the venue. In between, a concert involves an artist playing music and the audience responding. Audiences in concerts respond by dancing, standing still, singing along, requesting music, and in rare cases with indifference or anger.

There are expectations that go along with concerts, and tensions involved with those expectations. Will the band play the audience's favorite songs? Will the band be technically competent to produce the works as they sound in the recording studio—or will these surpass those expectations with the energy of the crowd? Will the band interact with the audience directly or indirectly? Will they respond in some way that acknowledges their geographic location?

Writing a good review involves engaging some or all of these expectations and telling the story of the concert.

The Analysis

Analyzing an album or song (or multiple albums) requires some of the same skills as analyzing a novel, short story, or collection of short stories; one has to closely "read" the album, try to come up with a main argument, and use the evidence gathered to bolster the argument.

The complications involved with a musical selection are the additions of musical components, which are harder to describe. But if you think about music being along a set of binaries, you might be able to draw some useful conclusions. For example you might ask whether a song is short or long, fast or slow, with lots of elements or few, slow or fast, distorted or clear. Such considerations help us determine what we think of a particular song, and these considerations might help us arrive at conclusions about an album.

The Researched Paper

Writing a researched paper on music involves the same type of work as the analysis does—finding a musical text and making sense of it. But in a researched paper, you use research to expand the scope of your paper; a research paper puts a lot of information into a paper, while in a researched paper outside sources supplement your own analysis. Such scope could include putting the album or artist in historical and generic context, writing about how social contexts such as race, gender, and class inform the reading, or even how production or technology influences the work. You can also use potential audiences as contexts.

For example, let's say you are writing about the band Nirvana and their album *Nevermind*. You could write about the way the band uses distortion and loudness to enhance the lyrics that often describe alienation and unsettledness. A research paper might undertake research about what the economy was like in the 1990s in the Pacific Northwest, where Nirvana was based. It might ask whether Nirvana's style and content match those of other bands of that era and in what ways. It might explore how production changes allowed the album to be done at all. It might focus on working-class ideals and art, or whiteness and class, or maleness and class.

Researching this would likely result in a combination of scholarly and non-scholarly sources. Scholarly sources have footnotes and are written by academics; non-scholarly sources can be written by a variety of people. Research can be included in a separate section from a paper called a literature review, or it can be mixed throughout the paper or both.

After compiling a literature review, one would do the analysis of the album through this lens through paragraphs that focus on songs from the album and their relationship to the lens. For example, one might focus on a particular aspect of alienation and use lyrics and sound from a song to prove a point. Or in the case of putting the band in context, one might use these paragraphs after the literature review to compare in more depth Nirvana with other bands.

As with other papers, a conclusion takes what you have already proven and speculates what this might mean to readers beyond the argument.

OTHER ESSAY IDEAS

1. Listen to a rap or country song in which the artist speaks in the first person about his or her experiences. Now go to an electronic database or a newspaper or magazine archive and find out something about the artist. Write a paper about what differences emerge and why or whether that matters.

2. Do an examination of an autobiographical song (or one that sounds like one). Do a literary analysis of the way the artist constructs the self.

3. Write a short definitional paper about a particular genre, using examples to define it. Or make up your own genre and define it.

4. Write a persuasive paper arguing for the abolition of genre considerations. What would the musical world look like in such a scenario?

5. Invent your own genre and write a speculative piece defining it. What would it sound like? Who would listen to it?

6. Listen to a favorite album of yours and write responses to a few songs. Are you surprised by the associations that come up during listening?

7. What other albums of a certain age deserve this type of revisiting? Name a few and talk about them in class.

8. Find an older album and reintroduce it to a younger crowd. What things might you have to consider about "youth" and "age" when doing this assignment?

9. Think about your criteria when choosing to listen to an album. How do they change when looking at an older album? Write a short paper about why you choose what you listen to.

10. If it's possible, go to the record collection of an older friend or relative and interview them about the experience with one of their favorite albums. Now go back and listen to it on your own and write a paper about your experience.

11. Write a persuasive paper about why authenticity should be the guiding principle in choosing which art to view or buy. Or take the opposite tack—write about why authenticity is overrated.

12. Write a definitional paper about the criteria people use to judge music as art.

13. Write a paper about the future of the use of authenticity.

14. Pick a song to decode in great detail. What is the mood of the music compared to its lyrics? Do they work well together? Why or why not? Are the lyrics more sophisticated than the music or vice versa? Write a paper that makes an argument about the compatibility of music and lyrics.

15. Find an album you do not know well. Study its cover, making notes on what the cover is saying to a potential listener. Now listen to the songs (reading the lyrics if you wish). Does the message behind the cover reflect the music? Why or why not? You can also do similar work with the band's name. Do they have any videos? If so, what arguments do the videos make? If you take the band's name, the content of their lyrics, the messages of their videos and look at the totality, does an argument or theme emerge?

16. Find a well-known song you like. How would you find out information about the song? What sources might be appropriate? How might you approach writing a paper if you had this information? As you think about this question, look for information on the song. When you have gathered enough information, think of arguments or ideas about the song about which you could write.

17. Take a band you like that has produced more than one album. Trace its critical history.

18. What elements of the band's work do the critics identify on a consistent basis? What is their general opinion of the band? How do they classify its genre? Now sit and think about whether you agree or disagree with these critics—and why.

19. Find two songs that have similar subjects. Compare and contrast their approaches to the subject, through both their music and lyrics. What approach do you favor, and why?

20. Find a band or bands with an explicitly political approach. Do you know their politics through their music or outside of it? Does their outside behavior correspond to their music? How do critics and other members of the media approach their relationship between politics and music? What do their fans think?

21. Find a movie or television show with a prominent soundtrack—does the music work well with the movie or TV series? What are your criteria? Is there a specific moment in the movie or television show that embodies the success or failure of the director's use of music?

RESOURCES

On the Web

Most major publications have music writers, and reading them can be very helpful. *Metacritic* indexes and links to reviews in a variety of publications (and also has user reviews). *Pitchfork* is great at covering modern music, and *Rolling Stone, Mojo, Spin,* and other music magazines are great.

Books

Here are a few books that might help develop your interest in music or serve as the beginnings of a researched paper.

The series 33 1/3 has books about many albums, both acknowledged classics and other interesting works.

Michael Azerrad, *Our Band Could Be Your Life: Scenes from the American Indie Underground 1981–1991*. A book that explores the nature of the growing independent music scene.

Bill Brewster and Frank Broughton, *Last Night a DJ Saved My Life: The History of the Disc Jockey*. Disc jockeys were the original curators of musical taste.

Jeff Chang, *Can't Stop Won't Stop: A History of the Hip-Hop Generation*. This book explores hip-hop culture and music.

Peter Guralnick, *Sweet Soul Music: Rhythm and Blues and the Southern Dream of Freedom*. Guralnick is best known for his books about Elvis Presley; this book is about the intersection between music, politics, and culture in the South.

Chuck Klosterman, *Fargo Rock City: A Heavy Metal Odyssey in Rural Nörth Daköta*. A book about a personal relationship with heavy metal.

Steve Knopper, *Appetite for Self-Destruction: The Spectacular Crash of the Record Industry in the Digital Age*. This book explores the rapid change of the record industry.

Daniel J. Levitin, *This Is Your Brain on Music: The Science of a Human Obsession*. This book explains how our brain processes music.

Evelyn McDonnell and Ann Powers, eds., *Rock She Wrote: Women Write about Rock, Pop, and Rap*. An anthology by women writing about rock.

Legs McNeil and Gillian McCain, *Please Kill Me: The Uncensored Oral History of Punk*. This book tells the story of punk through its musicians and other related industry people.

Greg Milner, *Perfecting Sound Forever: An Aural History of Recorded Music*. This book recounts the history of recording music.

Tricia Rose, *Black Noise: Rap Music and Black Culture in Contemporary America*. This book discusses the relationship between rap music and African American culture.

CHAPTER 23

READING AND WRITING ABOUT TECHNOLOGY

What does it mean to *read* technology? Technology is not a traditional text like a poem, nor does it have the clearly defined elements that public space and architecture possess. It's both the idea of technology—the often-symbolic elements that we think of when we hear the word—and the concrete applications that are worth reading, that on examination yield insight into how the world works. Most of us use technology without actively considering it. We often think about technology as computers, when in reality we use technology when we do any number of simple tasks, from washing our faces to turning on a light; from listening to music, to talking on the telephone; from riding our bike to running errands in our car. Even the places we live are built using technologies our ancestors could not have imagined.

At present, when politicians or Silicon Valley executives use the word "technology," they probably mean "computer technology," a broad term that can encompass mobile phones, tablets (like the iPad), robotics, and all of our many devices we use for music, directions, health monitoring, and surveillance. Reading these forms of technology requires an expanded vocabulary and some distance in order to make sense of these things as texts. Technology has never been closer to us, never been more embedded in our daily lives, and that makes writing about it with clarity difficult. This chapter will offer some direction for crafting smart, informed essays about this overwhelming topic.

Technology has artistic components. While technology is generally concerned more with function (how it works) than form (how it looks), we know by experience that design plays an important role in whether consumers purchase and use technology such as cars, computers, and even faucets. How technological elements look may not be a factor in how something works, but they may indeed be a factor in whether someone uses it. Indeed, the word technology comes from the Greek word *techne*, which means "art." The most practical car may not be the most beautiful—which is why not everyone owns a Volvo—and the more attractive computer may not be the most practical—not everyone owns a Macintosh. Yet technology relies on many of the same characteristics that we look for in art, such as symmetry, flow, exchange, and utility. We tend to forget that people create, design, and to some degree make tools, radios, Fitbits, cell phones, can openers, pens, and scissors. Elements of design go into the shape, weight, feel, and function of each of these items.

In the case of Apple products like computers, iPads, watches, and iPods, art and technology merge in interesting ways, making form almost as important as function. A great deal of time and effort goes into designing the machines, the operating system, and the components—even the speakers. Many users of Macs—both of us included—would argue that the artistic design and operation of the computers is an element of its technology. And because form and function work together, both can be "read," analyzed, evaluated, and written about.

Technology has both an intentional and an unintentional impact on people and environments. When a person invents something in response to a perceived problem or void—those are technology's intentional aspects. But with almost every invention comes a consequence that its inventor may not have considered, whether it's to the environment, to society's work or play habits, or to our domestic habits. Cell phones, for example, have made it more convenient to contact people and be contacted, but perhaps with this convenience has come safety and etiquette implications. Driving behind someone who is talking on the phone or texting can be as annoying as hearing a cell phone ring during a movie. Is the convenience of communication worth the inconvenience that accompanies it? The proliferation of the internet and home computing has had similar hard-to-measure effects. We get things done quicker, but we also have more to do. Cell phones, laptops, and email make it harder to get away from work. The degree to which social media and texting and messaging has impacted or even taken over our lives is, at this point in history, impossible to categorize. Facebook, Twitter, Snapchat, Tumblr, WhatsApp, and other social media platforms have completely changed the degree to which we are in touch with others and the manner in which that happens. Both authors have been scolded by friends and family members for not commenting on something that was posted on Facebook—as though we have an obligation to monitor others' lives by way of social media. These media have also had profound effects on people's lives through cyberbullying, sexting, and flaming. People seem willing to be meaner online than they would be in person, making social media particularly complicated. As the famous media critic Marshall McLuhan suggests, we are surrounded by technology—we have built it into our environment. The question persists: Does increased technology mean increased freedom or increased surveillance? More leisure or more work? Both? All?

Technology also has a complicated relationship with the environment. Our history is littered with the negative effects technology has had on the natural world, especially in its release of pollutants into the air and water, and the growing landfills that contain manmade elements that are not biodegradable. But often technology is marshaled against environmental problems as well—it was technology that helped fight technology's impact on our growing industrial world. We mention this only because it's important to recognize we often use technology against itself, whether it's solar power plants and windmills battling nuclear power plants, or ergonomic chairs battling carpal tunnel syndrome caused by overusing word-processing equipment. In a sense, technology is always confronting itself—which, in a sense, means humans are doing the same.

Technology has societal impacts, often involving race, gender, and class.

Especially in the era of the computer and the mobile phone, technological advances tend to affect individuals directly, whether it's the invention of the cell phone, the proliferation of home computers, or the widespread use of social media. But the accumulation of individual effects forces societal impact as well, whether it is driving with cell phones (or having them ring during class) or increased access to the internet. In turn, a more tuned-in populace forces employers to crack down on email use, forces advertisers to respond to an increased use of the remote control, requires movie theaters to post notices about cell-phone use, and even forces professors to implement no-social-media policies in class.

Then there are the specific effects on people. Individuals in various groups who do not have access to technological changes or are not prone to use technology are obviously affected by technological changes; they often make it harder to keep up with those who have increased access to such technology. Recent studies reveal a major digital divide between rich and poor and between white Americans and members of various ethnic groups, particularly African Americans and Hispanics. Men and women often have different and complicated relationships with technology. On the other hand, technology can be liberating to those who find that it can level the playing field; the young and skilled, whatever their identity, often have the advantage over the old and experienced when it comes to utilizing technology.

Another important topic is the relationship between technology and representation and the ease with which people can distort the images of each other with programs like Photoshop. We see this most often with celebrities—especially actresses—but it can happen to anyone. When Barack Obama was running for president, horribly offensive images of him were being sent around and posted. On a billboard alongside the road, he may have been able to do something about such an image, but the invisibility and slipperiness of technology makes removing and prohibiting troubling images nearly impossible. Social media has many positives, but it also has its drawbacks, many of which include its negative impact on women. People (usually men) post nude or semi-nude photos of women (and girls) without their permission. Stalkers leak illegally obtained images of celebrities in their homes or hotel rooms. Women are rated on their relative "hotness." Female journalists, writers, and bloggers regularly receive horribly violent sexist threats. How we represent each other by way of social media and technology is a new, uncharted area of ethics that can also make for fascinating (and consequential) essays.

Technology has changed the way we work and play. Whether it's constant access to others through cell phones or email, or the ability to do work from anywhere, technology has changed our lives in ways its inventors might not have been able to anticipate. Perhaps because of technology, the lines between work and play have blurred; emails are always waiting for us, and the cell phone can make us instantly available to both friends and colleagues. Many of us prefer this lifestyle, while others find it intrusive. Technological advances often make us think about these divisions, and accordingly, how we live our lives and why we do what we do, for better or worse.

Technology has also redefined work and play; the internet is the most prominent example. Match.com, Tinder, and other online dating services have completely altered how we meet partners. New remote video medical platforms are changing how medical attention is delivered in remote areas and third world countries. Facebook has altered how we communicate and keep in touch. Spotify, iTunes, and Pandora have transformed how we listen to music. Many businesses block employees from surfing the internet or employ website trackers that monitor the sites workers visit. Similarly, the proliferation of videos, digital music, streaming services, and video games have utterly changed our notions of play, relaxation, and entertainment. Contemporary Americans spend so much time intimately involved with technology, some critics have speculated about more direct connections between technology and the human body and what that is doing to our brains and nervous system, not to mention our attention spans and our literacy with older forms of media like books.

For the new edition of this book, the authors have relied on cell phones, the internet, laptop computers, Skype, and in a couple of instances, connections to GPS via Bluetooth. When we wrote the first edition, we used virtually none of these, yet it is impossible to imagine working without them now. Similarly, by the time you graduate from college, your interactions with technology will have come so far from those of your high-school days, you'll hardly recognize them.

Social media combines technologies in ways that have transformed everyday life, though it relies on the same relationship to advertising as more traditional media. Most of you don't remember a time when you were not using Facebook or Snapchat. How many times a day do you think you check your phone for texts, Instagrams, Snapchats, Twitter, or Facebook posts? 30? 50? 100? 200? According to a 2015 article in *Time*, the average American between the ages of 18–24 checks his or her phone 74 times a day.[1] If you are one of these people, consider how much a part of your life technology has become.

None of this comes for free. You pay for your cell phones either directly or through a minutes plan. But you pay for your social media through your attention to advertising (even if you try to ignore it). The infiltration of social media has been brought about through the growth of the smart phone and fast cheap cellular service. But technology costs money. For social platforms to be current, they need to make money. Just to keep Facebook up and running, hundreds of engineers and programmers monitor the site constantly. Developers are always working on making these platforms faster, easier, and more comprehensive. They are also always looking for ways to monetize technology. Facebook is now a major gateway to retailers; Twitter a major delivery mechanism for advertisers. Social media companies develop programs not only to facilitate communication but also to make money. As you scroll through Facebook or Twitter, pay attention to all of the attempts to divert your attention to ads, new games, or new products.

YouTube has become its own media platform. YouTube has become a medium for everything from discovering musical talent to watching cat videos, old commercials, games, and television shows, and increasingly capturing or even making news. In 2009, a video of Iranian student Nedā Āghā-Soltān being killed was uploaded onto YouTube and made the world aware of the riots following the Iranian elections. Subsequent videos in 2010 and 2011 led to the Arab Spring, a time when revolutions by young people spread across the region. Through YouTube, the world knows about Felix Kjellberg or PewDiePie, the video game commentator who has more followers than One Direction and Rihanna *combined*. Khan Academy offers nearly 1,500 free classes to anyone everywhere. It has over 500 million views and around 15 million online students. At the other end of the spectrum, terrorist organizations like ISIS use YouTube and other streaming video services to recruit impressionable young people to their cause. Put simply, YouTube has changed not only how information is disseminated but also how it is accessed.

Videogames have become an important part of American life. Videogames are at the cutting edge of technology, always trying to be more and more realistic (or even hyperrealistic). They have a place in homes, dorm rooms, and phones, and increasingly in cultural criticism. Back in the early 2000s, Peter Hartlaub became the first videogame critic for the *San Francisco Chronicle*, attempting to bring a level of discourse, critique, and evaluation to a pastime many people spend more time doing than reading, watching television, and listening to music combined. Now videogames are cultural touchstones; there are movies about them, and they have their own overwhelmingly popular

---

1   Lisa Eadicicco, "Americans Check Their Phones 8 Billion Times a Day," *Time*, 15 Dec. 2015.

YouTube channel, TwitchTV. There are professional videogame leagues, and sales of videogame-related materials are in the billions. Some people consider the day new versions of videogame franchises like Call of Duty (a shooter game) or Madden (the National Football League–sanctioned game) are released to be holidays. The questions of whether there are links between violence and videogames, or whether videogaming is social enough or whether it's misogynistic do hang over the medium. Still, the medium is now a crucial part of American life.

Here are some things to consider while reading technology:

Use: What is this piece of technology for? What does it do? What doesn't it do that it's supposed to do? That its designers imply it should do?

Need: What human needs does this technology attempt to meet? Does it meet those needs?

Design: What are the strengths of this piece of technology's design? Its weaknesses? What is artistic about the design?

Unintended effects: What are some of the unintended effects of this piece of technology? Could the designer have foreseen such effects? Can improvements to its design or function change these effects?

Societal impact: What impact has this piece of technology had on society? What impact will it have?

Personal impact: What impact has this piece of technology had on you? On those who you know? Can you see any future impact it may have?

WRITING ABOUT TECHNOLOGY: THE GENRES

The Personal Essay/Narrative

One can write about technology from a personal point of view by describing an experience one had while using technology and what that might say about both the technology and the author of the piece. To begin writing a personal piece, you should find a topic about technology you are interested in—it could be the first time you used GPS for directions, a difficult conversation you had by chat or Facebook messenger, or a disagreement you had with someone on your use of technology.

Let's say you decide to write about a difficult conversation through technology. First write out what happened with as much detail as you can. Make sure you not only tell the story but also explain the technology and its uses as you go along. Then ask yourself a few questions:

1. How universal is my experience? In other words, is this a common occurrence with people in my peer group or other social grouping?
2. What about this story might other people be interested in? This is related to the first question, except here you focus on the specifics of the story not just the general.
3. What might people learn from this story? What does my story say about technology and communication more generally?

We ask these questions or ones like them because they take what is a general story and expand its range and scope; instead of being about *you*, it's about *us*.

The Analysis

One can use technology as the lens to read a particular part of popular culture. A few texts like *Her*, about a man who falls in love with his operating system, *The Matrix*, about a world in which machines take over, *The Internship*, about older workers and their attempts to fit in at Google, *The Martian*, how a stranded astronaut uses technology and his own intellectual abilities to engineer his escape, and *The Terminator*, about a robot who goes back in time to kill the mother of a future rebel leader are obvious movies about technology. But other texts can be good subjects too, particularly if the director/writer uses technology to advance a theme or to impact the lives of her characters.

To write a paper like this, you should begin by watching or reading the text in question, taking notes about the use of technology. Then ask yourself a few questions.

1. What is the role of technology in the movie/television show? Does it contribute to a theme? Does it impact the characters?
2. What argument does the director/writer seem to be making about technological developments?

A QUICK GUIDE TO WRITING ABOUT TECHNOLOGY

1. Describe the function of the piece of technology.

2. Describe its physical appearance and design.

3. When using it, describe the knowledge you have to have before starting to use it (for example, for emailing or texting, you need to type. For a phone, you would need to know how to turn it on).

4. Compare the actual experience you have to the ideal experience you think the creators imagine you have. What accounts for the gap (if any)?

5. Consider its impact. Does it benefit the individual? Society?

3. What specific parts of the move make this argument?
4. What parts contradict it? (You include this as a way of anticipating others' arguments.)

After compiling this information, think about the organization of paragraphs, focusing each one on a specific point. Use your conclusion to talk about the implications of your analysis—what might this say about the movie genre or technology more generally?

If you want to write this kind of analytical paper but focus on a platform like Facebook or Instagram or Snapchat, you would go about it similarly. But, instead of focusing on theme you may want to think about functionality and utility. What do these platforms enable us to *do*? What kind of behavior do they encourage?

The Researched Paper

Like the analysis, the researched paper often involves finding a topic or text and using technology as a lens. A research paper adds a larger context to such work. So if we take the example of writing about *Her*, the movie about the man falling in love with an operating system, we might begin with similar work as the analysis—figuring out where the writer/director is making points about technology and what an argument about the text might be.

But where research papers are so useful is that they allow a larger context to emerge through reading outside stories. In the case of *Her*, research contexts could include artificial intelligence, machines and humans, and/or operating systems. Then you would analyze the text through that lens, by either focusing on one of the above categories like artificial intelligence and talking about how the movie uses the concept to make an argument about what being human means; you could do the same with the second category. The third category might lead you to compare your own experiences with computers to those of the main character in the movie.

Though cause and effect essays can be difficult to execute, you may be interested in writing a well-researched paper on the role of something like WhatsApp or YouTube in contemporary society. These kinds of papers can be fascinating to read and fun to write, but they rely on statistics, figures, and documentation in order to support your assertions.

These reviews of the literature associated with a topic are a staple of advanced academic papers, but where they are really useful is in understanding that those before you have grappled with the same issues. Sometimes students worry that they are not being original when using research, but we can assure you that being original comes when you incorporate previous work into your own points of view.

OTHER ESSAY IDEAS

1. Trace Technology

Find a technological advancement, modern or otherwise, and read media accounts of its invention through the present time. According to the initial invention, has the promise of this invention been fulfilled—why or why not? What mistakes in judgment did the inventors—and reporters—make when they first communicated about this technology? Do these mistakes represent a trend of any sort?

2. Read a Piece of Technology

Sit down with a piece of technology such as a computer, household appliance, your automobile, or anything. First, read the piece without thinking too much about its use. What messages does the technology give you in terms of design and function? Now think about its use. Do the messages coincide? If you were using this piece of technology for the first time, would you be disappointed with the execution of the technology compared to its promise? Is this important?

3. Find a Technological Hole

Can you think of something that you would like to do that a technological advance would aid? Why do you think the technology has not been invented? What might some of the implications of this particular advance be?

4. Read and Evaluate an Artistic Portrayal of Technology

Find a text such as *The Matrix* or another movie or television episode that has at its center technology as a subject. What do the writers think of technology generally? How do they show this stance in their portrayal? Do you agree with their assessment? If not, what might they not be taking into account?

Additional Essays

1. Write about a problematic relationship you have or had with a piece of technology. Or write about a bad experience by way of technology. Have you been a victim of cyberbullying? Has someone posted negative comments about you online? Have you initiated bad behavior online? Write about that process and what you learned and are still learning.

2. Write about an invention or design you find especially useful or helpful. What sets apart this design from more problematic designs?

3. Write an open letter to designers suggesting changes in the way they understand the consumer. Cite specific examples of poorly designed technology.

4. One of the most difficult things to do is design specifically for gender use without resorting to stereotyped behaviors. Write a short paper suggesting how designers address this problem.

5. Write a short piece recounting the history of recent technology from the viewpoint of an historian. What do you think history will remember about technology in this era?

6. Write a short paper about the shift in power that may have resulted from the popularization of the internet. In what ways do you think this is a positive development?

7. Do some lurking in chat rooms that purport to be devoted to a particular identity. What can or did you learn by being in these rooms that you might not have otherwise?

8. Write a short piece about your own relationship to the internet. Has the internet changed you? Brought out different facets of your personality? How have these changes manifested themselves?

9. No one has to tell you that email has changed the way we communicate with each other (even if you don't use it very much). In what ways is that a positive thing? In what ways is it a negative thing? How has this manifested itself in your own life and in those of your friends and family?

10. What technological advances do you think have been the most harmful in your lifetime? Do these advances have advantages too? How should we balance the strengths and weaknesses of technology? Through the free market? Government intervention?

11. Do you know people who resist new technology? What are their reasons for doing so? Do you find their logic convincing? Do you know people who embrace all new technology? Can you make any determinations of how they view the world from their ideas about technology?

12. How does the media portray technology—positively or negatively? Why?

13. How do movies and television portray technological advances? How about people who are fascinated with technology? Why?

14. During the Cold War, many Americans (and presumably people from all over the world) assumed that eventually there would be a nuclear war and that life as we know it would end. Do people still make the same assumption? How else might the world end? To what extent is technology regarded as a potential threat and to what extent is it regarded as a possible savior?

15. Keep track of how many times over one week you visit a particular social media site. At the end of each day, write in your journal what you learned and thought about during those visits. At the end of the week, craft an essay in which you examine what role that specific platform has in your life. How has it changed who you are? How has it altered your behavior?

RESOURCES

There are a number of excellent resources online and in print about technology. Two magazines/websites that we like are *Wired* and *TechCrunch*, but technology is covered by almost every mainstream periodical of note.

Books

Books are technology! Watch this funny Norwegian video, Medieval Helpdesk, with English subtitles, about this very subject: www.youtube.com/watch?v=pQHX-SjgQvQ.
   Otherwise, there is a wealth of books about technology covering a large variety of subjects:

Chris Anderson, *The Long Tail: Why the Future of Business Is Selling Less of More*. This book is about the way retailers like Amazon and streaming services like Netflix have changed the way we find content.

Mark Bauerlein, ed., *The Digital Divide: Arguments for and against Facebook, Google, Texting, and the Age of Social Networking*. This collection explores the nature of the divide between those with technology and those without it, commonly called the digital divide.

Nicholas Carr, *The Shallows: What the Internet Is Doing to Our Brains*. Carr explores what he thinks the internet is doing to our brains.

Mary Frank Fox, Deborah G. Johnson, and Sue V. Rosser, eds., *Women, Gender, and Technology*. This collection has a variety of pieces about technology and gender.

Walter Isaacson, *Steve Jobs*. In many ways, this is a modern history of computing, written about the cofounder of Apple.

Kevin Kelly, *What Technology Wants*. This explores the nature of technology in the world.

Donald Norman, *The Design of Everyday Things*. This is a great book about the way design impacts our everyday lives.

Henry Petroski, *The Pencil: A History of Design and Circumstance*. This book reminds us that technology is not just computers.

Clay Shirky, *Here Comes Everybody*. Shirky explains the new powers of social media.

Bruce Sinclair, ed., *Technology and the African-American Experience: Needs and Opportunities for Study*. This collection explores the ways technology has impacted African Americans.

Sherry Turkle, *Alone Together: Why We Expect More from Technology and Less from Each Other*. Turkle explores what it means to be in this digital age.

Siva Vaidhyanathan, *The Googlization of Everything (and Why We Should Worry)*. Vaidhyanathan explains the influence of Google beyond being a search engine.

PERMISSIONS ACKNOWLEDGMENTS

INDEX

From the Publisher

A name never says it all, but the word "Broadview" expresses a good deal
of the philosophy behind our company. We are open to a broad range of
academic approaches and political viewpoints. We pay attention to the
broad impact book publishing and book printing has in the wider world;
for some years now we have used 100% recycled paper for most titles.
Our publishing program is internationally oriented and broad-ranging.
Our individual titles often appeal to a broad readership too; many are
of interest as much to general readers as to academics and students.

Founded in 1985, Broadview remains a fully independent
company owned by its shareholders—not an imprint
or subsidiary of a larger multinational.

For the most accurate information on our books (including
information on pricing, editions, and formats) please
visit our website at www.broadviewpress.com. Our print
books and ebooks are available for sale on our site.

broadview press
www.broadviewpress.com